Living Skillfully

A Practical and Concise Commentary on Proverbs

By

William J. Finnigan, D. Min.

Living Skillfully: A Practical & Concise Commentary on Proverbs
©William J. Finnigan, D. Min.
October, 2015
Printed in the United States of America
ISBN: 978-0-9962591-6-3

Formatting, Editing and Publishing Assistance By:
The Old Paths Publications, Inc.
Cleveland, Ga 30528
www.theoldpathspublications.com
email: TOP@theoldpathspublications.com

1.0

Dedication

I dedicate this work to my faithful and loving wife, Chris, whose virtue is "far above rubies" (jewels). (Proverbs 31:10)

Acknowledgements

I'm also grateful to all that have contributed to the completion of this book. In particular, I'd like to thank Joseph Spera, Ph.D., who labored tirelessly on this project. His burden and enthusiasm to get this book to the public are now realized. Joe is a retired psychologist, and currently serves as the resident Chaplain at the Caprice Health Care Center in N. Lima, OH.

A special thanks is due to Dr. H.D. Williams and his lovely wife Patricia for their invaluable labor and expertise in the publication of this book. Their integrity, promptness, professionalism, and encouragement have been second to none. Their burden to help publish the works of relatively unknown authors, like myself, through "The Old Paths Publications," is admirable and appreciated. Indeed, they have been raised up by the Lord for such an hour as this.

William J. Finnigan
October, 2015

Table of Contents

Introduction

This Commentary is based on 46 years of my research and reflections on this fabulous book of wisdom. Its rules of conduct and action have molded, built, and challenged my life and ministry. While I've chosen to take a practical approach to my comments, I have labored over the Hebrew text to insure both accuracy and integrity. I've included the Hebrew text only when I thought it would be of practical value to nurture the reader's understanding. I recommend reading one chapter of **Proverbs** each day, corresponding to the day of the month. You will then read this book twelve times per year, and have a daily reminder of how to live skillfully.

I also believe that every word of the Bible is the Word of God.

> *"All Scripture is given by inspiration of God, and is profitable for doctrine, for reproof, for correction, for instruction in righteousness: That the man of God may be perfect, throughly furnished unto all good works." (2 Timothy 3:16, 17).*

All Scripture provides the totality of divine truth needed to live a godly life. Scripture corrects wrong behavior and provides training in godly behavior. I believe that **The Holy Bible, Authorized King James Version** (**KJV**) best translates the original text into the English language.

Right from the beginning, let me affirm my brief overview of this marvelous **Book of Proverbs.** The key word in **Proverbs** is *wisdom*; the ability to live life skillfully. However, a godly life in this ungodly world is no simple assignment. **Proverbs** provides God's detailed instructions for His people to deal successfully with the practical affairs of everyday life, including how to relate to God, parents, spouses, children, friends, neighbors, and government. Thus King Solomon, the principal author, uses a combination of poetry, parables, essential questions, short stories, and wise maxims to give the common sense and divine perspective necessary to handle life's issues.[1]

In this book, Solomon pulls together 513 of the most important proverbs from the 3,000 that he wrote (see 1 Kings 4:32), along with some proverbs from others influenced by his wisdom. Since the word "proverb" means "to be like," the book makes comparisons between the common and concrete descriptions of life's most profound truths.

These proverbs are simple, moral statements that illustrate and emphasize the realities of daily living. As a dear friend expressed to me, a proverb is "a nugget of wisdom from God." They were written by Solomon, who sought the Lord for wisdom (2 Chronicles 1:8-12), and to whom it was mightily granted. The Hebrew meaning of the name "Solomon" is "peaceable." He brought peace to his people. Solomon placed wisdom before any desire for wealth and fame. Thus, these were written that mankind might be motivated to fear God and live according to His wisdom (Proverbs 1:7). Ultimately, the whole masterpiece of wisdom points to the Lord, Jesus Christ, who is Wisdom personified. This is most evident from the Apostle Paul's declaration in:

> *"But of him are ye in Christ Jesus, who of God is made unto us* **wisdom**, *and righteousness, and sanctification, and redemption."* (1 Corinthians 1:30)

King Solomon ruled Israel from 971-931 B.C. and became the wisest man in the world (1 Kings 4:29-34). While most of the proverbs were personally written by Solomon, he also collected some proverbs from others. For instance, Proverbs 30 bears the name of Agur, and Proverbs 31 are the words of Lemuel. This collection of proverbs was later finalized under the reign of Judah's King Hezekiah (715-686 B.C.). Significantly, Solomon completed his proverbs prior to his lapse of faith recorded in 1 Kings 11:1-11, when his numerous wives turned his heart after pagan gods. His faith in God was later restored, and he went on to write Psalms 72 and 127,

---

[1] Selected from Introduction to Proverbs; Thomas Nelson Bible

along with the books of Ecclesiastes and the Song of Solomon.

Someone once said that wisdom is knowing what to do; skill is knowing how to do it; and virtue is doing it. With that in mind, let us consider what this sacred book reveals, and then how to practice its rules of conduct and action.

Just two major themes run through this book: *wisdom* and *foolishness*. They are often overlapping in the experiences of life. Solomon praises wisdom as being rooted in the fear of the Lord; i.e., reverence for God, leading to obedience to God's Word. On the other hand, foolishness constitutes everything opposite to wisdom; for instance, stupidity, deceit, meddling, rashness, and wickedness.

Many of the proverbs overlap in meaning with some repetition. However, the repetitions should not be considered unnecessary. Each proverb is divinely inspired, and any repetition is an instrument to emphasize its importance. The prophet Isaiah declared the need to teach God's wisdom. He then revealed the method of instruction, which is repetitive:

> "For precept must be upon precept, precept upon precept; line upon line, line upon line; here a little, and there a little." (Isaiah 28:10)

There are a number of helpful themes in **Proverbs**, as illustrated by the following outline:

I. Man's Relationship to God

A. His Trust	Proverbs 22:19
B. His Humility	Proverbs 3:34
C. His Fear of God	Proverbs 1:7
D. His Righteousness	Proverbs 10:25
E. His Sin	Proverbs 28:13
F. His Obedience	Proverbs 6:23

G. Facing Reward	Proverbs 12:28
H. Facing Tests	Proverbs 17:3
I. Facing Blessings	Proverbs 10:22
J. Facing Death	Proverbs 15:11

II. Man's Relationship to Himself

A. His Character	Proverbs 20:11
B. His Wisdom	Proverbs 1:5
C. His Foolishness	Proverbs 26:10-11
D. His Speech	Proverbs 18:21
E. His Self-Control	Proverbs 6:9-11
F. His Kindness	Proverbs 3:3
G. His Wealth	Proverbs 11:4
H. His Pride	Proverbs 27:1
I. His Anger	Proverbs 29:11
j. His Laziness	Proverbs 13:4

III. Man's Relationship to Others

A. His Love	Proverbs 8:17
B. His Friends	Proverbs 17:17
C. His Enemies	Proverbs 19:27
D. His Truthfulness	Proverbs 23:23

E. His Gossip	Proverbs 20:19
F. As a Father	Proverb 30:7; 31:2-9
G. In Educating Children	Proverbs 4:1-4
H. In Disciplining Children	Proverbs 22:6

Selected from the MacArthur Study Bible

1. Understanding the literary structure of Proverbs

The literary structure of Proverbs is quite unique. This rhythmic use of parallelism places truths side by side, so that the second line somehow enhances the first line. That means the second may basically repeat the first with some alteration of the words, or the second may further define, expand, complete, or even contrast the first. For example:

a. **Comparison** (Synonymous)—the simplest proverbial form where the second line repeats the first with similar words.

"My son, attend unto my wisdom,
and bow thine ear to my understanding." (5:1)

"The liberal soul shall be made fat:
and he that watereth shall be watered also himself." (11:25)

b. **Contrast** (Antithetical)—where the second member is in contrast to the first, showing the other side of the picture. This construction is very prevalent in Proverbs.

"In the multitude of words there wanteth (lacks) *not sin:*
but he that refraineth his lips is wise." (10:19)

"The thoughts of the righteous are right:
but the counsels of the wicked are deceit." (12:5)

c. **Completion** (Progression)—where the second member adds a progressive thought, thus completing or further defining the first.

"The eyes of the LORD are in every place,
beholding the evil and the good." (15:3)

"The name of the LORD is a strong tower:
The righteous runneth into it, and is safe." (18:10)

2. Understanding the nature (purpose) of Proverbs

The Proverbs are not commandments or inflexible laws. They are poetic statements of wisdom under the direction of the Holy Spirit (2 Peter 2:21). The most common mistake is to interpret Proverbs as promises rather than statements of principle. These are written by Solomon to grant guidance to those desiring to live wisely and successfully. To consider them to be direct promises of God will lead to frustration and error.

For example, Prov. 15:1 says:

"A soft answer turneth away wrath: but grievous words stir up anger,"

Generally speaking, a soft answer given to an angry person will temper his "wrath" (response), but that's no guarantee that he will stop his angry tirade. Thus, this statement is a *principle* rather than a promise.

Chapter 1
The Beginning of Knowledge

Prov. 1:1

"The proverbs of Solomon the son of David, king of Israel;"

The opening statement of this marvelous book identifies the author as Solomon, the son of David, the King of Israel. Like the parables of Jesus, proverbs depict earthly situations that point to heavenly applications, bywords, similarities, ethical wisdom, and popular moral sayings.

We could further define a proverb as a short meaningful statement of a general truth which boils down a common experience of life into a memorable form. In the next several verses, Solomon begins to define the purposes of these statements of wisdom:

Prov. 1:2

"To know wisdom and instruction; to perceive the words of understanding;"

To know wisdom and instruction; To "know" here is more than simple head knowledge. It speaks of inner perception of truth. **Wisdom** is the ability to use knowledge skillfully, along with seeing life from God's perspective. "**Instruction**" here has the idea of correcting a fault, which is the information needed for discipline and direction.

To perceive the words of understanding. The study of **Proverbs** can help one to discover or realize and distinguish the words of understanding in it. Thus, "**to perceive**" is the ability to separate information mentally and to make proper distinctions, leading to the right conclusions and actions.

Prov. 1:3

"To receive the instructions of wisdom, justice, and judgment, and equity;"

To receive the instructions of wisdom. Another purpose is to receive or take the instruction of wisdom. The word used for wisdom here also includes the idea of clever insight and thoughtfulness:

Justice is the word for that which is right (morally and legally), lining up with truth.

Judgment refers to the process of deciding what is right.

Equity is the idea of fairness, doing things right before God and man.

All of these virtues are the opposite of confusion, which prevails today in our society! Take away the Word of God, and there's no direction, clarity of purpose, or right procedure for living.

Prov. 1:4

"To give subtilty to the simple, to the young man knowledge and discretion."

To give subtilty to the simple. Subtilty is used to express cleverness or resourcefulness. This quality is especially needful to simple people, usually the young and inexperienced. Of course, such wise subtilty is essential in every stage of life. Jesus said that we were to be *"wise as serpents, and harmless as doves."* (Matthew 10:16)

To know how to function legitimately in society with wisdom is a necessity for every believer in Christ. The world is tricky and underhanded; it is essential to understand and cleverly respond to those who are sophisticated sinners.

To the young man knowledge and discretion. Significantly, **the simple** one is placed beside **the young man**, who is also unsophisticated and easily seduced. Most young men are impulsive, easily led astray and seduced by the sins of the flesh. **Proverbs** can provide **knowledge and discretion** to prevent one from being overtaken by subtle temptations of wickedness.

Discretion is the ability to "spot an evil plan." It knows where people are "coming from." Street people call it "vibes." This kind of wisdom is essential to a young person's well-being and future success.

Could it be that Solomon's main thrust of Proverbs is focused on **young people**? This seems evident when considering that he uses the term **my son** at least 23 times throughout the Book! (check the following examples: Prov. 1:8, 10, 15; 2:1; 3:1; 4:1 ("children"); 5:1; 6:1; 7:1, etc.

Solomon recognizes firsthand the vulnerability and immaturity of his children; thus, the utter necessity for them to be grounded early with wisdom and godly knowledge. This was probably the basis of his classic instruction in Prov. 22:6: *"Train up a child in the way he should go: and when he is old, he will not depart from it."*

Prov. 1:5

"A wise man will hear, and will increase learning; and a man of understanding shall attain unto wise counsels:"

A wise man will hear, and will increase learning. A fool doesn't listen! He disregards sound instruction and continues his journey to self-destruction. "I Did It My Way" is his theme song. But a wise man hears and heeds advice, thus enjoying the fruit of obedience (e.g., peace, clear purpose, confidence, etc.). This increase in learning includes advancement in understanding by experience, thus promoting growth in God's grace.

A man of understanding shall attain unto wise counsels. The wise man will continue to acquire wise counsel. The word "counsels" is plural, denoting the abundant availability of wisdom to steer one in the right direction. The practice of skillful living leads to a higher level of wisdom: "practice makes perfect," as the saying goes.

The Apostle Paul speaks of living from "faith to faith"; that is, as a believer exercises faith at his present level, it results in the development of faith at a higher level – the ability to trust God for greater things. (Romans 1:17) Wisdom comes from God through the knowledge of and obedience to His Word, the Bible.

Note: The 8th chapter of **Proverbs** fully describes wisdom as a person, typifying Jesus Christ who is Wisdom personified (1 Corinthians 1:30).

How foolish we are to pit ourselves against the Word of Wisdom. Men who are foolish and proud trust only in themselves, ending up in hopelessness and self-destruction. Everyone needs an anchor in life's stormy sea, and Christ alone is that Anchor and the Rock! Indeed, believers can sing triumphantly, "My Anchor Holds!"

Prov. 1:6

"To understand a proverb, and the interpretation; the words of the wise, and their dark sayings."

To understand a proverb, and the interpretation. Solomon wants us to not only read, but understand these statements of ethical wisdom. These words need to be "broken down" by the illumination of the Holy Spirit to be applied to our daily living. Sometimes these proverbs are hard to understand, so God sheds light on the subject.

The word **interpretation** has to do with figuring out what the statements are saying in order to properly comprehend them. We need to compare Scripture with Scripture, *"rightly dividing the word of truth"* (2 Timothy 2:15). The Apostle Paul was persistent in giving his maximum effort to impart God's Word completely, accurately, and precisely, applying it to all of Scripture.

This is powerfully illustrated as a future time when Solomon's temple was destroyed and later reconstructed in Jerusalem. Ezra, the Scribe, was commissioned to restore the spiritual life of the Jews, expounding the Word of God to the multitude gathered before the "Water Gate." A pulpit or platform of wood was built and Ezra stood before them. Nehemiah records the incident:

"And Ezra opened the book in the sight of all the people; (for he was above all the people;) and when he opened it, all the people stood up: and Ezra blessed the LORD, the great God. And all the people answered, Amen, Amen, with lifting up their hands:

and they bowed their heads, and worshipped the LORD with their faces to the ground."

"Also, Jeshua... and the Levites, caused the people to understand the law... So they read in the book in the law of God distinctly, and gave the sense, and caused them to understand the reading... For all the people wept, when they heard the words of the law," (Nehemiah 8:5-9)

O, for such a revival and reformation of the power of God's Word in this generation! May this volume on **Proverbs** lend itself to that lofty goal.

The words of the wise, and their dark sayings. Words from the lips of wise people may take the form of satire, perplexity, or obscurity; they may even be "dark sayings" that totally stump the average mind. Yes, these, too, must become understandable by the grace of God. Indeed, the Book of **Proverbs** is a life-time study and, along with the rest of Scripture, is as vast as God Himself.

Prov. 1:7

"The fear of the LORD is the beginning of knowledge: but fools despise wisdom and instruction."

The fear of the LORD is the beginning of knowledge: Since the LORD is the Author of all knowledge, our relationship to Him is all-important if there is to be understanding. Thus, the "fear of the LORD" is the essential ingredient in the fruitful understanding of God's truth.

The fear of the LORD is the underlying theme of **Proverbs** and is the prerequisite to godliness. A holy reverence and respect for Jehovah (the great "I Am" of Exodus 3:14) is the essence of salvation in Christ (See 2 Corinthians 7:1). Practically speaking, fearing God is taking Him seriously. In fact, it is directly connected to the believer's faith.

For example, it is said that **"by faith** Noah, being warned of God of things not seen as yet, **moved with fear**, prepared an ark to the saving of his house..." (Hebrews 11:7) Noah's faith caused him to move in the "fear" of God, obeying the Lord's command. True faith and holy fear are inseparable. To walk in faith and the fear of God yields the reality of true knowledge.

The word for "beginning" has the meaning of "first place, chief part, or principle thing." No one really knows anything apart from the fear of God. It is this particular fear that is the chief part of all knowledge, i.e., awareness of the facts.

The ABCs are the principle part of our language; one never gets past these letters no matter how educated he may be. All words from "cat" to "trigonometry" are but combinations of these basic letters. Likewise, no one ever gets past the fear of God.

It's been said that no doctor has ever really seen a body unless he has a sense of the fear of God: because we are *"fearfully and wonderfully made."* Without that fear, an astronomer is yet to see the wonder of a star in the universe. O, LORD, my God, "How Great Thou Art!"

Fools despise wisdom and instruction. Only fools (silly people) despise or scorn God's wisdom (skill) and instruction (discipline). O, what the world, including the Church, is missing by ignoring the One who made them and then came down to pay the awesome price of their redemption at the Cross!

Prov. 1:8

"My son, hear the instruction of thy father, and forsake not the law of thy mother:"

My son, hear the instruction of thy father. Immediately after the key verse of this book, we have divine instruction regarding the family. Solomon, as a concerned father, mentions first "my son," This is likely a reference to his son, Rehoboam.

Solomon tells us to listen to the corrections and warnings of our fathers. The father is not just the "sperm donor" and breadwinner, but the leader and instructor of the family. Along with the mother, he is the first representative of God to his children.

The previous verse spoke of the "fear of the Lord." This verse applies that instruction to the father and mother, who transfers it to their children. The reality of God's fear must begin and reside at home, in the family.

Forsake not the law of thy mother. While the father instructs, the mother gives rules of conduct and action to be followed. This is a marital team effort, setting the pace for the son's (child's) future. He is to "hear" or obey his father and not "forsake" his mother's teaching. That's two sides of the same coin: to obey is not to forsake or ignore. It's one thing to hear the words; it's another thing to heed the words. Parenting is a full-time job and so is growing up.

We see here the real foundation of a godly home, out of which comes true successful living.We spend too much time teaching children how to make a living without teaching them how to live. One of my mentors used to say, "If you ever learn how to live, you'll never have a problem making a living." No wonder there's been such a satanic attack against the family throughout history.

Prov. 1:9

For they shall be an ornament of grace unto thy head, and chains about thy neck.

Jewelry has never lost its charm. How precious and widespread are gold rings and necklaces. How apropos is this analogy to the elegance and spiritual charm of parental instruction. The law and instruction of parents shall be ornaments of **grace** around the **head** and **neck**.

The **ornament** is a wreath used as a crown of honor or **grace**. Barnes states here:

> "To the Israelite's mind no signs or badges of joy or glory were higher in worth than the garland around the head, the gold chain around the neck, worn by kings and the favorites of kings."[2]

(Refer to Genesis 41:42; Daniel 5:29.)

The **chains** were necklaces of honor, worn by kings and those

---

[2] Barnes Notes on Proverbs; e-Sword Program

honored by kings. Evidently, this practice was carried over into New Testament times in the Olympics, continuing even to this day. In a recent Games celebration in Greece, many garlands and gold metals were presented to the best athletes. Much time, energy, and discipline are given by athletes to win a gold medal and a crown of twisted vines.

Yet, it's all temporary and corruptible. How much greater is the incorruptible crown that lasts forever, given to those who faithfully obey the Word of God! Where does it all begin? It begins at home listening to the godly instructions of parents. Someone has said: "We are now what we have been becoming." Children obey your parents in the Lord, for this is not only right, but profitable in every way. (See Ephesians 6:1-3)

Prov. 1:10

"My son, if sinners entice thee, consent thou not."

Right up front, Solomon warns his son in regard to sinful peer pressure. This might indicate the vital importance of teaching **Proverbs** to children. He deals here with just saying "No!" to the temptations of the peer group. This works at any age. Wicked schemes are presented to us at every phase of life. As we say "Yes" to God, we can then say "No" to sinners.

Note the word "sinners" depicts offenders or criminals, not only weak individuals who easily fall into sin. These are wicked people who work at crime. See Genesis 13:13:

> *"But the men of Sodom were wicked and sinners before the LORD exceedingly."* (Refer also to 1 Samuel 15:18; Psalm 1:1, 5; 104:35)

Prov. 1:11

"If they say, Come with us, let us lay wait for blood, let us lurk privily for the innocent without cause:"

If they say... Here's the crowd, the cronies, the "peer pressure" group. They always have something to say, some scheme to present, or some mischief to do. Here their enticement comes in a verbal proposal: "Come with us"...for what? To **lay wait** (lie in ambush) **for blood**, to **lurk privily** or hide out in order to harm the innocent who are free from guilt. Yes, the wicked in their corruption and greed will prey on others **without cause**; that is, for no good purpose or valid reason (Refer to 1 Samuel 19:5; Job 2:3).

It is interesting that Solomon reveals up front how the wicked heart thinks and how essential it is to be right with God and obedient to His Word. But it's a fight to do right! The wise person must take a stand and not consent. This trap is set particularly for new believers who have recently made a break from their sinful lifestyles. However, that is not to say that mature saints in Christ do not face the temptation to compromise their own testimony in even more subtle ways.

Verses 10-19 serve as a commentary on Genesis 6:5:

"And GOD saw that the wickedness of man was great in the earth, and that every imagination of the thoughts of his heart was only evil continually."

This certainly defines man's utter depravity. Indeed, it is only through Christ that a sinful soul can be transformed and redeemed.

Prov. 1:12

"Let us swallow them up alive as the grave; and whole, as those that go down into the pit:"

Note the treachery: **swallow** (destroy) **them up alive as the grave.** It's similar to the terms "eat them up alive" and "bury them alive," Let's also destroy them entirely, and **whole.** There is no mercy shown whatsoever for these murderous and totally wicked thugs, who will go to the pit of hell.

Prov. 1:13

"We shall find all precious substance, we shall fill our houses with spoil:"

Here's the heart of the matter: the reason for the wicked, murderous scheme is MONEY! This is certainly another commentary on the love of money, which is the root of all evil. Note their cocky, arrogant confidence: **We shall find all precious** (valuable) **substance** (wealth), **we shall fill our houses with spoil.**

It is significant that this episode comes right up front in **Proverbs.** It follows right after the key verse on the **fear of the Lord** (1:7), and before the command to obey the instruction of father and mother (1:8, 9). A son who refuses to listen to God and his parents will follow the wrong crowd. Instead of being wise, he will be foolishly wicked. Who he listens to is of ultimate importance and consequence.

Prov. 1:14

"Cast in thy lot among us; let us all have one purse:"

The proposition continues: **Cast in thy lot** (your portion) **among us**, and we'll **have one** (common) **purse** (bag of money). Here's the commonality of thieves who think and act in wicked unity.

Yet, it must be noted how the initial, common purse becomes the instrument to divide and destroy the thieves themselves. They will even kill each other for their "common" purse, because their greed will not allow them to share. O, the ruthlessness of sin!

Prov. 1:15

"My son, walk not thou in the way with them; refrain thy foot from their path:"

Solomon pleads with his son to walk away from and reject the wicked proposal. Obviously, this is the **walk** of Psalm 1:1:

"Blessed is the man that walketh not in the counsel of the ungodly, nor standeth in the way of sinners, nor sitteth in the seat of the scornful."

Don't even think of walking in their wicked lifestyle, and don't even set foot on their path! Prevention is much better than cure. King David says it well:

"I have refrained my feet from every evil way, that I might keep thy word," (Psalm 119:101)

In other words, to **refrain** from evil is to obey the Word, and obedience to God will keep one from evil (Refer to Psalm 119:9, 11). Not to jump in the mud hole is much better than being delivered from it. "Flee youthful lusts"; i.e., run, run, run!

Prov. 1:16

"For their feet run to evil, and make haste to shed blood."

Why should we run from them? Because **their feet run to evil, and make haste to shed blood.** Begin walking with them, and you'll be running toward mischief and crime. This is another commentary on the wicked and sinful sell-out of the human heart. The prophet Jeremiah said:

> *"The heart is deceitful above all things, and desperately wicked, who can know it?"* (Jeremiah 17:9)

Prov. 1:17

"Surely in vain the net is spread in the sight of any bird."

Solomon magnifies the stupidity of the wicked by appealing to the positive instinct of birds. Birds are savvy to the danger of **the net** (trap) when it's spread out in their sight. In other words, even birds can sense danger and avoid it, especially when it is obviously in their **sight.** However, a foolish man goes headlong into the trap, made by his own wicked scheme.

Prov. 1:18

"And they lay wait for their own blood; they lurk privily for their own lives."

Not only do the wicked fall into their own trap, but their scheme backfires or boomerangs on them. They reap what they sow. While they **lay wait** to victimize others, it's only a matter of time before their **own blood** and **lives** are destroyed.

Consider the potent nature of this truth in the Book of Esther, and the story of Haman, whose plot against Mordecai boomeranged on himself. Haman was hung on the gallows that he prepared for Esther's uncle, Mordecai, an ultimate expression of God's justice (Esther 7). The adage: *"Be sure your sin will find you out,"* is clearly illustrated therein.

Prov. 1:19

"So are the ways of every one that is greedy of gain; which taketh away the life of the owners thereof."

Greed or covetousness is not only the root of robbery, but murder as well. Indeed, the love of money is the root of all kinds of evil. Greedy people will stop at nothing to get what they want, even to the utter destruction of others.

So is the condition of the human heart, which is "desperately wicked" (Jeremiah 17:9). Man is lost apart from the saving grace of God. No wonder Wisdom came one day to deliver fools!

Prov. 1:20

"Wisdom crieth without; she uttereth her voice in the streets:"

In spite of the wickedness described above, wisdom is not silent, but cries out in distress. In contrast to wickedness, wisdom has nothing to hide, and can be found in the most public of places, **the streets.**

J.F.B.'s Commentary comments that "Wisdom" here is in the plural, indicating fullness or magnification.[3] Some take this as the Christ, who is our Wisdom (refer to 1 Corinthians 1:30), crying out in the streets for folks to repent of their sin. This certainly fits the whole of Scripture. God is not indifferent to sinners and neither should we be. Lift up your voice as a trumpet and preach the Gospel in public places.

Prov. 1:21

"She crieth in the chief place of concourse, in the openings of the gates: in the city she uttereth her words, saying,"

A further description of Wisdom's aggression is crying out to the people. She cries in **the chief** (most prominent) **place of concourse** (noise or tumult). Her voice is heard where the traffic of humanity resides and travels (not in hidden places).

---

[3] Jameson, Faucet and Brown; e-Sword Bible Program.

These gates indicate the city fathers, the political leadership (refer to Proverbs 31:23). Wisdom seeks all people, all of whom will die without her.

Prov. 1:22

"How long, ye simple ones, will ye love simplicity? And the scorners delight in their scorning, and fools hate knowledge?"

Wisdom cries out to the **simple ones...the scorners** (mockers)**...and the fools.** This is an outright indictment indicating impending judgment, and an invitation to repent, as seen in the next verse. **How long**, she asks, will the wicked pursue their ungodly attitudes and actions? Simple ones are silly and ignorant; the scorners or mockers enjoy their scorning; and **fools hate knowledge**: they don't want to know the truth or the facts.

O, the corruption and rebellion of the human heart! Only the gift of saving faith can change such people. Man left to himself can only die and go to Hell.

Prov. 1:23

"Turn you at my reproof: behold, I will pour out my spirit unto you, I will make known my words unto you."

This seems like God's last call for simple fools to repent before they are turned over to a reprobate mind.[4] Here's an offer of grace in the midst of impending judgment. **Turn** (repent, return) **...I will pour out my spirit** (the Holy Spirit)...What a tremendous offer of mercy to rebels!

Note the sequence: 1st: Repent (**turn**); 2nd: The Holy Spirit will be **poured out** to you; and 3rd: Divine revelation of God's Word will be given to you. However, the next verse indicates that God's offer was not well received.

---

[4] A mind rejected by God, given over to sin; incapable of making right choices. Described further in Proverbs 1:26-31 and Romans 1:28-32.

Prov. 1:24

"Because I have called, and ye refused; I have stretched out my hand, and no man regarded;"

This solemn reprimand follows on the heels of an invitation to repent and receive God's mercy. The wicked failed to heed God's words. The Lord just made a loving plea, as in Isaiah 1:18-20:

"Come now, and let us reason together… though your sins be as scarlet, they shall be as white as snow… If ye be willing and obedient, ye shall eat the good of the land: But if ye refuse and rebel, ye shall be devoured with the sword…"

So here, Wisdom cries out: **Because I have called, and ye refused; I have stretched** (out) **my hand** (i.e., in mercy and love), **and no man regarded** (took heed). The Lord bemoans the stubbornness and rebellion of the wicked, but then announces the just consequences that follow.

It's significant that this somber and potent warning is in the first chapter—right up front. Whatever comes afterward, the Lord reveals and earnestly urges us to obey His Word from the very beginning. To fail here is to risk the possibility of hardening one's mind to the point of no return, as described in the following verses.

Prov. 1:25

"But ye have set at naught all my counsel, and would none of my reproof:"

In connection with the previous verse, Solomon reveals their depraved hearts (apart from their actions), which refused or ignored (**set at naught**) all of God's advice and His attempts to correct their faults. Here is another exposure of the depraved nature of mankind, which is bound to sin, unwilling to submit to God's correction. This commentary also applies to Genesis 6:5, Jeremiah 17:9, and Romans 3:10-12.

Prov. 1:26

"I also will laugh at your calamity; I will mock when your fear cometh;"

This has to be one of the most somber verses in Scripture. To invoke God's holy laughter at sinful rebellion is absolutely awesome! **I also will laugh at your calamity**...It's as if God is saying, "You have laughed at and refused my Word, now I will have the last laugh!" This statement reflects the Holy grief of a loving God who must respond with justice instead of mercy. (cf. Psalm 2:4; 37:13; 59:8)

Furthermore, God says He will **mock** or make fun of the wicked person's fear when he faces the consequences of his sinfulness. How this flies in the face of modern preaching that "God loves you, no matter what. Yes, God is love, but He hates wickedness. If a sinner repents, God will pour out His mercy. If a sinner does not repent, then God will pour out His wrath. Indeed, it's a fearful thing to fall into the Hands of the living, just God!

Prov. 1:27

"When your fear cometh as desolation, and your destruction cometh as a whirlwind; when distress and anguish cometh upon you."

There's hardly a way to understand, much less to explain, the judgment of God expressed here. When fear comes **as desolation** (complete ruin), and **destruction** comes as a **whirlwind,** etc., where do you run if this is God's doing? Where do the ungodly run? What an ultimate dilemma this is!

Indeed, *"it is a fearful thing to fall into the hands of the living God...For our God is a consuming fire"* (Hebrews 10:31; 12:29). Without faith in Christ and His blood atonement there is no refuge from the fire of God's justice and wrath.

Prov. 1:28

"Then shall they call upon me, but I will not answer; they shall seek me early, but they shall not find me:"

Like Esau, the son of Isaac, who sought his father's blessing with exceedingly great and bitter tears, but never received it (Genesis 27:34-40), so these God-haters cry out in anguish to no avail. What a contradiction to modern preaching which speaks "smooth words" with little mention of Hell's judgment.

Jesus is portrayed today as the one who is "always there" and "hears every prayer," No! There comes a time when folks will cross the deadline, having had opportunities to repent, but refused them. Yes, there is a time God says, "They shall call upon me, but I will not answer," How awesome is that statement?

Prov. 1:29

"For that they hated knowledge, and did not choose the fear of the LORD:"

The reason for God's rejection: *"...they hated knowledge* (the truth) *and did not choose the fear* (reverence) *of the LORD."*

Here is another description of man's utter rebellion and destitute condition. He doesn't just ignore truth—he hates it. True knowledge is contrary to his wicked heart (Jeremiah 1:9). Left to himself, he will never choose God, for he perceives himself to be god. That attitude began with Lucifer, who desired to replace God (cf. Isaiah 14:13f). When he fell from Heaven and became Satan, he successfully influenced Adam to play "god" as well (Genesis 3). Paul further depicts man's basic condition in Romans 3:10-12:

> *"As it is written, There is none righteous, no, not one: There is none that understandeth, there is none that seeketh after God. They are all gone out of the way, they are together become unprofitable; there is none that doeth good, no, not one."*

Prov. 1:30

"They would none of my counsel: they despised all my reproof."

Wicked men do not want God's advice or **counsel.** Their nature will not allow it, for the satanic world philosophy possesses them. Aren't they free to choose? Yes, but their choice is dictated by their fallen nature; therefore, they're bound to do wrong.

Not only do they refuse God's counsel, they despise or spurn His correction or **reproof.** Because of a wicked heart, man hates godly righteousness, and thus despises every admonition to change. This is depravity! He may be smart, cultured, and even religious, but he lives totally for himself. That's why Jesus confronted the elite religious teachers of Israel with the necessity of being "born again," a miraculous birth from on high (John 3:3). Apart from God's convicting and converting grace, man is totally self-absorbed, and headed for eternal destruction.

Prov. 1:31

"Therefore shall they eat of the fruit of their own way, and be filled with their own devices."

God doesn't give up on people, but will give them over to whatever they've sold themselves to (cf. Romans 1:24ff.). Solomon describes the result of the sinner's rejection of God's Word; i.e., **they shall eat of the fruit** (results) **of their own way** (lifestyle), **and be filled with their own devices** (or vices). Man must make a choice to go God's way or his own way. He cannot have it both ways. God's way is the only way that brings eternal blessings instead of judgment. Galatians 6:7, 8 verifies this concept:

"Be not deceived; God is not mocked: for whatsoever a man soweth, that shall he also reap. For he that soweth to his flesh shall of the flesh reap corruption; but he that soweth to the Spirit shall of the Spirit reap life everlasting."

Prov. 1:32

"For the turning away of the simple shall slay them, and the prosperity of fools shall destroy them:"

Instead of turning to wisdom, **fools** "turn away." They were exposed to truth, but didn't go with it. The **simple** foolishly do so to their own demise. There's a certain illusion of security or **prosperity** in which fools live; and it's a false security at best, leading to their destruction.

Fools live on "fantasy island," not willing, nor capable of facing their true condition. It's not like they have never heard the truth, but they can never escape the responsibility for their wrong actions. Their lives are destructive on earth, only to be faced with God's judgment in the end (refer to Hebrews 9:27).

Prov. 1:33

"But whoso hearkeneth unto me shall dwell safely, and shall be quiet from fear of evil."

A conclusive statement of comfort and hope is given to the wise. The one who **hearkens** (hears and obeys) **unto me shall dwell safely.** Here's a picture of abiding security in God. Not only that, but also he **shall be quiet from fear of evil (**peaceful rather than alarmed). What a contrast to the unrest, vulnerability, fearfulness, and final judgment of the foolish, who refuse to submit to the King of Kings!

Isaiah has a further word of comfort:

"Thou wilt keep him in perfect peace, whose mind is stayed on thee: because he trusteth in thee." (Isaiah 26:3)

Chapter 2
The Value of Wisdom

Prov. 2:1

"My son, if thou wilt receive my words, and hide my commandments with thee;"

Having given the key verse for all of **Proverbs** in 1:7 (*"The fear of the Lord is the beginning of knowledge"*), Solomon now sets out to reveal how that quality may be obtained. He affectionately addresses **My son,** which evidently refers to Rehoboam, but is certainly applied to all who follow the LORD. Keeping the Word is a family matter, even though Rehoboam failed to take his father's advice (1 Kings 12). Here he exhorts his son to **receive my words, and hide** (store or treasure) **my commandments with thee.** Note that the steps to the fear of God (F.O.G.) are conditional, preceded by "**if**." To acquire the fear of the Lord is basically a willing obedience to the Word. It comes down to what we think is most important in life or what has priority in our lives. David said:

"Wherewithal shall a young man cleanse his way? by taking heed thereto according to thy word.—Thy Word have I hid in mine heart, that I might not sin against thee," (Psalm 119:9,11)

Prov. 2:2

"So that thou incline thine ear unto wisdom, and apply thine heart to understanding:"

The quest for the "fear of God" continues. Key verbs in the previous verse were "receive" and "hide" the word within. Here in vs. 2, the progression involves inclining the **ear unto wisdom.** The idea is to pay strict attention to the words. The **ear,** as used here, indicates the inner, spiritual ear (the heart) whereby understanding takes place. How useless are the words that simply ring in the outer ear. Wisdom must have an impact on the soul. Therefore, God's Word must be taken seriously. **Apply thine heart to understanding:** as our ear and heart are stretched out and the Word of God is taken seriously, one can apply obedient faith to the heart. What is taken seriously in the heart will be manifest in every day behavior.

Prov. 2:3

"Yea if thou criest after knowledge, and liftest up thy voice for understanding;"

One's intense desire to know God is displayed by crying out and lifting up the **voice.** In times of emergency, one can't contain emotions. We let it "all hang out" when something is pressing us. What else is more important than knowing God?

Prov. 2:4

"If thou seekest her as silver, and searchest for her as for hid treasures:"

Here's a real test for intensity and desire to know the fear of the Lord. Do we want it more than riches? Is it really deemed valuable? Humans are possessed with seeking the wealth of the world. Just look at the "American Dream." Jesus told us that where your treasure is, there will your heart be also (Matthew 6:21).

O, to seek the Lord and His wisdom, as for **silver** (money) and **treasures!** How many stories have been written depicting pirates seeking hidden treasures, or men killing each other to find the gold? They will tediously follow the "treasure map" to find the hidden treasures.

O, that we could find it in our hearts to dedicate ourselves to an intense study the Word of God so as to know the God of the Word! What a wonderful difference that would make in our daily walk and in the holiness of the Church at large!

Prov. 2:5

"Then shalt thou understand the fear of the LORD, and find the knowledge of God."

Then shalt thou understand the fear of the LORD...! When? After the stated conditions of vs. 1-4 are fulfilled. This is more than just a desire or passing fancy; it's a determination to understand the Fear of God and **find** (attain) **the knowledge of God.** To fear Him is to know Him. To fear Him is to take Him seriously in every aspect of our lives. Such **knowledge** has to be the ultimate experience of any earth-bound saint.

The Fear of God is directly linked to faith in the New Testament. For instance, Noah by faith moved with fear and built the ark (Hebrews 11:7). Faith is not some passive "belief system," but an obedient response to God's Word.

All the heroes of faith in Hebrews 11 *did* something by faith that had never been done before. Somehow their faith was evidenced by a willingness to do God's will. This resulted from their awesome, reverential fear of God.

The fear of the LORD is indeed central to the Christian's life (2 Corinthians 7:1; Proverbs 1:7).

Prov. 2:6

"For the LORD giveth wisdom: out of his mouth cometh knowledge and understanding."

What is the Source of wisdom? Certainly, it is Jehovah Himself! **For** (because) **the LORD giveth wisdom.** There's an obvious connection between understanding the fear of the Lord (2:5) and the gift of wisdom (1:7). Wisdom is uniquely from the LORD. In fact, Christ **is** our Wisdom! Thus, apart from the fear of God and a right relationship with the Lord, true wisdom is impossible to attain.

Out of His mouth cometh knowledge and understanding: How we forfeit discernment and true knowledge when we fail to seek the Lord. Even as believers, we go to the wrong places and/or the wrong persons for direction. The fountainheads of the world seem to draw even the Church to its waters. God help us to come back to the Source of all wisdom and knowledge.

Prov. 2:7

"He layeth up sound wisdom for the righteous: he is a buckler to them that walk uprightly."

The Lord is the Treasury of all knowledge and wisdom (Colossians 2:3); therefore, He can dispense this **sound wisdom** (i.e., working knowledge) **for the righteous** (those who obey God). How wonderful that God reserves sound judgment for His children, and He has an infinite supply of it!

The words **layeth up** are the same as "hid" in Psalm 119:11: *"Thy word have I hid in my heart...,"*

The Lord has hidden or treasured up this wisdom in His Word. Thus, to hide the word in my heart is to draw upon the power and wisdom of God. Thank God for the unseen supply and abundance of wisdom that enables us to be effective servants of God (See 2 Timothy 3:16, 17; Hebrews 4:12; Matthew 6:33; Joshua 1:8). Note the word **righteous** is practical obedience, which parallels with **walk uprightly.**

In conjunction, the Lord is **a buckler** (shield or protector) to those who walk uprightly. God's supply equips and protects us. He gives us what we need, while protecting us from the enemy. (Refer to Psalm 18:1-2)

Prov. 2:8

"He keepeth the paths of judgment, and preserveth the way of his saints."

How wonderful that the Lord not only initiates His work of saving grace, but continues and consummates it (Philippians 1:6). Even as we obey His Word, we are totally dependent on His sustaining grace and strength. Thus, **He keepeth** (continually guards, protects) **the paths** (course of life or lifestyle) **of judgment.**

Judgment here means justice or rightness. Hence, God protects and maintains His character of Justice, along with those who walk uprightly in that justice. Indeed, He directs **the paths** of the obedient ones. God's Justice includes His hatred for what is wrong. His righteousness is His love for what is right.

Together, justice and righteousness comprise His Holiness. They are two sides of the same coin. That's why true believers hate what God hates and love what God loves. Before being born again or converted, we loved what God hated and hated what God loved. That's the fundamental issue of repentance: a total change of mind and heart, resulting in a godly attitude and godly actions.

And preserveth the way (course of life) **of His saints.** Here's the parallel thought of God's preserving grace regarding godly people (See Psalm 16:10).

Psalm 1:6, says: *"For the LORD knoweth the way of the righteous: but the way of the ungodly shall perish."*

God knows His children in the sense that He has set His love upon them, keeping them to the end which shall never end!

Prov. 2:9

"Then shalt thou understand righteousness, and judgment, and equity; yea, every good path."

The fruits of God's wisdom are many. The keeping and preserving power mentioned in the previous verse triggers further understanding of what is right. In addition, the believer will have the proper **judgment** in making decisions (refer to Abraham in Genesis 18:19; Leviticus 19:15).

"Equity" refers to what is even, smooth, not crooked or foul, and "on the level" as we put it. The same Hebrew word is translated "right things" in 8:6 and 23:16.

Yea, every good (excellent, pleasant) **path** you will **understand**. The emphasis here seems to be the ability to "see through the truth at hand" – the purpose behind the actions, not just the character qualities themselves. In other words, there's inner moral strength in understanding God's Word, rather than just running on sheer obedience.

Prov. 2:10

"When wisdom entereth into thine heart, and knowledge is pleasant unto thy soul;"

This verse gives the prerequisite to discretion and godly understanding (vs. 11). The entrance of **wisdom into thine heart** (or spirit), and the delight of **knowledge** to the **soul.** What grips us internally will be manifested externally in our conduct and actions. We are what we eat, physically and spiritually! We reap what we sow. In computer language: "garbage in, garbage out;" or likewise, "truth in, truth out."

However, note that simply being exposed to wisdom is not sufficient. There must be an "entrance" or penetration of godly wisdom into the **heart** or spirit. Then, spiritual knowledge becomes a delight, not a chore.

In Psalm 1, David deals with the blessed man who doesn't walk in the counsel of the ungodly (vs. 1) but he delights in and meditates on the Word of God day and night. That's the answer! There's no way to escape the power of this world apart from the power of God's Word, internally focused upon and rehearsed. Note the relationship between "success" and the Word of God in Joshua 1:8:

"This book of the law shall not depart out of thy mouth; but thou shalt meditate therein day and night, that thou mayest observe to do according to all that is written therein: for then thou shalt make thy way prosperous, and then thou shalt have good success."

Prov. 2:11

"Discretion shall preserve thee, understanding shall keep thee:"

When we really want to know, we can know. How good it is that God fixes our "wanter" when we repent and submit to Him. This process is depicted in the previous verse where "wisdom enters into the heart," A whole new vista is opened when this happens. For the first time, we want what God wants, instead of bucking His Word.

The result? **Discretion shall preserve** (guard) **thee, understanding** (skillful knowledge) **shall keep** (protect) **thee.**

This protection is essential in this big, wide, wicked world of ours. Whatever you may not have, make sure you do have God's wisdom, which produces divine, practical "know-how" in everyday life.

Prov. 2:12

"To deliver thee from the way of the evil man, from the man that speaketh froward things;"

Godly discernment is a means of deliverance from the evil ways of wicked men. We cannot escape the presence of wicked people, but we can refrain from getting caught up in their **evil** ways, especially their speaking **froward** (perverted) **things.** Evil men have an evil agenda and are always searching for others to join them in their schemes. It's better to never get involved, than to need deliverance later on. Wisdom sees the trap ahead and steers clear of it.

Prov. 2:13

"Who leave the paths of uprightness, to walk in the ways of darkness;"

Wicked men make a choice to **leave** or forsake the right paths of living. Even the unrighteous have a conscience, if not the written law found in the Bible. No one is totally innocent or ignorant. Thus, they **walk in the ways of darkness.** Every man walks down some road, either in the light of God's Word, or in the darkness of wickedness.

David said:

"Thy Word is a lamp unto my feet, and a light unto my path." (Psalm 119:105)

The Word = Right = Light! Anything else is **darkness**, leading to destruction.

Prov. 2:14

"Who rejoice to do evil, and delight in the frowardness of the wicked;"

O, the depth of depravity! Evil men do what they love to do:

Evil. The deceitful and **wicked** heart loves deceit and wickedness. How deep is this? How incurable is this condition apart from the mercy and miraculous power of God?

Evil men **rejoice to do evil, and delight in** willful perversion. This commentary on the sinner's attitude and philosophy is captured in Romans 1:32:

> *"Who knowing the judgment of God, that they which commit such things are worthy of death, not only do the same, but have pleasure in them that do them,"*

Everyone rejoices in something, depending on what he treasures in his heart.

Prov. 2:15

"Whose ways are crooked, and they froward in their paths:"

Solomon continues to describe the wicked, whom we must conquer through spiritual discernment. Perversion is the order of the day in this world. We use the term "pervert" for extreme or unusual cases, but such are really the ongoing ways of all sinners. In light of the standard of God's Law, their **ways** (course of life) **are crooked** (distorted).

The word **"froward"** is a synonym for crooked, depicting a turning aside or departure from the truth. See notes on 1:10-16.

Prov. 2:16

"To deliver thee from the strange woman, even from the stranger which flattereth with her words;"

Spiritual discernment not only delivers us from wicked men (2:12), but also from **the strange woman.** In our sex-driven society, these are practical and powerful words. Prostitution and immorality of all sorts are the order of the day, and believers are not exempt from Satan's fiery darts. Hanky-panky is not a stranger to the Church.

Note the enticing vehicle of flattery. O, the power of flattering words! Yet, how much greater is the power and cleansing of God's

Word? David addresses this issue in Psalm 119:9-11:

> *"Wherewithal shall a young man cleanse his way? By taking heed thereto according to thy word. With my whole heart have I sought thee: O let me not wander from thy commandments. Thy word have I hid in mine heart, that I might not sin against thee."*

The Apostle Paul adds:

> *"Flee also youthful lusts: but follow righteousness, faith, charity, peace, with them that call on the Lord out of a pure heart."* (2 Timothy 2:22)

Prov. 2:17

> *"Which forsaketh the guide of her youth, and forgetteth the covenant of her God."*

Who is this **strange woman**? She is someone's daughter who was **guided** in her **youth,** but has forsaken (refused) that vital instruction. More importantly, she has forgotten **the covenant** (the binding agreement) **of her God.**[5] She has turned from the pledge of purity before God.

Here is a grown woman, probably nurtured and instructed in Truth as a youngster, but chooses to go her own way. For instance, how many prostitutes are there today who come from Christian homes but have walked away from the Word of God?

Prov. 2:18

> *"For her house inclineth unto death, and her paths unto the dead."*

What a vivid picture of the "wages of sin" (Romans 6:23); namely, **her house inclined unto death;** i.e., it is sinking into the pit of death. It's like one caught in the sinking trap of quicksand. Death is sure, with no release or recourse!

In addition, **her paths** (tracks) are headed to a **dead** end. Her

---

[5] Covenant (Heb. *Bereeth*) used of a compact between God and man; e.g., Noah, Abraham, Moses, etc.

whole life is on the downhill trek to Hell.

Prov. 2:19

"None that go unto her return again, neither take they hold of the paths of life."

Here is verse 18 taken to the next level: Not only the incline to death, but the road of no return. Whoever gets involved with her is destined to ruin and death, with no way out. They can never break away (naturally), and will never **take hold of the paths of life.** What a warning and a horrible contrast to those who have abundant life in God. (See Psalm 16:11)

Prov. 2:20

"That thou mayest walk in the way of good men, and keep the paths of the righteous."

The effect of the above warnings culminates in the following earnest plea: **That thou mayest walk in the way** (lifestyle) **of good men and keep** (guard) **the paths of the righteous.** What road we travel makes a difference, and only the right road leads to the right place. Thus, *"The steps of a good man are ordered by the Lord"* (Psalm 37:23).

Prov. 2:21

"For the upright shall dwell in the land, and the perfect shall remain in it."

Here's a description of true prosperity for those who obey and walk with God. Who are they? They are **upright** (from *"yashar"*- "to go straight;" cf. Psalm 1:1, the root of *"blessed"*); they are **perfect** (not sinless, but complete, whole, and sound). See Psalm 37:3, 9, 11.

Prov. 2:22

"But the wicked shall be cut off from the earth, and the transgressors shall be rooted out of it."

In contrast to the upright, **the wicked shall be cut off** or destroyed. The **transgressors**, those who act treacherously, **shall**

be rooted out (plucked up) from this earthly existence. Thus, we have the basis for both Heaven and Hell.

There's an ultimate, eternal place for the righteous and one for the wicked. No one can have it both ways. Heaven and Hell are in opposite directions. To choose the right road is absolutely critical.

Chapter 3
Guidance for the Young

Prov. 3:1

"My son, forget not my law; but let thine heart keep my commandments:"

Here the admonition to Solomon's **son** is to **forget not my law;** i.e., don't ignore my Word, don't lay it aside. How many Bibles are on coffee tables or nightstands collecting dust, never read, much less, obeyed? We've never had more copies of the Bible than we do today. Yet, there has never been more compromise, worldliness, and unbelief.

He further states: **but let thine heart** (inner spirit) **keep** (guard or obey) **my commandments.** Here's an appeal to give priority to the Word and make it a matter of the heart that works from the inside out, rather than mere outward appearance. Religion always begins from the outside and works inward, but never far enough.

True salvation in Christ always begins on the inside and works outward. It's the divine "heart transplant" that makes us "new creatures" in Christ (2 Corinthians 5:17). Thus, the Apostle Paul says:

"...work out your own salvation with fear and trembling. For it is God which worketh in you both to will and to do of his good pleasure," (Philippians 2:12, 13)

In other words, the believer is "working out" what God is "working in."

Prov. 3:2

"For length of days, and long life, and peace, shall they add to thee."

After appealing to his son to obey God's law from the heart, Solomon now tacks on a promise similar to the 5th Commandment in Exodus 20:12: *"Honour thy father and thy mother: that thy days may be long upon the land which the LORD thy God giveth thee,"*

Ephesians 6:2 and 3 also says:

"Honour thy father and mother; (which is the first commandment with promise;) That it may be well with thee, and thou mayest live long on the earth,"

This is a general principle that must not be misinterpreted to mean that every obedient believer lives to an older age. It does mean that he will live a full and peaceful life with a godly quality.

The best way to have a long, full, and happy life is to walk in fellowship with God. Obedience is not bondage, but quite the contrary. To know God is to love and obey Him. Jesus said, *"If the Son therefore shall makes you free, ye shall be free indeed"* (John 8:36). The Apostle Paul said: *"For the law of the Spirit of life in Christ Jesus hath made me free from the law of sin and death"* (Romans 8:2).

Prov. 3:3

"Let not mercy and truth forsake thee: bind them about thy neck; write them upon the table of thine heart:"

Thank God for **mercy and truth** which capture the believer in Christ! Don't let them **forsake thee.** Better to lose every fortune of this world than to be stripped of these gifts from Heaven. The way to prevent this from happening is to **bind** (tie) **them about thy neck** and to **write** (engrave) **them upon the table** (smooth slab) of your **heart.**

In a world of violence and lies, we need to wear the character of God's mercy and truth as a necklace. It must be our heart's focus and the very principle of life (cf. Psalm 119:11; Joshua 1:8). What we do with the Word of God is what God will do with us (Colossians

3:16). The Church needs to display the character of God and the fruit of the Holy Spirit, to a world that's spiritually bankrupt. To forsake **mercy and truth** is to commit spiritual suicide.

Prov. 3:4

"So shalt thou find favour and good understanding in the sight of God and man."

Manifesting the fruit of the Holy Spirit attains favor and wisdom in the eyes of God and man. The Christian's life is full of favor, or grace, not only before God, but men as well. It's been said that "Good men are reasonable;" i.e., they respect those who are loving and kind. Walking with God and reaching out to people provide the most fruitful lifestyle one can live.

While there may be opposition from some who despise our testimony, the rank and file of mankind will favor our demonstration of love toward them. Our love of God and His Word spills over into our daily ministry with others. What better experience can there be except for Heaven itself?

Prov. 3:5

"Trust in the LORD with all thine heart; and lean not unto thine own understanding."

What an age-old formula of the believer's comfort, effectiveness, and hope!

Trust in the LORD. What? Put your whole confidence and security in Jehovah. How? **With all thine heart.** Put your whole spiritual weight down on Him. What a privilege and a comfort this is!

And lean not unto thine own understanding; don't trust or rely on yourself. Human reasoning alone is faulty. Our understanding of life and God's plan is insufficient and incomplete at best. While walking with the Lord we are often pleasantly surprised to see how He fits the pieces of our lives together, even the "puzzling" things come together for our benefit, and apart from our own plans. To Him be the glory!

Romans 8:28 says it best:

"And we know that all things work together for good to them that love God, to them who are the called according to his purpose."

Prov. 3:6

"In all thy ways acknowledge him, and he shall direct thy paths."

In all thy ways acknowledge Him. This statement has to do with a spiritual intimacy with God regarding every area of life. **Ways** include family, home life, business, buying things, recreation, etc. Our thought life is to be focused on Him. Bounce everything off of Him; i.e., we **acknowledge** our personal relationship with our Savior, seeking His wisdom and direction at every turn.

God then promises to **direct** our **paths.** He will make the road clear, direct, and it will be the right way. No detours will be needed. The journey may be difficult and trying, but we'll not travel alone. Moreover, we can be assured that the "right road leads to the right place," How wonderful is the thought of having God Almighty as our personal Director! (cf. Isaiah 9:6)

Prov. 3:7

"Be not wise in thine own eyes: fear the LORD, and depart from evil."

This follows on the heels of "leaning not unto thine own understanding" and "acknowledging him in all our ways," **In our own eyes**, we'd do ourselves and others a great injustice by judging things from outward appearances.

Pride is a horrible thing! It falsely enthrones us and dethrones God. Pride was Lucifer's downfall (Ezekiel 28), and can be ours as well. The **fear of the Lord** honors His Sovereignty as we bow in allegiance. We **depart from evil**.

"For all that is in the world, the lust of the flesh, and the lust of the eyes, and the pride of life, is …of the world. And the world passeth away, and the lust thereof: but he that doeth the will of God abideth for ever." (1 John 2:16-17)

Will we bow to our own interpretation of life or to the God of the Word?

Prov. 3:8

"It shall be health to thy navel, and marrow to thy bones."

Walking in the fear of the Lord affects not just our spiritual condition, but our physical body as well. There is healing in obedience to God. Taking God seriously **shall be health to thy navel** (the abdominal area). Prolonged disobedience can produce ulcers, colitis, etc.

There is much emphasis today on healthy food. While this is important to good nutrition for the body, the real issue is often not what we eat, but what is eating us! This is not to say that all gastrointestinal diseases are caused by sin, but there's probably a correlation. It's just another incentive for living right.

Solomon goes on to say that it shall be **marrow** (lit. moisture) **to the bones.** Marrow is soft tissue inside the bones, and bone marrow produces red blood cells. It is necessary for the skeletal frame of our bodies, and the circulatory system.

In addition, there is a synovial fluid in our joints which lubricates the skeletal system. Prolonged worry or resentment, for instance, can have a "drying" effect on that lubricant, triggering conditions like arthritis, bursitis, etc.[6]

Prov. 3:9

"Honour the LORD with thy substance, and with the firstfruits of all thine increase:"

Here is the answer to spiritual health: **Honour the LORD.** The word "**honour**" means to "glorify" (cf. Psalm 50:15; 86:12; 87:3; Job 6:3). So, the command is to glorify the LORD (Jehovah); to lift Him up in praise and worship. How? **With thy substance, and with the firstfruits of all thine increase.** This is more than lip service.

---

[6] My book, **Healing for the Mind**, examines these issues in more detail.

It gets down to the nitty gritty of everyday economics. God has prospered us with relative wealth and our use of this income reflects our attitude toward the One who gave it.

Firstfruits are the beginning or chief part of our prosperity. It's the same word translated as the "beginning" in Genesis 1:1 and Proverbs 1:7. We glorify God by giving back to Him a portion of our income UP FRONT – not what's left over. This is a gratitude offering.

Giving the tithe (at least 10%) is an Old Testament concept that has been carried into New Testament times as a starting point. In reality, 100% of our income is from the LORD. Thus, we demonstrate our worship and gratitude to Him in the way we use our wealth. It's the attitude of praise, not just an act or practice. Note, too, that the giving is from **thy substance** and **increase.** The Lord has made us stewards of what He has put in our hands.

Thus, if we have a house, it's our house, but, in reality, it's a gift from God, and we need to honor Him in the way we use that house. We also have seven days in a week, and one of those days is considered "the Lord's Day"; a day set aside to worship God. The Lord God of Israel said, *"for them that honour me I will honour"* (1 Samuel 2:30). Jesus said, *"But seek ye first the kingdom of God and his righteousness; and all these things shall be added unto you"* (Matthew 6:33).

The underlying issue here is to give God all the praise and credit for what we possess, living our lives accordingly. We must conduct ourselves in such a way that there's no question where our allegiance lies. As one has said, however we run our daily lives (home, business, finances, etc.), it should all make "Jesus look Great!" That may be the essence of what it means to "honor or glorify" God.

Prov. 3:10

"So shall thy barns be filled with plenty, and thy presses shall burst out with new wine."

Particularly in this agricultural economy, God's rewards were attached to the prosperity of the harvest. **Barns** were **filled with**

plenty and the **presses** (vats) bursting out with **new wine**. In this farming context, we embrace the principle of God's abundance by which He showed favor to His earthly people. This blessing was also reversed when the people were disobedient. (See Joel 3:13).

Jesus states a similar principle in Luke 6:38:

> *"Give, and it shall be given unto you; good measure, pressed down, and shaken together, and running over, shall men give unto your bosom. For with the same measure that ye mete withal it shall be measured to you again,"*

Care must be taken, however, not to use this verse as a sure-fire promise for every believer under every circumstance. Over the course of Church history, many "giving" believers have suffered great deprivation, and even martyrdom.

But the promise of Ephesians 1:3 has always been accessible:

> *"Blessed be the God and Father of our Lord Jesus Christ, who hath blessed us with all spiritual blessings in heavenly places in Christ."*

He has made full provision for His saints.

Prov. 3:11

> *"My son, despise not the chastening of the LORD; neither be weary of his correction:"*

This is the familiar passage used in Hebrews 12:5, regarding the believer's response to God's discipline. **My son, despise not** (never reject) **the chastening** (correction or discipline) **of the Lord...** Here is a family picture of God training his child. God disciplines or corrects, and it's essential that His children respond properly.

The verb is forceful (never reject or refuse) God's discipline! Contrary to modern thought, such discipline is a demonstration of the Father's deep love and concern for His child. We spurn His loving correction to our own demise and harm. This is illustrated in 1 Samuel 15:23, when King Saul was rejected by the Lord because of his (Saul's) rejection of God's instructions.

In addition, Solomon says **neither be weary of His correction.**

The word "weary" connotes "grief or distress," It is translated this way in Numbers 22:3, where *"Moab was **distressed** because of the children of Israel,"* BDB gives the meaning "to feel a sickening dread."[7] That should never be our response to God's discipline, since He knows exactly what we need and has our ultimate good in mind.

The word **correction** here is the same as the word **chastening**, but is more specifically "reproof or rebuke." Thus, we can trust our loving, heavenly Father, who is constantly motivated to develop and to complete that which He has begun in us (Philippians 1:6). God is for us, not against us, even when we miss the mark. We need not be anxious or fearful over His chastening.

The Apostle John tells us:

> *"There is no fear in love; but perfect love casteth out fear: because fear hath torment. He that feareth is not made perfect in love." (1 John 4:18)*

Prov. 3:12

> *"For whom the LORD loveth he correcteth; even as a father the son in whom he delighteth."*

Earthly fathers typify the ultimate example of our Heavenly Father who parents with perfection. Solomon continues his thought concerning the Lord's disciplinary process and why we should not reject it. **For** (because) **whom the Lord loveth He correcteth, even as a father the son in whom he delighteth.**

We have here the assurance of God's perfect motive and purpose for His correction. Again, as vividly portrayed in Hebrews 12:5ff, every good father trains his children; how much more does the Lord, as a faithful Father. In fact, that chastening is evidence of true sonship. Trials don't break us, but make us!

This all connects with Romans 8:28, 29:

> *"And we know that all things work together for good to them that love God, to them who are the called according to His purpose.*

---

[7] Brown, Driver & Briggs – Hebrew Lexicon on e-Sword Bible program.

For whom He did foreknow, he also did predestinate to be conformed to the image of his Son, that he might be the firstborn among many brethren."

True love wants the best for its object. So, the Father's love correlates with His delight in His child. The word **correcteth** in verse 3:11 has to do with rebuke or reproof, while in this verse it means "to make right." The former is to show our wrong or upside down position; the latter action is to make it right or to turn us right side up. What perfecting love is demonstrated here!

Prov. 3:13

"Happy is the man that findeth wisdom, and the man that getteth understanding."

One of Satan's chief lies is that a believer's life is miserable because God will take all the so-called "fun" away. Such thinking is not only foolish, but demonic. This word, **Happy,** is translated "blessed" in Psalm 1:1; 2:12; 34:8; etc., meaning "extremely happy." This is the ultimate of God's fulfilling satisfaction to His children this side of Heaven. It's likened to the Holy Spirit's fruit of "joy" (Galatians 5:22).

Note that this happiness is conditional; i.e., given to the man **that findeth** (has attained) **wisdom, and getteth** (produces or furnishes) **understanding.** This is another way of saying that the believer who walks with God is happy. Wisdom is lining up with God; living life skillfully and happily. As one writer has said: *"God is most glorified when we are most satisfied with Him,"* Amen.

Prov. 3:14

"For the merchandise of it is better than the merchandise of silver, and the gain thereof than fine gold."

If we're going to get into merchandising or profit-making, let it be with wisdom. For wisdom is the beginning of all knowledge and business. Its profitability is far beyond anything else this world offers. Yet, it is sought the least. Silver and gold catch the eye of mankind, and its lust ends in disaster. Wisdom is a matter of the heart, upon which all of life's transactions are made.

Again, it's not money that's evil, but the love of it. If we love Wisdom instead, the finances will fall into place. Jesus said:

"But seek ye first the kingdom of God, and his righteousness; and all these things shall be added unto you." (Matthew 6:33)

Praise God, from whom all blessings flow!

Prov. 3:15

"She is more precious than rubies: and all the things thou canst desire are not to be compared unto her."

Wisdom is better than silver, gold, and **rubies.** In fact, whatever our earthly standard of value may be, nothing is to be **compared unto her** (Wisdom). These are poetic expressions describing the ultimate and eternal value of possessing God's understanding. There is nothing like Wisdom, for Christ Himself is our Wisdom (1 Corinthians 1:30). O, if we only agreed, and practiced such truth!

Prov. 3:16

"Length of days is in her right hand; and in her left hand riches and honour."

Wisdom is pictured with two hands holding what is most precious to man: longevity of life in one hand; **riches and honour** in the other. The word for **honour** is translated "glory," expressing the idea of a weighty reverence. This depicts a person who exudes godly authority.

These qualities are the result of wisdom, not foolishness. One may obtain worldly riches, but without wisdom and a godly relationship, he has no intrinsic purpose or meaning. Here is another commentary on Matthew 6:33 (refer to Prov. 3:14).

Prov. 3:17

"Her ways are ways of pleasantness, and all her paths are peace."

O, the incomparable ways of wisdom! **Pleasantness** (delightfulness) and **peace** (wellness) are her fruits, rather than the misery and emptiness of sin. Yet, the sinful world still thinks it's having fun.

Prov. 3:18

"She is a tree of life to them that lay hold upon her: and happy is every one that retaineth her."

She is a 3rd person pronoun, which can be translated as "he" or "it," depending on the context. Wisdom **is a tree of life.** This source of life is manifested **to them that lay hold upon her.** To lay hold means "to seize or be strong." This pictures one who is resolved to firmly hold and depend upon wisdom for strength.

In conjunction, **happy** (truly prosperous) **is every one that retaineth** (holds fast, grasps) **her.** Genuine happiness comes only to those who are wedded to wisdom, and will not let go of it. The fool knows no such bliss, yet he is considered "normal" in a foolish world.

Study these verses on the "tree of life:" Genesis 2:9; Proverbs 11:30, 13:12, 15:4; and Revelation 2:7; 22:2; 22:14.

Prov. 3:19

"The LORD by wisdom hath founded the earth; by understanding hath he established the heavens."

Here is the exaltation of Jehovah, who created all things by wisdom. This is not only a statement of His eternal **understanding** in bringing all things into existence, but also the mediation of Christ, who is Wisdom personified.

In Genesis 1:3, it states: *"And God said, Let there be light: and there was light,"* Again, we see the Word's creative power in John 1:3: *"All things were made by him; and without him was not anything made that was made."*

Prov. 3:20

"By his knowledge the depths are broken up, and the clouds drop down the dew."

We see here what Barnes calls the "two storehouses of living water" that supply the needs of the earth.[8] By God's **knowledge the depths** or seas **are broken up** (make waves?), **and the clouds** (of the sky) **drop down the dew** (rain). God established the earth and then made ample provision to sustain it with water.

To deny the Creator's existence and power is to leave this process to chance, with no one in control. That's an unsettling thought!

Prov. 3:21

"My son, let not them depart from thine eyes: keep sound wisdom and discretion:"

People share and concentrate on what they are vitally interested in, or think is important. So, the author challenges his son to **let not**, or never let, **wisdom and discretion depart from thine eyes.** This must be his constant focus in life: the positive, powerful, precious Wisdom and Word of God.

Certainly, more is involved here than just eyesight. There is a reference here to the inner eyes of the soul, namely spiritual understanding. David rightly prayed:

"Open thou mine eyes, that I may behold wondrous things out of thy law," (Psalm 119:18)

The second phrase is the outworking of obedience flowing from the meditation of the heart. These spiritual insights must be guarded and maintained in daily life. O, to be absorbed with Truth, and thus to be free indeed to practice **sound wisdom and discretion** (discernment).

Prov. 3:22

"So shall they be life unto thy soul, and grace to thy neck."

What is the reason for guarding sound wisdom and discernment? They will continue to be **life unto thy soul** (actively flowing into and reviving your soul). Foolishness and sin drain the human soul and it

---

[8] Albert Barnes Notes on the Bible – e-Sword Bible Program.

ends up in eternal destruction or Hell. What a contrast with the life-giving flow and abundance of **grace** emanating from Wisdom!

The world is deceived and insane, energized by wicked selfishness and trying to find happiness in collecting stuff and personal power. That which emanates from humanity can only be consummated in death. God provides Life, and all that comes from Him consummates in abundant and eternal Life. In other words,

"The wages of sin is death, but the gift of God is eternal life through Jesus Christ our Lord," (Romans 6:23)

"Grace to thy neck" is a figurative expression of divine ornamentation or beauty. Gold neck chains are the order of the day for men and women. However, there's nothing more elegant than the display of God's wisdom in a human soul.

Prov. 3:23

"Then shalt thou walk in thy way safely, and thy foot shall not stumble."

Walking in grace and godly life insures stability and security. Here's the **way** (road) to confidence and hope. There's no substitute for steadily walking in obedience to the Word of wisdom.

Prov. 3:24

"When thou liest down, thou shalt not be afraid: yea, thou shalt lie down, and thy sleep shall be sweet."

Whether walking or sleeping, day or night, the word of wisdom sustains and secures the believer. To **lie down** without fear is a wonderful gift that need not be taken for granted. Even **thy sleep shall be sweet** (pleasant). The sweet peace of God is part of the believer's legacy.

Prov. 3:25

"Be not afraid of sudden fear, neither of the desolation of the wicked, when it cometh."

A further exhortation is given to the believer: Don't be fearful when **sudden** or unexpected **fear** comes, nor when the **wicked** are destroyed. There's an attending promise of comfort, as stated in the next verse.

Prov. 3:26

"For the LORD shall be thy confidence, and shall keep thy foot from being taken."

Fear is removed when we cast our burdens upon the Lord, who is our **confidence** (the hope expressed in Psalm 78:7). That confidence in God is an ongoing remedy against future disaster. Such hope is preservative, keeping our **foot from being taken** (snared in a noose). This speaks well of our walk with God or our wise lifestyle.

Prov. 3:27

"Withhold not good from them to whom it is due, when it is in the power of thine hand to do it."

The abundance of God's blessing is not to be heaped on ourselves alone, but shared with others in need. Love overflows and looks for those who are worthy of help; i.e., people who would be blessed and not spoiled by our assistance. Believers have the privilege of being a source of blessing and assistance to God's servants and others placed in our path.

Prov. 3:28

"Say not unto thy neighbor, Go, and come again, and to morrow I will give; when thou hast it by thee."

We must not just talk benevolence: words are cheap. We should give to others in need while we have the opportunity. What we do with what we have indicates who we really are. James uses this concept of giving to illustrate the evidence of true, saving faith:

"What doeth it profit, my brethren, though a man say he hath faith, and have not works? can faith save him? If a brother or sister be naked, and destitute of daily food, And one of you say unto them, Depart in peace, be ye warmed and filled;

notwithstanding ye give them not those things which are needful to the body; what doth it profit? Even so faith, if it hath not works, is dead, being alone. Yea, a man may say, Thou hast faith, and I have works: shew me thy faith without thy works, and I will show thee my faith by my works," (James 2:14-18)

Prov. 3:29

"Devise not evil against thy neighbour, seeing he dwelleth securely by thee."

Here's the flip side of the previous proverb: Don't do anything to hurt your neighbor (fellow citizen). Don't **devise** or fabricate evil against another, especially a close neighbor who feels safe with you nearby. God is for peace, not war.

Moreover, true love seeks the best for its object. In fact, Romans 13:8 says, *"for he that loveth another hath fulfilled the law."*

When filled with Christ's love, I will not break the moral law nor do anything that would harm another person.

Prov. 3:30

"Strive not with a man without cause, if he have done thee no harm."

Since there's war in the unsaved heart (James 4:1ff.), some people just like to fight. They thrive on conflict and, if there's nothing wrong, they'll trump up something. Today, people legally sue others over the most insignificant issues or trumped up charges. It's another manifestation of the world's depravity. For reasons of greed and resentment, folks will sue others without any justified cause. If there is a genuine or justified conflict, there are proper ways to settle them.

Prov. 3:31

"Envy thou not the oppressor, and choose none of his ways."

Solomon urges his people not to **envy** those who look down upon or persecute others, nor to select their evil ways of living. There's a tendency for human nature to follow an **oppressor** (cruel, violent person), especially when it seems profitable on the surface.

The reason for this prohibition is found in the next verse. There is still "right and wrong," with God's just response to man's choices and actions.

Prov. 3:32

"For the froward is abomination to the LORD: but his secret is with the righteous."

Don't follow or envy the oppressor, because he is **froward** (perverted), and, thus, **an abomination to the LORD.** That's good enough reason to not walk with the depraved. Plus, the Lord's **secret is with the righteous.** What a wonderful benefit for those walking in obedience to God!

Remember Enoch who *"walked with God"* (Genesis 5:22), and was taken straight to Heaven, bypassing the grave (Genesis 5:24)? The prophet Amos comments:

"Can two walk together, except they be agreed?...but he revealeth his secret unto his servants, the prophets." (Amos 3:3, 7)

Prov. 3:33

"The curse of the LORD is in the house of the wicked: but he blesseth the habitation of the just."

We see here that even the house is directly affected by the character of those who live there. In the **house of the wicked**, the wicked people make otherwise neutral things wicked; e.g., knives, guns, cars, cell phones, the internet, etc. can be used to commit evil deeds. Only the **wicked** can take legitimate items and make them "weapons of destruction."

In contrast, the house of those blessed by God will be marked by good living and pleasant surroundings. King David says,

"And he shall be like a tree planted by the rivers of water, that bringeth forth his fruit in his season; his leaf shall not wither; and whatsoever he doeth shall prosper," (Psalm 1:3)

Prov. 3:34

"Surely he scorneth the scorners: but he giveth grace unto the lowly."

We reap what we sow! The scoffer or mocker will meet with God's scorn. The proud will be put down. However, the Lord favors the humble or meek. Blessed are those who do not *"sit in the seat of the scornful"* (Psalm 1:1). James says, *"...God resisteth the proud, but giveth grace unto the humble"* (James 4:6). To the believer, the way up is the way down. God promotes the **lowly**.

Prov. 3:35

"The wise shall inherit glory: but shame shall be the promotion of fools."

What a contrast between the final condition of **the wise** and the foolish. The wise will inherit the glory of Heaven, while disgrace and Hell await sinful fools. Heaven and Hell are at opposite poles: no one can travel both roads at the same time.

Even **fools** want to receive a **promotion**, but there's no way to be a fool and receive the honor of a wise man. The Apostle Paul rightly stated,

"for whatsoever a man soweth, that shall he also reap." (Galatians 6:7)

The world may "promote" an unwise celebrity, but that "glory" will quickly fade. Jesus posed the question,

"For what shall it profit a man, if he shall gain the whole world and lose his own soul?" (Mark 8:36)

The wise believer, however, may not receive the accolades of this world, but his inheritance is up ahead! His reward is sure and eternal. Indeed, it can be said that his benefits are "out of this world!"

Chapter 4
Security in Wisdom

Prov. 4:1

"Hear, ye children, the instruction of a father, and attend to know understanding."

Solomon addresses **children,** the whole family, not just his son. He urges them to hear **the instruction of a father.** The family leader speaks, and the children are to listen with the intent of obeying him. Children will hear the words of instruction, but often do not heed them. Even unsaved fathers, who love their children and have some sense of morality, will give some positive instructions. How much more is this true of a dad who loves God, too?

It's obvious in **Proverbs** and the whole of Scripture that great priority is given to the home and family structure. We are witnessing a widespread failure of home life and the corresponding downplay of parental roles. No doubt, it follows on the heels of society's denial of the Bible in private and public life. Illegitimacy and fatherless homes abound, promoting moral and economic decline. The wholesome, two-parent family is at a premium. A loving, wise father is certainly a gift to his children, warranting their respect and submission.

Solomon also urges children to carefully listen, embrace, and **know understanding** or wisdom. What a challenge to children, not only to hear and obey, but to embrace the meaning and wisdom of what's being taught by their fathers. Obedience from the heart produces growth, maturity, and skills for the future. Obedient children are happy children.

Prov. 4:2

"For I give you good doctrine, forsake ye not my law."

What is the reason for obedience? It's because **I give you good doctrine** (teaching. In other words, my instruction is right and good, and will not lead you astray. You can't go wrong! Thus, **forsake ye not my law.** He's telling His children, "Don't walk away from my instructions, because it's good teaching and will create right thinking and action. You may not understand all the implications, but obey and heed my words,"

David, Solomon's father, said:

"Blessed is the man that walketh not in the counsel of the ungodly..." (Psalm 1:1).

It's interesting that another word for **good** is "precious." (See Psalm 133:2; Isaiah 39:1, 2).

Prov. 4:3

"For I was my father's son, tender and only beloved in the sight of my mother."

Solomon is not just speaking from a biological standpoint when he says, **I was my father's son...in the sight of my mother.** He was **tender and only beloved**; i.e., fragile and unique. This is a positive expression for a precious, specially loved, and flexible young man.

Notice, too, the position and camaraderie of both his mother and father. This is God's divine order of things; i.e., parental love. The family is the primary unit for man's earthly existence. No wonder Satan hates the home, and leads the attack toward its destruction.

Prov. 4:4

"He taught me also, and said unto me, Let thine heart retain my words: keep my commandments, and live."

Solomon testifies of how his father, David, taught him: **He taught me also....** The word "taught" literally means "to point out or to show." His father must have "zeroed in" with a direct method of instruction. Whatever it takes to teach the Word, let's use it; line by line, principle by principle.

However, the final issue lies with how we obey and **retain** His **words.** He earnestly urges us to **keep my commandments and live.** Abundant life comes only by taking God's Word seriously (Joshua 1:8). We receive all that God wants us to have when we are on the same channel with Him. We can never do any better than receiving what God has to offer. At its best, sin is no match for the goodness and grace of God! The idea that we can somehow succeed by disobeying God is a lie.

Prov. 4:5

"Get wisdom, get understanding: forget it not; neither decline from the words of my mouth."

Here is Solomon's continued urging to **get wisdom, get understanding;** i.e., pursue and attain skillful knowledge. This is a further plea to pursue that which is most valuable. **Forget it not:** don't ignore the priority of wisdom. Some things should be forgotten (i.e., past failures, sins, etc.), but not spiritual understanding. This **understanding** is unique to mankind; it relates to "God consciousness" and the ability to understand the Word. (See Genesis 2:7). This function is activated by the "new birth" or new life in Christ.

Neither decline from the words of my mouth. Don't turn aside or get side-tracked or end up off the right road. Let us follow hard after our Father's Word, refusing to exit off the King's Highway! (Colossians 3:16).

Prov. 4:6

"Forsake her not, and she shall preserve thee: love her, and she shall keep thee."

Wisdom here is likened to a child refusing a mother's love. What foolishness is it that would refuse such love and protection? Not only should we not **forsake** wisdom, but positively **love her.** What is it that gladdens your heart? What is the priority in your life? That's what you love. Remember, Jesus said your treasure is where your heart is also. Tell me what you love and what you hate, and I'll tell you what you are.

Preserve and **keep** are synonyms for guarding and maintaining the believer who walks in God's Wisdom. Here is a picture of walking with Christ, who **is** our Wisdom.

Prov. 4:7

"Wisdom is the principal thing; therefore get wisdom: and with all thy getting get understanding."

This is a great statement regarding the importance of wisdom: **Wisdom is the principal thing;** i.e., it's the first or chief part of real knowledge and life.

Proverb 1:7 uses the same word in the phrase:

"The fear of the Lord is the beginning (or chief part) *of knowledge..."*

Take away the fear of God, and you cannot have genuine knowledge. Take away wisdom, hinging on the fear of God, and you miss the best of what God offers.

Thus, we are commanded to **get wisdom** (attain it at all cost) and **with all thy getting get understanding** (the practical outworking of wisdom). There's so much emphasis on accumulating worldly knowledge, as though there's some guaranteed success in college degrees, etc. Bible knowledge tends to be devalued and despised. The fight is on between truth and error, between godly wisdom and worldly foolishness. Make the right choice without delay!

Prov. 4:8

"Exalt her, and she shall promote thee: she shall bring thee to honour, when thou dost embrace her."

Exalt (lift up) **her** (Wisdom), **and she shall promote thee:** Here's an interesting parallel – exalt wisdom and you will be exalted in the right way. Promote wisdom (e.g., Christ in 1 Corinthians

1:30), and you will be promoted or lifted up. What you do with wisdom is what God will do with you. The same is true with the Word in general (See Joshua 1:8).

She shall bring thee to honour or glory, **when thou dost embrace** (clasp) **her.** If you want to be honored or revered, then cling to wisdom. Weave wisdom into the fabric of your lifestyle. You will then be a weighty person with spiritual clout, as opposed to an "air-head" with no backbone. The wisdom of the Word can only bring one to honor; i.e., make one honorable.

The world has no substitute for this. It elevates and acclaims those who, otherwise, are wicked and devoid of wisdom. Our kingdom is of another world, heaven, and will not necessarily be appreciated by this world. However, we must let our light shine here, manifesting godly wisdom, so that our Heavenly Father will be glorified. We cannot serve "two masters" (Luke 16:13).

Prov. 4:9

"She shall give to thine head an ornament of grace: a crown of glory shall she deliver to thee."

Man has always been concerned about position and power. Earthly promotions are sought constantly, since all industrious people want to get ahead. Wisdom promotes the wise (vs. 4:8). In this verse, Wisdom **shall give to thine head an ornament** (wreath) **of grace** (honor or elegance).

Furthermore, **a crown of glory** (heavenly bliss) **shall she deliver to thee.** These are the jewels of wisdom: wreaths of honor and a crown of heavenly bliss. They are fit for a king! The Apostle John offers insight and praise regarding the believer's position in Christ:

"Unto him that loved us, and washed us from our sins in his own blood, And hath made us kings and priests unto God and his Father; to him be glory and dominion for ever and ever. Amen," (Revelation 1:5, 6)

The quest for expensive jewelry is prevalent these days. People want to "dress for success" and look beautiful, even though their inner lives may be in shambles. Wisdom enhances and beautifies the inner person and shines through his skin. The most beautiful people I've met are not the ones all "made up" externally, but those who have the glow of God radiating from within; i.e., the beauty of holiness.

Prov. 4:10

"Hear, O my son, and receive my sayings; and the years of thy life shall be many."

On the surface, Solomon seems to be saying that his son will live longer if he follows the Word. However, some of the greatest saints have had short lives. The phrase **shall be many** primarily refers to abundance, greatness, and enlargement, rather than mere quantity or length of time. Although longevity is inferred, the main thrust is quality of life.

Heeding the Word of God can only bring abundance to the soul, even though great trials and suffering attend one's path of life. It's not how long a man lives, but how well he lives that ultimately counts.

Prov. 4:11

"I have taught thee in the way of wisdom; I have led thee in right paths."

After Solomon urges his son to listen to his words, he now tells him why he should listen. Here, we have a declaration of a father who has been faithful in taking his responsibility of properly instructing his son. The word used for **taught** (the Hebrew word *yarah*) literally means to "throw, shoot, or pour." Thus, teaching is more than just exposure to information. It is more like "pointing out" or "shooting" the information so it hits the target (refer back to 4:4).

The same word is used in Exodus 4:12, 15), where Jehovah promises to put His word into Moses' mouth, specifically teaching him what to say. Again, the same word is translated "shoot" in Psalm 64:4, 7; also, "direct" in Genesis 46:28. Solomon is saying we should "shoot" our children with wisdom. What a vibrant thought!

Even more picturesque is the idea of the phrase **I have led thee....** The word for **led** (*darak*) means "to string or bend a bow," It's an archery term; thus, to "string" your son so as to shoot or guide him down the right path or track. What parental privilege and responsibility is resident here! We must do everything we can to lead our children by principles of conduct and example, while trusting our God to work grace into their hearts.

Prov. 4:12

"When thou goest, thy steps shall not be straitened; and when thou runnest, thou shalt not stumble."

Here, the wise man is described from a negative perspective: his **steps** will not be narrow or distressed (from the Hebrew word *vatsar* (see Genesis 32:7). The same word is translated *"vexed"* in 2 Samuel 13:2, but in 1 Samuel 30:6, David was distressed and *"encouraged himself in the LORD his God,"*

It's obvious that we can't press this verse to teach that a wise person will not experience pressure and stress or even defeat. Trials are a part of every saint's life, but how we "walk" through them is all important. The inference here is that wisdom promotes a wide and clear path of the believer, who, even under pressure, can "move skillfully" and effectively (see Psalm 18:36).

When thou runnest, thou shalt not stumble. Here, again, it is not literal running (as a track star), but moving quickly down the path of wisdom. We shall not falter, stagger, or faint. This includes not only the strength for the journey, but also protection from falling. The same grace that leads a believer is the same grace that keeps him.

The prophet Jeremiah depicts God's children during the Kingdom Age:

"...I will cause them to walk by the rivers of waters in a straight way, wherein they shall not stumble..." (Jeremiah 31:9)

Prov. 4:13

"Take fast hold of instruction; let her not go: keep her; for she is thy life."

When it comes to wisdom and skillful living, we must be aggressively serious. There's no room for passivity or "wishy-washiness." God's discipline and instruction are essential to our spiritual development and efficiency. Thus, Solomon commands us to **take fast hold of instruction.** This verb is used of the angels who "laid hold" of Lot's hand upon exiting Sodom, just prior to the fiery judgment (Genesis 19:16).

This same verb (the Hebrew word *chazaq*) is also translated several times in Joshua 1, as "to be strong." Joshua was urged:

"Only be thou strong and very courageous, that thou mayest observe to do according to all the law…" (Joshua 1:7).

In fact, this was the basis of the true success promised in Joshua 1:8. We are often too passive and indifferent regarding God's Word. We need to be aggressively firm and strong, showing faith in action. It's time for courage and unashamed allegiance to God's wisdom and ways.

Once we take hold of instruction, we dare not let go. Once we've put our *"hand to the plow,"* as Jesus once said (Luke 9:62), we must never turn back.

Furthermore, he says **keep her**; i.e., protect, guard or maintain wisdom, which is to be ongoing. We must not have a good start without a successful finish. It constitutes a life-long attitude. Why? Because **she is thy life.** It's fundamental; essential to life. It's not just a good idea, but a matter of life and death! This is the word translated as "life" and "living" in Genesis 2:7, given directly from God.

From the Christian perspective, Christ has not only given us eternal life, He Himself is our life. Regarding His words, Jesus said that *"they are life"* (John 6:63). Believing in Christ is a total lifestyle. To turn from His instruction, the Word, is to flirt with death, the opposite of life. The Apostle Paul says, in essence, "Christ is my life"

(Philippians 1:20, 21). Wisdom affects our lives personally, thus dictating the need to take it personally.

Prov. 4:14

"Enter not into the path of the wicked, and go not in the way of evil men."

Holding fast to godly instruction doesn't give much time, energy, or desire to move toward the **path of the wicked.** Yet, the command is given here in parallelism to **go not in the way of evil men.** Steer clear of the ungodly!

As we follow the dictates of our hearts, the decision to be separate from evil men should be easier if we're steeped in God's Word. Their way can only lead to a dead end!

Prov. 4:15

"Avoid it, pass not by it, turn from it, and pass away."

Here's a vivid example of the concrete nature of the Hebrew language. Unlike the Greek with its highly subjective and deep word meanings, Hebrew is full of illustration or concrete pictures of what and what not to do.

Notice the tremendous emphasis on the admonition regarding an evil lifestyle. **Avoid it...turn from it**; in other words, "don't get near it!" Solomon doesn't just say "don't go with the wicked," but spells it out in repetitive detail.

You can feel the intensity and urgency of his words. His warning is to not get involved with wicked people in any way, shape, or form. Steer clear of them! (See Psalm 1:1, 2) It's been said that "we can't prevent the birds from flying overhead, but we can keep them from making a nest in our hair." This applies primarily to our thought life, but certainly can also apply to relationships.

Prov. 4:16

"For they sleep not, except they have done mischief; and their sleep is taken away, unless they cause some to fall."

The writer is not speaking of casual contact with the wicked, but rather participation in their lifestyle and scheming behavior. They are characterized as being insatiable and driven in their wicked devices. **For they sleep not, except they have done mischief** (evil). What a description! They can't rest until they've done some sinful and hurtful deed. (Refer to Genesis 6:5; Jeremiah 17:9)

The second parallel statement reveals their motivation to cause others to **fall** or stumble. Evil devices always affect others personally. No man sins to himself; others are always unduly affected.

Prov. 4:17

"For they eat the bread of wickedness, and drink the wine of violence."

Everybody eats to live. The differences come in their choice of food. People have various tastes and appetites which dictate their choice of food. Spiritually, the principle is similar; we take in what our hearts desire. The Apostle Peter says,

"As newborn babes, desire the sincere milk of the word" (1 Peter 2:2).

The righteous desire the milk, meat, and drink of God's Word.

Not so with the wicked. Their sustenance is **the bread of wickedness, and the wine of violence.** They feed on what they are by nature; i.e., evil. As a man *"thinketh in his heart, so is he"* (Proverb 23:7). A person's words eventually reveal the attitude of his character and heart.

Prov. 4:18

"But the path of the just is as the shining light, that shineth more and more unto the perfect day."

What a beautiful picture of a saint's progressive walk from earth to Glory (Heaven)! **The path** (road or way) **of the just** (righteous one) **is as the shining** (brilliant) **light** (i.e., morning sun)**, that shineth more and more unto the perfect day.**

This poetic metaphor describes the joyous and spiritual brightness of walking with God. As the dawn appears, it gradually becomes brighter, until the sun is revealed in its glory. This relates to our growing in grace, and the progression of personal sanctification. Peter says it this way:

> *"But grow in grace, and in the knowledge of our Lord and Saviour Jesus Christ. To him be glory both now and for ever. Amen,"* (2 Peter 3:18)

This growing in grace is also referred to in John 8:12, and Revelation 21:23.

It's also used as a definition of prophecy:

> *"We have also a more sure word of prophecy; whereunto ye do well that ye take heed, as unto a light that shineth in a dark place, until the day dawn, and the day star arise in your hearts."* (2 Peter 1:19)

Prov.4:19

> *"The way of the wicked is as darkness: they know not at what they stumble."*

Solomon pictures the **wicked** as those who **stumble** in the dark, with no idea of where they're going. This is contrasted with those who walk in the light. Jesus said:

> *"If therefore the light that is in thee be darkness, how great is that darkness!"* (Matthew 6:23))

The path of wickedness is a murky road that can only lead to the abyss of eternal darkness.

Isaiah illustrates this condition referring to Israel's rebellion and judgment: *"...we wait for light, but behold obscurity; for brightness, but we walk in darkness. We grope for the wall like the blind, and we grope as if we had no eyes: we stumble at noonday as in the night; we are in desolate places as dead men."* (Isaiah 59:9, 10)

Prov. 4:20

> *"My son, attend to my words; incline thine ear unto my sayings."*

Again, the writer urges his son to reject the way of wickedness and hearken to his father's words. We must pay attention to someone, and that someone is all-important.

Incline thine ear. Stretch and extend your ear. There's no passivity here. Our senses are drawn in the direction of our hearts. Thus, the need for right choices is prompted by an obedient heart.

Prov. 4:21

"Let them not depart from thine eyes; keep them in the midst of thine heart."

Here is a very interesting expression of the believer's focus on the Word. **Let them** (my words) **not depart from thine eyes.** Initially, eyes refer to the physical (reading, etc.). However, David also prayed:

*"Open thou mine **eyes,** that I may behold wondrous things out of thy law."* (Psalm 119:18)

He was referring to the spiritual eyes or the spirit of man where understanding of the Word takes place. This is a heart focused on the Word.

The latter phrase further supports this understanding: **keep** (guard, protect) **them in the midst of thine heart.** Obedience is in the heart, then manifested in the mind and body. There's no substitute for the Word of God to fill and prosper the inner man.

Prov. 4:22

"For they are life unto those that find them, and health to all their flesh."

Why focus on the Word? Because **they** (God's words) **are life unto those that find them.** Since the Word emanates **life** from the Living Word Himself, then that life comes to the thirsty soul who receives the Word. But note the condition: **those that find them.** It's not an automatic thing. It must be sought.

Note even the physical results: **Health to all their flesh.** It must be said that the curing of the soul has a corresponding healing effect on the body. See notes on Prov. 3:5-8.

Prov. 4:23

"Keep thy heart with all diligence; for out of it are the issues of life."

Keep (guard) **thy heart** in which are the words of life (cf. 4:21). Solomon commands us to guard or protect our hearts **with all diligence** (concentrated effort). This is a serious situation, because out of the heart or spirit are **the issues**, outgoings, and source **of life**.

Most people live according to the flesh (self life), which fosters sensuality. The real issues of life come from the heart, which can only be made alive in Christ. The heart must be guarded in the fear of God. We must be serious about guarding the Word in our hearts, that we might not only refrain from sinning, but also glorify our God; (i.e., make it evident to others that God is Great!).

Prov. 4:24

"Put away from thee a froward mouth, and perverse lips put far from thee."

Guarding the heart results in the ability to **put away** or turn off perverted speech. **Froward** means to be intentionally or willfully crooked or distorted. The mouth is a great instrument of either praise or untamed perversion (James 3). Repeatedly in **Proverbs**, we see the connection of the heart to the tongue or mouth. The mouth does ultimately reveal the condition of one's heart.

Likewise, **perverse lips** need to be **put far from thee.** Whether we like it or not, we are betrayed or exposed by our speech. Note how various body parts are affected by the heart: the mouth (vs.24), the eyes (vs. 25), the feet (vs. 26, 27), and the hands (vs. 27).

Prov. 4:25

"Let thine eyes look right on, and let thine eyelids look straight before thee."

God likes "straight" rather than crooked behavior. He commands us to **look straight.** This verse warns against perverted **eyes.** The writer urges us to **look right** to the will and purpose of God; the road He's ordained for us (cf. Matthew 6:22).

There's much said in the Bible about the temptations or "the lust of the eyes" (1 John 2:16). We need to look straight with a Spirit-discipline that does not get side-tracked. As the Apostle Paul declared:

> "...but this one thing I do, forgetting those things which are behind, and reaching forth unto those things which are before, I press toward the mark for the prize of the high calling of God in Christ Jesus." (Philippians 3:13, 14)

This is not being narrow-minded, but rather single-minded to the Glory of God!

Prov. 4:26

"Ponder the path of thy feet, and let all thy ways be established."

The right path will lead to the right place. Thus, **ponder** (weigh mentally) **the path of thy feet, and let all** (the whole of) **thy ways be established** (firmly secured). The word "ponder" is a command, rather than just a suggestion. Truth must not be trivialized or treated lightly. Let's be careful in our daily walk, realizing that the road taken will make a profound difference in time and eternity.

Prov. 4:27

"Turn not to the right hand nor to the left: remove thy foot from evil."

Here we have a typical Hebrew way of emphasizing the importance of going straight on the right path: namely, **turn not to the right hand nor to the left.** In other words, if there's to be any turning, let it be **from evil.** Otherwise, just stay on the right road, which leads to the right place.

The Apostle Paul's earnest urging to the believer is apropos here:

> "I beseech you therefore, brethren, by the mercies of God, that ye present your bodies a living sacrifice, holy, acceptable unto

God, which is your reasonable service. And be not conformed to this world: but be ye transformed by the renewing of your mind, that ye may prove what is that good, and acceptable, and perfect, will of God." (Romans 12:1, 2)

Chapter 5
The Peril of Adultery

Prov. 5:1

"My son, attend unto my wisdom, and bow thine ear to my understanding:"

Again, as in Prov. 3:1, Solomon talks to his **son** (generic) and says **attend unto my wisdom** (seeing life from God's viewpoint); and **bow** (incline) **thine ear to my understanding** (discretion).

Here's another serious injunction to pay strict and undivided attention to God's wisdom and understanding. Again, this is attained through the absorption of God's Word. **Bow the ear** speaks to the attitude of heart; i.e., our spiritual "ears." Thus, the focus is the ongoing necessity of *inner* obedience and fellowship with the Lord.

Prov. 5:2

"That thou mayest regard discretion, and that thy lips may keep knowledge."

Embracing wisdom has this purpose: **That thou mayest regard** (respect) **discretion** (good judgment). By paying respectful attention to the Word, one protects and treasures God's plan for his life. This **knowledge** must then be kept or preserved by the **lips** (mouth).

What's in the heart comes out of the mouth. There's a direct and positive correlation between the two. A guarded mouth reveals a guarded heart. A right heart speaks right things. This is contrasted to the lips of the **strange woman** in the next verse (See James 3 for a comprehensive discourse on the untamed tongue).

Prov. 5:3

"For the lips of a strange woman drop as an honeycomb, and her mouth is smoother than oil:"

There's a need for discernment toward the advances of a **strange woman** (one other than your wife). The temptation of adultery is real and subtle, demanding discretion of the lips or what and how you speak. Her **lips** are described as dropping or oozing as **a honeycomb** dripping honey, and **her mouth is smoother** (more flattering) **than oil** (e.g., olive oil). In essence, he's saying such women will seek to destroy you through sexual advances.

Prov. 5:4

"But her end is bitter as wormwood, sharp as a twoedged sword."

This woman has a sweet approach or "come on," but a **bitter** end awaits her victim. **Wormwood** is an unused, bitter root, considered poisonous rather than medicinal. Thus, it was used to implement curses and death, very apropos for a harlot whose lips are as **sharp as a twoedged sword.**

How significant is this description? The same analogy of a two-edged sword is used for the Word of God in Hebrews 4:12. The Word is all powerful, and it cuts both ways (condemning or saving). It saves life for many, but brings death to others, depending on how the recipient responds to it (2 Corinthians 2:16).

So, the prostitute is sweet yet deadly at the same time! The power of an evil woman is uncanny, and so prevalent in Scripture history. How valiant were men like Sampson, David, and even Solomon himself, yet, they succumbed to the touches of women. How deep are the wounds of sexual impurity?

Today, prostitution and the "sex trade" are epidemic.[9] A

---

[9] Our government reports that the average prostitute starts her career between the ages of 12 to 14 years. 300,000 American children enter into the slavery of pornography and prostitution each year, based on reports from the U. S. Bureau of Missing and Exploited Children.

decadent society glamorizes the underworld and the base things of the flesh. Television exploits sexuality with such gusto, giving the impression that it's the ultimate of pleasure. In reality, sexual immorality leads to death and hell.

Prov. 5:5

"Her feet go down to death; her steps take hold on hell."

Her feet go down to death (to separation from real life, to the realm of dying); **her steps take hold on hell** (*Sheol* is the Hebrew word for the fiery place of departed spirits). Look at the tragic demise of the one prostituting her body and soul. It's like a beautiful flower that appears so attractive and fragrant for a brief time, then dies and rots. How sad; yet many men are deceived and trapped by lust, being devoid of wisdom.

There's so much confusion today about the role of the sexes. Women have become more like objects of lust, rather than the loving wives in marriage and the family. There are more men becoming more effeminate (e.g., homosexuals), while women are becoming more masculine (e.g., lesbians, "butches," etc.) This has fostered confusion, resulting in many women losing their God-given identity and purpose. What a tragedy! It's the result of rejecting God's Word, and His divine order of things.

There's a downhill trek to eternal destruction for the women of the underworld. What a horrible fate awaits them! The path to Hell may be paved with good intentions, but it's Hell nevertheless. There's also a gradual way to Hell, one step at a time. There's an evil subtlety that points to the deception of Satan himself. Just like the *"steps of a good man are ordered by the LORD,"* so the steps of the wicked are influenced by Satan. Life is a walk, not a race, and little decisions eventually affect one's whole destiny.

Death is a state of ruination. **Hell** is the domain of the damned, the underworld of the wicked dead. One thing is for sure, it's the opposite of Life and Heaven. Indeed, the wages of sin is death.

Prov. 5:6

"Lest thou shouldest ponder the path of life, her ways are moveable, that thou canst not know them."

Commentators vary on interpreting this verse. Some render it as the prostitute's inability to **ponder the path of life**, etc. But in context, **thou** must refer to the one taken up with the prostitute; i.e., the "customer," who is hood-winked by her bag of "tricks." This would explain the phrase **her ways are moveable** (changeable, deceitful, etc.).

She is well trained in her "trade." **Her ways** or sexual innovations captivate the man who is driven by lust and sexual fantasies. She would not want him to **ponder** (consider) **the** (right) **path of life,** because that might result in a loss of business.

This scenario illustrates the ploy of the underworld to sell its wares by tantalizing the flesh sufficiently to keep wayward people in its grip. The temptations attack from every direction. Even the gambling industry knows how to suck people in, using entertainment, lights, and sounds.

The lust of the eyes is basic in the underworld, to prevent folks from coming to Christ, the right path of life. The fight is on! The battle is for souls who can hopefully be rescued from Satan's deceptions through the Gospel of Grace. (e. g. Romans 1:16)

Prov. 5:7

"Hear me now therefore, O ye children, and depart not from the words of my mouth."

A forceful command to obey is injected here in the midst of the discourse on strange women. The word **children** refers to "sons," and they are being strongly urged to listen; to obey NOW! Solomon considers this a life or death situation. Certainly, with his many wives and concubines, he was a man with first-hand experience in this area.

The command is to **depart not from the words of my mouth.** As a father and mentor, he is pleading with his sons to obey his word, and not learn the hard way as did father Solomon. It's significant that so much of Solomon's writing addresses sexual sin. This earnest pleading is apropos for the present day, when genuine love has been substituted by "sleaze" and cheap sexuality.

Prov. 5:8

"Remove thy way far from her, and come not nigh the door of her house:"

To prevent catching a disease is more desirable than being cured. There's something better than being delivered from the "mud hole." It's not jumping in it to begin with! Thus, the admonition is to steer clear of sexual impurity. **Remove thy way far from her** (the prostitute). If necessary, cross the street and run for your life!

In essence, that's the theme of this proverb; not only to **Remove** oneself from her, but make no further plans to even get near to **the door of her house.** It would even be better to stay away from her neighborhood, for that matter.

The Apostle Paul says, *"Flee youthful lusts"* (2 Timothy 2:22). James says, *"Then when lust hath conceived, it bringeth forth sin: and sin, when it is finished, bringeth forth death"* (James 1:15). Solomon, along with David and Sampson, knew this principle first hand. It takes one to know one; so, we need to learn from the examples of others.

Prov. 5:9

"Lest thou give thine honour unto others, and thy years unto the cruel:"

Adultery (physical and spiritual) is a robber! It steals **honor**; that majestic glory which God has put within man. We give away our virtue (that which distinguishes us from animals) through illicit relationships. Something is lost through unfaithfulness, as a young lady who loses her virginity outside of marriage, never to regain it again. She's given away her honor. The adulterer dishonors himself and his God. How quickly it happens, and how eager is the harlot to snatch it away.

The word **honor** is used to describe God's glory (e.g., Psalm 8:1; 45:3, etc.). Somehow, in creating man, God put something of His majesty within him; i.e., a God-conscious spirit (Genesis 2:7, Heb. *neshamah)*. There is a dimension in man that is not found in animals. The conscience and spiritual understanding within man sets him apart, holding him responsible for his attitude and actions. We "give away" that honorable attribute when we sin; thus, the need for restoration and forgiveness. This **honor** also involves the "flower of youth" in a man, which can be squandered and further set the pattern for a wicked life of lust.

In addition, this verse says **thy years** (life time) are given **unto the cruel.** Adulteresses (harlots) can be cruel, even murdering their husbands. Thus a man can give away his life to their cruelty. His lustful lifestyle also plays into the hands of the cruel master of evil himself, Satan.

All through this passage, there's the application of the spiritual adultery associated with false doctrine (teaching). The Church has compromised the true Gospel of Grace, trying to cohabitate with worldly prosperity, pop psychology, and the New Age movement. Therefore, the clear Biblical message of man's lost condition and the necessity of being born again, has been severely adulterated and infected.

Prov. 5:10

"Lest strangers be filled with thy wealth; and thy labours be in the house of a stranger;"

Lust and adultery lead to poverty and slavery. It's just a matter of time, just like the seed and the harvest. Evil practices can only lead to evil consequences. The brokenness and hopelessness of those who squandered away their souls can be seen in ministering to those in a rescue mission setting. However, hope emerges when one repents and believes in the Gospel.

Lest strangers (harlots or adulterers) **be filled with thy wealth** (strength or power); **and thy labours** (painful, grievous toil) **be in the house of a stranger** (foreigner or alien). What a picture of the enemy's robbery of human souls. Sexual relationships with prostitutes can only lead to the decline of personal character and dignity. It is a picture of personal poverty, slavery, and hardship, resulting from sexual sin.

Prov. 5:11

"And thou mourn at the last, when thy flesh and thy body are consumed,"

Robbed of wealth and dignity, the lustful man is brought down to despair and decimation. The awful fruit of sin has matured. As James said:

"Then when lust hath conceived, it bringeth forth sin: and sin, when it is finished, bringeth forth death." (James 1:15).

So, this poor man faces death with sorrow and suffering (literally roaring like a lion, cf. 28:15; Isaiah 5:30). What a picture of agony! Here's extreme suffering **at the last** (end of life), when he could have been rejoicing in grace had he given his life to the Lord. To be sure, *"the wages of sin is death"* (Romans 6:23).

This verse describes the total demise and consumption of the person, **flesh and body.** In Clarke's commentary, he comments on the word "body" as:

"Signifying properly the remains, residue, and remnant of a thing: and is applied here to denote the breathing carcass, putrid with the concomitant disease of debauchery: a public reproach which the justice of God entails on this species of iniquity,"

A reference to the horror of sexually transmitted diseases (STD) is certainly included here.

Reader, take heed to this warning. Flee from sexual sin, and run to the Savior!

Prov. 5:12

"And say, How have I hated instruction, and my heart despised reproof;"

How tragic when a man waits until his deathbed to face the truth of his rebellion. He comes to a moment of truth, which is better late than never. He has **hated instruction** and loved his sinfulness. His **heart** (has) **despised** (scorned) **reproof** (blame or censure for his faults). No one could tell him anything. He was a "know-it-all,"

In the end, everything is tragically wrong. O, the awful price of disobedience!

Prov. 5:13

"And have not obeyed the voice of my teachers, nor inclined mine ear to them that instructed me!"

This man was instructed by people that were concerned about him. He candidly admits to not heeding **the voice of my teachers, nor inclined mine ear to them that instructed me!** He is reaping what he has sown, whether physically, mentally, or spiritually.

At least, he takes responsibility for his actions, which is a step toward repentance. He didn't blame his teachers, but his failure to follow their instructions.

Prov. 5:14

"I was almost in all evil in the midst of the congregation and assembly."

Solomon continues the saga of a man "saved by the skin of his teeth." He now sees that **in the midst** (sight) **of the congregation,** he **was almost** in total **evil;** i.e., a public disgrace. His peers saw him as one living in a "world of iniquity," sold-out to sin.

But note the verb **was**, which refers to a disgraceful *past*. Something happened! Could it be that he's repented and received God's forgiveness? Is this a direct inference of God's mercy and deliverance through the man's confession?

Prov. 5:15

"Drink waters out of thine own cistern, and running waters out of thine own well."

God said, "It is not good for man to be alone" (Genesis 2:18). Therefore, He provided Adam with his wife, Eve. A husband and wife in marriage is God's established institution (Genesis 2:24). The family is the basic unit of society. Children are a heritage from the Lord.

Therefore, **drink waters out of thine own cistern** (water hole)...and **thine own well.** Let a man procreate from his God-given marital relationship, and not involve himself with harlots, a recurring theme in **Proverbs.**

Prov. 5:16

"Let thy fountains be dispersed abroad, and rivers of waters in the streets."

The metaphor continues, regarding a man's productivity and procreation through his wife (**fountains,** off-spring). He is urged to let his children (**rivers of water**) be **dispersed abroad...in the streets.**

In other words, prepare children at home, and send them out to make their mark on the world. The basic purpose of marriage is to have legitimate children, who in turn procreate. King David said, *"Happy is the man that hath his quiver full of them"* (Psalm 127:5).

Prov. 5:17

"Let them be only thine own, and not strangers' with thee."

Again, the emphasis is on fidelity and having legitimate children, **not strangers** (i.e., bastards born through adultery or strange women).

Prov. 5:18

"Let thy fountain be blessed: and rejoice with the wife of thy youth."

Solomon extols the beauty and joy of procreation **with the wife of thy youth.** It's customary to wed at a young adult age and bear children. Here is encouragement for a monogamous, fruitful, and lifetime marriage. Such an intimate and lasting relationship is a blessing from the Lord Himself. There needs to be a resurgence of God-centered marriages in today's society.

Prov. 5:19

"Let her be as the loving hind and pleasant roe; let her breasts satisfy thee at all times; and be thou ravished always with her love."

The loving hind (doe) **and pleasant roe** (gazelle or young antelope), are descriptive of grace and beauty. So should be the love of a husband for his wife, **ravished always with her love** (and no other woman). There's neither room nor desire here for harlots.

Prov. 5:20

"And why wilt thou, my son, be ravished with a strange woman, and embrace the bosom of a stranger?"

It's ironic that Solomon should ask such a question in light of his many so-called wives. But the issue here is the validity and sanctity of the marriage vow and relationship. The fact remains that there's legitimate intimacy in marriage. A **strange woman** is in no way comparable to a God-ordained wife.

Sexual intercourse is reserved for a man's spouse, where there's true knowledge, friendship, and a covenant relationship. That's not true with a harlot. Here is where sex and love part ways. Sex can be bought or engaged in without true love and intimacy. That's not so with love, where two are joined in marriage with God's smile and with no guilt.

"Marriage is honourable in all, and the bed undefiled: but whoremongers and adulterers God will judge," (Hebrews 13:4)

Prov. 5:21

"For the ways of man are before the eyes of the LORD, and he pondereth all his goings."

One overriding issue with adultery is that it is all an open book before the Lord of Glory. There's nothing hidden from God. As Hebrews 4:13 states:

"...all things are naked and opened unto the eyes of him with whom we have to do,"

This includes not only specific acts, but all of **the ways** (lifestyle) **of man.**

God also ponders **all his** (man's) **goings** (deeds). The word ponder (to mentally weigh) denotes intensive and continual action on God's part. He is constantly weighing and evaluating our actions and the motives behind them. Wow! That's what will come out at the Bema or the Judgment Seat of Christ (2 Corinthians 5:10). This fact alone should motivate us to love the Lord with all of our heart, soul, and strength!

Prov. 5:22

"His own iniquities shall take the wicked himself, and he shall be holden with the cords of his sins."

This is a powerful and descriptive picture of the self-condemning punishment of man's own sin. God doesn't have to chastise man per se; all He has to do is take away His restraining grace, and man will self-destruct. Yes, **his own iniquities** (perversities) **shall take** (hold of) **the wicked himself, and he shall be holden** (seized) **with the cords** (ropes) **of his sin.**

Man is usually is own worst enemy. The fool hangs himself without any help. Sin binds, destroys, and kills, identifying with the Destroyer himself. However, Jesus came that we might have *"life, and …might have it more abundantly."* (John 10:10)

Prov. 5:23

"He shall die without instruction; and in the greatness of his folly he shall go astray."

What a finale to a wicked life! Bound up in his iniquities, the sinner dies in **the greatness** (abundance) **of his folly;** i.e., totally absorbed and intoxicated with the sins of the flesh. And he does so **without instruction**, meaning with no warning or restraint. He now faces the judgment of God and eternal damnation!

Solomon issues a similar warning in Prov. 29:1:

"He, that being often reproved hardeneth his neck, shall suddenly be destroyed, and that without remedy."

What can be more tragic?

Chapter 6
Dangerous Promises

Prov. 6:1

"My son, if thou be surety for thy friend, if thou hast stricken thy hand with a stranger,"

The first five verses of **Proverbs 6,** deal with further instruction to the writer's **son** in regard to risky personal and business transactions.

If thou be surety for thy friend indicates a co-signing or financial mediation for one's friend before a third party. **Surety** means a pledge, or loan in behalf of someone. This scenario arises when a friend cannot get a "legitimate" loan to purchase a commodity (e.g., car, appliance, etc.) which he wants, but can't afford. He then approaches his friend to mediate or "back him" financially. This is a bad idea!

If he has not established credit, nor has a steady income, who would be foolish enough to lend him the money? If someone is broke and yet wants to borrow funds, what makes him think he'll pay the money back with interest added?

It might be plausible, however, for a father to become **surety** (pledge, co-signer) for an ambitious son who needs to establish credit. The father signs a note at the bank, and allows the son to make the monthly payments. Thus, the son establishes his credit by paying the loan and establishing his own relationship with the bank.

However, this verse indicates that a mistake has been made, and Solomon is telling the son what to do **if thou hast stricken thy hand with a stranger.**

"The striking of the hand" must be like a handshake in our society. It was an open expression that a contract was made, in lieu of a notary seal. The **stranger** (like a strange woman or prostitute) is undesirable and not trustworthy, perhaps a "conman."

Prov. 6:2

"Thou art snared with the words of thy mouth, thou art taken with the words of thy mouth."

Solomon is saying, in essence, that his son is trapped or has "put his foot in his mouth" as far as this bad deal is concerned. If a man's word is his bond and a contract is sealed with a handshake, hopefully there would be some time period to escape or break the unfortunate agreement.

Prov. 6:3

"Do this now, my son, and deliver thyself, when thou art come into the hand of thy friend; go, humble thyself, and make sure thy friend."

Time is of the essence. Do it now! This situation is most serious and it is not a trivial loan. The borrower and co-signer are subject to the lender or creditor. Failure to pay back the loan could cost the co-signer his credit, house, family, or even time in debtor's prison! Thus, the desperate plea to **deliver thyself** (recover or rescue himself), and to plead his case to his **friend.**

Humble thyself, and make sure thy friend. Aggressively admit your mistake and plead with your friend, not taking "No" for an answer. The next couple of verses describe the intensity of trying to escape this awful mistake.

Prov. 6:4

"Give not sleep to thine eyes, nor slumber to thine eyelids."

Here is a parallelism which emphasizes how imperative it is to deal with this gross mistake quickly. Don't sleep or even close your eyes until you get this thing settled. There's too much at stake! The longer you wait, the more difficult it will become. When you get caught up in anything wrong or sinful, rebound quickly. Get right with God and others (1 John 1:9).

Prov. 6:5

"Deliver thyself as a roe from the hand of the hunter, and as a bird from the hand of the fowler."

Deliver thyself: The Hebrew verb here means "to tear oneself away." This is a command to escape the situation as quickly **as a roe** would run from a hunter. The second analogy is **a bird** escaping the hand of a bird snatcher (**fowler**).

It's interesting how intense are these words from Solomon. Running from debt entanglement is on par with fleeing from sin itself. Yet, how prevalent is debt and bankruptcy in our present society? Both financial and moral responsibilities are on a rapid decline.

Prov. 6:6

"Go to the ant, thou sluggard; consider her ways, and be wise."

Here Solomon injects an illustration from nature regarding the work ethic. Evidently, the whole co-signing idea hinged on laziness and/or greed; the desire to get something without working for it. **Go to the ant, thou sluggard.** You're indolent, slothful, and lazy.

There are too many people who "leech" on others and refuse to work. They're always on the receiving end, never working diligently. They have a "you-owe-me" or entitlement attitude, taking from others. It's like the "welfare mentality," which is geared to giving temporary help, but ends up becoming a lifestyle.

So, lazy people need to learn from the industrious **ant** and **consider her ways. Be wise** and learn something! It's amazing what we can learn from God's "lower" creatures. The small ant can do many "big" things. Observe their diligence and purpose, which is hard to find in human societies.

Prov. 6:7

"Which having no guide, overseer, or ruler,"

The ants have no leader, no officer over them, no king per se. An amazing fact! The work ethic is instinctively built into the ants, while indolent men remain lazy. People need someone over them to teach, direct, and make them work, but not the ant. Is it man's sin nature? The utopia of God's creation sometimes has the lowest ideals and energy. Yet, ants are diligent in their purpose.

How ironic. Sin has really cost us humans. That's why only the power of God can change a "lazy" man into a diligent worker with a lifelong purpose.

Prov. 6:8

"Provideth her meat in the summer, and gathereth her food in the harvest."

Without a leader, ants get their jobs done. They instinctively provide food **in the summer**, and make provisions for their sustenance in the winter, by working the **harvest** in the summer. These parallel thoughts simply state that ants "make hay while the sun shines." Ants are so small in size, yet so large in focus and labor. Man is so big in size, yet so small in sense and responsibility. O, the lessons we can learn from the little creatures of the dust! Facing the judgment of God, you'd think that man would be stirred into action.

Man, being the utopia of God's creation, somehow by choice lacks the instinctive genius of the animal kingdom. Sin has crippled man from making right choices and taking proper responsibility for himself and others. It's fascinating what ants accomplish by instinct, and how little man accomplishes with his accessibility to divine power.

Prov. 6:9

"How long wilt thou sleep, O sluggard? When wilt thou arise out of thy sleep?"

A pointed, convicting question is offered here: **How long wilt thou sleep, O sluggard? When wilt thou arise out of thy sleep?** The lazy man is addressed directly, now having been confronted with the diligent nature of the ant. If an insect, without a leader, can perform such faithful tasks, then what would hinder a human being who is under God's direction and power?

Remember, all earthly creatures are obedient to their Creator, doing what they were created to do, except mankind. Birds fly and build their nests; cows give milk; fish swim in the waters; and the ants are doing what they were created to do. Man is the culprit, the sinner who rebels against his Creator. Thus, the judgment of God is upon mankind and not animals.

> *"And as it is appointed unto men once to die, but after this the judgment,"* (Hebrews 9:27)

This passage really describes the process and results of laziness: 1) How long will he sleep before waking up; and 2) When will he actually arise out of bed? The inference is that he doesn't care. He seems content in sleeping his life away. What a commentary on man's depravity, which robs him of ambition and purpose. This is also characteristic of depressed people who "sleep" their lives away with their eyes shut or open.

Note the spiritual application of this problem by the Apostle Paul:

> *"Awake thou that sleepest, and arise from the dead...,"* (Ephesians 5:14)

Prov. 6:10

"Yet a little sleep, a little slumber, a little folding of the hands to sleep:"

This statement further describes excessive sleep, which may well be an escape from responsibility. Everyone needs sleep, but it must not be a substitute for diligent work. The flesh is naturally lazy and can easily submit to the temptation of irresponsibility.

Notice the graphic description of laziness in action: **a little sleep, a little slumber, a little folding of the hands to sleep.** O, just to get a little more sleep; just for a few more minutes; and hit the "snooze alarm" just another time! Anything but getting up to work! Such habits often lead to chronic unemployment and poverty. This is how the flesh operates if you let it. Nothing has changed from Solomon's day 'til now.

Prov. 6:11

"So shall thy poverty come as one that travelleth, and thy want as an armed man."

The lazy man is likened to a wayfarer who is either economically unstable or is a robber who steals because of his **poverty.**

Could the traveling man be poverty-stricken because of not being planted in one place, being unstable? The lazy man has need **as an armed man:** it doesn't say that he is in want because of an armed man. Rather, he is likened to an armed robber, who would not be known for his stability, uprightness, and economic security. See the same scenario in Prov. 24:34.

The remaining issue is that lazy people will suffer from neediness and poverty, because God ordained us to work diligently. Today, the welfare system has become a way of life for many, stripping people of self-worth and the initiative to work.

Prov. 6:12

"A naughty person, a wicked man, walketh with a froward mouth."

Here's an exposé of how **a wicked man** is revealed by his **mouth** and body language. **A naughty person** is one who is worthless, good for nothing, and unprofitable. The word "naughty" comes from the Hebrew word *"belial,"* as in "son of Belial" in Deuteronomy 13:13 and 1 Samuel 25:25. It's amazing how naughty people flaunt themselves, giving the impression that they have it all together. Such is the makeup of the world.

In addition, he's **a wicked man,** walking **with a froward mouth.** The word for "wicked" describes one who is troublesome, vain, and full of immorality. How bold and mouthy are the wicked! His mouth is **froward,** meaning perverted or crooked.

The reference to **mouth** is not primarily the body part itself, but what comes out of it. It's the "organ of speech;" literally, "a blowing or flow of words." How bold and mouthy are the arrogant who "blow hard" against God's authority! The mouth which is given to praise the Creator, is perverted by sin and becomes an instrument to blaspheme Him! No wonder there's a Hell.

There's a direct correlation between one's "walk" or lifestyle, and what comes out of his mouth. *"Out of the abundance of the heart the mouth speaketh,"* The believer is both revealed and judged by his speech. Note again James 3, the so-called "tongue chapter" of the Bible.

Prov. 6:13

"He winketh with his eyes, he speaketh with his feet, he teacheth with his fingers;"

Here's the epitome of body language, engaging the eyes, feet, and fingers. How expressive are these in communication. Note that this is a naughty person, who speaks non-verbally with his body language. The godly, Spirit-filled person speaks directly, letting his light shine. His face is sufficient to manifest the glory of God, attended by proper words. His "yea is yea;" i.e., he says what he means and means what he says.

However, the wicked man **winketh with his eyes, he speaketh with his feet, he teacheth with his fingers.** This is evidenced by the "sweet talker" on the street wooing a young woman, as well as salesmen and politicians who "sell" their wares through body language. All people engage in body language to some degree. Yet, the wicked are masters of it. Their approach smacks of condescending pride and deceit, overtaking their prey, and mesmerizing simple or foolish souls. Such activity is spawned in Hell from the Evil one himself.

Everyone has a message, whether they're consciously aware of it or not. We give ourselves away in both verbal and non-verbal communication. Some of the most wicked people are brilliant speakers; for instance, prisons are rampant with "smart" inmates who know how to play the system and manipulate others. Some crimes are impossible to commit unless you're well-educated or skilled in some area; e.g., one who is computer illiterate will never be locked up for computer "hacking" or internet fraud.

Prov. 6:14

"Frowardness is in his heart, he deviseth mischief continually; he soweth discord."

The body language finds its source in the heart. What we are inside manifests itself externally, unless we're masters of deceit. The wicked persons eyes, feet, fingers, mouth, etc. are connected to his inner heart. **Frowardness is in his heart:** his perverted, twisted, crooked heart will say and do wicked things.

He deviseth mischief (evil) **continually.** His mind is sold out to scheming. The word **deviseth** literally means "to carve or engrave; also "to be silent or quiet" (see Psalm 50:21). This is picturesque in describing the wicked man whose heart silently "cuts out" a plan of mischief. It's amazing how hard sinners work at sinning. Here's a man who illustrates Genesis 6:5:

"...every imagination of the thoughts of his heart was only evil continually." (Compare to Prov. 6:18).

As a result, **he soweth discord** (produces strife). His wicked activity can only create disunity and chaos.

"...for whatsoever a man soweth, that shall he also reap" (Galatians 6:7, again).

Some people just love to stir the pot and create chaos. In churches, these people see themselves as having the "gift of criticism." O, the depth of sin! How marvelous is the grace of God that can provide a "new heart" that produces rightness of life.

The word "devise" is also used in a good sense in Proverbs 14:22. Thankfully, the principle of sowing and reaping works on the positive side as well; e.g., "sow to the Spirit and reap life everlasting."

Prov. 6:15

"Therefore, shall his calamity come suddenly; suddenly shall he be broken without remedy."

Death and destruction sometimes come **suddenly** (from the Hebrew *pithome* - instantly), as in a **calamity** (disaster). Solomon emphasizes this tragedy by saying, **suddenly shall he be broken** (crushed) **without remedy** (cure). What a commentary on the destiny of those who hate God! Not to mention the Hell they will face for eternity afterward. What a tragedy!

All people die, but how they die makes a difference. Not long ago, there was a tsunami (killer wave) in Southeast Asia, killing over 150,000 people in a flash. They were swept away without warning. There was no time "to prepare to meet God,"

However, the Apostle Paul testifies in Philippians 1:21, that *"to live is Christ, and to die is gain,"* Death can be victorious and better when one walks with God. What a difference it makes, whether in life or death, to be a child of God!

Prov. 6:16

"These six things doth the LORD hate: yea, seven are an abomination unto him:"

God hates sin! His holiness is comprised of two basic characteristics: 1) Righteousness, or His love for what's right; and 2) Justice, or His hatred for the wrong. In verses 16-19, the writer portrays seven specific sins which are particularly an **abomination** to the LORD.

They are presented by using a Hebrew poetic apparatus for emphasis: **six things...yea, seven...** Compare a similar format in Proverbs 30:18, 21, 24, and 29.

Prov. 6:17

"A proud look, a lying tongue, and hands that shed innocent blood,"

Here are the first three of the list of seven: 1) **A proud look** (eyes); 2) **a lying tongue** (mouth); and 3) murderous **hands.** These characteristics amplify the body language mentioned in vs. 12-15, only now we have God's hatred for such.

Pride is mentioned first: the primary sin of Lucifer, leading to his ejection from Heaven (Ezekiel 28:12f.). **A proud look** conveys arrogance and self-exaltation. The expression of pride is deceit or **a lying tongue.**

This proud spirit or "god-complex" can easily lead one to **shed innocent blood** (murder). This may well explain why abortionists (especially doctors) can kill innocent babies without a cringe of conscience.

Prov. 6:18

"An heart that deviseth wicked imaginations, feet that be swift in running to mischief,"

The body follows the lead of the heart. **Wicked** deeds are devised in the **heart**, and **imaginations** are mental plans of the inner soul (Genesis 6:5). God hates **feet** that run unrestrained **to mischief** or evil.

On the other hand,

"How beautiful are the feet of them that preach the gospel of peace, and bring glad tidings of good things!" (Romans 10:15)

Prov. 6:19

"A false witness that speaketh lies, and he that soweth discord among brethren."

The last two characteristics hated by God are: A **false** (lying) **witness** and a sower of **discord.** Some wicked people major in these two areas. They have no rest until there's unrest and division among the brethren. They love lies and discord. It's another expression of the depth of depravity. (See vs. 12, 14).

Gossip is spreading detrimental news about someone to those who are neither part of the problem or solution. Many a church and family have been destroyed by such ungodly behavior. Problems are for solving, not to foster destruction. They need to be faced squarely by those directly involved.

Jesus spoke directly to this issue in Matthew 18:15, when he instructed the disciples to go directly to an offender; to privately confront him regarding his fault and hopefully getting things settled. The idea is to "solve the problem" and promote reconciliation.

Prov. 6:20

"My son, keep thy father's commandment, and forsake not the law of thy mother:"

See the commentary on Prov. 1:8.

Prov. 6:21

"Bind them continually upon thine heart, and tie them about thy neck."

This proverb is similar to Prov. 3:3. God's Word needs to be etched and fastened to our very being, internally (**heart**) and externally (**neck**), that we may be totally secured. It's like a godly addiction to the Bible. What's wrong with brainwashing if you have the right "wash?"

Moses speaks to this truth in Deuteronomy 6:6-8, which is called the "Shema" (meaning "hear"):

"And these words, which I command thee this day, shall be in thine heart: And thou shalt teach them diligently unto thy children, and shalt talk of them when thou sittest in thine house, and when thou walkest by the way, and when thou liest down, and when thou risest up. And thou shalt bind them for a sign upon thine hand, and they shall be as frontlets between thine eyes."

Prov. 6:22

"When thou goest, it shall lead thee; when thou sleepest, it shall keep thee; and when thou awakest, it shall talk with thee."

The inseparable connection with God's Word will produce complete protection and guidance day and night. Even during the vulnerable state of sleep, God assures us of His divine security. Furthermore, **it shall talk with thee.** The Word speaks to us profoundly. What a blessed provision is this? The word "talk" is used for "meditate," as in Psalm 1:2. Speaking of the blessed man, David says:

"But his delight is in the law of the LORD; and in his law doth he meditate day and night,"

What we make of the Word, God will make of us. There's no better companion like the Word. Don't leave home without it!

Prov. 6:23

"For the commandment is a lamp; and the law is light; and reproofs of instruction are the way of life:"

God's Word is the believer's **lamp, light,** and **way of life.** Every aspect of the Word gives clarity and direction as we walk through this dark world. In fact, the Word is the very "way" or path of abundant life itself.

David said:

"Thy word is a lamp unto my feet, and a light unto my path" (Psalm 119:105).

It was customary to use small clay pots filled with oil and strapped to each foot. The wick was lit, enabling a person to "light their path" down a dark road; an ancient "flashlight," if you will. Significantly, Jesus is both the Living Word and the Light of the World, becoming:

"The way, the truth, and the life..." (John 14:6).

Note that the commandments not only render positive instruction, but negative as well; i.e., what we should not do. The Apostle Paul says, the Word of God is *"profitable for doctrine, for reproof, for correction, for instruction in righteousness"* (2 Timothy 3:16). The Word reveals what is wrong so it can be made right.

Prov. 6:24

"To keep thee from the evil woman, from the flattery of the tongue of a strange woman."

It's interesting how Solomon again zeros in on the evil woman. Only a Heavenly perspective can keep a man from avoiding the enticing **flattery** of **a strange woman** (1 Corinthians 10:13). The **evil woman** has an agenda of preying on the weaknesses of men.

Prov. 6:25

"Lust not after her beauty in thine heart; neither let her take thee with her eyelids."

Lust begins in the **heart**, which leads to action; thus, Solomon's warning. Her painted **eyelids** aggravate the problem, deceitfully enhancing **her beauty.** Don't **let her take** (seize) you! Not much has changed to this day, except for the proliferation of pornography by print, photography, and internet technology. The lust of the flesh can only be overcome by the fullness of the Holy Spirit. The Apostle Paul admonishes: *"Flee also youthful lusts"* (2 Timothy 2:22).

James also warns:

"Let no man say when he is tempted, I am tempted of God: for God cannot be tempted with evil, neither tempteth he any man: But every man is tempted, when he is drawn away of his own lust, and enticed. Then when lust hath conceived, it bringeth forth sin: and sin, when it is finished, bringeth forth death. Do not err, my beloved brethren." (James 1:13-16.)

Prov. 6:26

"For by means of a whorish woman a man is brought to a piece of bread: and the adulteress will hunt for the precious life."

This is a picture of a whore hunting for prey. She is not passive, but aggressive about it. Men are easy targets by nature, and are destroyed or swallowed like **a piece of bread.**

His **precious life** or soul is at stake. How the Destroyer can use a determined woman of the street to destroy lives! However, men must take personal responsibility for their actions, including their vices. (Refer to Psalm 119:9, 11.)

Prov. 6:27

"Can a man take fire in his bosom, and his clothes not be burned?"

Speaking of the whore hunting for a man's life, Solomon uses the analogy of a man placing **fire in his bosom**, wrongly thinking that **his clothes** will remain untouched by the flame. No way! To play with fire is to get burned. Lust is fire out of control. To think otherwise is foolishness or deception.

Prov. 6:28

"Can one go upon hot coals, and his feet not be burned?"

Here's another analogy where the writer asks a question which has an obvious answer. However, many believe they are "fire-walkers," who can rise above the burning consequences of fiery temptation. Again, the easiest person to deceive is one's self.

Note Paul's admonition and metaphor in 1 Corinthians 7:9:

"for It is better to marry than to burn,"

He's speaking of sexual lust and the need to marry, rather than committing fornication. Yet, it must be said that marriage itself is no automatic deterrent from further sexual sins, like adultery.

Prov. 6:29

"So he that goeth in to his neighbour's wife; whosoever toucheth her shall not be innocent."

Starting with the word "so," this verse is linked to the previous two illustrations depicting the "burning of lust." (See vs. 27, 28) The two verbs "going in" and "touches" indicate an extramarital affair. Such activity is not only foolish, but sinful and very risky. (See vs. 32).

Prov. 6:30, 31

Men do not despise a thief, if he steal to satisfy his soul when he is hungry; But if he be found, he shall restore sevenfold; he shall give all the substance of his house."

While sin is an offense before God, society's crimes vary in seriousness (e.g., there's "murder one;" 2nd degree murder; and manslaughter involving degrees of motive, violence, etc.). Stealing bread and stealing a neighbor's wife in adultery are both wrong but differ in degree of severity.

Note the severity of the punishment: 1) Restitution, restoring **sevenfold**; 2) Surrendering whatever **substance** (wealth or equity) he has in his house. This is proper in keeping with the law, and necessary in reclaiming his personal reputation. That's a steep penalty; yet, the awful results of committing adultery are even greater.

Prov. 6:32

"But whoso committeth adultery with a woman lacketh understanding: he that doeth it destroyeth his own soul."

Bread can be restored, but what happens in adultery cannot be restored. The man who has sex with another man's wife is described here in serious terms. He's not only wrong, but **lacks understanding** (lit. "heart"). He's spiritually destitute or "beside himself" (insane)![10]

Moreover, the adulterer is **destroying his own soul;** i.e., his inner person. How serious is that? The terrible consequences are now described.

Prov. 6:33

"A wound and dishonour shall he get; and his reproach shall not be wiped away."

A wound (from the Hebrew *nega,* used to describe a leprous spot or plague) **and dishonour** (loss of grace, disgrace) **shall he get. His reproach** (shame) **shall not be wiped away.** O, he can find forgiveness with God through repentance, but not with people!

There's something about adultery that's never forgotten. People will have some pity on a hungry man for stealing bread, but there's only contempt for a wife-stealer.

Prov. 6:34

"For jealousy is the rage of a man: therefore he will not spare in the day of vengeance."

---

[10] Translation by Keil & Delitzsch Commentary, e-Sword Bible Program

It's hard to imagine anything more offensive to a man than finding the wife he loves lying with another man. Therefore, he's not going to show compassion in his revenge. Such **jealousy** or **rage** fosters blind fury in a man, who will not rest until justice is served, even at his own hands.

Prov. 6:35

"He will not regard any ransom; neither will he rest content, though thou givest many gifts."

So deep is this man's wounded heart, that nothing, even a bribe (**ransom**), will cover the wrong done to him. Neither will he be made **content** with a showering of **many gifts**. Vengeful justice is the only option.

The number of bloody homicides relating to such marital "triangles" is myriad. The worst sinners have a sense of justice. It reflects their God-given conscience. Even a heathen, who has never heard of the 10 Commandments, knows it's wrong to run off with another man's wife. It all points to the Holy One who has revealed Himself to all of mankind (cf. Romans 1:18; 2:14, 15).

Chapter 7
My Son, Keep My Words

Prov. 7:1

"My son, keep my words, and lay up my commandments with thee."

Again, there's the ongoing, earnest urging to his son to **keep** (attend to) **my words, and lay up** (treasure) **my commandments with thee.** There's the constant repetition regarding the necessity of obedience; not because God wants to "beat us over the head" with it, but rather to assure the blessings and positive results that follow obedience.

Prov. 7:2

"Keep my commandments, and live; and my law as the apple of thine eye."

The writer is not saying: "Keep God's commandments and be saved from sin." That would contradict the whole of Scripture. (See Galatians 2:16; Titus 3:5) Rather, **Live** here refers to the abundant life which results from a believer's obedience to the Word. This fruit is a *product* of being saved by grace; it's God's doing, not man's. It is living life to the full! (John 10:10)

The apple of thine eye refers to the pupil of the eye. It relates here to the believer's spiritual eye or heart. There's a focus that goes beyond the physical. Jesus said, *"If, therefore, thine **eye** be single (focused), thy whole body shall be full of light."* (Matthew 6:22)

This has to do with meditating (focusing, concentrating) on the Word (e.g., Joshua 1:8; Psalm 1:2). It is sure to produce godly results; i.e., the fruit of the Holy Spirit (Galatians 5:22, 23). Being filled with the Word has the same effect as being filled with the Holy Spirit (cf. Ephesians 5:18f. with Colossians 3:16, 17). A believer truly filled with the Holy Spirit will be filled with the reality of the Word, and vice versa.

Prov. 7:3

"Bind them upon thy fingers, write them upon the table of thine heart."

Bind them upon thy fingers, or tie them on your hands. Our hands are usually busy and engaged in some activity. They need to be sanctified for the glory of God, not for our own selfish purposes. We need to do what our hands find to do with God in mind, serving Him with all our might.

The key statement is to **write them upon the table** (polished tablet) **of thine heart.** The heart dictates what the hands do. We are to be absorbed and motivated by the principles of the Word. External righteousness emanates from inward righteousness.

Prov. 7:4

"Say unto wisdom, Thou art my sister; and call understanding thy kinswoman:"

This verse speaks to the intimate, family relationship of wisdom and understanding. Wisdom is in the feminine gender, a sweet **sister** who befriends the brother in Christ. Family members love and fight for each other. So does wisdom for the brother who struggles with lust. (cf. vs. 5)

We need to get well acquainted with Wisdom and the Word, if we're to be "overcomers,"

"Thy word have I hid in my heart, that I might not sin against Thee," (Psalm 119:11)

Take authority over the world, the flesh, and the Devil by faith. Faith is the victory that overcomes the world, and wisdom enables us to live skillfully in the process. Amen.

Prov. 7:5

"That they may keep thee from the strange woman, from the stranger which flattereth with her words."

Family members take care of and guard each other. It's noteworthy to see how often wisdom is essential in matters of sexual impurity. The harlot cannot overtake a man who's putting wisdom to use. Linked with the fear of God, wisdom sees through the emptiness of the prostitute.

The beauty of a woman is not "skin deep." The most beautiful women are not those who just look fine, but those who exude the glory of God. It takes more than makeup and smooth talk to be beautiful.

We must make an application of "smooth talkers" in the religious realm: those who eloquently parade their false teachings. These charmers claim to be "super apostles and prophets" with anointed tongues, who fleece the crowds with their "health and wealth" schemes.

Prov. 7:6

"For at the window of my house I looked through my casement,"

The author cites his experience of watching how the "simple ones" fall into the prostitute's snare. **For at the window of my house I looked** (peeped) **through my casement** (latticed window). Here's a demonstration of the downward process of sin, given for our admonition.

Prov. 7:7

"And beheld among the simple ones, I discerned among the youths, a young man void of understanding,"

The saga continues. It's as though Wisdom speaks directly to the situation, watching the procedure of temptation upon the foolish **simple ones**, particularly **among the youths.** He focuses on **a young man void of understanding**, empty of wisdom and good sense. This is the young man of Prov. 1:4, for whom the **Proverbs** were written. He's the young man of Psalm 119:9, who needs to cleanse his lifestyle by taking heed to the Word (vs. 11).

Sexual sins are not unique to the young, but there's an intensity of hormonal activity in lustful youths. The desire for marriage and procreation begins in late adolescence, according to God's plan. Thus, discernment and godly sensitivity is especially warranted for young people. Today, that quality is being thrown to the wind, creating a horrible wave of immorality. The great need is for more wise young people who will refrain from promiscuity, awaiting God's life partner.

Prov. 7:8

"Passing through the street near her corner; and he went the way to her house,"

This verse pictures the simple young man, who is about to fall into the trap of lust. He's **passing through the street near her corner**, or "cruising" near where the harlots gather. He wants to get as close as possible without making his intent obvious.

Then, **he went the way** (road) **to her house**, her place of business. There's trouble ahead, for sure, but the flesh's temptation must have its way. After all, he has "needs," and they must be "satisfied." Yes, needs are legitimate, but must be satisfied legitimately, if at all.

Prostitution is legalized in some places in America, and promiscuity has become more socially acceptable. Marriage is disdained by some people, who simply live together with no embarrassment. Marital fidelity has been thrown to the wind. Same-sex confusion is rising, which is not from God. In conjunction to the increasing lawlessness in the world, it would appear that the Coming of the LORD in judgment is imminent.

Prov. 7:9

"In the twilight, in the evening, in the black and dark night:"

The simpleton operates **in the twilight** (dusk), **in the evening, in the black** (literally, the pupil of the eye) **and dark night.** All of this shady action takes place at night. Satan and sin love to operate in the dark of the night. As "the Prince of Darkness," Satan hates the light.

Children of the world are "in the dark," desiring to sin without exposure. They, too, hate the light, because "their deeds are evil." (cf. John 3:19) But the believer is a "child of the light," with nothing to hide. He is lined up with what is right. So whether in the light or the night, he does right, with no shame or fear.

Prov. 7:10

"And, behold, there met him a woman with the attire of an harlot, and subtil of heart."

How deep runs the subtlety of the whore. This woman was not just a "street walker," but a married woman (cf. 7:19). She comes in the **attire** (dress) **of an harlot, and subtil of heart** (cunning and shrewd). This woman is a "pro," selling her body in a subtle manner. The foolish man is set up for the kill. How deceitful is the game of illicit sex! Its consequences are widespread and destructive.

Prov. 7:11

("She is loud and stubborn; her feet abide not in her house."

Solomon describes the harlot's demeanor, stemming from her inward agenda. (vs. 10) She is **loud** and **stubborn**. The "loudness" here is not simply the volume or sound. The word means "to murmur; to cry aloud in rage; to be troubled." It describes a disgruntled, bitter woman, which is characteristic for a harlot.

The Hebrew word translated **stubborn** is *sarar,* meaning "to turn away from what is moral; to rebel," She is rebellious against God and will not budge; her mind is made up, explaining why she can promote her trade without shame. Her obstinate heart prevents any change in her lifestyle, apart from God's intervention.

Consequently, **her feet abide not in her house** because she's busily engaged in the streets away from her family. She is not a normal woman assuming home responsibility. She is experienced and subtle, which makes the lustful simpleton an easy victim.

Prov. 7:12

"Now is she without, now in the streets, and lieth in wait at every corner.")

This "streetwalker" is like an animal on the prey, waiting to lure another fool into her deceitful trap. **Now is she without** (outside), **now in the streets, and lieth in wait at every corner.** This gal is busy: inside one minute and outside the next. She takes to the streets, and then lurks as one ready to ambush another. She knows the "tricks of the trade," and the lustful hearts of men. As long as there's unbridled lust, the prostitute will always be employed.

Although her sin does pay in a perverted sense, one day it's "wages" will be death! God has ordained marriage, and the Gospel serves to deal with sexual lust. Yet, prostitution is considered "the oldest occupation," still flourishing today. What a challenge for the virtuous woman to consider as she ministers in her home. (cf. 1 Timothy 5:14; Titus 2:3-5)

Prov. 7:13

"So she caught him, and kissed him, and with an impudent face said unto him,"

He chased her until she **caught him!** Sounds like a trap springing shut on its prey. More accurately, the Hebrew word for "caught" (*chazak)* means "to prevail; be strong;" and this woman is strongly resolved in her quest. It's amazing how committed people are in their sin.

She further subdues him with a kiss, and then speaks to him **with an impudent face** or "hard look." This is her profession, and she does her thing with no embarrassment.

Prov. 7:14

"I have peace offerings with me; this day have I payed my vows."

The brazen harlot offers him food left over from **peace offerings** (Leviticus 7:15). She has done her "religious" duty by paying her **vows,** a way of covering up her guilt before engaging in her sinful trade. Is this not the same attitude that prevails all too often in the modern Church, where professing believers attempt to serve two masters; God and the world? It's time to get "off the fence," and choose whom we will serve.

Matthew Henry's commentary is well taken:

> "It is sad that a show of piety should become the shelter of iniquity (which really doubles the shame of it, and makes it more exceedingly sinful) and that men should baffle their consciences with those very things that should startle them. The Pharisees made long prayers, that they might the more plausibly carry on their covetous and mischievous provisions."

So, this prostitute hid behind her "religiosity" to further defile and sear her conscience. Amazing how religion can harden the heart, rather than making it alive and receptive! Indeed, the same sun that melts butter, hardens clay.

Prov. 7:15

"Therefore came I forth to meet thee, diligently to seek thy face, and I have found thee."

How intensely the harlot seeks her prey, especially when armed with the deceitful justification by religious duties performed (vs. 14). Unashamed, she testifies of her evil conquest: **Came I forth to meet thee, diligently to seek thy face, and I have found thee.** Note that the religious feast is the entrée to the evil sexual liaison.

She came with a peace offering of food, easing her conscience. The subtle scheme was to make this sexual encounter a religious experience. The world and even the Church are filled today with such deceitful engagements. Shame is almost a thing of the past.

Prov. 7:16

"I have decked my bed with coverings of tapestry, with carved works, with fine linen of Egypt."

How clever is the temptress! She's not only aggressive, but careful to set the stage and atmosphere for her sexual trade. She appeals to the senses, almost like the serpent did to Eve in the

Garden of Eden. The bed looks good and smells good.

How could anything be wrong that looks, smells, and feels so good? How our senses can deceive us when we are not steeped in Truth. To what lengths she has gone to make wickedness appear to be "lily white," Her bed is exquisite to the eyes, but deadly to the soul.

Prov. 7:17

"I have perfumed my bed with myrrh, aloes, and cinnamon."

The bed is sprinkled with intoxicating spices, which help to ensnare the harlot's prey. **Myrrh** (fragrant gum from the bark of a tree), **aloes** (tree)**, and cinnamon** (a fragrant bark of a tree) all heighten sensuality. These fragrant spices all have legitimate uses, but are used here to cover the stench of evil sexual activity.

Likewise, elaborate sights, sounds, and smells can serve to "cover up" false religious worship. How easily good things can be perverted!

Prov. 7:18

"Come, let us take our fill of love until the morning: let us solace ourselves with loves."

After all the tantalizing preparation, she invites him to **Come, let us take our fill of love** (or become intoxicated with sex) **until the morning.** She leaves no stone unturned. She's a master in the art of seduction. It's similar to Satan's ploy in the Garden of Eden (Genesis 3), making the forbidden fruit of the tree so desirable.

The true meaning of "love" is used in the Song of Solomon; an expression of a beloved and legitimate relationship between a man and a woman (cf. Song 1:14; 2:3; 4:10). Illicit, adulterous lust is far removed from true love. This is how sin works: it is pleasurable, deceitful, temporary, and ultimately unsatisfying, not to mention the aftermath of guilt and judgment.

Prov. 7:19

"For the goodman is not at home, he is gone a long journey:"

She's telling him that the **goodman** (lit. "the man") is not at home and won't be back for awhile. Rather than saying "my husband," she uses this evasive term, likened to the modern usage of "the ol' man." The scenario is that **he is gone (on) a long journey** (trip), and won't be home anytime soon; therefore, there's no one at home to catch them in their evil act.

This reveals again the depth of human depravity; for when a person is overcome by evil and lust, there's no concern that God sees all, and will someday demand accountability. That state of denial, however, will not change the fact. *"Be sure, your sin will find you out!"*

Prov. 7:20

"He hath taken a bag of money with him, and will come home at the day appointed."

She's comforted by the fact that her husband is on a business trip with enough money to not have to come home until **the day appointed** (i.e., the new moon). She's calculated the length of his trip, and has schemed accordingly.

Prov. 7:21

"With her much fair speech she caused him to yield, with the flattering of her lips she forced him."

Here's the power of her persuasion in action. With a mouth "smoother than oil," she **caused him to yield** or surrender to her advances (cf. Prov. 5:3). With her sweet talk, **she forced him;** (literally, "to intensely push or thrust away"). This suggests that she seductively conquered or dispelled any moral consciousness possessed by the man.

John Gill comments:

"Her charming voice, and flattering lips, had more effect upon him than her kisses"[11]

---

[11] John Gill's Exposition of the Bible; e-Sword Bible Program

It reminds one of the power of Delilah over Sampson, who could take on an army of Philistines but couldn't handle one seductive and deceptive woman! (Judges 16:4-22)

Prov. 7:22

"He goeth after her straightway, as an ox goeth to the slaughter or as a fool to the correction of the stocks:"

Who is the "weaker sex" anyway? This duped fellow is effectively drawn into her clutches. Just as the unsuspecting ox goes to the slaughter, or the fool nonchalantly takes his punishment (stock or stripes), so the lust-filled man is led to his destruction.

The idea of **straightway** is suddenness. He is taken suddenly, with no recourse or deliverance. How powerful and subtle is sin!

Prov. 7:23

"Till a dart strike through his liver; as a bird hasteth to the snare, and knoweth not that it is for his life."

How beautiful is the woman of God's choice (i.e., a wife), but how deadly is the prostitute. The writer likens the man to a bird who hastens to **the snare** or net. He has no inkling that his life is at stake, until the arrow or **dart** pierces **his liver** (i.e., vital organ). What tragedy!

Prov. 7:24

"Hearken unto me now therefore, O ye children, and attend to the words of my mouth."

In light of his prior, repeated warnings of impending danger, Solomon exhorts his children to "listen up" **and attend to** his **words.** Children do not have to learn everything the hard way or by experience. It's wise to listen and learn from parents and others. Certainly, Solomon learned the hard way and had "been there" with all of his sexual encounters, and he was considered the wisest man on earth.

Prov. 7:25

"Let not thine heart decline to her ways, go not astray in her paths."

His earnest urging progresses from "ears" to the "heart"; and from "words" to **ways.** There's great emphasis of impending danger. Don't let your **heart decline** (or incline) **to her ways; go not astray in her paths.**

There's a conscious choice involved in pursuing fornication and adultery. In the present day, the Biblical standard has been blurred by those who have a man-centered, rather than a God-centered, philosophy of Scripture.

Prov. 7:26

"For she hath cast down many wounded: yea, many strong men have been slain by her."

What an apt description of the casualties of sexual warfare! There's no question about who wins, **for she hath cast down many wounded: yea, many strong men have been slain by her.** How the mighty have fallen at the hands of an evil woman!

This "victory" has been repeated incessantly over the course of human history. Barnes' commentary rightly describes this scene: "The house of the harlot is now likened to a field of battle strewn with the corpses of the many slain."

"Flee also youthful lusts" is Paul's command; that is, "run for your life!" It's better to run away from the cesspool, than to jump in and be delivered later.

Prov. 7:27

"Her house is the way to hell, going down to the chambers of death."

The wounded and slain from **her house** end up in **Hell** (Sheol – world of departed spirits). Here are **the chambers of death:** the eternal and infernal world. What a finale for sin and Satan-possessed souls. Sin always pushes downward, away from God's life.

What a tragedy to spend eternity in the chambers (cells) of the damned; i.e., eternal death!

Chapter 8
The Excellence of Wisdom

Prov. 8:1

"Doeth not wisdom cry? and understanding put forth her voice?"

The 8th chapter is a revelation of wisdom in principle (vs. 1-11), and then as personified in Christ (vs. 12-36).

Doeth not wisdom cry (surely call out loudly)? God's wisdom is not silent, and it's crying out for man's attention and observance. Not only did God reveal His Law through Moses, but God offers His remedy for wickedness. God could have been silent, and let man go to Hell. In His marvelous grace, He has taken the initiative to save mankind.

The next parallel phrase compliments the first: Wisdom is sounding out to all who will take it. God is assertively addressing mankind; He is the same Lord who one day gave His only begotten Son, so that sinful humanity might access everlasting life (John 3:16).

Prov. 8:2

"She standeth in the top of high places, by the way in the places of the paths."

Notice the universality of wisdom: it stands **in the top of high places** (mountains); it is seen **by the way** (road); it is **in the places** (homes); and it is in the **paths** (beaten tracks). So, from the highest altitudes to the lowest, remote place, wisdom is available.

Prov. 8:3

"She crieth at the gates, at the entry of the city, at the coming in at the doors."

In poetic style, Solomon is describing the all-encompassing

desire of wisdom to be acquired. **She crieth at the gates, at the entry** (entrance) **of the city,** as well as at all **the** open **doors** of the city. Wisdom covers every nook and cranny, with universal coverage.

Gates of the city also speak of political power and leadership (e.g., Lot in Genesis 19:1). *"Be wise, now therefore, O ye kings....Kiss the Son, lest he be angry..."* is the warning of Psalm 2. If the leaders of the city are foolish, how great and widespread is their foolishness. Our own country of America is losing its foundational morals upon which we have been previously blessed. Wisdom and truth have "fallen in the streets." Repentance, reformation and revival are the needed order of today.

We can apply the Lord's promise to Solomon in another place:

> *"If my people, which are called by my name, shall humble themselves, and pray, and seek my face, and turn from their wicked ways; then will I hear from heaven, and will forgive their sin, and will heal their land," (2 Chronicles 7:14)*

Prov. 8:4

Unto you, O men, I call; and my voice is to the sons of man.

Note here the change in person from "she" (3rd person) to "I" (1st person). Wisdom zeros in on **men** and **the sons of man.** Wisdom now cries out to the people themselves. Christ, our Wisdom, did not die for gates, doors, trees, city walls, and buildings. He died for precious souls. He calls for men to be saved. Once saved, they still need to come for wisdom (James 1:5).

Prov. 8:5

"O ye simple, understand wisdom: and, ye fools, be ye of an understanding heart."

Again, he urges the **simple** and **fools** to **understand wisdom** and have **an understanding heart.** It's out of the heart that wisdom comes. The Holy Spirit grants spiritual understanding and discernment to those filled with the wisdom of God's Word. Christ is the Treasury of all wisdom and knowledge. (Colossians 2:3)

Prov. 8:6

"Hear; for I will speak of excellent things; and the opening of my lips shall be right things."

Hear is the command to listen and obey from the heart. Why? The **excellent things** of Wisdom are from the King of Glory Himself, therefore, they are not only worthy to be heard, but absolutely **right**. To meditate on God's wisdom insures **right** thinking which, in turn, promotes **right** speaking.

Moses knew this truth when he told Joshua:

"This book of the law shall not depart out of thy mouth; but thou shalt meditate therein day and night...for then thou shalt make thy way prosperous, and then thou shalt have good success," (Joshua 1:8)

Yet, how ironic that man rebels against the wisdom and Word of God! He would rather listen to the ungodly forces and concepts of the world. O, the utter depravity of man's heart which causes even the greatest of intellects to reject the Word, and manifest rebellion and foolishness. Such an attitude leads to perplexity and eternal damnation.

Prov. 8:7

"For my mouth shall speak truth; and wickedness is an abomination to my lips."

The Source of true wisdom is Christ Himself (1 Corinthians 1:30). Wisdom only speaks the **truth**, whereas **wickedness is** thoroughly revolting; **an abomination.** James 3 speaks at length about the power of the tongue, which reveals the inner human spirit.

The Hebrew word for "speak" is *hagah*, also translated as "meditate" in Joshua 1:8, and Psalm 1:2. Thus, wisdom **speaks truth** because it ponders truth. It ponders truth because it is Truth; i.e., Christ who is (embodies) both Truth and Wisdom. So it follows that the Christian will be a person of truth and wisdom, totally opposed to wickedness. This would also infer that a believer has the Spirit's control over his speech.

"My brethren, be not many masters, knowing that we shall receive the greater condemnation. For in many things we offend all. If any man offend not in word, the same is a perfect man, and able also to bridle the whole body." (James 3:1, 2)

Prov. 8:8

All the words of my mouth are in righteousness; there is nothing froward or perverse in them.

All the words of my mouth are in righteousness. Not simply "words," but the whole content proceeding from the mouth of wisdom is right, never wrong. Justice and rightness always result from wisdom, which is pictured in Christ Himself. He will never lie, nor lead one down the wrong path. Rightness reflects the prosperity of being right with God, and manifesting that rightness in everyday living.

To emphasize the character of God's wisdom, Solomon describes the "flip-side;" i.e., **there is nothing froward or perverse in them.** He not only tells us what wisdom is, but also what it is not: **froward** (twisted, as twine); **perverse** (distorted or crooked), thus false.

This "flip-side" often describes the philosophy of this troubled world we live in! That's why to love the world is to be at odds with God. The fight is on between good and evil; truth and error. The choice must be made between loving Wisdom or embracing the distorted mindset of this world.

Prov. 8:9

"They are all plain to him that understandeth, and right to them that find knowledge."

The Word of God is not obscure or puzzling. With God's grace, it can be **plain.** The words of wisdom are straightforward **to him that understandeth.** This understanding, however, takes the operation of the Holy Spirit dwelling in the believer. Paul states:

"Now we have received...the Spirit which is of God; that we might know the things that are freely given to us of God." (1 Corinthians 2:12)

The Apostle goes on to say that the Lord has given us *"the mind of Christ."* (1 Corinthians 2:16) How incredible is that? He has made supernatural provision by the Holy Spirit for us to begin thinking like Jesus thinks! Amazing!

On the other hand, those without Christ have no such promise or reality. Because *"the natural* (unsaved) *man receiveth not the things of the Spirit of God: for they are foolishness unto him: neither can he know them, because they are spiritually discerned,"* (1 Corinthians 2:14) One must know the God of the Word personally before he can really know the Word of God.

The words of wisdom are **right to them that find knowledge.** How wonderful to be **right** (lit. straight) with God, being able to understand His **right** rules of conduct! This is the by-product of His saving grace.

An unbeliever rejects God's truth until he's arrested by that Truth. To find this knowledge of Truth is the ultimate of understanding and salvation (cf. John 17:3). Thank God, we can be led in a **plain** path while living in a confused and perverted world!

Prov. 8:10

"Receive my instruction, and not silver; and knowledge rather than choice gold."

We're confronted again with one's sense of priority or value. Silver and gold are not sinful per se, but people will do sinful things to acquire them. Money is not evil, but the love of money is (cf. 1 Timothy 6:10). It's safe to say that most people who love money don't have much of it. This explains the craze for gambling, robbery, and greed in general.

One can be wealthy financially without being rich in soul (e.g., the rich young ruler that Jesus confronted in Luke 18:18). Wisdom says, **Receive my instruction...and knowledge,** rather than giving money priority. According to 1 Corinthians 1:30, to seek Wisdom (Christ) is not only wise, but essential to Salvation. God can supply what money can't, while still taking care of financial needs (cf. Matthew 6:33).

Prov. 8:11

"For wisdom is better than rubies; and all the things that may be desired are not to be compared to it."

Set forth here is the reason for choosing wisdom over money. It provides an inner spiritual wealth far beyond anything that **rubies** can buy. A person devoid of wisdom, although financially rich, is poor indeed! The best things in life are free!

However, God's gifts of **wisdom** and salvation, though received freely, were divinely provided at tremendous price. Salvation has come as the result of Christ's redemptive work on the Cross. (cf. 1 Corinthians 15:3, 4; 1 Peter 1:18, 19)

Prov. 8:12

I wisdom dwell with prudence, and find out knowledge of witty inventions.

The Lord is making a personally defining statement. First, **I** (for emphasis) **wisdom dwell with prudence.** Here's a Scriptural co-habitation of wisdom and prudence; if you see one, you see the other. **Prudence** means positive, Biblical cleverness. It might be described as "common sense" on a higher spiritual level, correlating with Jesus words, *"Be ye therefore wise as serpents, and harmless as doves."* (Matthew 10:16) Walking with God makes one "supernaturally natural," rather than some "religious oddball."

Secondly, wisdom finds out **knowledge of witty inventions.** "Witty" is translated as "devices" or as "discretion," For instance, in Psalm 10:2, the wicked are *"taken in the devices that they have imagined,"* However, in Prov. 2:11, Solomon says, *"Discretion shall preserve thee."* The meaning of the word depends on the heart attitude from which the statement emerges.

There's a sense in which wisdom discerns both wickedness and righteousness. In fact, there is a wisdom that's not godly, but rather *"earthly, sensual, devilish"* (James 3:15). James goes on to say that *"the wisdom that is from above is first pure, then peaceable, gentle, etc.;"* i.e., it is positive and godly, as well as skillful and effective (James 3:13-18). Thus, the wise believer must utilize the "gift of discernment" when evaluating the deeds of others.

You can see the struggle between the devices of God and those of Satan. It's all part of the warfare between good and evil, right and wrong, truth and error. Indeed, the spiritual fight is on! (It might be helpful to reflect on Satan's attack and strategy against Jesus in Matthew 4.) Godly wisdom Is essential if we're to survive the wiles of Satan (cf. Ephesians 6:10-18).

Prov. 8:13

"The fear of the LORD is to hate evil: pride, and arrogancy, and the evil way, and the froward mouth, do I hate."

Here's another definition of the fear of God: **to hate evil** (cf. Prov. 1:7). To love God is the "first commandment;" but, if that's a reality, we begin to love what God loves. Likewise, we hate what God hates. These are two sides of the same coin. What we *love* and what we *hate* indicates who we are. Walking in the "fear of the Lord" promotes a godly, balanced attitude.

This love-hate relationship is the basis of God's Redemptive plan, including the ultimate destinies called Heaven and Hell. An awesome reverence for the Lord deeply affects our attitude toward sin. It's impossible to love God and to love sin at the same time. In a day of compromise, carnality, and worldliness, this truth needs to be emphasized among those who profess to love God.

Wisdom is still exhorting us here as He describes sin:

1st: **Pride** (the Hebrew word is *geah*, used only here. Evidently, this usage includes every form of pride or arrogance, finding its source in Lucifer himself (Ezekiel 28:15). Pride is the "bottom-line" sin that started the warfare in Heaven. The one referred to as Satan, the "Deceiver," was expelled from Heaven because of his egotism in attempting to take God's place.

That kind of pride is resident in every human being from birth. *"All we like sheep have gone astray; we have turned every one to his own way..."* Pride's theme song is "I Did It My Way!" That's why the sinner must be "killed" at the Cross, and raised in newness of life (Romans 6:6).

2nd: **Arrogance**: literally meaning "an offensive sense of superiority." This surely describes the pompous self-presentation. How amazing that "dust people" can be so arrogant and self-sufficient. That's why nothing less than the divine sacrifice of the Son of God could remedy the situation.

3rd: **The evil way:** An evil heart produces evil fruit.

4th: **The froward mouth:** the evil fruit of a perverted mouth.

Jesus said, *"For out of the abundance of the heart, the mouth speaketh"* (Matthew 12:34). Note that the true saint's hatred for evil pertains not only to what he sees in others, but also to what he sees in himself as well.

Prov. 8:14

"Counsel is mine, and sound wisdom: I am understanding; I have strength."

Here, again, is Wisdom speaking of Himself in the first person "I," To relegate these words to Christ may be a stretch, but the following verses support this claim: Isaiah 9:6; Isaiah 40:14; John: 1:9; Romans 11:33, 34; 1 Corinthians 1:24, 30; Colossians 2:3. Christ not only gives wisdom, He is the Source and very essence of it. (cf. John 1:1)

I am understanding; I have strength (might). All discernment and understanding is found in Wisdom (see 1 Corinthians 1:30). Men are searching for wisdom only in religion or philosophy, when it is only found in one Person: Jesus Christ.

Prov. 8:15

"By me kings reign, and princes decree justice."

Talk about the utter necessity and uniqueness of Wisdom! **By me kings reign...**That's emphatic; i.e., only by wisdom, nothing else, can kings rule properly. How essential is wisdom to the common man if kings can't reign without it (Him)? No wonder wisdom is far beyond earthly treasure and power.

Furthermore, by the same wisdom, **princes decree justice**

(from the Hebrew word *tzedek,* which means "right, equity or just"). **Princes** (rulers) need the wisdom of God to **decree** (prescribe) the right decisions on behalf of others.

In the New Testament, believers are made "kings and priests unto God" (Revelation 1:6), becoming recipients of Christ's wisdom (cf. 1 Corinthians 1:30). What a great inheritance is ours!

Prov. 8:16

"By me princes rule, and nobles, even all the judges of the earth."

The list of dignitaries continues and is governed by Wisdom. Rulers must submit to the law if they are to govern others properly. Our judicial system is based on the Ten Commandments, without which we have no standard of rule. Human nature rebels against authority, wanting to embrace its own "rules." Not surprisingly, there's been an ongoing movement to obliterate the Commandments from any public view. The height of corruption is when judges disregard the law, and begin making the "rules" as they go; not to mention the lack of wisdom emanating from their decisions.

As in the Book of Judges, there is no king in the land per se, and *"every man did that which was right in his own eyes,"* (Judges 21:25)

Prov. 8:17

"I love them that love me; and those that seek me early shall find me."

I love them that love me. What a beautiful statement of reciprocal love! *"We love him, because he first loved us."* (1 John 4:19). Wisdom also declares love to those who love God. This divine transaction can also be seen in the following verses: John 14:21, 23; 16:27.

Solomon further states, **those that seek me early shall find me.** This is in both timing and priority. Not only early in the day (e.g., Psalm 63:1), but early in life (Ecclesiastes 12:1). Jesus said:

"Blessed are they which do hunger and thirst after righteousness: for they shall be filled," (Matthew 5:6)

Prov. 8:18

"Riches and honour are with me; yea, durable riches and righteousness."

Everything has a price and/or consequence. **Riches and honour are with me;** while sin leads to poverty and disgrace, wisdom produces the opposite. We are urged to:

"But seek ye first the kingdom of God…and all these things shall be added…" (Matthew 6:33*).*

Unlike the consequences of sin, **riches and honour** are valuable and enduring. In contrast to the vain and destructive nature of foolishness, wisdom produces superior and perpetual qualities.

Prov. 8:19

"My fruit is better than gold, yea, than fine gold; and my revenue than choice silver."

This verse further clarifies the previous one, defining riches as spiritual **fruit** rather than money per se. His **revenue** (income) is better **than choice silver.** While Solomon had riches galore, he repeatedly concludes that godly qualities or **fruit** (Galatians 5:22, 23) are far more valuable than money.

God is not opposed to material wealth, for He's the Provider of it. The issue is seeking God HIMSELF first and foremost, rather than the wealth He provides us. What a difficult lesson to learn! Solomon himself is a classic example of this critical principle.

Prov. 8:20

"I lead in the way of righteousness, in the midst of the paths of judgment:"

Wisdom walks before, leading us on the right way; this **way of righteousness** is always in the context of proper **judgment.** The Hebrew word *mishpat* means "justice, or the right verdict in a case," Wisdom is not only more valuable than money, but it protects and directs us down the right road of life. In other words, wisdom will never lead us down the wrong road, even though we may experience injustices while traveling the right road.

The right road will always lead to the right place, never leaving us in the "ditch" of destruction. Why? Wisdom finds its source in God Himself. David said:

> "...he leadeth me in the paths of righteousness for his name's sake. Yea, though I walk through the valley of the shadow of death, I will fear no evil: for thou art with me..." (Psalm 23:3,4)

Prov. 8:21

> "That I may cause those that love me to inherit substance; and I will fill their treasures."

This verse further verifies the truth of Matthew 6:33. Wisdom says **I may cause those that love me to inherit substance** (treasure)**; and I will fill their treasures.** These are great words of truth and comfort. No matter the amount of the **treasure** (wealth) received, we can never lose out by loving, seeking, and obeying our God!

Prov. 8:22

> "The LORD possessed me in the beginning of his way, before his works of old."

This statement not only personifies Wisdom, but also His eternality and relationship with Jehovah. In Psalm 2:7, the LORD says to the Messiah (Christ), "...Thou art my Son; this day have I begotten thee." Wisdom is **possessed** by the Father; i.e., co-habiting with God **in the beginning.**

This correlates with John 1:1-3:

> "In the beginning was the Word, and the Word was with God, and the Word was God. The same was in the beginning with God. All things were made by him, and without him was not any thing made..." Wisdom was **before His works of old.** This portrays the mystical relationship of the Godhead prior to creation.

Prov. 8:23

"I was set up from everlasting, from the beginning, or ever the earth was."

This further describes Wisdom's (or Christ's) deity. The Hebrew form is emphatic, reading: *"From everlasting was I set up..."* This underlines Wisdom's eternality, always existing.

The verb "set up" comes from the root meaning "to pour out"; thus, "to be anointed," This correlates with the description of Christ in Hebrew's 1:8-10:

"But unto the Son he saith, Thy throne, O God, is for ever and ever: a scepter of righteousness is the scepter of thy kingdom. Thou hast loved righteousness, and hated iniquity; therefore, God, even thy God, hath anointed thee with the oil of gladness above Thy fellows. And, Thou, Lord, in the beginning hast laid the foundation of the earth; and the heavens are the works of thine hands."

Prov. 8:24

"When there were no depths, I was brought forth; when there were no fountains abounding with water."

Eternal Wisdom **was brought forth** before the **depths** (abyss of the seas). This describes the Everlasting and Only Begotten Son joyously anticipating His creation of all things (John 1:1-3).

Before **there were no fountains abounding** (lit. heavy) **with water,** Christ was there waiting for the outworking of the divine plan of the Godhead.

Prov. 8:25

"Before the mountains were settled, before the hills was I brought forth:"

In a picturesque manner, Solomon poetically describes the grandeur of **the mountains** and **the hills** as a backdrop to the preeminence of the Son prior to creation. The Psalmist exclaims:

"Before the mountains were brought forth, or ever thou hadst

formed the earth and the world, even from everlasting to everlasting, thou art God," (Psalm 90:2)

Prov. 8:26

"While as yet he had not made the earth, nor the fields, nor the highest part of the dust of the world."

He further affirms Wisdom's preeminence over creation. **The highest part of the dust of the world** could refer to mountains or man himself, who was made of the dust of the earth (Genesis 2:7).

Prov. 8:27

"When he prepared the heavens, I was there: when he set a compass upon the face of the depth:"

The Apostle John says of the Word:

"The same was in the beginning with God. All things were made by him; and without him was not any thing made that was made," (John 1:2, 3)

Now we have a series of "when clauses:" When **he prepared the heavens** (the expanse of heaven or sky); and **when He set a compass...** (circle). Could this be the forming of the earth as a circle, with its containment of **the face of the depth** (seas)?

Clarke's commentary sheds some light on this thought:

"Does not this refer to the establishment of the law of gravitation? by which all the particles of matter, tending to a common center, would produce in all bodies the orbicular form, which we see them have; so that even the waters are not only retained within their boundaries, but are subjected to the circular form, in their great aggregate of seas, as other parts of matter are."

However explained, we have Divine creation by Intelligent Design, which far supersedes anything propounded by the theory of evolution. God has the first and final Word in creation!

Prov. 8:28

"When he established the clouds above: when he strengthened the fountains of the deep:"

From the highest (**clouds above**) to the lowest **fountains of the deep** (subterranean water), the omnipotent (all-powerful) hand of God operates. Every level of the universe has been **established** and sustained by the Creator. Refer to Genesis 1:7-11.

Prov. 8:29

"When he gave to the sea his decree, that the waters should not pass his commandment: when he appointed the foundations of the earth:"

What a mighty God we serve! He incredibly set the boundaries of the seas, while **He appointed the foundations of the earth.**

As the Sovereign of the universe, He rules the "beach fronts" of the world. Significantly, He occasionally allows a tsunami (gigantic tidal wave) or hurricane to strike land, demonstrating both His power and man's pathetic weakness at the same time.

Prov. 8:30

"Then I was by him, as one brought up with him: and I was daily his delight, rejoicing always before him;"

In poetic terms, this is a description similar to the prologue of John 1:1-3, regarding the relationship between God and the Word.

Immediately, the Father's statement during the Transfiguration comes to mind:

"This is my beloved Son, in whom I am well pleased." (Matthew 17:5)

Prov. 8:31

Rejoicing in the habitable part of his earth; and my delights were with the sons of men.

Here's Wisdom "touching down" to the earth where man is to live. The One co-existing with God, now intermingles **with the sons of men.** Notice that Wisdom is **rejoicing** (laughing) as he **delights** (enjoys) the interaction with earthly creation.

Compare Genesis 2:4, where God the Creator now involves Himself with man (Genesis 2:7), being revealed by His Name: "the LORD God." The Creator touches lowly man, which becomes a display and type of God's redeeming grace.

Prov. 8:32

"Now therefore hearken unto me, O ye children: for blessed are they that keep my ways."

With access to such Wisdom, the believer is urged to **hearken unto me** (the Lord) now! He addresses them tenderly as **children,** stating the promised reward; i.e., **blessed** or happy **are they that keep** (obey) **my ways.** Submitting to God and His Word brings ultimate joy and success (cf. Psalm 1).

Obedient children are the happiest (most blessed), both in a family setting and in the family of God. Rebellion may bring a temporary thrill, but always leads to permanent misery and disaster. True freedom is not a license to do wrong, but the liberty to do right!

Prov. 8:33

"Hear instruction, and be wise, and refuse it not."

In typical Hebrew fashion (striking both sides of an issue), Solomon says to obey **instruction and be wise,** but don't dismiss or reject what you've learned. This illustrates the essence of the fear of God: taking Him and His Word seriously. How one responds to God's Word reflects the difference between saints and sinners, or Heaven and Hell.

Prov. 8:34

"Blessed is the man that heareth me, watching daily at my gates, waiting at the posts of my doors."

Can someone be too serious about heeding God's Word? We are **blessed** (happy) by listening, **watching,** and **waiting,** i.e., "hanging out" at His door with eager anticipation. What a picture of keeping our ear to the door, not missing a word.

Look how absorbed we are in worldly things (music, television, the internet, magazines, books, the breaking news, etc.). The world system is a temporary and fleeting fantasy, at best, but the heavenly world, revealed in the Bible, leads us to God who is all Wise and Eternal.

Prov. 8:35

"For whoso findeth me findeth life, and shall obtain favour of the LORD."

What a find! Everything in this world will eventually be lost or die. "You can't take it with you," as the saying goes. However, the abundant and eternal **life** is hinged upon the Lord's **favour** or grace.

What a beautiful statement: **whoso findeth me findeth life.** The choice is ours to make.

Prov. 8:36

"But he that sinneth against me wrongeth his own soul: all they that hate me love death."

What a contrast to the previous verse! Sin not only offends God, but wrongs or violates the sinner's **own soul.** The Lord has made a way to change a sinful lifestyle: repentance and faith in the Lord Jesus Christ.

The last phrase is sobering: **all they that hate me love death.** As sinners, we love what God hates, and hate what God loves. When converted, or born again, we begin to hate what God hates, and love what God loves (i.e., the process of sanctification).

The wicked don't just bypass the truth, they **hate** it. Therefore, they prove that they **love death**, the alternative to everlasting life with God. This is so profound. How deceitful is the human heart! (Jeremiah 17:9)

Chapter 9
The Way of Wisdom

Prov. 9:1

"Wisdom hath builded her house, she hath hewn out her seven pillars:"

Personified **Wisdom** has constructed **her house** with **seven pillars** or columns carved out of stone or wood. Seven is the number denoting "perfection," This is an impressive building, a structure of prominence to be sought by all.

Prov. 9:2

"She hath killed her beasts; she hath mingled her wine; she hath also furnished her table."

This verse describes Wisdom's house as the banquet hall for hungry souls. It's a picture of Christ preparing the "wedding feast"; butchering the meat, enhancing the taste of the **wine**, and setting **the table**.

This could be likened to Jesus' parable of the king's "marriage feast" for his son (Matthew 22:2f.). The servants are sent out to invite folks to come and partake of the banquet delicacies, honoring the son, *"But they made light of it and went their ways."*

So is the attitude today when folks are bidden to embrace the Son of God, who became the Supreme Sacrifice for sin at the Cross. However, as believers, we gather at the Lord's **table**, partaking of the elements that celebrate His blood atonement in our behalf.

Prov. 9:3

"She hath sent forth her maidens: she crieth upon the highest places of the city,"

Wisdom sends out her servants, who **crieth upon the highest places of the city.** Like Luke 14:7-24, sinners, the poor, maimed, and blind are invited to the feast. Let the needy come to Wisdom because, *"Blessed are they which do hunger and thirst after righteousness: for they shall be filled."* (Matthew 5:6)

Prov. 9:4

"Whoso is simple, let him turn in hither: as for him that wanteth understanding, she saith to him,"

The command is given by Wisdom for those who are **simple** (easily seduced) and lack understanding. The arrogant and sophisticated need not apply! Come to the banquet hall and feast on wisdom's provisions. Food for the soul is essential for spiritual life, as earthly food is for the body.

Prov. 9:5

"Come, eat of my bread, and drink of the wine which I have mingled."

Now, the invitation is given for the unwise to become wise and the needy to be filled. It sounds like Jesus saying, *"Come unto me, all ye that labour and are heavy laden, and I will give you rest."* (Matthew 11:28). I AM the Bread of Heaven: eat! I AM the Wine of Heaven: drink!

The Song of Solomon says: *"Let him kiss me with the kisses of his mouth: for thy love is better than wine. (1:2) He brought me to the banqueting house* (the house of wine)*, and his banner over me was love."* (2:4)

Pictured here is the intimacy of the believer and Christ, who is our Wisdom. Wine speaks of the fruit of the Holy Spirit (Galatians 5:22, 23).

Wine is to the world what the Holy Spirit is to the believer. To be intoxicated with wine is a worldly "joy." However, we are not to be *"drunk with wine, wherein is excess; but be filled with the Spirit"* (Ephesians 5:18). The best that the world has to offer does not begin to compare with the fullness of God's Elixir.

Prov. 9:6

"Forsake the foolish, and live; and go in the way of understanding."

Cut loose from silly people! That's the idea behind the phrase **forsake the foolish.**

> *"Blessed* (happy) *is the man that walketh not in the counsel of the ungodly, nor standeth in the way* (lifestyle) *of sinners"* (Psalm 1:1).

Casual contact with the **foolish** is inevitable, but do not "hang out" with them. Instead, choose "life" by rejecting the lifestyle of "death." **Go in the way of understanding;** i.e., walk in the way of godly understanding or wisdom. This is a matter of right attitude and character, which produces right conduct; thus, to **live** in God's fullness.

Prov. 9:7

"He that reproveth a scorner getteth to himself shame: and he that rebuketh a wicked man getteth himself a blot."

Verses 7-9 form a trilogy in reference to dealing with scorners or mockers. There are many who just disregard the commandments because of their sinful lifestyles. Then, there are those who aggressively mock the things of God. Such people are the ones Jesus spoke about when He told the disciples not to cast pearls before swine (Matthew 7:6).

It's a real battle to **reprove** or attempt to correct a **scorner.** The backlash that comes seems futile. There are some people you must leave alone, at least at that time. Discernment is paramount, for what may be received by one may be rejected by another.

Rebuking or reprimanding may get us a "black eye" or **blot.** We must be careful how and when we confront someone who mocks God. It's imperative to rely on the guidance of the Holy Spirit in our dealings with them.

Prov. 9:8

"Reprove not a scorner, lest he hate thee: rebuke a wise man, and he will love thee."

Mockers hate to be confronted, and you're likely to end up despised and rejected. On the other hand, **a wise man** welcomes the light of rebuke and godly instruction. He has dealt with sin and pride, thus, he is open for any correction that would make him more effective in his witness and testimony. This **love** refers to appreciation and affection. His wisdom allows him to recognize true love in the one who rebukes him. A true friend confronts another friend in brotherly love.

Prov. 9:9

"Give instruction to a wise man, and he will be yet wiser: teach a just man, and he will increase in learning."

Not only will a **wise man** take rebuke and love you for it, but **he will be yet wiser.** Such a man is both submissive and teachable, thus fertile ground for further growth and understanding. Trying to teach the unteachable is an exercise in futility.

A just man, i.e., one right with God, desires to be right and do right. Thus, he's ready to listen. On the other hand, the rebellious "Cain spirit" that plagues humanity is too often manifested, rejecting God's authority. The fear of the LORD is absent, preventing the use of godly wisdom (see vs. 10). Whatever worldly wisdom these people have becomes folly in the long run (refer to James 3:14-16).

Prov. 9:10

"The fear of the LORD is the beginning of wisdom: and the knowledge of the holy is understanding."

The production of true **wisdom** in one's life finds its source in **the fear of the LORD** (see 1:7). Extract the reverential fear of and obedience to the Lord, and there's no godly wisdom. A humble attitude is essential to knowing God's ways. That's also the parallel thought of **the knowledge of the holy**, as the foundation of **understanding.**

Holy refers to the Holy One, God. Therefore, this **knowledge** or perception of the Holy One constitutes genuine, spiritual understanding. Knowing God is actually one definition of eternal life

(John 17:3), initiating a glorious and endless process of **understanding** Him.

King David said, *"The fear of the Lord is clean, enduring for ever: the judgments of the LORD are true and righteous altogether"* (Psalm 19:9). **The knowledge of the holy** is inseparately linked with an **understanding** of the written Word, the Bible (cf. Joshua 1:8; Psalm 1).

Prov. 9:11

"For by me thy days shall be multiplied, and the years of thy life shall be increased."

Since the wages of sin is death, all men die. By wisdom, however, one's **days shall be multiplied** (enhanced). Solomon's picture is one of abundant living, not merely length of days. Some wicked people live many years, but they are likely to be sorrowful and unfruitful. A believer may live a brief time on earth, but know the fullness of God's blessings and a glorious eternity.

Living skillfully in reverence before God guarantees fullness of spiritual life, regardless how long someone spends on this earth. The issue is not how long one lives, but *how* he lives. This principle is found throughout **Proverbs** and the whole of Scripture. (cf. Prov.3:1, 2, 16; 10:27; Deuteronomy 6:2)

Prov. 9:12

"If thou be wise, thou shalt be wise for thyself: but if thou scornest, thou alone shalt bear it."

Being a believer has abundant, personal benefits. God wonderfully rewards those who walk in obedience to His Word. It's not just a matter of giving to and living for others. There's something in it for the believer as well. But to scorn or despise the wisdom of God is to pay a great price.

If thou be wise, thou shalt be wise for thyself; i.e., we make a personal choice to be wise or foolish, depending on our response to Truth. The fruit of wisdom is reaped on ourselves and those around us.

On the other hand, the scorner not only reaps heartache and trouble, but he **bears** them **alone**. The arrogant man (mocker) is so full of himself that it leaves him empty and estranged from others. This illustrates the wrong response to wisdom. What futility!

It does "pay" to serve God, even if the benefits aren't readily apparent. The heart of the wise man is filled with godly treasures. To be wise in Christ is the only sane way to cope with life in this sin-filled world.

Prov. 9:13

"A foolish woman is clamorous: she is simple, and knoweth nothing."

The counterpart of a foolish man is **a foolish woman.** She is characterized not as glamorous, but **clamorous** or noisy, loud, in an uproar. **She is simple**, meaning naïve, easily seduced, and open to all forms of evil. This could be a reference to the original woman, Eve, who was seduced by Satan to eat the forbidden fruit (cf. 2 Corinthians 11:3; 1 Timothy 2:14).

She **knoweth nothing**; i.e., she's a picture of ignorance and folly. Her ignorance is willful and reckless. She knows how to be a harlot, but her detachment from God's grace renders her a failure.

Prov. 9:14

"For she sitteth at the door of her house, on a seat in the high places of the city,"

The foolish woman is camped at **the door of her house** so she can see all and be seen by all, awaiting her next customer. **Her house** is **in the high places of the city**; i.e., on an elevation or hill overlooking the city. She doesn't have a legitimate purpose in life, but thrives on stealing the life force of others. Notice the contrast to Prov.9:1, where wisdom's house is stately and exalted. Fools try to imitate wisdom in their own folly, but only to their own detriment.

Prov. 9:15

"To call passengers who go right on their ways:"

The harlot lives on a thoroughfare or street corner where people constantly pass by (**passengers**) on their way to work, to their homes, etc. The harlot sits on her "lofty seat" (vs. 14), calling (lit. shouting) to potential takers. Her shamelessness is amazing! However, such is the depth of the sinful heart.

Prov. 9:16

"Whoso is simple, let him turn in hither: and as for him that wanteth understanding, she saith to him,"

If you're a simpleton or fool, go ahead and **turn in** to her! This strange woman will also be glad to speak further words of temptation to anyone that **wanteth** (lacks) **understanding** or heart. It takes courage to withstand temptation.

Furthermore, she can sense a man's weakness, and can cleverly use her expertise to entice him into her trap.

Prov. 9:17

"Stolen waters are sweet, and bread eaten in secret is pleasant."

Her alluring word is: Stolen waters are sweet... She knows human nature and the power of lust. Her "sweet talk" is intensely seductive. Something forbidden seems so **sweet** and **pleasant.** This factor is so prevalent in marital infidelity.

How our senses deceive us when our hearts are not right! It's better to make the right choice up front, then to need deliverance later. In fact, the Apostle Paul urges us to *"abstain from all appearance of evil"* (1 Thessalonians 5:22).

Prov. 9:18

"But he knoweth not that the dead are there; and that her guests are in the depths of hell.

As an unsuspecting fly caught in a spider's web, so is the simpleton who flirts with a seductress. **He knoweth not that the dead are there; and that her guests are in...hell** (*Sheol*, the world of departed spirits). His ignorance doesn't change the fact or the outcome: sin leads to death and Hell (cf. Prov. 2:18, 19; 7:27).

Again, there's an application to the seduction of false prophets and doctrine. Sincere, but ignorant men, have been sucked into anti-Biblical teaching which will destroy them and their unsuspecting followers. (Galatians 1:6-9)

Chapter 10
Wise Sayings of Solomon

Prov. 10:1

The proverbs of Solomon. A wise son maketh a glad father: but a foolish son is the heaviness of his mother.

The proverbs of Solomon continue after two chapters on wisdom per se. **A wise son maketh a glad father.** How true! Nothing brightens and rejoices a father's heart than to see virtue and godly skill demonstrated in his son. Although worldly success of children is measured by income, assets, and social clout, it's not so with God. All the worldly "toys" will one day vanish, and then the true character of godliness, or the lack of it, will be revealed (cf. 1 Corinthians 3:11f.). God is not opposed to financial success, but even material wealth will be used and properly prioritized by a wise son (Matthew 6:33).

Note how **a foolish son** brings **the heaviness** (grief or depression) to **his mother.** There's usually none more involved or close to a son than his mother. Even good and faithful mothers have sons who make wrong choices, affecting themselves and those who love them the most deeply. There's a whole sermon here, beginning with the story of Cain and Abel (Genesis 4), which set the stage for all of human history.

Prov. 10:2

"Treasures of wickedness profit nothing: but righteousness delivereth from death."

What a concise statement of fact! **Treasures** are in the store house, laid up, or invested. They have no **profit** if a man is wicked, because they never bring satisfaction, nor can they buy what he needs. Plus, investments cannot deliver one's soul **from death.**

Only **righteousness,** or rightness of life, provides ongoing victory over the flesh and the snares of Satan. Righteousness is a result of the justifying grace of Christ. Obviously, riches can buy things, but ultimately they have no value in light of our standing with God.

> *"For what is a man profited, if he shall gain the whole world, and lose his own soul?"* (Matthew 16:26)

Prov. 10:3

> *"The LORD will not suffer the soul of the righteous to famish: but he casteth away the substance of the wicked."*

The LORD has a unique relationship with His children, **the righteous,** and makes special provisions for them. He **will not suffer the soul of the righteous to famish** (hunger). God has committed Himself to meet the needs of those who honor and obey Him. This is a general principle, seeing that some saints in history have died hungry, while some sinners feast.

> *"For the LORD knoweth the way of the righteous: but the way of the ungodly shall perish"* (Psalm 1:6).

We don't serve God for material gain and physical wellness, although they can be by-products of obeying Him (cf. Matthew 6:33). King David had this testimony:

> *"I have been young, and now am old; yet have I not seen the righteous forsaken, nor his seed begging bread."* (Psalm 37:25)

It's **the soul of the righteous** ones that will not **famish.** On the other hand, God **casteth away** (expels) **the substance** (lusts or naughtiness) **of the wicked.** Solomon is describing the results of either obeying or disobeying God.

How foolish is the foolishness of a fool! He is fighting against the only One who can satisfy the human spirit. The enemy (Satan) has duped him into thinking that he can be happy and successful by living "his own way," rather than God's way. What a lie!

The Apostle John summed it up when he said:

> *"And the world passeth away, and the lust thereof: but he that doeth the will of God abideth for ever."* (1 John 2:17)

Prov. 10:4

"He becometh poor that dealeth with a slack hand: but the hand of the diligent maketh rich."

God's ordained means to prosperity is WORK! Unfortunately, many do not work legitimately, but are "con-artists," dealing **with a slack** (or deceitful) **hand**. The same word also refers to a lazy person; i.e., a "slacker." Both of these conditions will eventually lead to poverty, or even jail time.

One thing is for sure: **the hand of the diligent maketh rich,** in more ways than financial (cf. Prov. 12:24, 27; 21:4-5). The word for "diligent" here is used in Isaiah 28:27 for a "sharp threshing instrument." That's significant. Diligent people are usually "sharp" people of purpose and effectiveness. May God give us many more of these kinds of people to work in His Kingdom.

Prov. 10:5

"He that gathereth in summer is a wise son: but he that sleepeth in harvest is a son that causeth shame."

Another challenge requiring hard work is to gather the **harvest** in the summer.

What a shame for a farmer to plow, plant, and cultivate, only to have the crop die in the field! The last thing an industrious farmer needs is a lazy son who shamefully sleeps during the **harvest,** leaving his father in a bind.

Wise children work and help support the family when needed. Too many adolescents and young adults are pampered and lazy. Farms are conducive to family life, with a built-in opportunity to work together. Today, home life is crumbling, resulting in the corresponding demise of the unique family work ethic. However, **wise** children still contribute and bear responsibility.

Prov. 10:6

"Blessings are upon the head of the just: but violence covereth the mouth of the wicked."

The righteous man has **blessings upon** his **head**, while the wicked man is covered or filled with the **violence** in his **mouth.** The head and the mouth are significant parts of the body. Psalm 133 speaks of the anointing oil placed on Aaron's head that flowed down to his beard, etc. **Upon the head of the just**, the **blessings** of God are poured out.

James 1:17 says:

"Every good gift and every perfect gift is from above."

These gifts can be physical, material, and spiritual. One's character has some connection with God's abundance. Here is an overflow of **blessings** ("good things") coming upon a **just** (right-living) man, making him happy.

The opposite is true of the wicked: their injurious mouths give away their sinful attitude and lifestyle. Indeed,

"For the Lord knoweth the way of the righteous: but the way of the ungodly shall perish." (Psalm 1:6)

O, to have a new heart through regenerating grace; and, thus, to have a new mouth too!

The word **covereth** is graphic, meaning "to fill up or overflow." The mouth of the wicked is overflowing with offensive, injurious, violent speech. A heart full of sin runs out from **the mouth of the wicked.**

Prov. 10:7

"The memory of the just is blessed: but the name of the wicked shall rot."

Saints live and die differently than the wicked. **The memory** (memorial and eulogy) **of the just is blessed** (from the Hebrew word *barak*, a source of praise and happiness). Those touched by their lives are quick to testify and share that influence with others. Their godly legacy continues to be commemorated by those who appreciate righteousness.

However, **the name of the wicked shall rot** (fade away into decomposition or decay by worm-eating). What a contrast between the two!

The wicked are buried quickly, often without a memorial service or eulogy; they are soon forgotten, unless their violence was traumatic to their victims. Character has a lasting effect, not only on the present generation, but on those that follow.

Prov. 10:8

"The wise in heart will receive commandments: but a prating fool shall fall."

How one responds to the commands of God (or anyone in authority) reveals the condition of his **heart.** Some folks are "wise guys," who give lip service to the commands, but never exhibit heart obedience. Wise-hearted people are teachable and eager to obey God's **commandments.** They are a rare breed, even in today's Church.

The word **receive** means to "lay hold of." There's no passivity here, but rather an active, latching on to the Word. It's a joy, for instance, when a son really desires to hear the instructions of his father, knowing that the advice will enhance his life, and gladden his father's heart. So it is with our Heavenly Father. His commands are instructions from His loving heart, which only has His and our best interests in mind. O, for an epidemic of such wisdom in our homes and in the Church!

But a prating (silly, know-it-all, "running at the mouth") **fool shall fall.**

Talk is cheap, and the fool "mouths off;" he does it *his* way, and falls. What a contrast between the wise and the foolish.

Prov. 10:9

"He that walketh uprightly walketh surely: but he that perverteth his ways shall be known."

Integrity and security go together. **He that walketh** (lives) **uprightly** (with integrity) **walketh surely** (securely). The safest place to be is walking in the perfect will of God. No matter where the path leads, it will be right and secure. This is the essence of freedom and confidence (cf. Prov. 3:5, 6).

But he that perverteth (distorts) **his ways shall be known** (found out). Those that live a perverted lifestyle will eventually be discovered. A man's sinful lifestyle will not only be found out, but will ultimately be judged (cf. Hebrews 9:27).

Prov. 10:10

"He that winketh with the eye causeth sorrow: but a prating fool shall fall."

Who's worse, the "winking" man or the "prating fool"? While the latter destructively "runs at the mouth," he may not be as dangerous as the "winker." Prov. 6:13 describes how wickedness is communicated non-verbally through body language; e.g., winking the eyes. This person, through his conniving and deceptive motions, causes great **sorrow** (lit. pain or wounds).

We can agree that the mouthy **fool shall fall** or be overthrown in the end (cf. comment on vs. 8); however, the "winker's" activity will be more damaging to others because of his subtle agenda. "The dog that bites is not always the dog that barks," says Matthew Henry.

Prov. 10:11

"The mouth of a righteous man is a well of life: but violence covereth the mouth of the wicked."

A person whose heart is right with God, speaks right. A heart filled with abundant **life** will readily express it. His **mouth** will become a pipeline blessing; i.e., a vehicle stemming from the well-spring of the inner **life.**

Jesus said:

"He that believeth on me, as the scripture hath said, out of his belly shall flow rivers of living water." (John 7:38)

A man speaks what is in his heart, whether a saint or a sinner. Thus, the **wicked** speak **violence.** (Refer to Prov. 10:6).

Prov. 10:12

"Hatred stirreth up strifes: but love covereth all sins."

The heart of an evil-doer is marked by hate. He not only loves strife or discord, but instigates it. Isaiah rightly expresses this condition:

> *"But the wicked are like the troubled sea, when it cannot rest, whose waters cast up mire and dirt. There is no peace, saith my God, to the wicked."* (Isaiah 57:20, 21)

In contrast, **love covereth all sins** (transgressions). This does not say that love "covers up" or excuses sin, whether personally or in others. Sin must be acknowledged and confessed so that God will apply His forgiveness through the blood sacrifice. (cf. Leviticus 16) Ultimately, God's love provided the Cross, where Christ Himself atoned for sin; there it was that all sin was "covered" (forgiven) for those who have believed in Him." (John 3:16)

In this proverb, the person who "loves" **covers all sins**; i.e., he covers what God has covered, not bringing it up again! He doesn't "stir up" past situations, especially where the "peace of God" has been applied. The Apostle Paul said:

> *"Charity (agape love or God's love) suffereth long, and is kind...(Love) rejoiceth not in iniquity, but rejoiceth in the truth."*
> (1 Corinthians 13:4, 6) (See also James 5:20 and 1 Peter 4:8).

Prov. 10:13

"In the lips of him that hath understanding wisdom is found: but a rod is for the back of him that is void of understanding."

There is emphasis here on the fruit of **wisdom**, being in and coming from the **lips** or mouth of a wise man. The man possessing wisdom will act wisely. The fool may attempt to "talk big," but his ignorance and emptiness of soul will soon be detected. The one that **is void** (lacking) **of understanding** becomes the recipient of **a rod** (judgment and correction with a stripe). However, even after many stripes with a whip, he probably won't change. He still doesn't get it! He doesn't have even common sense. (cf. Prov. 17:10).

In contrast, just a word of correction will get the attention and acceptance of the wise.

Prov. 10:14

"Wise men lay up knowledge: but the mouth of the foolish is near destruction."

Wise men treasure **knowledge.** What do you treasure? The answer to that question reveals whether you're wise or foolish. In contrast, the fools empty heart and **mouth** are on the brink of **destruction.** His tank is "running on empty," with little spiritual resource to sustain his life.

Prov. 10:15

"The rich man's wealth is his strong city: the destruction of the poor is their poverty."

The general attitude of this verse may have to do with man's station in life. Earthly **wealth** grants **the rich man** a strong fortress, making him a strong force in the community. On the other hand, **the destruction** (ruin) **of the poor is their poverty.** The poor are weak, wanton, subservient, disadvantaged, and constantly "on the short end," so to speak. Their poverty could be the result of a wicked lifestyle. Thus, they've lost out all the way around. Yes, there is power in the wealth of money, but without true wisdom, one is spiritually poor no matter how much money they possess.

Prov. 10:16

"The labour of the righteous tendeth to life: the fruit of the wicked to sin."

Everyone reaps from their labor, whether good or bad. **The labour of the righteous tendeth to life**, because of the spiritual life within the person. A right attitude and purpose will use income for the right causes. The way one uses money correlates with the lifestyle and values of the spender.

In contrast, **the fruit** (income) **of the wicked is sin.** The wicked will spend money on what feeds his sinful purposes. Again, *"...the wages of sin is death"* (Romans 6:23). The loss, not gain, of sin is death, so sin is the opposite of life. That's why Christ, the Life, died for our sins, so that we might not die, but have everlasting life!

Prov. 10:17

"He is in the way of life that keepeth instruction: but he that refuseth reproof erreth."

The believer **in the way of life** embraces and practices truth, guarding instructions. Since godly instruction is based on God's Way (John 14:6), then he that obeys God demonstrates that **he is in the way of life.**

On the other hand, the one who refuses **reproof** (censure) errs or goes astray. Correction is necessary to get a sinner back on the right track. Only fools despise such **instruction.** O, for a heart that is sensitive to and accepts God's Word!

Prov. 10:18

"He that hideth hatred with lying lips, and he that uttereth a slander, is a fool."

Some people are very clever in hiding **hatred with lying lips.** What you hear from someone does not always reveal their inner heart. People will cover up their true feelings, unless the brain filter is flawed through the effects of drug or alcohol intoxication, dementia, etc. However, the sinful heart is a master of deceit.

The second part of this verse points to **a fool** who utters his hateful sentiments by **slander** or defaming others. Whether one covers up his hatred or speaks his hateful mind, both harbor murderous hatred in God's sight. The Apostle John said:

"We know that we have passed from death unto life, because we love the brethren. He that loveth not his brother abideth in death. Whosoever hateth his brother is a murderer: and ye know that no murderer hath eternal life abiding in him. Hereby perceive we the love of God, because he laid down his life for us: and we ought to lay down our lives for the brethren." (1 John 3:14-16)

Prov. 10:19

"In the multitude of words there wanteth not sin: but he that refraineth his lips is wise."

How revealing are our words, and the frequency with which they are spoken! The glaring principle of this proverb is that the more one talks, the more potential there is for sin. James says that controlling the mouth is a quality of perfection (James 3:1). Such a person can speak in abundance and not sin. Solomon commends the wise man who refrains **his lips** or keeps his mouth shut at the right time. Sometimes the one who listens quietly is considered wise, while the talker reveals his foolishness quickly. The Apostle Paul says, *"...study to be quiet and to do your own business."* (1 Thessalonians 4:11) Don't underestimate the power of words.

Prov. 10:20

"The tongue of the just is as choice silver: the heart of the wicked is little worth."

How precious is a tongue that speaks truth and justice. It is likened to **choice silver**, pure without defiling elements. How right words minister, comfort, and build up others! The sowing of righteousness can only build up.

In contrast, **the heart of the wicked is** (has) **little worth.** Notice **the tongue of the just** compared to **the heart of the wicked**. As mentioned many times in the Bible, the mouth reveals the heart. So the **just** express their godly hearts openly, while the inner hearts of the wicked are empty or worthless. How powerful is the tongue, sometimes even deciding between life and death (cf. James 3).

Prov. 10:21

"The lips of the righteous feed many: but fools die for want of wisdom."

The righteous person (saint) speaks words that **feed many** souls. As a shepherd feeding his flock (cf. Jeremiah 3:15), so believers have a ministry of spiritually feeding others with the Word. Too often the saints engage in idle chatter rather than edifying or building up one another. In contrast, **fools die for want of wisdom,** lacking heart or understanding.

Jesus said:

> *"...the words that I speak unto you, they are spirit and they are life."* (John 6:63).

Prov. 10:22

"The blessing of the LORD, it maketh rich, and he addeth no sorrow with it."

The prosperity which God bestows upon His obedient children takes various forms. The believer is "blessed with all spiritual blessings in Christ" (Ephesians 1:3), which makes his soul **rich.** We're told to *"Let the word of Christ dwell in you richly* (Colossians 3:16), which far surpasses material wealth. Yet, these spiritual riches do not nullify monetary wealth. Solomon himself was known as the wisest and richest man in the world.

God will often shower His children with external abundance by free grace. He has given us all things to enjoy, without any guilt on our part, because we're living the right life. There will always be trials and difficulties, and His blessings are given in the midst of our troubles.

God blessed godly Abraham with riches (cf. Genesis 12:2; 13:2). Wealth can be a blessing or a curse. It all depends on how you acquired it and use it.

Prov. 10:23

"It is as sport to a fool to do mischief: but a man of understanding hath wisdom."

Sports, like football and baseball, are the craze of many people. There is also the illegitimate **sport** of the **fool to do mischief.** The text speaks to the attitude of one who is gleefully caught up in profane or ungodly living. The word "sport" means "defiant laughter." The **fool** finds great pleasure in mockery, while delighting in his scheme of lewdness (**mischief**).

Yet, **a man of understanding hath wisdom.** He delights in and practices what is dear to his heart, the Word of God. Jesus said that you will know a wise and righteous man by their fruit (Matthew 7:17).

Barnes has a helpful note: "As the fool finds his sport in doing mischief, so the man of understanding finds in wisdom his truest refreshment and delight."

Prov. 10:24

"The fear of the wicked, it shall come upon him: but the desire of the righteous shall be granted."

What is the result of the fool's "sport?" **Fear...shall come upon him.** This may not be an immediate consequence, but it'll catch up with him.

Likewise, the believer will reap the results of his right actions: his godly desires **shall be granted.** The believer will have his Day of Glory, while the futile whims of the wicked will be dashed to pieces as he faces destruction. O, to realize this principle while one still has the time to do something about it!

Prov. 10:25

"As the whirlwind passeth, so is the wicked no more: but the righteous is an everlasting foundation."

The **wicked** are described as being destroyed by a **whirlwind** (hurricane or tornado). This verse vividly describes the horrendous storm of God's judgment upon a wicked world (cf. Psalm 1:4; Psalm 37:9, 10, 36).

In contrast, the **everlasting foundation** of **the righteous** shall not be moved! Jesus spoke the parable regarding the man who built his house on the rock, as opposed to the one who built his house on sand. The former stood firm in the storm, while the latter was destroyed (cf. Matthew 7:24, 25).

Blessed is the man who is firmly fixed on the Rock, Jesus Christ!

Prov. 10:26

"As vinegar to the teeth, and as smoke to the eyes, so is the sluggard to them that send him."

This verse describes the frustration imposed on those who have to deal with a lazy messenger. Such an individual is useless and troublesome. He is likened to the deteriorating effect of **vinegar to the teeth** and the irritation of **smoke to the eyes.** Some relationships are just flat-out painful. How blessed it is to move among people with ambition and godly purpose. Clarke's note is helpfully expressive:

> "The acid softening and dissolving the alkali of the bone, so as to impair their texture, and render them incapable of masticating; and as smoke affects the eyes, irritating the tender vessels, so as to give pain and prevent vision; so (is) the sluggard, the lounging, thriftless messenger, who never returns in time with the desired answer."

Prov. 10:27

"The fear of the LORD prolongeth days: but the years of the wicked shall be shortened."

In general terms, there's no question that believers (i.e., those that **fear the LORD**) are granted a quality of life that surpasses the **wicked**. The "prolonging" of days is more than years on earth. It carries into eternal life, which applies to those saints who have had a short stay on Earth (cf. Prov. 9:11).

Prov. 10:28

"The hope of the righteous shall be gladness: but the expectation of the wicked shall perish."

The hope of the righteous believer is anchored in God's promise of **gladness. The wicked** also have **the expectation** or hope that things will turn out right, but their hope **shall perish**, ending in disaster (cf. Psalm 1).

Biblical **hope** is that calm anticipation and confidence that God is on the Throne, and all will be right in the end. In contrast, the wicked live for the "now," and only "hope" that things will turn out right. That's nothing more than fantasy or wishful thinking. The believer perseveres by faith, because his future is secured in Christ. How wonderful and exuberant is the believer's hope. We need to appropriate the Apostle Paul's prayer:

"Now the God of hope fill you with all joy and peace in believing, that ye may abound in hope, through the power of the Holy Ghost." (Romans 15:13)

Prov. 10:29

"The way of the LORD is strength to the upright: but destruction shall be to the workers of iniquity."

The way of Jehovah has two sides: mercy and justice to **the upright** (those full of integrity), which is a source of **strength; but destruction** or ruin **to the workers of iniquity.** The same sun that melts butter hardens clay. The Gospel is a *"two-edged sword":* a taste of life for some and death for others (cf. 2 Corinthians 2:15, 16).

A modern analogy could be driving on the right side of the highway so that all have freedom to travel both ways. To travel down the left side would end up in disaster for the driver and those coming the other way. Freedom is not license to do wrong, but liberty to do right. There's **strength** and reward in following God's Way.

Prov. 10:30

"The righteous shall never be removed: but the wicked shall not inhabit the earth."

The righteous shall never be removed (shaken or overthrown). A believing Israel will inhabit the Promised Land. This is not true of **the wicked** who **shall not inhabit** that Land. Those who belong to the Messiah (Christ) steadfastly inherit God's kingdom, while those who reject Christ, **the wicked,** will not inherit His kingdom. Jesus addressed this issue with a religious teacher of Israel, Nicodemus, when He said:

"Verily, verily, I say unto thee, Except a man be born again, he cannot see the kingdom of God...He that believeth on the Son hath everlasting life: and he that believeth not the Son shall not see life; but the wrath of God abideth on him." (John 3:3, 36)

Prov. 10:31

"The mouth of the just bringeth forth wisdom: but the froward tongue shall be cut out."

The words used in this verse suggest a garden setting, with fruit-bearing trees and plants. **The mouth of the just** brings forth the fruit of the heart or godly **wisdom.** James beautifully describes this heavenly quality:

"...the wisdom that is from above is first pure, then peaceable, gentle, and easy to be intreated, full of mercy and good fruits, without partiality, and without hypocrisy." (James 3:17)

In contrast **the froward** (perverted) **tongue shall be cut off.** It's a picture of "rooting up" a dead plant, which cannot produce anything living or useful. The wicked are not only devoid of wisdom, but their perverted tongues will be destroyed.

Prov. 10:32

"The lips of the righteous know what is acceptable: but the mouth of the wicked speaketh frowardness."

A **righteous** man knows **what is acceptable** in any given situation. He has spiritual common sense, which is absent in the wicked (cf. 1 Corinthians 2:14-16). Furthermore, the word **know** contains the idea of sustenance. Psalm 1:6 says:

"For the LORD knoweth the way of the righteous, but the way of the ungodly shall perish." (cf. Colossians 4:6).

In contrast, **the mouth of the wicked speaketh frowardness.** He is caught up verbally with wickedness. He expresses what's in his wicked heart, which is overflowing with sin. As the saints need to be truthful and obedient, the fruit of holiness and revival needs to overflow from the Church in a "bigger way."

ca

Chapter 11

Dishonest Scales are an Abomination

Prov. 11:1

"A false balance is abomination to the LORD: but a just weight is his delight."

A merchant using a fraudulent scale of weight is a crook. This practice is an **abomination** (a revolting practice that is disgusting) **to the Lord.**

A just weight is His delight. The Lord delights in a genuine, balanced testimony or lifestyle. The issue is between integrity vs. perverseness; hypocrisy vs. truthfulness; a false front vs. genuineness. Jesus let the Pharisees know in no uncertain terms His disgust and indignation for their hypocrisy (cf. Matthew 23). Their profession did not match their possession.

God is looking for those who worship Him *"in spirit and in truth"* (John 4:23). Some fools evidence spirit with little truth, while others have truth with little evidence of the Spirit. We need "two wings" to fly spiritually: the Holy Spirit and the Truth. Those who have the balance of the Truth and the Holy Spirit will GROW UP and become spiritually mature!

Prov. 11:2

"When pride cometh, then cometh shame: but with the lowly is wisdom."

Pride or arrogance produces **shame** or disgrace. When the one comes, so does the other. What we sow, we reap. A farmer cannot plant corn to get barley. We cannot sow wickedness and get righteousness: right produces right, and wrong produce wrong. We can't go wrong serving our Righteous God!

With the lowly (humble) **is wisdom.** Those who walk humbly with God learn to live skillfully, sharing their wisdom with others. On the other hand, the world says, "Do your own thing; live for yourself; get what you can; and everything is open to one's own interpretation, including the Bible." How contrary is that self-centered attitude to the Word of God!

Prov. 11:3

"The integrity of the upright shall guide them: but the perverseness of transgressors shall destroy them."

The **upright** have integrity and innocence, while **transgressors** have corruptness. Integrity will **guide** those doing right, while the crooked thinking of the sinners will lead to self-destruction and ruin. As men make their own rules according to their own opinions of what's true, lawlessness and corruption prevail.

This was the situation in Israel after the demise of Joshua. Judges 21:25 states: *"In those days there was no king in Israel: every man did that which was right in his own eyes."*

In our day, many people feel entitled to their own opinion as far as what is right or wrong, with little regard for God's Word, the Bible. All kinds of perversion exists, producing heartache and confusion. Even the God-given institution of marriage between a man and a woman is in question, resulting in a rise in same-sex marriage (refer to 1 Corinthians 6:9-13). Sexual taboos are flourishing in proportion to the demise of God's Biblical authority in our society. There can only be destruction on the horizon.

Prov. 11:4

"Riches profit not in the day of wrath: but righteousness delivereth from death."

It's not how long a person lives, but how he lives! It's not how he begins, but how he ends. **Riches profit not in the day of wrath.** Jesus said:

"For what is a man profited, if he shall gain the whole world, and lose his own soul?" (Matthew 16:26).

How tragic it is to witness the wicked rich who, as paupers, head for the Judgment Day! How sobering to watch wicked people with abundance of wealth withering away with age; finding out the hard way; powerless over their tragic destiny.

But righteousness delivereth from death (eternal condemnation; see Romans 8:1); the righteousness given to us through Christ's sacrifice on the Cross. There is no substitute for being righteous in the face of death. In a word, money is no substitute for being right with God!

Prov. 11:5

"The righteousness of the perfect shall direct his way: but the wicked shall fall by his own wickedness."

The right road leads to the right place. So the fruit of righteous living leads to the right end. What we are will be apparent in our actions of righteousness or wickedness. **The perfect** (mature or complete) believer's lifestyle is directed by **righteousness.** The mature Christian is right within and without, while **the wicked shall fall by his own wickedness.** It mirrors the principle: what a man sows, he reaps. Righteousness in Christ is a positive, active force; wickedness is negative, causing a downhill course without effort. It's been said that any dead fish can swim downstream, but it takes a vitality of life to buck the tide upstream. Our sin is sure to betray us somewhere along the way. We are either on the road to Heaven or on the road to Hell. There's no in-between.

Prov. 11:6

"The righteousness of the upright shall deliver them: but transgressors shall be taken in their own naughtiness."

There's deliverance in righteous character, producing the right attitude and action. The rightness of the **upright** will rescue and preserve them. **Transgressors**, however, will be trapped in their own perverted desires and ways. Basically, we not only sow what we reap, but also what we are within our hearts. We could say that the rightness of the upright delivers him before he gets into trouble, while the wicked fall headlong into sin. In other words, prevention is better than the cure. Even if we fool others regarding our character, we never fool God.

Prov. 11:7

"When a wicked man dieth, his expectation shall perish: and the hope of unjust men perisheth."

How wonderful it is to be filled with genuine, eternal hope! **Hope** is that calm, assuring expectation and anticipation that all will one day be well. God Almighty is on the Throne of the universe and everything will come out right. In the light of this Biblical hope, one can walk by faith in the present. In 1 Thessalonians 1:3, believers had faith that worked, and a love that labored because of a hope that endured.

The world has **expectations,** but they are couched by worldliness or fleeting, ungodly pursuits, which never fully satisfy, or are temporary at best.

Christ is the "Hope of Glory," insuring an eternal harvest. We need to settle our eternal destiny in Christ, then live daily with eternal purpose. The sinner's life is indeed a colossal exercise in futility. There's nothing worse than a false and fleeting **hope** that perishes in the end.

Prov. 11:8

"The righteous is delivered out of trouble, and the wicked cometh in his stead."

Job 5:7 says:

"...man is born unto trouble, as the sparks fly upward,"

Believers likewise are tried and tested with **trouble**, yet they are **delivered** from it. The **trouble** (distress, adversity, or anguish) is usually the consequence of sin.

The righteous escapes the distress that overtakes the **wicked.** Clarke's commentary offers a helpful statement:

"The wicked cometh in his stead – Often God makes this distinction; in public calamities and in sudden accidents He rescues the righteous, and leaves the wicked, who has filled up the measure of his iniquities, to be seized by the hand of death. Justice, then, does its own work; for mercy has been rejected."

There's also a blessed thought here of divine intervention and substitution.

> "For he hath made him to be sin for us, who (Himself) *knew no sin; that we might be made the righteousness of God in him." (2 Corinthians 5:21)*

Our Savior was identified with our sin and bore it **"in** our **stead,"** the just for the unjust. Thus, *"...he was wounded for our transgressions, he was bruised for our iniquities: the chastisement for our peace was upon him."* (Isaiah 53:5)

Prov. 11:9

> *"An hypocrite with his mouth destroyeth his neighbour: but through knowledge shall the just be delivered."*

Again we're faced with the power of the **mouth** (tongue). We can either build up or tear down others (cf. James 3). The mouth can destroy a neighbor's reputation, family life, job, etc. It bears repeating that more wounds have been inflicted verbally with the edge of the tongue, than by the edge of the sword. Hypocrites thrive on taking others down to the pit.

But through knowledge (i.e., cunning awareness) **shall the just be delivered.** The believer has a "weapon" too: a mind that's intellectually and spiritually prepared for war against evil.

Interestingly, the Hebrew word *"chalats,"* translated *"be delivered,"* is used of Israel being *"armed for war"* (cf. Numbers 32:20, 21). By superior wisdom and discernment, we are equipped for warfare against Satan. The believer's armor includes the "helmet of salvation" (Ephesians 6:10). Psalm 18:19 says:

> *"He brought me forth also into a large place; he delivered me, because he delighted in me."*

Note also that *"chalats"* is also translated as "prepared" in Joshua 4:13 and 2 Chronicles 17:18. Thank God for all the divine preparation that He gives to the believer who obeys Him. There are many a **hypocrite** in the pulpits, so-called religious cultists, television personalities, etc. who are destroying people with heresies. We need to be armed with the armor of salvation and prepared to make a stand, rightfully using our mouth as weapons of God's Truth!

Prov. 11:10

"When it goeth well with the righteous, the city rejoiceth: and when the wicked perish, there is shouting."

To some degree, there's a fundamental and universal sense of justice built into even the worst of men: it's called the conscience (cf. Romans 2:14, 15). Righteousness or lawfulness is the positive essential to the sustenance of any unit of society (i.e., home, township, city, state, and country). Wickedness is negative destructiveness, and cannot stand on its own. Even the ungodly know what's right. The leadership of **righteous** men will bring prosperity to the city; so much so that **the city rejoiceth** or "jumps for joy," Even those who are not righteous reap the benefits of the righteous. In contrast, **when the wicked perish, there is shouting** (gladness over the removal of evil men). The world may fight the Word of God and personal righteousness, but still it is aware of the positive power of goodness.

Prov. 11:11

"By the blessing of the upright the city is exalted: but it is overthrown by the mouth of the wicked."

The upright people made a positive difference in **the city.** Those who walk rightly (*"yashar"* or straight) influence the place where they live. To elevate or exalt a city, there must be those whose lives are on a high moral plane. Individuals affect the whole of society, whether for right or for wrong.

The righteous exalt a good moral standard, while the wicked fight against anything godly. If a nation doesn't legalize that which is moral, then immorality becomes "the law." Our country needs to ponder this truth.

Prov. 11:12

"He that is void of wisdom despiseth his neighbour: but a man of understanding holdeth his peace."

Our treatment of others reveals how wise we are. What is in us will eventually come out of us. He who lacks wisdom despises or scorns his neighbor. A man of discretion doesn't voice his contempt, but keeps the peace if at all possible. James 3, the "tongue chapter of the Bible," is comprehensive in describing the power of the tongue. A mature man, **a man of understanding,** holds **his peace.** He not only refrains from mocking his neighbor, but also commends him when he can. He will also proclaim the truth, but keep silent when necessary.

Prov. 11:13

"A talebearer revealeth secrets: but he that is of a faithful spirit concealeth the matter."

Confidentiality is a rare quality. How difficult it is to protect the reputation and privacy of others. **A talebearer** (or "scandal monger") loves to expose or reveal the **secrets** of others. He has an insatiable pleasure in spreading gossip, and, in turn, reveals his ingenuous nature.

On the other hand, he that possesses **a faithful spirit** (genuine inner character) is concerned about the reputation of others; he conceals **the matter** or keeps it confidential. Indeed, this is a faithful friend. The talebearer is unfaithful, and not a true friend.

Prov. 11:14

"Where no counsel is, the people fall: but in the multitude of counsellers there is safety."

People, like sheep, must have guidance and **counsel** to succeed. Left to ourselves we can only go astray and **fall** (fail). Thus, God has ordained the role of parents, teachers, pastors, and counselors to grant direction and wise counsel. Jesus said:

"My sheep hear my voice… and they follow me." (John 10:27)

He has also granted us the counsel of others who follow Him. **There is safety** (salvation) in **the multitude of counselors.** Notice having a good number of advisors brings safety. This even surpasses the proverbial "second opinion." Godly counsel cannot be overdone.

How many marriage, family, and business decisions would have turned out differently if the proper counsel had been sought? It's always better to be safe, than sorry.

Prov. 11:15

"He that is surety for a stranger shall smart for it: and he that hateth suretiship is sure."

This proverb correlates with Prov. 6:1, emphatically warning against being a co-signer for another, even a friend. However, in the present verse, to be **surety for a stranger** is even worse. In fact, Solomon says the co-signer **shall smart for it** (will suffer miserably for it).

Gill's commentary renders this idea of "smart" as a complete breaking process..."one ruined and undone; becoming a bondsman for one whose circumstances he knew not; and these being bad bring a load upon him, such a heavy debt as crushes him to pieces," Yet, is this not what Jesus Christ did on the Cross when He was "crushed to pieces," becoming our Surety," and bearing our unbearable load of sin? Hallelujah!

In contrast, the only real surety in this imperfect world is hating **suretiship** (i.e., not putting up security for someone you don't know). This alone will ensure hope and confidence, keeping one out of debt and disaster.

Prov. 11:16

"A gracious woman retaineth honour: and strong men retain riches."

Notice how **gracious** and **honour** go together. A woman full of grace (kindness) is elegant and charming in the truest sense. Thus she **retaineth** or maintains honor. The Hebrew word for "honor" is "*kabod*," meaning glory or dignity. One with honor carries dignity, respect, and trust. This is a woman of excellence indeed. She has found and maintained her glorious place in God's economy. Honor is a key to mental health as well, which is often lacking today in those who are striving for "self esteem."

And strong men retain riches (wealth). The Hebrew for "strong" is "*ariyts*" meaning "mighty," or "awesome." Some translate this verse: "A gracious woman retains honor as strong men retain riches." This sets up a comparison in the tenacity and character of each. There's also a hint of a wife's relationship to her husband, and the compatibility of both in their roles.

Prov. 11:17

"The merciful man doeth good to his own soul: but he that is cruel troubleth his own flesh."

Significantly, a **man** who is **merciful** shows mercy to others and winds up doing **good** to himself. What goes around comes around. So it is with the **cruel** man who reaps trouble. Galatians 6:7-9 states:

"Be not deceived; God is not mocked: for whatsoever a man soweth, that shall he also reap. For he that soweth to his flesh shall of the flesh reap corruption; but he that soweth to the Spirit shall of the Spirit reap life everlasting. And let us not be weary in well doing: for in due season we shall reap, if we faint not."

It's no accident that merciful, loving people are blessed by others, while the wicked are miserable and draw miserable "friends" around them. We can live any way we want to, but we only get one chance to live a life. The judgment of God is at the end of life's road.

Prov. 11:18

"The wicked worketh a deceitful work: but to him that soweth righteousness shall be a sure reward."

The contrast between the fruit of the wicked and the righteous continues. All people work or produce a product in their lives, but it's ultimately a result of the condition of their heart. **The wicked**

worketh (produces) **a deceitful** (false or untruthful) **work; but to him that soweth righteousness** (right deeds) **shall be a sure** (true) **reward.** The strong inference is that works of deceit can never be right, true, or rewarding.

Prov. 11:19

"As righteousness tendeth to life: so he that pursueth evil pursueth it to his own death."

This verse can be reduced to two contrary principles: **Righteousness** leads **to life; evil** produces **death.** Saints build up their own lives and the lives of others, rather than tearing them down. Likewise, the one who is pursuing **evil** does so to his own demise, and fails to bring life to others. The evil man ultimately heaps **death** and self-destruction upon himself.

Prov. 11:20

"They that are of a froward heart are abomination to the LORD: but such as are upright in their way are his delight."

God's heart is moved by both the wicked and the righteous. He's angry with the wicked. To say that "God loves everyone" is misleading. The word "love" must be interpreted in light of John 3:16; He so loved the world that He made a way to save those who believe in Him. A perverted heart is an **abomination** (disgusting thing) **to the Lord**.

On the other hand, the **upright in their way** (lifestyle) **are His delight.** What a contrast! We can delight God's heart by a whole-hearted devotion to Him, which affects our daily walk. What a great privilege to walk with God, as did Enoch and Noah of ancient days (cf. Genesis 5:24, 6:9).

Prov. 11:21

"Though hand join in hand, the wicked shall not be unpunished: but the seed of the righteous shall be delivered."

While most people would concede that God will judge individual sinners, how will He deal with great numbers of **the wicked** who are joined together hand-to-hand? Such is the questioning of a rebellious society which shakes its unbelieving fist in God's face. They do so to their own destruction. The so-called "strength in numbers" is no obstacle to the Word of God, who will not hold any guiltless who have sinned. King David said:

"The wicked shall be turned into hell, and all the nations that forget God." (Psalm 9:17)

In contrast, **the seed of the righteous shall be delivered** or saved. Again, the need to repent and be saved cannot be overlooked. The unconverted will be cast into Hell fire, while those who are right with God will be saved forever. While the righteous may suffer, and the wicked "go free," in the present life, the Day of Judgment will bring eternal Heaven or Hell.

Prov. 11:22

"As a jewel of gold in a swine's snout, so is a fair woman which is without discretion."

This verse is a great commentary on the importance of a woman's inner beauty. Beauty can just be "skin deep." It's impossible to be a "fair" or beautiful **woman**, but have no **discretion.** How tragic! This scenario is likened to a ring of gold hanging from a pig's snout. There's something wrong with that picture. Gold and pigs don't go together; neither should an "air-head" mentality go with a beautiful woman. Some of the most beautiful women may be physically "homely" or plain; but their inner quality shines through. This principle is so important for young people to realize. Looks can be deceiving. We have a potential treasure in our bodies, even though they crumble with age. The inward treasure of a believer is being renewed day by day (2 Corinthians 4:7, 16). The issue is not having a good outward appearance, but the supernatural projection of a Christ-like image.

Prov. 11:23

"The desire of the righteous is only good: but the expectation of the wicked is wrath."

With the believer's "new birth" comes a new nature that desires **good** (an essence of godliness). It wants the best for others, because God's love is focused on the welfare of others. In contrast, **the expectation** (motivation) **of the wicked is wrath** (selfishness and anger). The "Cain spirit" produces wrath toward others.

Prov. 11:24

"There is that scattereth, and yet increaseth; and there is that withholdeth more than is meet, but it tendeth to poverty."

This proverb illustrates the contrast between the hilarity and abundance of giving versus the spirit of restraint or the tightfisted mentality. The one who "scatters" or broadcasts his possessions to those in need, will reap a harvest. God blesses that attitude with abundance (cf. 2 Corinthians 9:5-11). Indeed, God loves a cheerful giver (2 Corinthians 9:7).

On the other hand, the one who **withholdeth more than is meet** (fair or right) will end up in **poverty.** Ironically, godly giving to others can never be lost. It's interesting that the root word for "miserable" is "miser." One who is a miser tends to be miserable. In God's economy, he that sows bountifully will reap bountifully, while he that sows sparingly, shall reap sparingly. Thus, the cliché: You can't outgive God.

Prov. 11:25

"The liberal soul shall be made fat: and he that watereth shall be watered also himself."

The freedom and joy of giving is a beautiful thing. It expresses God's heart: *"the giving God"* (James 1:5) and the One who *"gave His only begotten Son"* (John 3:16). The promise of giving is to **be made fat** (a picture of abundance and insurmountable blessings).

The parallel thought is, **he that watereth shall be watered also himself.** Watering is an expression of blessing from above; e.g., rain and dew. What a privilege to water dry and thirsty souls around us with both spiritual and material sustenance, only to heap blessings on our own heads. Jesus said:

> *"Give, and it shall be given unto you; good measure, pressed down, and shaken together, and running over, shall men give into your bosom. For with the same measure that ye mete withal it shall be measured to you again."* (Luke 6:38)

Prov. 11:26

"He that withholdeth corn, the people shall curse him: but blessing shall be upon the head of him that selleth it."

In the same context, those blessed with abundance often become greedy. A farmer withholds the sale of **corn** (grain) to those in need. This restraint may be a scheme to wait for a drought which would increase the demand, so that the farmer could overcharge and make more money (cf. Amos 8:4-6).

Whatever the case, the **people** will **curse him.** There's a God-given sense of justice and fair play in every soul and people will react accordingly, whether negatively or positively. Thus, we see a positive **blessing...upon the head of him that** sells the grain at a reasonable price. Despite their own sinfulness, all people hate to be "ripped off," even thieves! Likewise, there is a sense of appreciation when receiving kindness from others.

Proverb 11:27

"He that diligently seeketh good procureth favour: but he that seeketh mischief, it shall come unto him."

Again, we have the principle of sowing and reaping: **He that diligently** seeks good receives favor, while **he that seeketh mischief** will find evil.

Seeketh occurs twice in the translation, but they are two different words. The first *"shachar"* suggests earnestness or diligence. That's what's needed to acquire what is good. The second is *"darash"* suggests following a downhill path. The <u>Keil & Delitzsch Old Testament Commentary</u> renders this verse well:

> "He that striveth after good, seeketh that which is pleasing;
> and he that searcheth after evil, it shall find him."

Proverb 11:28

"He that trusteth in his riches shall fall: but the righteous shall flourish as a branch."

"Trusting in riches" is the basic problem here. Money has its place, but is not to be trusted or "become one's god." Covetousness is indeed a cancer to the soul, and can only bring disaster (**fall**).

On the other hand, **the righteous shall flourish as a branch.** They will bear the fruit of the Holy Spirit, making them rich indeed. It's a matter of priority. There's nothing wrong with wealth in itself. However, it matter's whether it takes God's place, or results from seeking God first. Matthew 6:33 fits so many scenarios:

"But seek ye first the kingdom of God, and his righteousness; and all these things shall be added unto you."

Saving grace puts our priorities in the right perspective. Our primary focus must be on Christ, trusting Him to supply the "stuff" needed to function in this chaotic world. The issue is not what we possess, but what possesses us! Legitimate things can be used and enjoyed, but we must never let them overcome us. For instance, a house and a car are helpful, but they must not become an end in themselves. They are earthly provisions to be used for our good and God's glory; for instance, a house can be used to have a weekly Bible study group, or a car could be used to pick someone up for church.

Proverb 11:29

"He that troubleth his own house shall inherit the wind: and the fool shall be servant to the wise of heart."

The troublemaker in his own family will end up with nothing! Whatever he covets or has will have no lasting value.

In conjunction, he will play the **fool** who will become **a servant to the wise of heart.** Instead of being a self-controlled, successful man, he becomes a slave to those who conduct their lives skillfully in wisdom and spirit.

Prov. 11:30

"The fruit of the righteous is a tree of life; and he that winneth souls is wise."

Again, as in 11:28, we have the metaphor of a flourishing garden; the godly man bears **the fruit....a tree of life.** Herein is portrayed the stability and abundance of God's life in the believer; i.e., the fruit of the Spirit; e.g., love, joy, peace, etc. (Galatians 5:22, 23). This person is not only righteous, but one who produces practical, outward qualities that promote life-giving happiness. (Psalm 1:1-3) One of the great by-products of such fruit is "winning souls." Solomon was commending spiritual fruit-bearing which wins and influences people positively.

The Hebrew word translated "winneth" is "*laqach*," meaning "to take, fetch, lay hold of." This indicates more than just "letting our light shine" on others. Wisdom motivates the "soul winner," Believers can win souls by being winsome or cheerful, but only God can save souls. Jesus said:

"Follow me, and I will make you fishers of men." (Matthew 4:19)

Daniel also spoke of wisdom's necessity, saying:

"And they that be wise shall shine as the brightness of the firmament; and they that turn many to righteousness as the stars for ever and ever." (Daniel 12:3)

Prov. 11:31

"Behold, the righteous shall be recompensed in the earth: much more the wicked and the sinner."

This verse starts with a complex statement regarding the believer's reward on earth, prior to death. Yet, so much of Scripture points to future reward, beyond the grave. The word **recompensed** has the idea of being paid or repaid (as in Job 21:31). It is also translated "rendered" in Job 34:11. So, righteous people are blessed for acts of obedience while on earth, although they can be disciplined for any disobedience. Likewise, good things happen to bad people, while bad things come upon good people.

If the righteous man is repaid or dealt with justly, how **much more** will God deal justly with the wicked and the wayward sinner (cf. 1 Peter 4:17,18). Life in this world is unfair, at best. Injustices abound. Yet, *"Vengeance is mine; I will repay, saith the Lord."* (Romans 12:19)

Chapter 12
Whoso Loves Instruction Loves Knowledge

Prov. 12:1

"Whoso loveth instruction loveth knowledge: but he that hateth reproof is brutish."

How we respond to correction and rebuke reflects our true heart. **Instruction** indicates discipline and training: **knowledge** that molds and develops one's character. Thus, it sparks an ongoing desire to learn more. Rebuke a wise man and he will love you for it. The purpose of the Word of God is that it is *"profitable for doctrine, for reproof, for correction, for instruction in righteousness: That the man of God may be perfect, throughly furnished unto all good works"* (2 Timothy 3:16, 17).

But he that hateth reproof is brutish. The Hebrew word for "brutish" is *"baar"* which is used to describe a "stupid fool or brute beast." Clarke comments: "He is a bear; and expects no more benefit from correction than the ox does from the goad," The wise wants to know, the fool doesn't; the wise is gladdened by instruction, the fool is turned off. In essence, the fool says, "Don't confuse me with the facts, my mind is already made up!"

Prov. 12:2

"A good man obtaineth favour of the LORD: but a man of wicked devices will he condemn."

What is **a good man**? Romans 3:12 says: *"There is none that doeth good, no, not one."*

In a general sense, there are good people; i.e., those who are concerned for others, and do not manifest ill-will toward others, etc. Yet, Biblically, there are none completely good before God; i.e., sinners cannot please God nor possess a right relationship with God in this life. Thus, the Cross of Calvary comes into play, where Christ bore mankind's sin, opening the Way to God forever. True goodness comes only from God Himself; "good" relates to "godly."

Therefore, **a good man obtaineth favour of the LORD.** Notice the covenant Name of Jehovah (**LORD),** the Great I AM. One can only receive acceptance from Him through the only One who has been accepted of the Father: Jesus Christ (Ephesians 1:6). What an incentive to be right with God!

The above explanation is a New Testament one. However, Solomon could have been referring to common people with "good natures."

The **man of wicked devices** will be troubled in the end. We know that the wicked will be condemned in the Final Judgment (2 Thessalonians 1:7). There's no substitute for walking in the goodness of Christ, and having favor with God. Wicked men manifest their wickedness by **wicked devices** that are evil plots with an evil heart purpose. Everyone has a purpose of some sort, for out of the heart are the issues of life. A person's life is geared in the direction of what's important to his heart. Give a $20 bill to each of six men, and they will each spend it in a different way, depending on the priorities of their hearts.

Prov. 12:3

"A man shall not be established by wickedness: but the root of the righteous shall not be moved."

This verse describes the tremendous difference between the sinner and the saint. **Wickedness** will never establish or insure stability to a man. Isaiah 53:6 says:

"All we like sheep have gone astray; we have turned every one to his own way..."

Man's basic sin is pride and selfishness; doing things his way. A famous singer used to sing, "I did it my way," explaining his self-centered destiny. Only God's Way will establish a man's life. Christ alone is the "Rock of Ages," the Cornerstone and Foundation of the Church. To stand upon that Rock is to be secured and firm, but woe be to the person upon whom that same Rock falls.

Thus, **the root of the righteous shall not be moved.** The saint, fixed on Christ, will be:

> *"Like a tree planted by the rivers of water, that bringeth forth his fruit in his season; his leaf also shall not wither, and whatsoever he doeth shall prosper."* (Psalm 1:3)

> *He can be "stedfast, unmoveable, always abounding in the work of the Lord." (1 Corinthians 15:58)*

Speaking of being **moved**, sinners need to be moved from wickedness unto godly repentance; they need to turn to God from their idols, to serve the true and living God. Likewise, backsliding believers need to be moved from their lethargy, if they are to bear the fruit of the Holy Spirit.

The theme song of many "Christians" today is: "We shall not be moved!" Only a divine convicting power of God can shake them from their spiritual stupor!

Prov. 12:4

> *"A virtuous woman is a crown to her husband: but she that maketh ashamed is as rottenness in his bones."*

Solomon's wisdom and experience causes him to commend the excellence of a **virtuous woman** to her husband. The King also knew the devastating consequences of a wife who brought shame to the household. This was first hand knowledge to Solomon, seeing that he had multiple wives (see 1 Kings 11:3). This might be the place to mention the ethical concerns posed by Solomon's wives. God did not condone Solomon's polygamous life-style, evidenced by the many sad consequences that resulted. (See I Kings 11:4, 7, 8) While the Lord allowed this unusual arrangement in the king's palace, it doesn't mean that God approved if it.

Solomon started out well, heeding the counsel of his father David (cf. 1 Kings 2:2-3). Eventually, he lost sight of his own counsel and wisdom. God allowed him freedom to make choices, right or wrong. This illustrates how God can use a flawed individual to advance His Kingdom. While this is no excuse to sin, it's good to know that God is merciful and uses people in spite of themselves. Someone has said, "God can use a mighty crooked stick to draw a straight line." Again, that's not to promote license, but rather an encouragement to follow hard after God.

As stated above, Solomon knew the value of a **virtuous** wife, as opposed to one with a "shameful" spirit. Virtue is defined by excellence, efficiency, and strength of character. Such a wife is sure to be a **crown** of special jewels to her husband. (Consider a fuller description of the **virtuous woman** in Prov. 31:10f.) Needless to say, a resurgence of these qualities would help to revolutionize the present-day state of marriage and family life.

Prov. 12:5

"The thoughts of the righteous are right: but the counsels of the wicked are deceit."

A heart that's right with God produces **right thoughts,** including right intentions and imaginations. We can't live and conduct ourselves any higher than we think. Hypocrites attempt to manifest something that's not really a part of them; e.g., they act the part of being **righteous.**

The thoughts also mean advice and counsel that comes from the **righteous:** those right with God. Again, Psalm 1 warns against seeking the "advice of the ungodly." **But the counsels of the wicked are deceit.** Not only are the wicked deceptive in their counsel, but the very essence of their advice is deceptive and fraudulent. In other words, they speak what they are in their deceitful and wicked hearts (cf. Jeremiah 17:9).

Prov. 12:6

"The words of the wicked are to lie in wait for blood: but the mouth of the upright shall deliver them."

Men speak of their interests, plans, exploits, etc. **The words of**

the wicked are to lie in wait for blood. The "Cain spirit" is full of murder and lurks to shed blood; it's not a disease per se, but a corrupt heart or character. There's also power in words, which project the sinful heart to others. That's why peer pressure is so tempting. "Birds of a feather flock together" (cf. Prov. 1:10-19).

On the other hand, **the mouth of the upright shall deliver them.** The mouths of believers speak truth and stand against evil, resulting in deliverance and self-preservation. This is a blessed man, indeed.

The vital lesson of this verse is that speech will eventually reveal the person. Not only that, but there is power and authority in our words (cf. James 3), not to create but to affirm, declare, and stand up for what is right.

Prov. 12:7

"The wicked are overthrown, and are not: but the house of the righteous shall stand."

The wicked and **the righteous** are contrasted in many ways in Scripture. Not only are their lives different here on earth, but also in eternity (what Heaven and Hell are all about). We now witness the difference between one's stability and longevity while on earth. **The wicked** (ungodly) **are overthrown, and are not;** their reign is very temporary and soon comes to nothingness. How ironic it is that the wicked can rise to power in this world only to be decimated and destroyed. What makes headlines down here on earth may be an abomination up there, before God. The result of living a selfish life for the present is an exercise in futility and hopelessness.

Conversely, **the house of the righteous shall stand.** This security not only pertains to the **righteous** man himself, but to his **house**hold, which is rightly influenced by his rightness. Wickedness is destructive and eventually meets with destruction. Righteousness stabilizes and endures the pitfalls of the world. This is another illustration of Paul's principle of sowing and reaping found in Galatians 6:7, 8:

"Be not deceived; God is not mocked: for whatsoever a man soweth, that shall he also reap. For he that soweth to his flesh

shall of the flesh reap corruption; but he that soweth to the Spirit shall of the Spirit reap life everlasting."

Prov. 12:8

"A man shall be commended according to his wisdom: but he that is of a perverse heart shall be despised."

A man shall be commended according to his wisdom, rather than by his wealth or station in life. This is a statement of godly success. The <u>Keil & Delitzsch Old Testament Commentary</u> indicates the order of the sentence, denoting emphasis: "According to the measure of his intelligence is a man praised." A man is commended or praised according to his knowledge steeped in the fear of God. Even the world acknowledges and respects genuine, righteous character.

But he that is of a perverse heart shall be despised. A crooked and perverted heart produces perverted fruit which is not commendable. In fact, it is **despised**, contemptible, and disrespected. Excellence of character is important!

Prov. 12:9

"He that is despised, and hath a servant, is better than he that honoreth himself, and lacketh bread."

The one **despised** or scorned is a righteous man who is not held in high esteem by this world. Yet, he has been blessed with **a servant**, which indicates economic stability. He is contrasted to the man who **honoureth himself, and lacketh bread** (food). The second man appears to be conceited and self-glorifying but is poor. The K&D render this verse clearly: "Better is he who is lowly and has a servant, than he that makes himself mighty and is without bread," When seen from God's perspective, what the world considers success may turn out to be misery and failure. God will honor His servants in due season.

Prov. 12:10

"A righteous man regardeth the life of his beast: but the tender mercies of the wicked are cruel."

Salvation even affects one's attitude and treatment toward animals, especially his own. He **regardeth the life of his beast** (animal, cattle). The Hebrew word for "regardeth" is *"yada,"* meaning "to know with concern and care (cf. Psalm 1:6). This text is not teaching "animal rights" per se. It does say that believers not only love God and people, but also have compassion for animals. The so-called **tender mercies of the wicked are cruel.** The wicked do not have compassion at all. Their selfishness is cloaked in emotion and/or empty words. They're cruel because they lack sincerity and genuineness. In a word, the attitude one has for people has direct bearing on his response to animals.

Prov. 12:11

"He that tilleth his land shall be satisfied with bread: but he that followeth vain persons is void of understanding."

Not only is it right to work, but it's satisfying. Work is an honorable grace given by God. Adam was placed in the Garden of Eden *"to dress...and to keep it."* (Genesis 2:15). Farming is the "oldest profession" and is not a curse. The curse of "sweat" came after the Fall of man in Genesis 3. Man had purpose and a means of sustenance, being satisfied with food. This work ethic has never changed to this day. Paul exhorts:

"...if any would not work, neither should he eat." (2 Thessalonians 3:10)

In spite of this God-given provision, some refuse to work, for whatever reason. Interestingly, they work at something, even if it's illegitimate. The text says that these are running after worthless, empty people, evidencing their lack of understanding or heart. They're not only foolish and unfruitful, but their idleness will lead to deeper trouble. Idleness is "the devil's workshop." A man must be involved with something; if it's not something good and wholesome, it will be evil and wasteful. God blesses hard work! (cf. Prov. 28:19).

Prov. 12:12

"The wicked desireth the net of evil men: but the root of the righteous yieldeth fruit."

There's power and security in the underworld. The wicked gravitate to their own evil system. They desire **the net** (network) **of evil men** (cf. 2 Corinthians 10:4). Wicked men live in their own evil world, finding camaraderie but no trust or friendship.

On the other hand, **the root of the righteous yieldeth fruit.** Those rightly related to the Lord have new desires to bear the fruit of the Holy Spirit, turning their backs on the nets of evil. They have been delivered from the bondage of sin. Herein is stability, security, and happiness (cf. Psalm 1:3; Prov. 11:30).

Prov. 12:13

"The wicked is snared by the transgression of his lips: but the just shall come out of trouble."

The mouth of the wicked not only gets him in trouble, but also reveals his trouble. **The wicked is snared** (hanged) **by the transgression of his lips.** Out of a wicked heart comes wicked talk and actions, eventually hanging the transgressor, whether in society, the courts, or future judgment.

For instance, a liar's tongue should be connected to a superb memory, lest he forget what he lied about the last time, and entrap himself. It's only a matter of time before the sin will be revealed. On the other hand, the **just** will be vindicated, or **come out of trouble**; i.e., his right-speaking (integrity) will be acknowledged by others, enabling him to escape and/or avoid trouble (cf. Prov. 11:8).

Prov. 12:14

"A man shall be satisfied with good by the fruit of his mouth: and the recompense of a man's hands shall be rendered unto him."

K&D captures the emphasis of this verse:

"From the fruit which the mouth of the man bringeth forth is he satisfied with good."

How important and influential are words! One can build up or tear down with a word. This man is an encourager, who blesses and benefits many. Thus, he's rewarded and **satisfied with good** things. Furthermore, there's a **recompense**, or reward, for the work of his **hands.** A man who is gifted by the Lord in his words and the work of his hands is blessed and an example of righteousness (cf. Prov. 13:2; Matthew 12:37).

Prov. 12:15

"The way of a fool is right in his own eyes: but he that hearkeneth unto counsel is wise."

Again, the popular song of another era said, "I Did It My Way," That's the fool's motto, because he assumes his **way** is **right** and he will not be deterred from his self-centered path. Furthermore, he will not seek **counsel** or advice from others, who may know which way to go. **He that hearkeneth** (heeds) **unto counsel is wise.** Wise people, unlike fools, are "all ears" when it comes to wise advice and godly direction. O, what travesty and disaster has resulted by doing it "my way!"

Prov. 12:16

"A fool's wrath is presently known: but a prudent man covereth shame."

A fool doesn't hide his anger. It **is presently known** or apparent at once. There's no restraint or discretion when a fool is offended; he lets it "all hang out." The **prudent** or wise **man** covers **shame**; i.e., he doesn't hastily over react. He is *"slow to wrath,"* as James 3 says. He bears offense patiently. It's not only our actions that reveal our character, but also our reactions. Responding with deliberation is more effective than reacting hastily.

Prov. 12:17

"He that speaketh truth sheweth forth righteousness: but a false witness deceit."

Truth is transparent, while lies are covered up. Truth can stand alone, openly and undaunted. Falsehood must sneak around, trying not to be detected. Truth can stand in the sunlight with no need or desire to deceive. So, a righteous man speaks truth, because that is his nature. He speaks what's in his heart, what he is! But **a false**

witness (speaks) **deceit.** How careful a liar must be! Not only must he have a deceitful heart, but a good memory. A fraudulent witness has to really work at it to make sure no one finds out.

Prov. 12:18

"There is that speaketh like the piercings of a sword: but the tongue of the wise is health."

There are those who are masters at using their tongues **like the piercings of a sword.** They inflict deep wounds into the spirit of others. The Hebrew word translated "speaketh" is *"batah,"* meaning to speak harshly (used only five times in the Bible; cf. Psalm 106:33).

The old adage says, "Sticks and stones will break my bones, but words will never hurt me." The truth is that words can be injurious, especially coming like **the piercings of a sword** from a vile tongue. Stab wounds can heal much better and faster than severely injurious words which penetrate impressionable souls. Some folks wrestle a lifetime with cruel words spoken to them as children. The opposite is true of **the tongue of the wise**, which fosters **health** or healing (cf. Prov. 4:22; 16:24; Malachi 4:2). Out of a righteous heart, the wise person speaks instruction with graciousness. What great power is in the tongue! James 3 devotes the whole chapter on the subject.

Prov. 12:19

"The lip of truth shall be established for ever: but a lying tongue is but for a moment."

The **truth** is **established for ever** because it's God's character, and God is eternal. To speak the truth is to project the authority of God.

On the other hand, **a lying tongue is but for a moment.** It creates a brief stirring and then fades away. What a contrast between truth and lying!

Yes, truth endures forever, while lies are momentary. However, the tongue can choose to be an instrument of either, depending on one's heart.

Prov. 12:20

"Deceit is in the heart of them that imagine evil: but to the counsellers of peace is joy."

Deceit (fraud, treachery) **is in the heart** (behind) **of them that imagine** (devise) **evil.** Since *"the heart is deceitful above all things, and desperately wicked"* (Jeremiah 17:9), it's no surprise that it produces evil schemes. As water cannot rise above its source, so man cannot live above his depraved nature, except for God's saving grace.

But to the counselors of peace is joy. So, the result of counselors who promote peace is joy, rather than the misery of the evil. The K&D commentary says:

> "Deceit is in the heart of him who deviseth evil, but those who devise peace cause joy."

Prov. 12:21

"There shall no evil happen to the just: but the wicked shall be filled with mischief."

As a general principle, Solomon promotes the faithfulness of God's plan and purpose, which will not allow anything **evil** to befall **the just**, except that which brings ultimate good. In other words:

> *"...all things work together for good to them that love God..."* (Romans 8:28).

On the other hand, **the wicked shall be filled with mischief** (from the Hebrew *"ra'ah"* meaning misery).

Again, this is a general principle, for we know that the wicked seem "trouble free" at times, while believers suffer. Yet, without hope in God, the wicked person's life is shallow and meaningless, with the future damnation by God staring him in the face.

K&D interpret the word "evil" as "sorrow"; the sorrow of sin (cf. Isaiah 59:4). The godless are full of evil, for the moral evil which is their life-element brings out of itself all kinds of evil on themselves.

Prov. 12:22

"Lying lips are abomination to the LORD: but they that deal truly are his delight."

A liar is simply expressing his nature, and yet lying is listed with the most heinous sins (cf. Revelation 22:15). On the other hand, God is Truth, and can only express Himself accordingly. When converted by God's grace, a believer is joined inseparably to Truth. Since Christ, the Truth, abides in the believer, the believer begins to manifest that new truthful nature (cf. Prov. 12:17).

Want to bring **delight** to God's heart? Live, walk, manifest Christ-like Truth! In other words, live every aspect of your life for the glory of God; i.e., your lifestyle will honor Christ, letting others know that He is Great!

Prov. 12:23

"A prudent man concealeth knowledge: but the heart of fools proclaimeth foolishness."

A similar principle is illustrated in Prov. 11:13 and 12:16. One of wisdom's strengths is the ability to conceal **knowledge,** rather than blurting out silliness or **foolishness** as does **the heart of fools.** Those who really have something to say are often silent and discerning, while the foolish must say something. Again, this is another illustration of James' discourse on the tongue (cf. James 3:10).

Prov. 12:24

"The hand of the diligent shall bear rule: but the slothful shall be under tribute."

There's freedom and reigning power in **the hand of the diligent.** Such a person is powerful, independent, and demonstrates an overcoming spirit. He rules his own spirit, and, therefore, can oversee others or **rule.**

In contrast, the **slothful shall be under tribute.** The deceitful slacker is an expert in avoiding labor or self-exertion. Professing freedom to take life easy, he's really **under tribute** (burden or force to work). There's a price to pay when refusing to work. Laziness leads to personal and financial bondage. It destroys self-worth and motivation. For example, those who depend on the welfare system, often taking the "easy road," become stagnant at best. Assuming one is able, diligent work is liberating.

Prov. 12:25

"Heaviness in the heart of man maketh it stoop: but a good word maketh it glad."

Without question, what is in the heart affects one's entire being, including the body. **Heaviness** (anxiety) **in the heart maketh it stoop** (depressed). In contrast, **a good word** (kindness or encouragement) **maketh it glad** (cheerful). How powerful are words! A word can make the difference between victory and defeat, as well as joy and sorrow. The word "stoop" is primarily used for worship or bowing down before God. This verse pictures a **heart** bent to depression, thus affecting his physical position (cf. Cain in Genesis 4). **Heaviness** of **heart**, along with aging, can weigh down a person in every aspect. How fine it is to get **a good** uplifting word from someone. What hope and joy is fostered by such words. What rejuvenation of the soul is rendered by an encouraging word! (cf. Prov. 15:13, 15, 23; 17:22; 18:14)

Prov. 12:26

"The righteous is more excellent than his neighbour: but the way of the wicked seduceth them."

The phrase **is more excellent** literally means "to seek, select or explore, especially in a business transaction." It pictures the believer's character to lead **his neighbor** or friend into something beneficial or successful. It's an expression of love. On the other hand, **the way** (lifestyle) **of the wicked seduceth them,** leading them astray. This seduction may be subtle, passed off for real love, but the true character of deceit will be manifested in the end.

Prov. 12:27

"The slothful man roasteth not that which he took in hunting: but the substance of a diligent man is precious."

The idea of this verse is that a man acts in line with what he thinks is important or valuable. One's character dictates how he deals with life, even in regard to **hunting.** Thus, **the slothful** (lax) **man roasteth not that which he took in hunting.** This is more than just a sporting event. The man hunts for food, not having abundance. Yet, slackness prevents him from preparing or roasting his meal. How lazy can one be? Note that the word "slothful" can also mean "deceitful" (cf. Psalm 120:2), inferring a conniving and scheming spirit of the slacker.

But the substance (wealth) **of a diligent** (sharp) **man is precious** (valuable). Unlike the lazy man, the diligent man is decisive and ambitious, which explains his wealth; but he also values what he has and what it can accomplish. Here's a man with purpose and uses his money without waste. He has money, but doesn't love it. He will honor the Lord and help others with his abundance (cf. Prov. 12:24; 13:4).

Prov. 12:28

In the way of righteousness is life: and in the pathway thereof there is no death.

The concluding verse of this chapter is a great summation of the believer's journey and final reward. The road he travels is the right road, leading to eternal life. However, this **way of righteousness** not only leads to life; it **is life!** To follow the Just One, Christ, is to experience abundant life now (John 10:10).

Chapter 13
A Wise Man Heeds His Father's Instruction

Prov. 13:1

"A wise son heareth his father's instruction: but a scorner heareth not rebuke."

A wise (discerning, skillful) **son heareth** (heeds) **his father's instruction** (warning). In Prov. 12:1, notice that instruction (discipline) fosters knowledge. Godly instruction is both positive and negative, telling what to do and what not to do; thus, developing a balanced life (cf. Prov. 11:1). In Prov. 10:1, *"a wise son maketh a glad father,"* but the wisdom comes by the son's humble reception of it, and the father's dedicated teaching.

But a scorner heareth not rebuke (blame for a fault). The scorner is a mocker (arrogant talker, who refuses to hear instruction or censure). Being the opposite of wise, he has the "Cain spirit" of rebellion. Not like the young lad Samuel; who, when hearing God's voice wisely said, *"Speak LORD; for thy servant heareth."* (1 Samuel 3:9) Likewise is the blessed man of Psalm 1:1, 2, who doesn't sit in the seat of the scorners, but delights in the Word of God, thus bearing the fruit of true prosperity.

Prov. 13:2

"A man shall eat good by the fruit of his mouth: but the soul of the transgressors shall eat violence."

Obviously, the "eating" in this verse is figurative. The idea is "receiving or obtaining," as one would eat food. The inference regarding the first man is that he's righteous or **good**, thus, what comes from **his mouth** is not only a blessing to others, but also to himself. Again, we reap what we sow.

On the other hand, **the soul of the transgressors shall eat violence** (cruelty). **Transgressors** are those who act treacherously or deceitfully. Their wickedness may be covered up, but it's there. They will manifest their true colors in time. They also will wreak havoc on others, and eventually upon themselves.

We like to "eat" what we enjoy. That's true spiritually, as well. A righteous heart wants to feed on the Righteous Word, which will bear righteous fruit. An unrighteous soul craves that which satisfies his unholy desires, and thus reaps cruelty, a sinful harvest.

Prov. 13:3

"He that keepeth his mouth keepeth his life: but he that openeth wide his lips shall have destruction."

The wrong words can kill you. The man **that keepeth his mouth keepeth his life.** What power is in the tongue! On the positive side, a man's very life can be saved or preserved by guarding what he says to others.

However, talk to spies, crooks, and undercover agents, and see what happens. The negative aspect of this proverb is that one who "runs his mouth," the incessant talker, or "big mouth" exposes his foolish heart, leading to self-destruction. Jesus said:

"For out of the abundance of the heart the mouth speaketh" (Matthew 12:34).

How revealing is our speech! Listen to a man for five minutes and you can discern his character. There's a direct pipeline between the heart and the mouth. (Again, cf. James 3, the "tongue chapter.")

Prov. 13:4

"The soul of the sluggard desireth, and hath nothing: but the soul of the diligent shall be made fat."

Both the lazy and the diligent have desires, but only the latter succeeds. By virtue of being human, the **sluggard** wishes and dreams like anyone else. However, his dreams will never materialize because he will not take responsibility. Thus, **the soul of the sluggard desireth, and hath nothing.** No plowing and sowing, no reaping! God ordained the work ethic from the beginning of creation. The first man "tilled the ground" even before his Fall (Genesis 2). After the Fall, work became a chore and a choice. To refuse to work brings dissatisfaction to life.

But the soul of the diligent shall be made fat. The lazy man dreams, but the diligent man works the dream and it becomes true.

Diligence reflects definite goals, determined actions, and precise decisions. Zacchaeus not only had a desire to see Jesus, but a diligent determination to see Him when denied access by the crowd. So, he climbed a sycamore tree to see Jesus (Luke 19:1). That speaks volumes to a sluggard!

Prov. 13:5

"A righteous man hateth lying: but a wicked man is loathsome, and cometh to shame."

There are many differences between the righteous and the wicked. Basically, the godly individual not only loves what's right, but he hates what's wrong. Thus, Solomon describes the basic character of **a righteous man:** he hates **lying.** What we love and what we hate reveals our character. On the other hand, **a wicked man is loathsome** (stinks), and he will be shamed.

Interestingly, even the godless world has a sense of justice. It has an aversion to those who live in deception, falsehood, and wickedness. If that were not so, there would be no justice system.

However, the thought here is that wickedness has a stench in the present, and shame in the future Judgment. All things will "come out in the wash." This is why Christ's sacrifice on the Cross is essential to salvation. There are pleasures in sin, but only for the moment. How much better it is to live with eternity in view, knowing that whatever a man sows, he shall reap.

Prov. 13:6

"Righteousness keepeth him that is upright in the way: but wickedness overthroweth the sinner."

There's a preserving and protecting ministry of God's righteousness.

To be right is to live right, and end up right. So the writer says, **Righteousness keepeth him that is upright in the way** (lifestyle). It's like personifying righteousness: a Person maintaining and preserving His children; i.e., Christ, our Righteousness.

The word "upright" refers to being complete and morally innocent. Moral virtue is the result of godly righteousness, and makes one complete. Sin destroys self-worth and integrity of character. No wonder there's an epidemic of psychological problems in society.

In contrast, **wickedness** (moral wrongness) **overthroweth** (ruins) **the sinner. So is the existence of a wicked man.** There's no preservation or protection for the wicked, except by God's common mercy. There's certainly a vast difference between the righteous and the wicked.

Prov. 13:7

"There is that maketh himself rich, yet hath nothing: there is that maketh himself poor, yet hath great riches."

What a beautiful illustration of the contrast between riches and true wealth. **There is that maketh himself rich, yet hath nothing.** This pictures the self-centered, self-made man, who heaps the world's riches upon himself. Yet, this man has nothing of real value. Money cannot satisfy and make one truly wealthy like the second man in this verse. **There is that maketh himself poor, yet hath great riches.** This man has the right priorities, not heaping upon himself riches, yet blessed with true wealth and abundance. He shares what he has with others, and gives himself to God, making himself "poor" from a worldly perspective. God will meet his every need, making him genuinely rich and prosperous.

Prov. 13:8

"The ransom of a man's life are his riches: but the poor heareth not rebuke."

This verse expresses the thought that a rich man needs to obey the law because his wealth is at stake if he doesn't. The poor man with nothing to lose can disregard reprimands (cf. Prov. 13:1). Society is filled with such people.

"How much is he worth"? That is a common question, because a **man's life** seems directly related to **his riches.** This wealth is his **ransom** or cover, when he gets in trouble. On the other hand, the poor are disregarded by and large, with few lawsuits coming their way. If the poor break the rules, there's no financial risk to them.

Prov. 13:9

"The light of the righteous rejoiceth: but the lamp of the wicked shall be put out."

This concept is profound. **"The light of the righteous"** has to be more than physical. We know that the Word of God is a light to our paths, leading and instructing in righteousness. But how can that light "rejoice" or be glad in itself? This must be some function within the righteous man. Jesus said:

"The light of the body is the eye: if therefore thine eye be single, thy whole body shall be full of light." (Matthew 6:22)

Again, was He referring to the physical eye? If so, then that would leave out a blind person. It must be the spirit, or the heart sealed by the Holy Spirit (Ephesians 4:30). When that's "made alive," the light shines throughout the body, producing joy and gladness.

But the lamp of the wicked shall be put out (extinguished). In the same context as above, Jesus said:

"If therefore the light that is in thee be darkness, how great is that darkness!" (Matthew 6:23)

Whatever glimmer of light is in a wicked man can only wane and **be put out** (judged). That's why believers are called "children of the light" (Ephesians 5:8), and do not walk in darkness.

Prov. 13:10

"Only by pride cometh contention: but with the well advised is wisdom."

Contention or quarreling is a fruit of pride or arrogance. **Pride** must have the final word! It is contentious and argumentative even when wrong. Humility may contend with or defend a true position, but will remove itself from the arrogant, rather than quarrel.

Wisdom and humility are connected; thus, wisdom is with the one who is **well advised** or has received good counsel. Humility receives and submits to counsel. Pride does not.

K&D's commentary renders this verse as:

> "Nothing comes by pride but contentions; but wisdom is with those who receive counsel."

Prov. 13:11

"Wealth gotten by vanity shall be diminished: but he that gathereth by labour shall increase."

The acquisition of wealth is not wrong in itself, but the motive and method may be wrong. The thrust of this proverb is the blessing of the work ethic. A lasting and increasing wealth can be obtained by honest **labor.**

Wealth gotten by vanity (illegitimate work, gambling, stealing, welfare fraud, etc.) **shall be diminished** (decreased, become small).

The sinful mind wants something for nothing. However, easy come, easy go! Work is God's way to sustain one's self and family (cf. Prov. 20:21; Psalm 128:2).

Prov. 13:12

"Hope deferred maketh the heart sick: but when the desire cometh, it is a tree of life."

Hope is a longing expectation for something or someone. When it is **deferred,** it will make **the heart sick** (grieved). Just observe those who suffer under the load of shattered dreams. Hopelessness is indeed a root cause of depression, particularly to those who have no trust in the Lord.

Generally speaking, just the future anticipation of hope can sicken the heart; i.e., depressively wondering if the fulfillment will ever come.

But when the desire cometh, it is a tree of life. The remedy for being "heart sick" is a **tree of life**, the source of strength, happiness, and inner healing. Hope fulfilled is a glorious event!

This applies to the ultimate Hope, which is Christ (Colossians 1:27). He is also the Tree of Life (Revelation 22:14), and one Day we will see Him face to face. Indeed, Christ is the Ultimate Hope of Salvation!

Prov. 13:13

"Whoso despiseth the word shall be destroyed: but he that feareth the commandment shall be rewarded."

One's attitude toward The Word of God is all-important. "Despise" (disrespect) it and **be destroyed. Fear** (revere) it, and **be rewarded.** What we do with the Word of God is what God will do with us. Yet, the world doesn't believe that. There are some in the Church who don't believe it either.

The Hebrew word "destroyed" is *"chabal,"* which means "to wind tightly as a rope." This describes the disobedient man as being "bound tightly with no freedom" to enjoy God's blessings. Serving sin appears to be "freedom" up front, but it is only a matter of time before the bind comes, and the "noose" of God's judgment tightens.

Prov. 13:14

"The law of the wise is a fountain of life, to depart from the snares of death."

What one believes is all important. It determines one's lifestyle and ultimate end. Solomon extols **the law of the wise** as **a fountain of life;** i.e., the wise man finds his source of life in the Law (*torah*). As Jesus said:

"...out of his belly (inner being) *shall flow rivers of living water."* (John 7:38)

The right doctrine leads to the right destination; i.e., life instead of death!

Thus, there is a God-given remedy allowing a person **to depart from the snares of death.** To reject the Word of God is not only unwise, but eternally damning to one's soul.

Prov. 13:15

"Good understanding giveth favour: but the way of transgressors is hard."

Good (pleasant, agreeable) **understanding** (discretion) **giveth** (bestows) **favour** (grace). Godly wisdom always has positive results in the long run, even when the immediate results appear to be negative. There's **favour** with discernment, because it rightly understands people and their condition. There's an element of true love here, which desires the best for others. A godly servant is gracious.

However, the **transgressors** are bent on violating and taking advantage of others. The result is a perpetual life of difficulty (hardness or toughness). There's no undergirding grace, nor the fullness of God's love. It's a "rough road!"

Prov. 13:16

"Every prudent man dealeth with knowledge: but a fool layeth open his folly."

One of the characteristics of a wise or prudent man is his desire and ability to deal properly with life; i.e., he takes responsibility and does the right thing with what he knows.

On the other hand, **a fool layeth open** (disperses, scatters) **his folly** (silliness). First, his foolishness is **open** for all to see. He has no discretion.

Second, he scatters his problems to others, blaming the consequences of his folly on others. How prevalent is this attitude in this day of irresponsibility and victimization. What a challenge for believers to be courageous and deal squarely with life's responsibilities!

Prov. 13:17

"A wicked messenger falleth into mischief: but a faithful ambassador is health."

The scene depicts two messengers sent on a mission. The **wicked messenger** ends up in trouble along the way. The **faithful ambassador** soundly remains in good **health.** The one fails, while the other succeeds. **Mischief** is the bad fruit of the **wicked.** On the other hand, **health** attends the messenger who is **a faithful ambassador.** This proverb illustrates the fact that we do what we do, because we are what we are. Our character is manifested by our deeds.

Prov. 13:18

"Poverty and shame shall be to him that refuseth instruction: but he that regardeth reproof shall be honoured."

How we respond to **instruction** and **reproof** is all important. Fools despise instruction. A wise man is eager to learn in order to be more effective and fruitful in life. **Poverty and shame** result from rejecting right instruction. There's a price to everything, and it's not only a matter of finances, but also embarrassment. Eventually, fools reap the negative results of their poor decisions.

In contrast, the one who **regardeth reproof** (censure) **shall be honoured** (the Hebrew word is *"kabod,"* meaning "respected"). Heeding reproof is a mark of humility, another fruit of righteousness. In turn, this promotes honor or respect in the eyes of others.

Prov. 13:19

"The desire accomplished is sweet to the soul: but it is abomination to fools to depart from evil."

Everybody dreams, even fools! They desire to accomplish something legitimate which, in turn, would be **sweet to the soul.** So, what's the issue? **Fools** won't **depart from evil.** In fact, it's an **abomination** (disgusting) for them to do such. "Abomination" is a strong word, indicating that the fool is wed to the idolatry of wickedness. Talk about the depravity of man!

A fool is so selfish and sold-out to sin, that he will not make any break from it in order to live legitimately. He will not pay the price to have genuine satisfaction and the blessing of God. The J.F.B. commentary says, "Self-denial, which fools will not endure, is essential to success."

Prov. 13:20

"He that walketh with wise men shall be wise: but a companion of fools shall be destroyed."

The Apostle Paul says, "*...evil communications* (companions) *corrupt good manners* (character)." (1 Corinthians 15:33) Solomon speaks of the same principle from both a positive and a negative standpoint. One who "walks" with **wise men shall be wise.** As a result, they will grow wiser, because *"iron sharpeneth iron"* (Prov. 27:17).

But a companion of fools shall be destroyed. On the opposite side of the equation, to walk with fools can only lead to destruction and judgment. A man becomes like his companions. The proverb validates the common adage: "Birds of a feather flock together!"

Prov. 13:21

"Evil pursueth sinners: but to the righteous good shall be repayed."

Evil is not neutral. It's not a matter of take it or leave it, for it is held in Satan's hand (cf. 1 Corinthians 15:56; Hebrews 2:14). In Genesis 4:7, sin is personified as a wild beast, lurking at the door of the human heart, and eagerly desiring to devour his soul (K&D). Peter warns us:

"Be sober, be vigilant; because your adversary the devil, as a roaring lion, walketh about, seeking whom he may devour." (1 Peter 5:8)

Sin, along with its consequences, tracks down the sinner. It's on the offense! **But to the righteous good shall be repayed.** Again, we have illustrated the law of sowing and reaping from Galatians 6.

Prov. 13:22

"A good man leaveth an inheritance to his children's children: and the wealth of the sinner is laid up for the just."

God not only ordained that we have children, but grandchildren as well. Interesting is the concept of **a good man** leaving an inheritance for his grandchildren. This man is looking out for the second generation, as well as his own children. Meanwhile, the **wealth of the sinner** can end up in the hands of the righteous. Money gained by the wicked can still be "converted" and used to the glory of God. By His grace, God continues to bring "fruit out of a garbage pail," so to speak.

Prov. 13:23

"Much food is in the tillage of the poor: but there is that is destroyed for want of judgment."

Indeed, there is **much food** (abundance of crop) **in the tillage of the poor;** i.e., the plowed field of the diligent poor man has great potential. He need not beg nor join the welfare role, but by God's nature, he can sustain himself.

The second clause can refer to the poor farmer whose crop is destroyed by poor decisions. A more likely meaning would be a reference to a farmer who, although rich, loses his wealth through unscrupulous business practice. Therefore, the land is **destroyed for want of judgment.** Through foolish and/or greedy management, the crop is destroyed.

In summary, we see the potential of prosperity for a poor farmer who works his land diligently. In contrast, there's the farmer with the same potential, but he fails because of flawed character or faulty discernment.

Henry's commentary nails the truth as follows:

> "The poor, yet industrious, thrive, though in a homely manner, while those who have great riches are often brought to poverty for want of judgment."

Prov. 13:24

"He that spareth his rod hateth his son: but he that loveth him chasteneth him betimes."

Corporal discipline is scriptural. Of course, it warrants wisdom and steady emotions, but, nevertheless, it is an integral part of raising children properly. In fact, Solomon says that failure in this area is to "hate" the child. Strong words! To **spareth the rod** (branch or stick) is to withhold or refuse proper discipline. The parent might say, "I love my son too much to spank him!" Such a philosophy is twisted, even leading some to "child abuse," when the son's rebellion becomes unbearable.

The other alternative is just to surrender to the child's "lordship" and trust that changes will occur later. This is not to say that all children are the same. There are various kinds and degrees of discipline for different children. Therefore, wisdom is essential in child-rearing. God's way is to **"loveth"** the child so much that his need for discipline is essential for correction and training (cf. Prov. 22:6). Thus, we are to **"chasteneth him"** (discipline him) **betimes** (quickly); i.e., in early childhood. True love wants God's best for its object, even though it may entail distasteful and difficult actions (See Prov. 3:12; 23:13; 29:15).

Prov. 13:25

"The righteous eateth to the satisfying of his soul: but the belly of the wicked shall want."

There's a "God-shaped" vacuum in every soul that only God Himself can fill. This "eating" process is a figurative term which pertains to the "soul." A man who is right with God is satisfied spiritually, no longer living the selfish life. This has physical and emotional benefits as well. He is content with God's provisions, for godliness with contentment is great gain. Not so with the wicked, who constantly search for self-satisfaction. His **belly** (the seat of hunger and emotional faculties) is never satisfied. He's always in "want," but never getting enough. O, the wages of sin that not only reap eternal damnation, but also bring sinners up short in this temporal existence! Indeed, "sin is the blast that doesn't last!

Chapter 14
The Wise Woman Builds Her House

Prov. 14:1

"Every wise woman buildeth her house: but the foolish plucketh it down with her hands."

This verse expresses the phenomenal power and influence of a godly woman (refer to Prov. 31:10ff.). The "house" here refers to the wise woman's household and family. A man can build a house, but a godly woman can make a home. Money can buy a house, but only God can establish and maintain a real home. **Every wise woman** (no exceptions) **buildeth** (establishes, causes to continue) **her house.** The man may be the breadwinner, but it's **her house.** He's to be the king, but she's the queen.

On the other hand, a foolish woman will destroy a home quickly if she's side-tracked from her responsibility. O, the difference a godly woman makes in a family! No wonder God said, *"It is not good that the man should be alone"* (Genesis 2:18). Marriage is a covenant between a man and a woman, even if that concept is contested these days.

In the context of **Proverbs**, the home was the primary responsibility of the wife and mother. In this day of technology, mothers can once again work out of their homes, as did the woman of Proverbs 31. There's no substitute for a wise and godly woman. It's been said many times: "The hand that rocks the cradle, rules the world." There's not a man on earth that doesn't owe his existence to a mother. How we need a resurgence of God's divine order for marriage and family.

Prov. 14:2

*"He that walketh in his uprightness feareth the LORD: but he that
is perverse in his ways despiseth him."*

"Walketh" indicates a frame of mind or attitude. It is not just one who is taking literal, physical steps. A bed-ridden believer can "walk" with God. The *"eth"* is the old English for "ongoing action," Therefore, it depicts one who is constantly walking in rightness (integrity, goodness, etc.).

A truly righteous lifestyle indicates one who **feareth the Lord.** The LORD has his rightful place in a God-fearing or righteous man. The Apostle John said, *"…he that doeth righteousness is righteous."* (1 John 3:7)

The counterpart is the one who **is perverse in his ways** (course of life); i.e., he is perverting or turning aside from Truth. Furthermore, he **despiseth him** (the LORD), holding Him with contempt and not taking Him seriously. Just as a child despises his parents by rebellion, so does a fool despise God. Our attitude and lifestyle reveal who we are.

Prov. 14:3

*"In the mouth of the foolish is a rod of pride: but the lips of the
wise shall preserve them."*

In the mouth of the foolish (perverse) **is a rod of pride** (arrogance, haughtiness): **but the lips of the wise shall preserve** (keep or guard) **them.**

Could the "rod" in our text not have the connotation of the perverted "majesty" of pride? Perhaps, using the mouth as a "weapon" to beat others down? Speaking great and swelling words which eventually are his undoing? Could it be an arrogant "lashing out" toward others? All of these are valid suggestions.

In any case, the "rod of pride" belongs to the "fool" which eventually leads to his demise, after aggravating those around him. In contrast, the wise will guard their lips with a right spirit, which "preserves" them from embarrassment and eventual judgment.

Prov. 14:4

"Where no oxen are, the crib is clean: but much increase is by the strength of the ox."

Where no oxen (cattle) **are, the crib** (manger or feeding trough) **is clean** (empty)**, but much increase** (produce, yield, or crops) **is by the strength** (power or force) **of the ox.** This is a principle relating to the work ethic of the farmer. God has not only ordained work "by the sweat of the brow," but also in conjunction with beasts of burden. One of those faithful animals is the ox. Clarke's commentary on the ox is enlightening:

"The ox is the most profitable of all the beasts used in husbandry. Except merely for speed, he is almost in every respect superior to the horse:

1. Scarcely liable to any diseases.

2. He is steady, and always pulls fair in his gears.

3. He lives, fattens, and maintains his strength on what a horse will not eat, and therefore is supported on one third the cost.

4. His manure is more profitable.

5. When he is worn out in his labor his flesh is good for the nourishment of man, his horns of great utility, and his hide almost invaluable.

6. It might be added, he is little or no expense in shoeing, and his gears are more simple, and much less expensive, than those of the horse.

In large farms, oxen are greatly to be preferred to horses. Have but patience with this most patient animal, and you will soon find that there is much increase by the strength and labor of the ox."

Thus, Solomon is saying that the farmer's investment in the ox will bring great increase if he works the field. Two are better than one, seeing the great strength and endurance of the beast. With no ox, he can save on the feed, but the harvest will be skimpy too. There is an economic strategy of fruitful production taught here. It could follow that the greater the increase, the more feed would be available to expand the whole operation, etc.

Prov. 14:5

"A faithful witness will not lie: but a false witness will utter lies."

A "witness" is someone who sees and hears something, and may be called upon to express it. More fundamentally, the witness expresses what they are: whether **faithful** or **false.** This verse is another illustration of how "out of the abundance of the heart, the mouth speaks." A trustworthy person will not lie, because he is true and faithful of heart. An "untrue" witness will speak untruths or lies. In other words, a person is not a liar because he lies, but he lies because he is a liar. Likewise, we call a man a thief when he steals, but he steals because he's a thief in his heart. "As a man thinketh in his heart so is he." A man cannot live any higher than his thoughts and his heart attitude.

Putting all of the above aside, this text deals primarily with one called upon to testify in court, etc. or relate what he has witnessed. One's lifestyle and trustworthiness will greatly affect his witness. The person who walks in truth tells the truth. He who follows lies and false doctrine reveals that with his mouth.

Prov. 14:6

"A scorner seeketh wisdom, and findeth it not: but knowledge is easy unto him that understandeth."

A scorner (mocker) **seeketh wisdom, and findeth it not.** The attitude of the heart is everything. Without a heart for God, one can never understand the Word of God.

> *"...the natural man (unsaved and full of self) receiveth not the things of the Spirit of God...neither can he know them, because they are spiritually discerned."* (1 Corinthians 2:14)

This is why brilliant minds (e.g., scientists, professors, and scholars) may lack wisdom or just plain common sense. They are devoid of understanding because they are in rebellion to the One who is the Author of all understanding and wisdom.

But knowledge is easy unto him that understandeth (i.e., one with discretion and wisdom). The Apostle John defines Eternal life as knowing God personally and intimately, thus becoming a recipient of His understanding (John 17:3). Consequently, the ministry of the indwelling Holy Spirit provides "easy" understanding of the Word. The flesh cannot produce this in our lives (cf. John 16:13-15).

How blessed is the most insignificant child of God who can understand God in a way that puzzles and frustrates intelligent mockers of this world! A college professor, who doesn't know Christ, is no spiritual match for a young Sunday school child who knows Christ. Even John 3:16 is an absolute mystery to an unsaved scholar who may seek understanding but can never find it, because of an unbelieving heart.

Prov. 14:7

"Go from the presence of a foolish man, when thou perceivest not in him the lips of knowledge."

Simply put, walk away from a man the moment you discern that he speaks foolishness. It takes wisdom to detect fools. Who we spend time with is a reflection of our own character. Just like a bad book or movie, we need not spend any more time with a foolish man than necessary. Some people will just not be helped. Thus, we cannot force wisdom on those who have no desire or capacity for it.

So the writer says: **Go** (walk away) **from the presence of a foolish man, when thou perceivest not in him the lips of knowledge.** Notice that the second phrase characterizes the first; i.e., the **foolish man** is one who lacks **knowledge.** His foolishness is evident by his speech.

Life is too short to spend one's time and effort on those who are full of themselves. Spend time with those who have a desire to know the Truth.

Prov. 14:8

"The wisdom of the prudent is to understand his way: but the folly of fools is deceit."

Evidently, wisdom within a **prudent** (sensible, shrewd) man enables him **to understand his way** (i.e., to discern or deal wisely with his lifestyle). Wisdom is the ability to live skillfully, using our God-given gifts effectively for the glory of God (e.g., Philippians 2:13; 4:13). Part of that "understanding" is to know God's purpose for being here on Earth, and living accordingly. The fool has no such knowledge, nor the desire to know.

Thus, **the folly** (silliness) **of fools is deceit.** The word "deceit" is used of falsehood (cf. Prov. 20:23). Deceit is believing a lie and acting like it's true. Wisdom looks in God's Mirror, the Word, and judges right from wrong, choosing truth. Fools don't want to know the truth. They don't want to be confused with the facts. It's easier for them to be silly than sober.

Prov. 14:9

"Fools make a mock at sin: but among the righteous there is favour."

This is a progression from the previous verse. The fool's deception leads him further into mockery and scoffing in regard to the reality and power of sin. Since that's his lifestyle, sin can't hurt him. What arrogance accompanies wicked folly! If he can't conquer sin, then he joins it, even to the point of denial. **But among the righteous there is favour.** The righteous find favor with God and man. There's still enough sense in the world to admire and accept the integrity of people who do right. Plus, the righteous have settled their sin with God Himself, receiving and enjoying the divine favor of saving grace.

Prov. 14:10

"The heart knoweth his own bitterness; and a stranger doth not intermeddle with his joy."

This statement expresses the ultimate in personal, intimate privacy. **The heart** (spirit) **knoweth** (witnesses within) **his own** (soul) **bitterness** or trouble. There's a personal communication between the heart and the soul, known by no other person. King David was known to "talk to himself," as illustrated in Psalm 42:5.

He said, *"Why art thou cast down, O my soul...?"* His heart was speaking to his soul, reflecting on his trouble. He had inner conflict, known by none other than God Himself. But he could speak a word of "hope in the Lord" to himself, rather than listening to the accusations of Satan. So it needs to be with us. The principle of "joy" in the soul is no different. It's known and experienced only by the individual.

A stranger doth not intermeddle with his joy. The Arabic word "intermeddle" is a business term used in exchanged collateral, like mortgages. It has to do with sharing or having fellowship with another. Thus, one's intimate joy of soul is not exchanged or entered into by another. It's a totally private matter.

Prov. 14:11

> *"The house of the wicked shall be overthrown: but the tabernacle of the upright shall flourish."*

Following the lead of Proverb 12:7, this is another description of prosperity and the longevity of the saint, in contrast to the destruction of the wicked. Even though **the wicked** live in a **house**, that household **shall be overthrown** or destroyed. Whatever prosperity and security comes his way, they will perish.

But the tabernacle (tent) **of the upright shall flourish.** The believer may have few earthly possessions, but God will establish his "tent," and he shall flourish. The Hebrew word for "flourish" is *"parach,"* meaning "to bloom." God's people are "bloomers," who are filled with the fruit of the Holy Spirit, regardless of worldly belongings.

In Psalm 92:12-14, King David said:

> *"The righteous shall flourish like the palm tree: he shall grow like a cedar in Lebanon. Those that be planted in the house of the LORD shall flourish in the courts of our God. They shall still bring forth fruit in old age; they shall be fat and flourishing."*

Better to live in a tent with the Lord, than to live in a palace without Him.

Prov. 14:12

"There is a way which seemeth right unto a man, but the end thereof are the ways of death."

Here is a powerful principle regarding self-deception. This man is devoid of the Word and wisdom, leaning only on his own understanding. He is simply following **a way** or course of life which seems **right** to him. In reality, his **ways** lead to **death.** This is true in every aspect of one's life: personal, family, "religion," etc. Many are sincere, yet deceived by their own religious beliefs, including those of cults. God has given us the Bible as our "Manual for Living," our Roadmap from Earth to the Glory of Heaven (cf. Prov. 3:5, 6).

As mentioned previously, King David said: *"Thy word is a lamp unto my feet, and a light unto my path."* The Bible gives direction and safety along the road of life, which cannot be mustered by man himself. Christ is the Way. Let's follow Him!

Prov. 14:13

"Even in laughter the heart is sorrowful; and the end of that mirth is heaviness."

Laughter is a beautiful gift from the Lord. How often it has been used to ease tense and difficult times. However, laughter often hides a grieving heart. Years ago, there was a popular song called, "Laughing On the Outside (Crying On the Inside)," What we see on the face is not always reflective of the heart. It has been said that comedians are profoundly serious actors who have been deeply hurt. Saints and sinners can experience the reality of a sorrowful and heavy heart. The verse may indicate a "backslider," who attempts to laugh his way through a miserable lifestyle. **Mirth** (gladness or pleasure) is wonderful when it's genuine and heart-felt. However, it's both sad and fruitless to attempt faking this emotion without the inner reality.

Prov. 14:14

"The backslider in heart shall be filled with his own ways: and a good man shall be satisfied from himself."

This proverb contrasts **the backslider in heart** and **a good man.** The former is estranged from God, an unsaved man, while the other is a godly man rightly related to God. The backslider is full of himself, self-sufficient in his own course of life. The good man is satisfied with the fruit of righteousness, stemming from his redeemed heart. The inference is that a man can be full of himself and miserable; thus, being ineffective for good. The good man filled with rightness, results in being satisfied with himself and effective in touching others.

Prov. 14:15

"The simple believeth every word: but the prudent man looketh well to his going."

Solomon describes the gullibility of the **simple** or foolish, who **believeth every word** spoken by his cohorts in crime (see Prov. 1:10ff.). How quickly a fool will listen to the schemes of those bent on his destruction. How silly it is to heed the words of those whose only interest is to use others for their own benefit. An early American sage used to say, "There's a sucker (fool) born every minute!" In contrast, **the prudent** (sensible or shrewd) **man looketh well in his going** or step. He discerns and understands where he's going, and acts accordingly with wisdom (cf. Prov. 13:16).

Prov. 14:16

"A wise man feareth, and departeth from evil: but the fool rageth, and is confident."

This proverb is a practical outworking of Prov. 1:7 and 3:7, regarding the true nature of wisdom. **A wise man feareth and departeth from evil.** First, the wise man has a reverential fear of God which leads to good actions. Second, that reverence motivates him to depart or steer clear from evil. The Apostle John describes this principle as follows:

"Whosoever is born of God doth not commit sin; for his seed remaineth in him: and he cannot sin, because he is born of God."
(1 John 3:9)

But the fool rageth and is confident. The attitude of the fool is the opposite of the wise. He is raging or intensely angry, while exuding "confidence" or a cock-sure, bold attitude. The fool is constantly pushing the limits with bold disobedience. Just as wisdom becomes a lifestyle, so does sin become a foolish way of life.

Prov. 14:17

"He that is soon angry dealeth foolishly: and a man of wicked devices is hated."

Impatience is not a virtue. Solomon describes the foolishness of one who **is soon angry** or "short fused, losing his temper quickly," Anger has its place (Ephesians 4:26), but most of the time people are angry for the wrong reason. Such anger makes one act **foolishly,** lacking temperance or self-control (Galatians 5:23).

A man of wicked devices is hated. Foolish anger and conniving go together. How prevalent are "con-men" who cleverly plot to do evil. Such people are hated by those that they abuse or victimize. God hates a deceitful heart, and so do the upright.

Prov. 14:18

"The simple inherit folly: but the prudent are crowned with knowledge."

Some inheritances are a curse rather than a blessing. **The simple inherit folly** (silliness). He possesses and manifests more of what he already is. In contrast, **the prudent are crowned** (surrounded by) **knowledge.** In Psalm 142:7, King David cries:

"Bring my soul out of prison, that I may praise thy name: the righteous shall compass me about; for thou shalt deal bountifully with me."

The idea is being "enclosed" or secured by godly knowledge.

Prov. 14:19

"The evil bow before the good; and the wicked at the gates of the righteous."

Righteousness will prevail, either in the present and/or in the future. In spite of their wickedness, **evil** men **bow before the good** (the godly or upright). There's a sense of justice in all men, even though they themselves break the law. For instance, it is not uncommon for prison inmates to take out their "righteous" anger against a pedophile inmate. Likewise, **the wicked (**bow) **at the gates** (authority) **of the righteous.**

Prov. 29:2 sheds further light on this principle:

> *"When the righteous are in authority, the people rejoice: but when the wicked beareth rule, the people mourn."*

The wicked learn to appreciate the benefits of good, righteous leadership, in spite of their own immorality. Ultimately, the ungodly will admit and acknowledge right from wrong before the Righteous One Himself! In the end;

> *"every knee should bow… and that every tongue should confess that Jesus Christ is LORD…!"* (Philippians 2:10, 11)

Hell will be inhabited by perpetual rebels against God, while forced to recognize His Sovereign Lordship.

Prov. 14:20

> *"The poor is hated even of his own neighbour: but the rich hath many friends."*

Money does talk! A poor man is generally despised and hated, even by his neighbors. Human nature is such that we gravitate to those who are wealthy, and thus able to give us something. No one wants to personally associate with what society calls "a loser." Only true love ("*agape*" or godly love) can see the worth of a poor man and act accordingly. It's just a fact that **the rich hath many friends** or acquaintances. However, that can be deceiving, for a person of means cannot be sure of the motivation of those who pose as his friends. When one is financially broke and bankrupt, he will find out who his true friends are!

Prov. 14:21

> *"He that despiseth his neighbour sinneth: but he that hath mercy on the poor, happy is he."*

One's attitude and response to the poor or needy reveals his own character. To be disrespectful and condescending to the poor is wicked. The worth of a person has nothing to do with his financial status. Moreover, showing **mercy on the poor** is not only right, but produces happiness. Selfishness is not only a curse, but the opposite of love. God grants all kinds of opportunities to be gracious to others.

Remember the acrostic: **JOY** – **J**esus first; **O**thers second; **Y**ourself last!

Prov. 14:22

"Do they not err that devise evil? but mercy and truth shall be to them that devise good."

The question intensifies the stated truth. Yes, those that **devise evil, err** (go astray). Those who **devise good** will reap **mercy and truth** (cf. Galatians 6:1ff.).

Prov. 14:23

"In all labour there is profit: but the talk of the lips tendeth only to penury."

The expression "Talk is cheap!" can rightly find its source in this verse. Man was made to **labour** from the beginning; e.g., Adam labored in the Garden, resulting in **profit** or gain. God blesses diligent labor, but "big talk" only produces poverty and misery. Many "talk the talk," but do not "walk the walk," There are those who **talk** about "pipe dreams" that never materialize. Some say, "Put your money where your mouth is!" There's a price to pay either way: work brings **profit** while talk without work brings only **penury** or impoverishment.

Prov. 14:24

The crown of the wise is their riches: but the foolishness of fools is folly.

Wealth itself is not evil. In fact, **the crown of the wise is their riches.** The wise will increase their opportunity to engage in wise enterprise which will benefit others. In turn, their reputation will be enhanced because their wealth is used properly. Not so with **fools.** Whether rich or poor, their **foolishness** only produces more foolishness. Thus, whatever money they have will only feed their foolish hearts.

The foolishness of fools is folly (foolishness). Wisdom does not produce wealth, or vice-versa. By God's grace, Solomon had both wisdom and wealth, but that's not the norm. However, a wise man will make a living, and what he does with his money will be wise. On the other hand, fools will be fools and nothing but fools, no matter how much wealth they possess.

Prov. 14:25

"A true witness delivereth souls: but a deceitful witness speaketh lies."

There's something to be said about the correlation between truth and deliverance. Jesus said:

"And ye shall know the truth, and the truth shall make you free," (John 8:32)

The battle rages between Truth and deception; between God and Satan. **A true** (faithful) **witness delivereth** (constantly rescues) **souls: but a deceitful** (false or fraudulent) **witness speaketh lies.**

Lies or deceptions do not rescue souls from sin. Yet, deceived people are not deterred from peddling their falsehood. Satan is the "father of lies," opposing Truth on every hand. Thus, the warfare continues while we attempt to proclaim the Truth, trusting the Holy Spirit to rescue souls from the clutches of Satan.

Prov. 14:26

"In the fear of the LORD is strong confidence: and his children shall have a place of refuge."

The fear of the LORD is many things, as seen repeatedly in **Proverbs.** Here it is the believer's **strong confidence** or security. Confidence is comprised of hope, trust, and assurance, all products of faith in and reverence for **the LORD.** What a refuge from the onslaughts of sin and Satan!

Such security in Christ is contagious. It influences others around us, especially our children. The security of a parent becomes a source of confidence for children. Reverence for God is the true basis of a secure home within a troubled and insecure world.

Prov. 14:27

"The fear of the LORD is a fountain of life, to depart from the snares of death."

Not only is **the fear of the LORD** our strong confidence and security, but it also wells up within us **a fountain of life.** There's an overflow from the inner flow of God's Spirit that brings abundant blessing to self and others. Jesus said to His disciples:

"He that believeth on me, as the scripture hath said, out of his belly (innermost being) *shall flow rivers of living water."* (John 7:38)

O, the gushing forth of indescribable joy from those who believe God and take Him seriously! We can't separate fearing God from believing God, or obeying Him. Noah is described as the man who;

"By faith (believing) *Noah, being warned of God of things not seen as yet, moved with fear, prepared an ark to the saving of his house."* (Hebrews 11:7)

Notice how his faith moved, or obeyed, motivated by the fear of God.

So the fear of God (FOG) not only offers inner security (confidence), but provides escape from that which would kill us. Believing (fearing) God not only insures abundant life, but consequently keeps us from the **snares of death** (cf. Prov. 13:14).

Prov. 14:28

"In the multitude of people is the king's honour: but in the want of people is the destruction of the prince."

In the multitude (abundance) **of people is the king's honour** (beauty). The king's honor goes beyond his authority and wealth; it has to do with the loving support of his people. A righteous ruler will draw the right kind of subjects. Such was the life of King Solomon himself, who had the hearts of the people (1 Kings 4:21).

The contrasting scene is one of demise and **destruction of the prince**, for lack of the people's support. No reason is given, but no ruler can endure for long without a faithful following. How rewarding it is to have the hearts and loyalty of the people you lead. The Apostle Paul expresses this sentiment in Philippians 4:1, when addressing his..."*brethren dearly beloved and longed for, my joy and crown.*"

Prov. 14:29

"He that is slow to wrath is of great understanding: but he that is hasty of spirit exalteth folly."

This statement is an example of and urging to longsuffering, one of the fruits of the Spirit (Galatians 5:22, 23). Being **slow to wrath is of great understanding**, a gracious virtue. The Hebrew word translated "wrath" means "nose or nostril," depicting rapid breathing, accompanied by anger.

Suffering long with others is a gift of God's enabling. However, sometimes getting angry for the right cause is also a matter of grace.

In contrast, the writer proclaims the **hasty** (short tempered) **of spirit exalteth** (promotes) **folly** or foolishness (cf. Prov. 14:17; 16:32). James speaks clearly to this issue:

"Wherefore, my beloved brethren, let every man be swift to hear, slow to speak, slow to wrath....But the wisdom that is from above is first pure, then peaceable, gentle, and easy to be intreated, full of mercy and good fruits, without partiality, and without hypocrisy," (James 1:19; 3:17)

Prov. 14:30

"A sound heart is the life of the flesh: but envy the rottenness of the bones."

How the heart and body are intertwined and synchronized! **A sound heart is the life of the flesh** (body). Whether it's the physical or spiritual heart, it is influenced by its relationship to the LORD who gave it. The Hebrew word "*marpay*" means "sound, a wholesome cure." A heart right with God has a reviving effect on the body. Jesus came *"that they might have life, and that they might have it more abundantly."* (John 10:10).

One thing is for sure: **envy** (jealousy) is **rottenness** (decaying) to **the bones.** A covetous, selfish heart will decay the bones. The spiritual condition of a person directly affects the physical condition, one way or another. Inner peace serves as a medicine to one's entire being.

cf. sound	Prov. 4:23; Psalm 119:80; 2 Timothy 1:7
rottenness	Prov. 3:8, 12:4, 17:22

Prov. 14:31

"He that oppresseth the poor reproacheth his Maker: but he that honoureth him hath mercy on the poor."

The central thought of this verse is that one's action and attitude toward the poor reveal his love or hatred for God, the Creator. Since the Lord has **mercy on the poor** (cf. Prov. 19:17, 22:22, 23), those who oppress or defraud them reproach (defy) his (the poor's) **Maker.** Likewise, the one who honors (*"kabadh"* or glorifies) **him** (God) **hath mercy on the poor.**

Thus, as we walk with God, we carry and reflect His burdens. What concerns Him, concerns us. Therefore, we extend His love to others, including the poor, as He would if He were still present on Earth. As believers, we are the extension of His heart and life. (John 15:1)

Prov. 14:32

"The wicked is driven away in his wickedness: but the righteous hath hope in his death"

There's a difference between the life and death of both the wicked and the righteous! This is the recurring theme, not only in the book of **Proverbs**, but the whole **Bible!**

In this verse, there's a relatively unique thought regarding the "driving force" of sin (See Prov.13:21). The ungodly do not always simply "fall" into sin. There's such a thing as "supernatural flesh"; i.e., the work of Satan who takes advantage of sinful flesh and "drives" one into greater sin and darkness. This is illustrated in Genesis 3, when the serpent pressured Eve to eat the forbidden fruit. Certainly, King Saul was demonically driven in his hateful attempts to kill David (1 Samuel 18:9ff.).

As it is in life, so it is in death. The wicked is overcome by his wickedness, and then faces the judgment of God at the end (Hebrews 9:27). He has no refuge and no hope then! What a horror! Thank God **the righteous hath hope in his death.** Our hope is in the Lord, who alone applies the righteousness of Christ to all who trust Him. Hallelujah! What a Savior!

Prov. 14:33

"Wisdom resteth in the heart of him that hath understanding: but that which is in the midst of fools is made known."

For sure, **wisdom resteth in the heart of him that hath understanding.** His conduct, expressions, discussions, etc. reflect that inner understanding. Much of the time, it is manifested silently by his attitude and touch. On the other hand, **that which is in the midst of fools is made known.** Regardless of where people are coming from, it will betray them eventually. Fools are quick to reveal their lack of wisdom. Thus, foolishness runs rampant **in the midst of fools** (cf. 12:23; 13:16; 15:2).

Prov. 14:34

"Righteousness exalteth a nation: but sin is a reproach to any people."

Solomon ends this chapter on a national level, which he himself understood. His kingdom was unique in that it was a reign of peace and relative righteousness. It pictures the coming Millennial reign of the "Greater than Solomon," Jesus Christ, who will reign in perfect righteousness. Thus, the character of the king has tremendous bearing on the quality and direction of his kingdom. In the course of history, **righteousness exalteth** (raises on high) **a nation: but sin is a reproach** (disgrace) **to any people.** Godly leaders affect their country for good, while the reign of sin is an abomination to all, including God. Sin destroys!

Prov. 14:35

"The king's favour is toward a wise servant: but his wrath is against him that causeth shame."

A wise man delights in wisdom found on any level, whether among peers, children, or employees. This was true with Solomon, whose wisdom was injected into his servants, thus reaping delight in his soul. Such is the case with a father toward his son (e.g., Prov. 15:20). **The king's favour** could include benevolent blessing and favorable deeds toward his servants, placing them on the status of his "sons" (See Prov. 17:2). However, the same king is angry toward those who **causeth shame** or disgrace. No man sins to himself. He always affects others. A wise man knows these facts.

Chapter 15
A Soft Answer Turns Away Wrath

Prov. 15:1

"A soft answer turneth away wrath: but grievous words stir up anger."

This is a sound principle (not a promise) concerning the power and tone of speech. **A soft** (tender, gentle) **answer** (response, reply) **turneth away** (defuses) **wrath** (heated anger). It's so easy to fight fire with fire, but a kind or gentle response to another's angry words can take them off guard. Again, this is a principle, not a promise; i.e., it may not always work. But it certainly is in line with the earnest urging "not to render evil for evil, but overcome evil with good" (Romans 12:17-21). Solomon speaks further of wrathful men in Proverbs 10:12, 15:13, 28:25, and 29:22.

But grievous (hurtful, painful) **words stir up anger** (angry puffing of the nostrils). Words are powerful and incite various reactions, even a *"world of iniquity,"* according to James 3. Great care must be taken in how and what we speak. It's been said that more wounds have been inflicted by the edge of the tongue than by the edge of the sword. One difference is that sword wounds heal, but tongue wounds may never heal!

Prov. 15:2

"The tongue of the wise useth knowledge aright: but the mouth of fools poureth out foolishness."

Wise people have wise tongues. We basically speak what we are and what we think. Thus, **the tongue of the wise useth** (continually uses) **knowledge aright** (i.e., to make glad or well; skillfully).

But the mouth of fools poureth (gushes forth) **foolishness** (folly or silliness). Knowledge is always with us and can either be used or abused. Like material things, a godly man will use words to bring positive help to others. There's a great need to build-up one another in the faith.

James 3 is a whole chapter devoted to this subject. How revealing and powerful is man's tongue. It is either a blessing or a blight! Indeed, he that doesn't offend with his tongue is a mature man. Listen to someone speak for a time and they will reveal their hearts!

Again, Jesus said, *"out of the abundance of the heart the mouth speaketh,"* Thus, the need to be "born again," receiving a new heart and a renewed tongue.

Prov. 15:3

"The eyes of the LORD are in every place, beholding the evil and the good."

If **the eyes of the Lord are in every place,** then He is all-seeing and all-knowing or omniscient. This characteristic of God is not a quality of mankind.

The issue in this proverb is that our God beholds (observes) **the evil and the good.** Nothing good or bad escapes His all-seeing eyes. What man does openly or in secret does not go unnoticed by the Omnipresent LORD! That can work both ways, either for or against us. Unlike man, God sees the heart and the motivation of deeds. The evil will one day be exposed openly in the Judgment for unbelievers. The secret things done by believers will be rewarded openly at the Judgment Seat. (See the example of Asa in 1 Kings 15:11, and Omni in 1 Kings 16:25).

This verse extols the Lord's Omniscience, but the matter of **beholding the evil** needs further explanation. The "evil" is not necessarily sin or wickedness. The Hebrew word "*raah*" can also be translated as "unpleasant or miserable." See Isaiah 45:7 and 47:11, and Prov. 12:21 and 13:17. Thus, the Lord sees EVERYTHING, good or bad, so there's nowhere to hide! (Psalm 139:7-10).

236

2 Chronicles 16:9 says:

"For the eyes of the LORD run to and fro throughout the whole earth, to shew himself strong in the behalf of them whose heart is perfect toward him. Herein thou hast done foolishly: therefore from henceforth thou shalt have wars."

Prov. 15:4

"A wholesome tongue is a tree of life: but perverseness therein is a breach in the spirit."

A wholesome (healing, healthy, sound) **tongue is a tree of life.** A tongue connected to a wise and sound heart becomes a tree planted firmly, giving forth spiritual life. The tongue of a Spirit-filled believer ministers grace and vitality to the hearer. Therein is the power of life and death. We either build up or tear down when we speak (James 3).

To the contrary, **perverseness** (crookedness) **therein is a breach** (fracture, breaking, shattering) **in the spirit** (*"ruach"* or mind). Again, what power the tongue has! A perverted, vile tongue kills! Words can and do hurt us. Some wicked people are powerful and effective communicators, influencing badly the weak souls to sin.

Prov. 15:5

"A fool despiseth his father's instruction: but he that regardeth reproof is prudent."

How a child responds to his immediate authority (e.g., parents) indicates whether he's foolish or wise. **A fool despiseth** (scorns) **his father's instruction** (discipline). God has established the family unit not only to procreate children, but to train and nurture them. A child is a fool if he will not listen to his father, who represents God in that family. The father represents and encourages a humble attitude when confronted by the Lord Himself in saving grace. We're in a spiritual family where our Heavenly Father trains or chastens His children. Hebrews 12:5 says:

"My son, despise not thou the chastening of the Lord...."

On the positive side, **he that regardeth** (heeds, observes)

reproof is prudent. Submission and obedience to what's right is the foundation of right and effective living. *"To obey is better than sacrifice"* (1 Samuel 15). Religious activity (going to church, Bible reading, good deeds, etc.) is no substitute for obeying God, and that obedience begins at home. Even salvation is a matter of obeying *"from the heart"* the Gospel of Christ (Romans 6:18). True faith is DOING what God commands! How we respond to parents is how we respond to God. That's the real issue of parental discipline: preparing children to submit to the Holy Spirit's call.

In regard to "reproof," training is both positive and negative. 2 Timothy 3:16 and 17, reveals the Source and purpose of the Word of God.

> *"[It] is profitable for doctrine, for reproof, for correction, for instruction in righteousness...."* (3:17)

The total picture of God's training program is: "doctrine" – basic information for the soul; "reproof" – showing what's wrong with our lives; "correction" – how to remedy what's wrong; "instruction in righteousness" – taking us on from the starting line, down the right road of spiritual maturity.

Thus, to obey parental teaching and to submit to godly discipline are "prudent" or wise. "Prudent" means "to be subtle or shrewd," That can certainly be a positive quality in grace. There's discernment in the affairs of life, where we must be as *"wise as serpents, and harmless as doves."* The great need in our day, especially in the Church, is the gift of discernment.

Prov. 15:6

> *"In the house of the righteous is much treasure: but in the revenues of the wicked is trouble."*

Whoever lives in a house determines what kind of household it will be. A house, like a car, is neutral. It's the family that makes the difference. This verse contrasts the "righteous" versus the "wicked" family.

The **righteous** family has **much treasure** (abundance, wealth). Riches are not always wealth. A little is much when God is in it.

Having excessive amounts of money does not constitute success or happiness (refer to Ecclesiastes 2). The "much treasure" in the "righteous" household has to be genuine wealth and blessing, as opposed to riches. Needs are met when a family seeks first the Kingdom of God (Matthew 6:33). If there's an abundance of money, it will then be used for the glory of God.

In contrast, **the revenues** (income, gain) **of the wicked is trouble** (stirred up). This may be legitimate income, but the wickedness within brings trouble and not blessing. Lifestyle dictates the use of money; e.g., smokers and drinkers spend well-earned dollars on sinful and health-destroying habits. Thus, they reap what they have sown.

Prov. 15:7

"The lips of the wise disperse knowledge: but the heart of the foolish doeth not so."

Among other things, lips are an instrument of communication, good or bad. Every time one opens his mouth, the words are either building up or destroying, blessing or cursing. Here **the lips of the wise** illustrate the treasure of the righteous in Prov. 15:6. They spread true knowledge or that which builds one up. Prov. 11:30 states:

"The "fruit (lips) *of the righteous is a tree of life...."*

A right heart will produce right fruit, manifested through the lips (See Prov. 7:10; 8:6; 10:13, 21, 32).

On the other hand, **the heart of the foolish doeth not so.** A fool can only communicate foolishness or what's in his foolish heart. You can't speak higher than you think and live (James 3:6). Solomon refers a lot to the harlot who sells her wares via her lips that drip honeycomb; i.e., she's a sweet talker. The effective street walker must be a sweet talker! So are many fools who must make up for lack of content by sordid, smooth words.

It must also be said that a foolish heart is revealed by what is not said. Some speak knowledge, but leave out the weighty matters of the whole truth. For instance, some preachers speak a positive gospel without ever offending the sinner by dealing with sin and God's judgment.

Prov. 15:8

"The sacrifice of the wicked is an abomination to the LORD: but the prayer of the upright is his delight."

We have a tendency to judge people by their external deeds and religious activities. However, God judges according to the heart. This proverb illustrates this truth. It's not uncommon to hear lost people say, "I say my prayers every night," or "I give to the Rescue Mission." In fact, the Apostle Paul spoke of the futility of one "giving his body to be burned" (sacrificed) without love *(agape)*; i.e., sacrificing oneself without glorifying God. "*...whatsoever ye do, (*in word or deed), *do all to the glory of God."* Anything else is an abomination!

So religious exercise without Christ in your heart is unacceptable to God.

"Not by works of righteousness which we have done, but according to his mercy he saved us, by the washing of regeneration, and renewing of the Holy Ghost." (Titus 3:5)

How religious some sinners try to be! It's to no avail.

In contrast, **the prayer of the upright is His delight.** The Hebrew word for "upright" is *"yashar,"* meaning "straight." It's translated "blessed" in Psalm 1:1. The prayer of the blessed delights the heart of the LORD! Amen.

Prov. 15:9

"The way of the wicked is an abomination unto the Lord: but he loveth him that followeth after righteousness."

Not only is the "sacrifice" of the wicked an abomination to the LORD, but **the way** (lifestyle) **of the wicked** is too. Perverted religious deeds stem from a perverted lifestyle from a perverted heart. Only God fully knows the heart. However, *"by their fruits ye shall know them,"* The fruit of the wicked manifests a wicked heart. Thankfully, God is the final Judge (Matthew 7:1).

But he loveth him that followeth after righteousness. This is a beautiful statement of God's delight in His obedient children; i.e., those who have been declared righteous or justified by faith. We are the friends of God who have been born into His family; the result of a new lifestyle, evident by a heart's desire to follow after God (Philippians 3:13).

Israel grieved Jehovah's heart by its unrighteous deeds (Isaiah 1:1, 11). In contrast, those who constantly "follow after" the Word bring God great delight. This describes His ongoing love and affection toward His children who obey. For instance, a good father loves his children unconditionally, but there's a special delight and expression of love toward children who love to obey.

Prov. 15:10

"Correction is grievous unto him that forsaketh the way: and he that hateth reproof shall die."

The wayward cannot handle correction! Someone once said: "A man convinced against his will, is of the same opinion still." One who **forsaketh** (refuses) **the way** (the right path of life), refuses **correction.** Any **reproof** or discipline is **grievous unto him** (unpleasant to him). Righteousness is foreign to an unrighteous man. It rubs him the wrong way! He is only comfortable doing what his wicked heart dictates.

The second clause gives the reason for his grief. He hates **reproof.** He refuses to do right, thus, he doesn't want to hear what's wrong. Therefore he **shall die** (physically and spiritually). *"For the wages of sin is death"* (Romans 3:23). A rebuke could be a godsend to someone who wants to repent. Thank God for the preaching which can save the lost, turning souls *"from idols, to serve the living and true God"* (1 Thessalonians 1:9).

Prov. 15:11

"Hell and destruction are before the LORD: how much more then the hearts of the children of men?"

This is a vivid and powerful description of the LORD's

omniscience (all-knowingness). Even the depths and mystery of **Hell and destruction** cannot escape His all-seeing eyes! What chance, then, does puny man have to dodge the One in whose presence all things are naked? Not just the actions of men, but their very hearts are totally exposed before Him. That which is spoken in secret, will be "shouted from the roof tops" one day. (Job 26:6, 38:17)

Psalm 9:17 leaves no doubt that hell is a place of punishment. God's justice will be glorified in Heaven, as well as Hell.

Prov. 15:12

"A scorner loveth not one that reproveth him: neither will he go unto the wise."

The gist of this verse is that a mocker doesn't like the one who attempts to set him straight; nor will the **scorner** want to get near to a **wise** man. When you're wrong, you despise those who are right. In addition, a fool doesn't "buddy up" with **the wise.** (See Prov. 9:7, 8; 15:10).

For the same reason, a disobedient saint dislikes preaching about righteousness. He not only rejects the message, but the messenger as well. Interestingly, when a scorner repents, he then desires fellowship with the wise. We desire to be with those who are like us.

Prov. 15:13

"A merry heart maketh a cheerful countenance: but by sorrow of the heart the spirit is broken."

A joyful heart is normally manifested by a happy face, just like a heavy heart is reflected by a sad facial expression. Of course, there are those who just always put on a happy face, like the song: "Smile Though Your Heart is Breaking." However, **by sorrow of the heart the spirit is broken.** The Hebrew word for "spirit" (*ruach*) is not synonymous with "heart," but indicates the mind or the inner flow of life. It has to do with courage and vitality.

Prov. 15:14

"The heart of him that hath understanding seeketh knowledge: but the mouth of fools feedeth on foolishness."

The heart seeks its own; i.e., the nature of man feeds on that which further stimulates that nature or **heart.** That's why a new babe in Christ will desire the pure milk of the Word (1 Peter 2:2). His heart now gravitates to the new knowledge of grace, because he has a new understanding (discernment).

In contrast, **the mouth** (foolish talk) **of fools feedeth on foolishness.** With a constant desire to talk, and not think, the fool feeds on what motivates him, foolishness! Wesley's commentary says, "Foolishness – Wickedness is meat and drink to them (fools)."

Prov. 15:15

"All the days of the afflicted are evil: but he that is of a merry heart hath a continual feast."

The "afflicted" means "depressed in mind and circumstances; needy or weak. Thus, **all the days of the afflicted are evil** (bad). This describes the unrighteous and foolish person whose life is filled with affliction.

In contrast, one with **a merry** (good, glad, or happy) **heart hath a continual** (ongoing or constant) **feast** (banquet). The joy of the Lord proceeds as a river from the wise man's heart. Merriment is the perpetual fruit of a heart right with God. Even work and unfavorable responsibilities still bring pleasure because of the grace of the Lord (Philippians 4:13, 19; Psalm 1). On the surface, the God-fearing life may look like a famine, and the sinful lifestyle like a feast, but, in reality, the very opposite is true!

Prov. 15:16

"Better is little with the fear of the LORD than great treasure and trouble therewith."

This principle is so contrary to the secular and material world view! "Stuff" seems to be the object and goal of life, regardless of the corresponding heartache. Solomon emphasizes living in **the fear**

of the LORD (Prov. 1:7) as primary, regardless of financial wealth. Solomon speaks from experience since he had both *"treasure and trouble"* (see Ecclesiastes 1 and 2).

So, many people live for money rather than God. Even some churches focus on the abundance of "health and wealth" at the expense of witnessing as faithful saints of God. Whatever happened to: *"...seek ye first the kingdom of God, and his righteousness!"* Indeed, little is much, when God is in it! Remember, it's not money itself that's the problem, but the LOVE of it! (1 Timothy 6:10)

Prov. 15:17

"Better is a dinner of herbs where love is, than a stalled ox and hatred therewith."

How many people enjoy the choice (**stalled**) cut of meat (**ox**), but find it tasteless because of a bitter spirit (**hatred therewith**). In contrast, it's **better** to eat meagerly (**herbs)** while sitting in an atmosphere of **love.**

What a commentary on family meal time, where the emphasis is on love, rather than the meal itself. Hatred destroys family enjoyment and gives the enemy (Satan) an opportunity to "eat our lunch," (or rob proper digestion).

Prov. 15:18

"A wrathful man stirreth up strife: but he that is slow to anger appeaseth strife."

Fire begets fire! **A wrathful man** (heated with anger) **stirreth up strife.** The world is filled with such people. It's hard to have an angry heart without it being manifested. However, the angry man instigates and enjoys stirring up contention. Some folks wouldn't know how to live if they couldn't fight about something.

On the contrary, the man who **is slow to anger** (long-suffering) **appeaseth** (quiets or settles) **strife.** He is a mediator, one who settles a dispute and brings peace. He is a peace-maker, rather than a peace-breaker!

Prov. 15:19

"The way of the slothful man is as an hedge of thorns: but the way of the righteous is made plain."

This verse describes two different roads traveled by two different men. First, the **slothful** or lazy **man** is on a rough road or course of life, riddled with **thorns.** Everything is difficult for him because it involves the expenditure of energy, which is contrary to his lazy lifestyle. To those looking for the easy road, nothing is easy!

In contrast, **the way of the righteous is made plain** (smooth). The K&D commentary translates "plain" as "paved." O, the beauty and blessing of obeying God! (cf. Isaiah 40:3, Psalm 1:3)

Prov. 15:20

"A wise son maketh a glad father: but a foolish man despiseth his mother."

This proverb correlates with Prov. 10:1: *"A wise son maketh a glad father,"* The Hebrew word for "glad" is *"samach,"* from the root "to brighten up." To watch a son order his life aright brightens up his father, bringing great joy. Some things are just beyond monetary wealth! To the degree that a wise son gladdens his father's heart, the opposite is the heart of the grieved **mother** of **a foolish man!** Instead of expressing gratitude, the fool despises or dishonors his mother.

Prov. 15:21

"Folly is joy to him that is destitute of wisdom: but a man of understanding walketh uprightly."

Ignorance can be "bliss," but not without disastrous results! The fool and the righteous have different perspectives on life. Rich or poor, a fool lives for this world and himself, with no regard for eternity. Thus, he can have **joy** in his **folly,** without concern for consequences.

On the other hand, **a man of understanding walketh uprightly.** He makes the right choices, and has an upright lifestyle. It is not "whatever makes you happy" that brings true happiness or holiness. Decisions are not to be made by emotion, but by a sanctified will.

Martin Luther said: *"We need to live as though Christ was crucified yesterday, risen today, and coming tomorrow."* A great challenge!

Prov. 15:22

"Without counsel purposes are disappointed: but in the multitude of counsellers they are established."

Input and communication with wise people is good advice. It enables one to glean from the experiences of others, promoting safety and confirmation of proposed plans or **purposes.** (cf. Prov. 11:14, 20:18) Many a man goes "half-cocked" into a business endeavor without wise **counsel**, only to end up **disappointed.**

On the other hand, **in the multitude** (abundance) **of counselors they** (purposes or plans) **are established** (confirmed to succeed). It's just wise to seek wise advice. We need not learn everything the hard way. Let us learn from the mistakes and successes of others.

Prov. 15:23

"A man hath joy by the answer of his mouth: and a word spoken in due season, how good is it!"

Words have great power and influence, especially when spoken at the right time. That's the gist of this verse. More specifically, one's proper **answer** produces **joy.** The latter part says **a word spoken in due season, how good is it** (how pleasant and valuable it is)! Solomon says:

"To every thing there is a season, and a time to every purpose under the heaven" (Ecclesiastes 3:1).

Abigail's mediation on behalf of King David is a beautiful example (1 Samuel 25:32, 33). *Jamieson-Fausset-Brown Commentary* on this verse says, "Good advice blesses the giver and the receiver."

Prov. 15:24

"The way of life is above to the wise, that he may depart from hell beneath."

Life reaches heavenward from its Source. Even nature's plants, trees, flowers, etc. generally grow toward the sun. So, a wise man's **way of life** or lifestyle emanates from **above**, where *"Where Christ sitteth on the right hand of God"* (Colossians 3:1). His **way of life is above** because he's born again from **above.** Thus, his journey on Earth is focused on a heavenly perspective. He lives with eternity in view. That's wisdom!

Hell is in the opposite direction or **beneath.** The believer has been delivered from an eternity in **hell**, but currently is influenced by it from the flesh (Romans 7). Thus, he must *"seek those things which are above"* so as to avoid the sinful magnetism of the underworld. The wise man will, *"Walk in the Spirit and ye shall not fulfil the lust of the flesh"* (Galatians 5:16). Hell must be shunned, whether in the present or future. Therefore, *"...seek ye first the kingdom of God"* with face toward Heaven and back toward Hell.

Prov. 15:25

"The LORD will destroy the house of the proud: but he will establish the border of the widow."

The Lord destroys, but He also establishes or restores. Indeed, **the proud** or arrogant man will one day meet with God's judgment. Here, the emphasis is on the destruction of his household, not merely his **house** per se. The arrogant and lofty sow seeds of evil, which negatively affect their families. The so-called famous of this world often fall as quickly as they arose, dying without dignity or an honorable legacy.

In contrast, the Lord loves the righteous **widow** and establishes her **border** (house, land, welfare, and legacy). The inference is that she has a humble, obedient spirit toward **the LORD**, which He loves. Catch God's attitude toward the widows in the following verses: Deuteronomy 10:18, Psalm 68:5, Psalm 146:9, and James 1:27).

Prov. 15:26

*"The thoughts of the wicked are an abomination to the LORD:
but the words of the pure are pleasant words."*

God sees the heart! He weighs intentions, motives, and imaginations. The wicked are first wicked in their heart, from which comes sinful actions and words. Thus, **the thoughts of the wicked are an abomination** (disgusting idolatry) **to the LORD.** Let's face the fact that God hates the wicked! "God *is angry with the wicked every day"* (Psalm 7:11). *"The wicked shall be turned into hell, and all the nations that forget God"* (Psalm 9:17) Try as we may, we can't water this down.

Yes, Christ died for the ungodly so that by repentant faith those separated from God could be reconciled to Him (cf. Romans 3:22f.). Jesus said:

"...except ye repent, ye shall all likewise perish." (Luke 13:3, 5)

That's why even a top-notch religious man like Nicodemus needed to be "born again"; i.e., receive a new heart to replace the wicked one (John 3:10). In contrast, the **pure** heart (regenerated by grace) produces **pleasant words.** Gracious words are the fruit of a new heart, pleasing God. There is a vast difference between the wicked and the righteous, between sinners and saints, and between the lost and the saved.

Prov. 15:27

"He that is greedy of gain troubleth his own house; but he that hateth gifts shall live."

Greed can only destroy in the long run! The words **greedy of gain** come from the same Hebrew root *"batsa,"* meaning "to covet, plunder or gain through unrighteous means," It pictures one given over or controlled by the lust of covetousness; i.e., he's determined to get what he wants, no matter the cost or effect on others. Thus, he **troubleth** (disturbs) **his own house** (household), having no regard for their well-being and tranquility. Surely, no man sins to himself. His sin always involves others.

In contrast, **he that hateth gifts** (bribes) shall live (prosper). Everyone loves legitimate gifts, but not those received with "strings attached"; i.e., for illicit purposes. A wise man will do right even when tempted to get "rich quick" by unlawful means.

Prov. 15:28

"The heart of the righteous studieth to answer: but the mouth of the wicked poureth out evil things."

A righteous heart will express itself righteously, because *"out of the abundance of the heart, the mouth speaketh."* The mark of a godly man or woman is the maturity and carefulness of his speech. He **studieth to answer;** i.e., he is careful to ponder or think through what his answer will be. The Hebrew word for study, *"hagah,"* translates "meditate" in Joshua 1:8, and Psalm 1:2. One who thinks before he speaks is the "perfect" or mature man to which James 3:1 refers.

In contrast, **the mouth of the wicked poureth** (gushes forth) **evil things.** Again, what is in the heart comes out, but in this case it gushes out with no forethought. How our words give us away! Indeed, the tongue has the capability to bless or curse, to build up or tear down, to foster life or death!

Prov. 15:29

"The LORD is far from the wicked: but he heareth the prayer of the righteous."

Among other things, this verse teaches that prayer is communication with the LORD, but one must be **righteous** to get an audience with Jehovah. He **is far** (removed) **from the wicked**, even though they may say prayers. Religion is an attempt to contact God Almighty without having a saving relationship with Him. This is an exercise in futility! Only the prayer of repentant faith in Jehovah's Son, Jesus the Messiah, will be honored by the Lord. (See Romans 10:9, 10, and 13). Those saved by Christ have personal access to the True and Living God, Who invites us to prayerfully enter His presence. Jesus said:

"...And when thou prayest, thou shalt not be as the hypocrites are: for they love to pray standing in the synagogues and in the corners of the streets, that they may be seen of men. Verily, I say unto you, They have their reward. But thou, when thou prayest, enter into thy closet, and when thou hast shut thy door, pray to thy Father which is in secret; and thy Father which seeth in secret shall reward thee openly." (Matthew 6:5, 6)

The Psalmist, King David, put it this way:

"The LORD is nigh unto all them that call upon him, to all that call upon Him in truth. He will fulfil the desire of them that fear him: he also will hear their cry, and will save them. The LORD preserveth all them that love him: but all the wicked will he destroy." (Psalm 145:18-20)

Prov. 15:30

"The light of the eyes rejoiceth the heart: and a good report maketh the bones fat."

This verse displays the tremendous influence of the eye and ear gates. How powerful is **the light of the eyes** to rejoice **the heart** (soul)! Solomon says in Ecclesiastes 11:7:

"Truly the light is sweet, and a pleasant thing it is for the eyes to behold the sun."

What a privilege it is to be blessed and joyous within through what we see. How awesome it is to stand on the brink of the Grand Canyon at sunset and behold the incredible, inexplicable handiwork of the Creator! Yet, this is only a foretaste of divine glory, when we stand before God who is the majestic and eternal Light of Heaven itself! (Revelation 21:23; 22:5). The Apostle John says:

"...we shall be like him; for we shall see him as he is." (1 John 3:2)

In like manner, how good is **a good report** (good news) to the soul. It's "medicine" to the body (Prov. 17:22) and *"cold waters to a thirsty soul"* (Prov. 25:25). Moreover, it **maketh the bones fat,** a term meaning spiritual prosperity. How enriching it is to hear the Word of God, the Good News of the Gospel! How well this message affects every aspect of one's life!

Prov. 15:31

"The ear that heareth the reproof of life abideth among the wise."

Everyone enjoys a "good report," (vs. 30), but the test of our character is how we receive a message (teaching) of **reproof** or correction. Some words do not "sound good" on the surface, but "hearing" (heeding) them will enrich our lives. **The reproof of life** is that instruction which "tends toward life," instead of death. The Word of God rebukes our sin so as to lead us to repentance and new life. It seems negative on the service, but when received by humble faith can save us forever!

The physician reveals to the patient that he has a cancerous tumor in his lung that must be removed to save his life. What a distasteful report! Yet, after a second opinion, he decides to "receive" the diagnosis and submit to the surgery. He does so to the saving of his life. So it is with receiving and heeding a word of rebuke to the soul. To obey here is to **abideth** (continue to dwell) **among the wise,** to demonstrate godly grace and skillful conduct.

Prov. 15:32

"He that refuseth instruction despiseth his own soul: but he that heareth reproof getteth understanding."

If receiving reproof "tends to life," then **he that refuseth instruction** (chastisement or warning) would "tend to death" or separation from life. Solomon depicts this principle as **despiseth his own soul** (spurning himself). God's rebuke and instruction, when heeded, result in abundant life and wholeness of soul. To refuse such is to not only sin against God, but also to damage one's self. Later, in Prov. 29:1, Solomon further warns: *"He, that being often reproved hardeneth his neck, shall suddenly be destroyed, and that without remedy."* Life and death have everything to do with obedience to God's Word (See Prov. 1:24-33 and 8:33-36).

On the other hand, he who **heareth reproof getteth** (procures, attains) **understanding** (*"labe"* or heart, moral character, determination). There's great reward in obeying God; viz., courage, wisdom, discretion, and further challenge to serve Him! Being a servant of the Most High God is a "win-win" situation!

Prov. 15:33

"The fear of the LORD is the instruction of wisdom; and before honour is humility."

According to the Hebrew construction, this first phrase can read: "The fear of the LORD is the instruction or discipline to wisdom"; i.e., the fear of God is the essential element that disciplines one in the school of wisdom (skillful living). Taking God seriously and walking by faith through life's obstacles develops God's wisdom (spiritual understanding) in one's soul. That's why *"The fear of the LORD is the beginning* (chief part) *of knowledge (and wisdom)"* (Prov. 1:7, etc.). Thus, "hearing reproof" (vs. 32) is essential to that process.

Likewise, **before** (in the face, in front of) **honour is humility;** i.e., submissiveness or meekness is prerequisite to honor ("*kabod*," weightiness, glory) before the Lord. This is the opposite condition reflected in Prov. 16:18:

"Pride goeth before destruction, and an haughty spirit before a fall."

Somehow, the self life (flesh) of the believer must suffer a "death blow" before he comes to a place of spiritual authority. *"For God resisteth the proud, and giveth grace to the humble"* (1 Peter 5:5).

Someone has said that before God really uses a man, He hurts and humbles him. The great Apostle Paul exemplifies this principle regarding his infirmities received after his "revelation" of Heaven. He sought the Lord three times to remove his "thorn in the flesh," only to hear God say:

"My grace is sufficient for thee: for my strength is made perfect in weakness."

To which Paul responds:

"Most gladly therefore will I rather glory in my infirmities, that the power of Christ may rest upon me....For when I am weak, then am I strong." (2 Corinthians 12:9, 10)

Luther adds:

"And ere one comes to honor, he must previously suffer."

Indeed, for the Christian, the way up is the way down; the way to receive is to give; the way to gain life is to give it away; to die to self is to live!

Chapter 16
The Preparations of the Heart Belong to Man

Prov. 16:1

"The preparations of the heart in man, and the answer of the tongue, is from the LORD."

At first glance, it seems that whatever is in man's heart (spirit) and tongue are ordered by the LORD. Jesus said that out of the abundance of the heart, the mouth speaks. So man's inner thoughts are projected by his tongue. However, this is not to say that man is a robot, with no thoughts of his own. Dictated by his nature, he has his own plans, etc., but his ability to answer or speak comes from the LORD.

In light of 16:2 and 9, this verse seems to indicate that whatever man's scheme or plan (of the heart), the Lord has the last word and is in full control. See Prov. 19:21; 21:1. Although difficult to understand, this statement extols God's ultimate sovereignty in the affairs of men.

At the very least, this verse teaches that the very ability to think and/or speak originates in God, the Creator. Certainly He reigns supreme over every thought and word of His creatures. As Jesus so aptly stated in John 15:5, *"Without me ye can do nothing"* (No Thing)!

Prov. 16:2

"All the ways of a man are clean in his own eyes; but the LORD weigheth the spirits."

All the ways (lifestyle, actions) **of man are clean** (right, pure) **in his own eyes** (estimation). We don't see ourselves as other do, especially how God sees. Amazingly, sin's depravity seems to blind us of our impurity and wickedness. We can't be objective because we are self-centered and myopic (short-sighted). It's "me, myself, and I"!

Man judges his acts on his own "standard," not God's. Thank God for conscience which may restrain man to some degree (see Romans 2:14, 15). But left to himself, man has a blurred sense of righteousness; and even when he knows what's right, doing it is another matter. "*For all have sinned and come short of the glory of God*"! (Romans 3:23)

The LORD, on the other hand, **weigheth** (constantly pondering, measuring, evaluating) **the spirits**"(*ruach* or inner spirit). God sees and judges on a different level or dimension. Man looks at the outside, but God looks at the heart. He judges motive and intent (Hebrews 4:12), while man is concerned about how he looks in front of others (or himself in the mirror).

We may be counting our good deeds, but God is weighing our hearts. Christian leaders may be counting "how many" are at the church meeting, while God is asking "how much." Outward deeds change, but without the new birth, the heart is still dead in sin. The focus must be on God, and what He sees. To be right in the vertical or upward relationship with God, is to be right in the horizontal relationship toward others.

Prov. 16:3

"Commit thy works unto the LORD, and thy thoughts shall be established."

This verse emphasizes the importance of exercising our redeemed will in action and thus affecting our thought life. That is the essence of FAITH. This is the other side of "thinking and thus doing." **Commit** (lit. roll upon) **thy works** (activity, deeds) **unto the LORD, and thy thoughts** (plan, purpose) **shall be established** (fixed or set up).

This word **"commit"** is used also in Psalm 37:5:

> *"Commit thy way unto the LORD; trust also in him; and he shall bring it to pass."*

There's the element of faith here in obeying God in our actions (regardless of feeling); thus, to establish our **thoughts**. The Apostle Paul says:

> *"...work out your own salvation...For it is God which worketh in you both to will and to do of his good pleasure."* (Philippians 2:12, 13)

God works from both ends! We must choose to do God's will, trusting His enabling grace. There is a mystical element here, but there's also a very practical lesson: It's all of God and all of us! We need to work like it all depends on us, while believing that it all depends on God.

There is also the idea here of developing new habits to replace the old. A man saved from alcoholism or drug addiction must now become "addicted" to the Word of God. Old habits must now be replaced by prayer, meditation and personal application to God's Word. Habits are good if they are the right ones. Do Right by choosing Right until Right becomes the norm. Of course, one can only do right *"through Christ which strengthenth me"* (Philippians 4:13).

Prov. 16:4

> *"The LORD hath made all things for himself: yea, even the wicked for the day of evil."*

This beautiful verse extols the LORD's sovereignty! He has **made all things for himself**; *The heavens declare the glory of God and the firmament sheweth his handywork* (Psalm 19:1); He even made *"man in his own image."* and, we are *"the sheep of his pasture...,"* etc. Revelation 4:11 states:

> *"Thou art worthy, O Lord, to receive glory and honour and power: for thou hast created all things, and for thy pleasure they are and were created."*

Not only has He made all things, but they were made for Him. God is Self-sustaining and needs nothing because He's God, but somehow He has ordained to "need" us; e.g., *"I am the vine, ye are the branches...."* He has ordained to bear His fruit in and through believers—what a divine privilege. COL 1:16

But more controversial is the latter part of the verse, stating that He's made **even the wicked for the day of evil**. This is not to say that God is the author of evil or sin—that was "found" in Lucifer who rebelled against God in heaven (see Ezekiel 28:13). But certainly God allowed and does allow Satan and the wicked to exist in this world. This is the **"day of evil"** which could refer to the whole scope of human history under the curse of sin, or could be related to times of judgment and calamity when the wicked were ordained to punish His people. (E.g., Babylonian captivity, Lamentations, etc.)

Whatever the case, *"the LORD God omnipotent reigneth"*! Nebuchadnezzar was used of God to punish Judah's wickedness, but he himself was later judged by God and eventually humbled by saving grace (Daniel 4). What a mighty God we serve!!

Prov. 16:5

"Every one that is proud in heart is an abomination to the LORD: though hand join in hand, he shall not be unpunished."

Pride is a horrible sin! In fact, it's the #1 sin, if there's any such thing. Lucifer fell from Heaven because of pride (Isaiah 14:12ff) and man has followed suit. Unbelief (e.g., Adam) issues from pride and self-trust. The "Cain spirit" was quickly manifested in Adam's children and confronts us to this day! Pride is that desire to take God's place and become gods ourselves.

Note that it's a matter of the **heart,** not just external show. Many **proud** people come off as humble souls so as to fool others. Judas talked about "feeding the poor" with the treasury, while scheming to betray the Saviour! How deceitful is sin!

Pride **is an abomination to the LORD**; i.e., God is disgusted (lit.) with it. It invokes His wrath and is counted as idolatry. Note that the issue isn't with drugs, booze, stealing, etc., but an inflated attitude of the heart. It's the root of all sin(s) and certainly explains the horrible condition of man; *"there is none that doeth good, no, not one"* (Romans 3:12).

Some feel that the strength of sin is in numbers. If enough of us hang together in our wickedness, we shall prevail. That was the attitude at Babel (see Genesis 11), when an army of men attempted to build the tower to Heaven. (e.g., United Nations). God judged them, confusing their language and ability to communicate. Wicked leaders "ganged up" on Jesus at the Crucifixion, but judgment is forth coming (Psalm 2); Man at his "best" and in conspiracy with a host of others, is no match for God. **...though hand join in hand, he shall not be unpunished.** None can escape the all-seeing eye of God and, thus, will never escape His impending Judgment! The only "escape" God has provided man from his sin is the Ark of Salvation; the Lord Jesus Christ, Who took the penalty of sin in our behalf! Amen.

Prov. 16:6

"By mercy and truth iniquity is purged: and by the fear of the LORD men depart from evil."

While pride (and all sin) is an *"abomination to the LORD"* and will meet with His judgment (vs.5), there is a remedy for sin. Thank God that **by mercy and truth iniquity is purged**. Psalm 85:10 is a commentary on this thought:

"Mercy and truth are met together; righteousness and peace have kissed each other."

This illustrates what happened at the Cross where these attributes culminated in Christ to bring about salvation for sinners.

At the Cross, the truth of man's condition (sin) was met by God's **mercy**! "Mercy there was great, and grace was free"! Sin could not be overlooked, but had to be dealt with in condemnation. Christ alone became the "Sin-offering" so that **iniquity** could be **purged** (lit. covered, atoned for—*Kaphar*; e.g., Leviticus 16). Here man's true state was remedied by God's **"mercy"** alone; *"Not by works of righteousness...but according to his mercy he saved us"* (Titus 3:5).

Mercy and grace are two sides of the same coin. By mercy, we do not get what we deserve—Hell and judgment; in grace, we receive what we don't deserve—Heaven and forgiveness! All this came into play at the Cross. David goes on to say: *"righteousness and peace have kissed each other."* What a romance of God's grace! God's righteous nature demanded the payment of sin if man was to have peace with God. That was accomplished at the Cross, prophesied by Isaiah 53:5, 6:

> *"But he was wounded for our transgressions... the chastisement of (for the purpose of) our peace was upon him; and with his stripes we are healed. All we like sheep have gone astray... and the Lord hath laid on him the iniquity of us all.*

Amen! In Christ, the righteous demands of God were met so that the sinner could be reconciled to the Holy God! *"Therefore, being justified (declared righteous) by faith, we have PEACE with God through our Lord Jesus Christ"* (Romans 5:1). At the Cross, "righteousness and peace kissed each other." Glory to God!

The second part of this proverb seems to be the result of justifying grace—"departing from evil." There's not only justification at the Cross, but sanctification as well. (See 1 Corinthians 1:30). "The fear of the LORD (Jehovah—the "I AM") is another expression of true faith—taking God seriously. Because of the **"purging"** of sin, I can now **depart from evil.** I have power over sin because I have become a "new creature" in Christ (2Corinthians 5:17). Greater is he that is in me, than he that is in the world (Satan)! True salvation always produces true righteousness (practical). *"As ye have therefore received Christ Jesus the Lord, so walk ye in him."*

Salvation is not just a profession; it is a possession of Christ. Thus, it must be somehow manifested in everyday life. Another way of saying that justifying grace is always followed by sanctifying obedience. (Ephesians 2:8-10).

Prov. 16:7

"When a man's ways please the LORD, he maketh even his enemies to be at peace with him."

It's significant that Jesus drew the "common people who gladly heard him." The early church also had "favor with all the people (i.e., common)" (Acts 2:47). While the religionists hated Christ and His followers, they had trouble finding fault with their lives. Their attack had to be against their "religious views," as was the case with Daniel of old.

So in a hostile world, there's a sense in which a God-fearing man can live in peace with those who oppose the Gospel. This proverb is a simple statement of how a godly lifestyle ministers to others. It speaks of the fruit of love, etc. coming forth from the believer that reaches out for even his enemies. That disarms unbelievers! So today, we can be *"full of grace and truth"* as was Jesus. He demonstrated "grace" which led to speaking the "truth" to sinners.

Our lifestyle is an entree to the Gospel. We are to love people as people, with no hidden agenda. "What the world needs now is love, sweet love," so the song goes. They respond to that love, regardless of their religious views. In addition, we need to *"overcome evil with good"* in dealing with our enemies.

Prov. 16:8

"Better is a little with righteousness than great revenues without right."

What a commentary on the rightness of living right regardless of financial increase! In a day when money is god, people make major decisions solely on "how much does it pay." Integrity and wisdom are after-thoughts when God's Word is left out. But Solomon puts it all in perspective when he says, **"Better is a little with righteousness** (rightness, virtue) **than great revenues** (lit. abundant increase) **without right** (justice, as in a right verdict)."

What a man is, is more important than what he possesses. That's not to say that all wealthy people are void of integrity, however, in a fallen world that duo seems rare. The believer's emphasis needs to be on virtuous character, trusting God for resources (Matthew 6:23). We can "make it" on little when walking uprightly. It's been said: "Little is much when God is in it."

Great wealth is not wrong in itself, but when obtained illegitimately, it can never satisfy. The best things in life are free, the song says, thus, selling our soul for money is not only unwise, but dangerous. Again the word of Jesus is apropos: *"For what shall it profit a man, if he shall gain the whole world, and lose his own soul?"* Many people may be wealthy financially who are paupers in God's sight. Material wealth does not insure true riches.

Prov. 16:9

"A man's heart deviseth his way: but the LORD directeth his steps."

Along with 16:1, this could be considered a mystical statement—especially if the man is wicked. **"Deviseth"** means here "to think upon, plan, consider" (piel imperf.), rather than the negative inference of "plotting or scheming." So it's safe to say that this is a righteous man, thinking through his **way** or path of life; he plans to do thus and so, if it be God's will.

In the final analysis **the LORD directeth** (lit. establishes) **his steps.** We plan, but God directs (3:5, 6). Indeed, *"the steps of a good man are ordered by the Lord."* Here is man's responsibility and God's sovereignty coming together. I work like it all depends on me, while trusting God like it all depends on Him!

K&D has a helpful observation here:

> The result and issue are thus of God, and the best is, that in all his deliberations one should give himself up without self-confidence and arrogance to the guidance of God, that one should do his duty and leave the rest, with humility and confidence, to God.

Prov. 16:10

"A divine sentence is in the lips of the king: his mouth transgresseth not in judgment."

We have here a statement of the God-given authority of a king. Solomon could be referring to himself regarding the wisdom of his decrees; but there may be the ultimate reference to Christ, the

Perfect King—the One whose **mouth transgresseth not in judgment** (verdict).

Divine sentence (*qesem*) is used primarily for "divination"; e.g., Balaam; Numbers 22:7. But it can be used in the positive sense of the oracles spoken by a king. This is the sense of this proverb which depicts the authority and finality of the king's verdict or judgment of a matter. In Balaam's case he spoke the truth, but led Israel astray through his compromised advice (i.e., intermarriage with Moabites, etc.).

Suffice to say here that the king was the final authority in all matters. What he said and did was law, even if it was wrong. You don't question the king! That's why a benevolent "dictator" is ideal, like David and Solomon, who sought the Lord for wisdom, etc. This pictures the future reign of Jesus, the Messiah and Perfect King!

Prov. 16:11

"A just weight and balance are the LORD'S: all the weights of the bag are his work."

God sets the standards. The laws of physics, math, science, etc. all come from Him. This includes weights and measures. More specifically, this verse deals with the balance scales and bag of weights (stones) used to weigh out commodities. The Lord has provided "just and balanced" weights and measures for man's welfare. To attempt to cheat or change the standard is an abomination before God and fraud before men. See note on 11:1.

Prov. 16:12

It is an abomination to kings to commit wickedness: for the throne is established by righteousness.

Kings have the grave responsibility to reign uprightly. He is the law and example to the subjects; to be unrighteous and wicked is out of character to the position, like a mean and unloving father to his children. Not only so, but a ruler's practice of **wickedness** is not only a bad example, it is **an abomination.**

Reason? **For the throne is established by righteousness.** Governments and kings are established by God Himself (see

263

Rom.13). The Lord is sovereign in the affairs of men—He sets up kings, and puts them down. Each one has been **established by righteousness**, and thus obligated to do right and assume an upright life and a lawful reign.

Prov. 16:13

"Righteous lips are the delight of kings; and they love him that speaketh right."

Since "the throne is established by righteousness"(vs.12), then kings who want to do right take **delight** in **righteous lips.** Such kings desire truth and integrity and loyalty, rather than flattery and deceit. Thus, the parallel phrase: **"and they love him that speaketh right** (lit. straight).**"**

The Hebrew structure reverses the thoughts for emphasis: "The delight of kings are righteous lips"; "and him that speaketh right they love." (see K&D).

Prov. 16:14

"The wrath of a king is as messengers of death: but a wise man will pacify it."

The king's **wrath** or anger doesn't lie dormant for long. Because of his position and influence his "death penalty" can be dispatched (by messengers) quickly and effectively. To be the object of the king's anger was not only foolish, but life-threatening.

The **wise man will pacify it**; i.e., he that may be the one accused who attempts to appease or appeal to the king. This proverb indicates the angry king's sentence coming upon the accused as an overwhelming host of judges, ready to condemn him. If he's wise, he will not just take it "lying down," but will try to make atonement or appeasement so as to pacify and receive forgiveness from the king.

Prov. 16:15

"In the light of the king's countenance is life; and his favour is as a cloud of the latter rain."

Here's the opposite of the previous verse (vs.14); the former is a scene of the king's anger and subsequent judgment of death. Now we see **the light** (lumination) **of the king's countenance** (face) which **is life.** This is a vivid picture of the king's appeasement and satisfaction making it possible to pour out his blessing. Thus, life is enhanced and preserved.

The parallel statement which further describes the king's deportment is: **His favour** (desire, pleasure) **is as a cloud of the latter rain.** His desire to bless his people is like the cloudburst bringing the "latter rain"; i.e., the rain which precedes the harvest of crops (see Deuteronomy 11:14). "Showers of blessing" come from the heart of our King as we walk with Him! That's when the "fruit of the Spirit" is most evident. (See John 15).

Prov. 16:16

"How much better is it to get wisdom than gold! and to get understanding rather to be chosen than silver!"

Gold and silver may be good, but wisdom and understanding are better! Solomon, a man of experience, knew the difference. He prayed for wisdom up front and God gave him his request, plus the gold, etc. But he learned shortly that the money was no substitute for the wisdom of obedience! (See Ecclesiastes 1, 2). The wealth is only an effective blessing when the heart is right with God. See 4:7; 8:10.

Prov. 16:17

"The highway of the upright is to depart from evil: he that keepeth his way preserveth his soul."

The true believer (upright) travels the "high" road which overcomes evil. This "highway" (course of life), though filled with exits leading to sin, is characterized by departing (turning away) **from evil.** The word translated **"depart"** (*soor*) is lit. "to turn off." The righteous should be "turned off" by sin because he's alive unto God! (See Romans 6:1ff.)

Furthermore, **he that keepeth** (constantly guards) **his way** (life) **preserveth his soul.** This is the outworking of the previous statement; i.e., the righteous lifestyle of departing from evil guards his way, thus preserving (protecting) his soul (inner man—*nephesh*). Surely there's no substitute for obeying God and His Word.

Prov. 16:18

"Pride goeth before destruction, and an haughty spirit before a fall."

This proverb finds its source in Lucifer's fall (Isaiah14; Ezekiel 28). It was not so much what he did, as much as what he became in spirit when "sin was found in him." **Pride** is the basic sin of man—the desire to usurp God's authority. Such arrogance precedes **destruction** (ruin, lit. "crash, crushing, fracture"). How wickedly proud is man, apart from any wicked deed per se! The "peacock" mentality is resident in all humanity, strutting its stuff!

Likewise is the **haughty spirit** (high, exalted) **before a fall** (lit. a stumbling, calamity). A wise man knows the "pit from which he was dug," and walks humbly before his God. It was this attitude that brought the flood upon the earth (Genesis 6ff). It's this same attitude to sends people to Hell! Thus, the utter necessity of sinners to be broken at the foot of the Cross!

Prov. 16:19

"Better it is to be of an humble spirit with the lowly, than to divide the spoil with the proud."

Here's the antidote to the warning against pride in vs. 18. It is **better it is to be of a humble** (lowly) **spirit** (*ruach*—breath, disposition) **with the lowly** (meek, poor, suffering ones), **than to divide the spoil** (booty, riches) **with the proud** (arrogant, lofty ones).

How apropos is this admonition for today! The world is basically arrogant and self-absorbed—the "Cain spirit"! Humility is all but passé, even in the Church. How to "get ahead," succeed, and become wealthy, are popular themes. The "love of money" reigns. Success is who can die with the most "toys."

We need to reach out for the **lowly**, those who can't pay back, rather than "hob-nobbing" with the arrogant rich and lusting after their worldly gain. There is nothing wrong with wealth gained by hard work and humble service to the Lord, but the issue here is ATTITUDE—the lofty, arrogant spirit originating with Lucifer (Isaiah 14:12f.).

Prov. 16:20

"He that handleth a matter wisely shall find good: and whoso trusteth in the LORD, happy is he."

He that handleth a matter wisely (vb. to be prudent, circumspect) **shall find** (attain) **good** (prosperity). A sowing and reaping principle—do right, receive right reward. But the ability to act wisely is hinged on "trusting the Lord." (cf. 13:13)

Whoso trusteth (lit. puts confidence and hope) **in the LORD** (Jehovah-"I AM THAT I AM"), **happy** (extremely happy and blessed) **is he.** (cf. Psalm 1:1)

Ahsher is the Hebrew word here in the O.T., trans. "blessed" 27 times and "happy" 18 times. Those people are happy who:

1. Don't walk in the counsel and lifestyle of the ungodly - Psa.1:1

2. Kiss the Son (worship) and trust Him - Psa.2:12

3. Know sin's forgiveness and freedom from guilt and hypocrisy - Psa.32:2

4. Are chosen as God's inheritance - Psa.33:12

5. Have experienced salvation and trust in God - Psa.34:8

6. Has a burden for the poor (he will be delivered in trouble) - Psa.41:11

7. Dwell in God's house, praising Him - Psa.84:4

8. Know the "joyful sound" and walk in His light - Psa.89:15

9. Are chastened (disciplined) and taught by the Lord - Psa.94:12

10. Do right constantly - Psa.106:3

11. Live holy lives - Psa.119:1

12. Obey His Word with their whole heart - Psa.119:2

13. Fears the Lord; i.e., takes Him seriously in obedience - Psa.128:1

14. Listens intently for God's voice - Prov.8:34

15. Wait (lit. adhere or stick) for Him - Isa.30:18

16. Saved by the LORD - Deut.33:29

17. Stood before the king (Solomon) and heard his wisdom – 1Ki.10:8

18. Corrected by God--don't despise it - Job 5:17

19. Have large family - Psa.127:5 ("quiver full")

20. Destroy God's enemies - Psa.8, 9

21. God is the LORD - Psa.144:15

22. Hope is in the LORD - Psa.146:5

23. Finds wisdom and gets understanding - Prov.3:13

24. Has mercy on the poor - Prov.14:21

25. Fears or stands in awe - Prov.28:14

26. Obeys the Law - Prov.29:18

Prov. 16:21

"The wise in heart shall be called prudent: and the sweetness of the lips increaseth learning."

True wise men gain a reputation for being **prudent** or discerning. Likewise, the **sweetness** or pleasantness coming from their lips augments or activates learning in others. See Prov.1:5; 9:9. Wisdom begets wisdom; i.e., wise people desire to listen to and learn from those who possess and can dynamically present truth. A wise man has learned to live skillfully and there are always those who want to sit at his feet (to learn).

Prov. 16:22

"Understanding is a wellspring of life unto him that hath it: but the instruction of fools is folly."

Heart attitude and character determines how we process instruction. The believer who possesses **a wellspring** (fountain) **of life** (*chay*—something fresh, flowing, alive) will manifest or yield **understanding** (discretion, wisdom).

But the instruction (*musar*—reproof, warning) **of** (given to) **fools is folly** (i.e., silly to him). The fool is bent on foolishness, so that when confronted with serious and weighty information, it is interpreted as foolishness! (cf. 1:7) That's why fools do foolish things, because they're fools! Only the converting grace of God can change a "fool" into a wise man!

Prov. 16:23

"The heart of the wise teacheth his mouth, and addeth learning to his lips."

The heart of the wise teacheth his mouth; i.e., wisdom contained in the heart will be manifest through the mouth. There's a direct pipeline between the heart and the mouth. Wisdom "addeth" (augments) instruction which in turn is expressed by the lips. How and what we speak basically reveals what is in our hearts.

Prov. 16:24

"Pleasant words are as an honeycomb, sweet to the soul, and health to the bones."

Pleasant words (lit. sayings) **are as an honeycomb, sweet to the soul** (*nephesh*—inner man**), and health** (healing, medicine) **to the bones.** As in 3:8 and 4:22, (also 15:13, 15) words (incl. the Word) produce not only sweet joy within, but affect the health of the physical body as well. Here is an example of the tremendous power of the tongue, which can speak healing and edification or destruction! Not that we "speak things into existence," as some teach, but that we can rightly bless and positively influence the lives (actions) of others.

In 17:22, Solomon says, *"A merry heart doeth good like a medicine...,"* The heart is definitely influenced by words, which in turn stirs the flow of life-giving juices (e.g., blood, chemicals, etc.) in the body. Only a fool would deny that the body and soul greatly affect each other. Even "chemical imbalance," in my opinion, is directly related to one's response to words and events. *"As he* (a man) *thinketh in his heart, so is he."*

Prov. 16:25

"There is a way that seemeth right unto a man, but the end thereof are the ways of death."

See notes on Proverbs 14:12.

Prov. 16:26

"He that laboureth laboureth for himself; for his mouth craveth it of him."

Somehow hunger and work go together! A man's **craving** (urge) to fill his **mouth** should dictate the need to **labor for himself**; i.e., God ordained that man work for a living, or else starve! (cf. 2 Thessalonians 3:8-10) This is the natural remedy for human appetite. (Note: "He" is *nephesh*—a breathing soul). Only lazy fools will attempt to side-step this basic life principle, or else attempt to satisfy their need by illegitimate means. (e.g., welfare, stealing, con-artistry, etc.). Of course, this proverb presupposes that the person is healthy and able to work.

Note that Adam worked before the Fall (Genesis 2:15), but this was work without sweat and toil. That changed after the Fall.

Prov. 16:27

"An ungodly man diggeth up evil: and in his lips there is as a burning fire."

"Yet man is born unto trouble, as the sparks fly upward," says Job 5:7. We have here (vs.27-30) a commentary on how sin is manifested by the unrighteous. **An ungodly** (*beliel*— lit. worthless, cf. 6:12; 19:28) **man diggeth up evil** (*ra'ah*— trouble, misery).

This is his wicked nature motivating and gravitating to trouble! A worthless man produces worthless activity, majoring in wickedness. His pastime is spent in "digging up" trouble. He loves what God hates.

His **lips** follow suit, for they simply manifest the **fire** in his heart. James speaks of having a tongue *"set on fire of hell"* (3:6). There's a direct pipeline from the heart to the mouth. A person full of "Hell" will surely verify that in words. Listen to people talk for any length of time and you can tell where their heart is.

How believers need to have a "tongue of fire," inflamed by the Spirit of God and charged by a heart that beats for the Lord—fed by "digging" into the Word! (Joshua 1:8; Psalm 1)

Prov. 16:28

"A froward man soweth strife: and a whisperer separateth chief friends."

Sinful men fall into wickedness, but evil or **froward** (perverted) men have an agenda to **sow strife.** They are not content in just "sinning" themselves, but love to divide others—even friends. They will **whisper** (i.e., slander) behind the backs of others, **separating chief** (familiar, personal) **friends.** Such people cannot stand unity and peace, which come from God. They are peace-breakers, rather than peace-makers.

Prov. 6:14 exposes this divisiveness as a heart problem which results in sowing discord among others. This further indicates that there is war in the human heart because of the Fall. The "Cain spirit" prevails, which hates God and men. There's really no other explanation of human sinful behavior. Evolution is stymied to explain this phenomenon.

Prov. 16:29

"A violent man enticeth his neighbour, and leadeth him into the way that is not good."

Here is the previous verse (28) taken to another level. The man here is not just sinful but **violent**; i.e., aggressively unjust. These kinds of people are not content in the sphere of their own wickedness, but work at **enticing** (lit. "opening, deceiving") others. This activity is depicted well in 1:10-14, against which Solomon gives grave warning. David also cries out to the LORD to, *"preserve me from the violent man..."* (Psalm 140:4).

Note the progression: **and leadeth** (lit. walk) **him** (i.e., his neighbor) **into the way that is not good.** The evil (violent) man not only entices his neighbor by his con-artistry, but then "walks" him down the path of destruction. Certainly, with friends like that, we do not need enemies!

Both the wise and the wicked lead others, but the means and the destination are distinctively opposite! How we, as believers, need to *"let your light so shine before men, that they may see your good works and glorify your Father which is in heaven"*; thus, "enticing" (in a right way) others to follow our God!

Prov. 16:30

"He shutteth his eyes to devise froward things: moving his lips he bringeth evil to pass."

Described in this verse is the source and thinking process behind this violent man's action. So vivid is the picture of the one who **shutteth** (lit. fasten) **his eyes to devise** (plot, fabricate) **froward** (perverted) **things: moving** (lit. biting) **his lips he bringeth evil to pass.** Watch this man as he plots his evil plan, squeezing his eyes and biting his lip. Wicked men work at what they do. The verbs "shutting and moving" are participles, indicating constant action. This is habitual to the wicked who major in "bringing to pass" (i.e., completing) their evil scheme. (See 6:12-14; 16:27)

This reminds me of the criminal who spends most of his time plotting his next "perfect" crime. But every individual apart from saving grace is focusing on something selfish and/or sinful. No one can ever understand or plummet to the depths of human depravity! Only the Word of God tells it like it is; e.g., Genesis 6:5:

"And GOD saw that the wickedness of man was great in the earth, and that every imagination of the thoughts of his heart was

only evil continually." (Also Jeremiah 17:9; Isaiah 1; Romans 1)

Indeed, as a man thinks in his heart, so is he. No one can live any higher than he thinks; thus all are candidates for the "new birth."

The above revelation of man's heart is most difficult for us to accept, which is another indication of our own depravity and inability to see ourselves as God does. Thanks be to God, for His infinite grace that provided salvation to lost sinners, in spite of our ignorance of the depth of sin. (Romans 5:8)!

Prov. 16:31

"The hoary head is a crown of glory, if it be found in the way of righteousness."

What beauty and honor is manifest in **the hoary** (gray, aged) **head** of one who has walked with God over the years! Such **is a crown of glory** or a "bright diadem" (K&D), reflecting the mature character and wisdom of a godly lifestyle. Solomon is not extolling the gray head (hair) per se, for most old people are still selfish, immature and ungodly. Old age is not necessarily beautiful, unless it exemplifies and demonstrates the "righteousness" (fruit) of Christ Himself. What a challenge this is for "seasoned citizens" who may lose sight of ministry and worth in the "sunset" years of this earthly pilgrimage!

In a turbulent day, when such lawlessness and disrespect abounds, we must have a resurgence of godly senior saints who command the respect of the younger generation. O, for an army of young people who follow hard after God, walking in the **way of righteousness** and one day demonstrating the "glory" of the gray head! (Compare notes on 20:29)

Prov. 16:32

"He that is slow to anger is better than the mighty; and he that ruleth his spirit than he that taketh a city."

Here we have the true definition of a warrior. We usually characterize a "mighty man" by his exploits in battle, but Solomon makes one a hero who is **slow to anger** (i.e., longsuffering, patient) and has his "spirit" under control. This is the essence of inner strength and meekness, ultimately exemplified so beautifully by the Lord Jesus Himself.

It takes genuine courage to check one's passion of anger. Anyone can "fight" in the flesh, but ruling one's spirit in conflict is valiant indeed. Most of us will never be in position to "take a city" by storm, but on a daily basis we have great opportunity to overcome trial and adversity by the power of the Holy Spirit. (Galatians 5:22, 23). This truly exemplifies "fighting the good fight of faith."

Prov. 16:33

"The lot is cast into the lap; but the whole disposing thereof is of the LORD."

This seems to be a statement of providence, ending this great chapter. Yes, **the lot is cast** (down, pitched) **into the lap; but the whole** (totality) **disposing** (lit. verdict or decision) **thereof is of** (from) **the LORD.** The "lot" was small, rough stones used like our modern dice to make certain choices or decisions. (See notes on 18:18).

But, in the final analysis, the outcome is not only in God's hands, but the decision originates in and by Him! That sounds like a statement of Sovereignty—the LORD ruling over all things! One might say, "I don't understand that," or "that's mysterious," etc. Finite man wants to figure out everything, but is only humbled by God's infinite providence. Paul sums it up by exclaiming:

"O the depth of the riches both of the wisdom and knowledge of God! How unsearchable are his judgments, and his ways past finding out." (Romans 11:33)

Amen!

Chapter 17

Better is a Dry Morsel with Quietness

Prov. 17:1

"Better is a dry morsel, and quietness therewith, than an house full of sacrifices with strife."

Life's happiness is not dependent on food, pleasure and material things. Solomon says that it is better to have a **dry morsel** (tasteless piece of food) with peace and contentment, than a **house full of sacrifices** (best of flesh given for sacrifice or offerings) **with strife** (or contention). In other words, little is much when God is in it. A house can be filled with "stuff," but a real home is a quiet or peaceful place. Some things just cannot be bought—they're gifts from above. Paul said:

"For the kingdom of God is not meat and drink; but righteousness, and peace, and joy in the Holy Ghost." (Romans 14:17)

So many today are scraping and searching for the "finer things" of life, only to lose their souls in the end. It's what we ARE that counts, not what we have. Now if God has blessed us with earthly possessions, let's keep the priority straight and use them for His glory in the ministry of souls.

Prov. 17:2

"A wise servant shall have rule over a son that causeth shame, and shall have part of the inheritance among the brethren."

We really can't chose our station in life; i.e., our race, nationality, birthplace, IQ, etc. Some are born in palaces and others alongside a dumpsite in Ethiopia. There are things out of our control and we can only function the best we can in our capacity. In this text, **a wise servant** can "break out of the mold," by taking advantage of his opportunity in the family.

It's the "son" who is in line for the "inheritance," but has forfeited his part through shameful actions. In the skill of wisdom, the servant takes charge over the son, and by correction, discipline, etc., he is used to straighten out the son. Therefore, he (the servant) becomes partaker of the inheritance, just as if he were one of the family ("brethren")! Originally born a "slave," but now adopted as a "son." Wow! Sounds like redemption in Christ!

How we need to make the most of our opportunity, regardless of our station in life. Quit blaming others, family, environment, race, etc. Let us do what our hand finds to do with all our might, trusting God to make us all that we should be for His glory! The son here had privilege, but "blew it" through shameful living. Thus, a wise servant took advantage of the situation, restored the son, and then received part of the inheritance! That's a display of loving wisdom.

The Prodigal's elder brother did not have this spirit. He criticized the father for receiving the repentant son back, rather than helping his brother get right. Thus, he could not enter into the joy of the occasion. What a contrast to this wise servant here in the text.

Prov. 17:3

"The fining pot is for silver, and the furnace for gold: but the LORD trieth the hearts."

Here's an analogy of the refining process of silver and gold as it relates to the Lord's trying or testing of man's heart. What the furnace and crucible are to silver and gold, so is the LORD to hearts. Several observations:

1. Metals are refined to burn away the dross and reveal their true worth or substance. So the is the innermost part of man tried by the Lord.

2. Precious metals can withstand the heat, but "wood, hay and stubble" (1 Corinthians 3) cannot. Thus one day the true

heart-salvation and ministry of the saints will be revealed "so as by fire."

3. It is not the head, for instance, that is tried, but the "heart"—for out of it are "the issues of life."

4. God is not primarily interested in outward actions, so much as the heart motive. He wants to know not just what we do, but why we do it.

5. "If we judge ourselves, we shall not be judged" (1 Corinthians 11). We must guard our hearts, knowing that all things open before Him. Let us not cover up sin, but submit to His "trial or testing." David cried, *"Search me, O God, and know my heart: try me, and know my thoughts: And see if there be any wicked way in me..."*

6. Finally, the emphasis of Hebrew word order unfolds thusly— what the furnace is to gold, the LORD (Jehovah) is to the heart; i.e., it's the Lord and no one else who tries our hearts. That's a work unique to Him and Him alone! Amen.

Prov. 17:4

"A wicked doer giveth heed to false lips; and a liar giveth ear to a naughty tongue."

This verse can serve as the basis of common expressions like: "Birds of a feather flock together," or "We do what we do, because we are what we are." Who we listen to indicates where our heart is. Here, **A wicked doer giveth heed to false** (lying) **lips, and a liar giveth ear to a naughty** (very wicked, perverted) **tongue.** Yes, we take in what suits our fancy and love people who speak forth what we love.

It's not a mystery that the world loves to hear people of the world! Hollywood, through its films, caters to the base nature of society which clamors for the next box office hit. We gravitate to those who are like us. That works also in a godly sense, where as new babes, we desire to hear more of the milk of the Word. But that's not the theme of this proverb. Suffice to say that people reveal their heart's desire by the type or character of those to whom they gravitate. Profess whatever you like; you expose who you are by who you listen to.

Prov. 17:5

"Whoso mocketh the poor reproacheth his Maker: and he that is glad at calamities shall not be unpunished."

How we respond to those less fortunate than us is tell-tale of our character and our relationship with God. In this case, **Whoso mocketh** (derides, scorns) **the poor** (needy, destitute) **reproacheth** (defies, rails upon) **his** (the poor's) **Maker** (*asah*—to make, produce; ref. to God). How we treat people is how we treat their Creator. What we do for people who cannot do anything in return reveals our love and character. God has a special love for the poor and widows (see James 1:27; 2:1-7).

He further states: **and he that is glad** (gleeful) **at calamities** (misfortune**) shall not be unpunished** (acquitted). Pride would take pleasure in the misfortune of others. Man always wants to be on "top" because of his insecurity. When you don't know who you are in Christ, you envy those who are richer or more successful than you. Likewise, you despise those who are poor and destitute, because they have nothing to offer you. Since money is the root of all evil, and it "talks" in a corrupt society, then people without money are not important nor desired for friends. After all, what good are you if you have nothing to give me?!

This attitude offends God and will surely be judged accordingly. By the way, this verse indicates that we'll always have poor people, as Jesus said, *"For the poor always ye have with you."* They are not second-rate citizens, but never-dying souls who, as well, are recipients of God's common grace.

Prov. 17:6

"Children's children are the crown of old men; and the glory of children are their fathers."

Children's children (i.e., grandchildren) **are the crown of old men.** A man knows how well he raised his children by observing his grandchildren. What a commentary on the legacy of a father and sanctity of the home! There's just something about that "second" generation that's special and rewarding. The "crown" and "old men" seem to relate, for the gift of grandchildren makes the senior years fulfilling—the "crowning" years, if you please.

A grandfather can revel in the grace of God which made possible the success of his children in raising their children. How this speaks of the perpetuity of the family which is under severe attack these days. Homosexuality, for instance, cannot produce such a legacy. Marriage between a man and a woman is ordained of God, not only for immediate results, but to be a "crown" of joy even in old age!

And the glory (honor, beauty) **of children are their fathers.** What an honorable position and privilege is a father! This is more than being the bread-winner of the family. He is revered by his children, but even more, he becomes their ornament of honor and security. A godly father is indeed a gift from God Himself. Blessed is the child that understands this and acts accordingly.

Prov. 17:7

"Excellent speech becometh not a fool: much less do lying lips a prince."

"Thy speech bewrayeth thee," they said to Peter. What is in our hearts eventually is revealed through our mouths. Our talk somewhere along the way will match our walk, unless we're a first-class hypocrite. (e.g., Judas)

Thus, **excellent speech** (lit. lips) **becometh not a fool** (*nabal*—stupid, impious); i.e., superior speech not only doesn't fit or match a stupid man, it doesn't "beautify" or make him any better. He is what he is, regardless of how he tries to impress others. Some people may try to "talk big," while they live "little."

Likewise, **much less do lying lips a prince.** The word for "prince" is used for a noble person in mind and character, not merely in rank. Thus, lying lips certainly do not fit or are not becoming to a virtuous man.

Solomon is arguing from the greater to the lesser: If excellent lips are not becoming to a fool, then much less are lying lips to a noble man. What standard of character and virtue are portrayed in this statement. How believers in Christ need to take heed, that our testimony (walk and talk) is one of truth and integrity.

Prov. 17:8

"A gift is as a precious stone in the eyes of him that hath it: whithersoever it turneth, it prospereth."

A difficult verse in light of no immediate context. The **gift** (*shachad*) here is definitely a "bribe" determined by the overwhelming usage in the O.T. (see Deuteronomy 27:25; 16:19; Prov. 17:23; 18:16; 19:6; Psalm 26:10; "bribes"; Ecclesiastes 10:19, etc.).

This bribe (present) **is as a precious stone**; i.e., something "gracious or well-favored" (*chanah*—word for "Grace"—Hannah). The "stone"(*eben*) here is not necessarily a jewel, but a precious stone of sorts (cf. Exodus 25:7); certainly something of value, otherwise it would not be a favorable gift.

It is said to be precious **in the eyes of him that hath it.** The word for "hath" is *baal*, meaning "master or owner"; the difficulty is knowing whose "eyes" are referred to here, the giver or receiver of the gift? After further reflection, I would opt for the former, the original owner, who sees the value and convincing power of his "precious stone."

Whithersoever (lit. "with the whole" or "every which way") **it turneth, it prospereth** (gives insight, causes to prosper). If it were a gem, it could be said that every position it is turned toward the sunlight gives off a different hue or sparkle. That would certainly be an evidence of its intrinsic value, but does is explain the accurate meaning here? It can mean that the gift used by the owner has power and influence to accomplish the owner's purpose. The word **"turneth"** is also translated "look" (cf. 2 Samuel 9:8; Isaiah 56:11) or "respect" (Leviticus 26:9). Thus, however you "look at it," it prospers or has good success. Hence, we see here the subtle power of a bribe.

However, if this gift is not a bribe, then the whole verse has another meaning. If the **eyes** belong to the receiver of the gift, then he will prosper at every turn. This will take further reflection.

Prov. 17:9

"He that covereth a transgression seeketh love; but he that repeateth a matter separateth very friends."

"Love (charity) shall cover the multitude of sins," says 1 Peter 4:8. This present verse deals with the same principle. Note it doesn't say, "He that covers up a transgression (sin)..." Some would take this to mean that love just covers up our neighbor's sins, never dealing with anything that would offend. In street talk it would be "narking" or "squealing"; i.e., telling the authorities.

But here the **love** aspect has to do with **covering** or not exposing the sins of others which have been dealt with properly. If I have had an issue with someone and we resolve it before God and each other, it should never be brought up again. That's a true expression of love.

See the contrast, however, in the one who **repeats** or brings up the matter again. In fact, this verb, *shanah* is a Qal. part. meaning to "change." This may indicate not only repeating, as such, but altering or exaggerating the matter to others (friends). The participle indicates ongoing action or repetition. So bringing up the matter to certain people can do great damage to their friendship. This is not an action of love! How wicked and selfish the tongue can be! See 16:28 and James 3; also on this verse: Prov.10:12; Psalm 32:1.

Prov. 17:10

"A reproof entereth more into a wise man than an hundred stripes into a fool."

Just a word of rebuke will quickly and deeply penetrate the heart of a wise man! His heart is always ready and open for instruction—that's his nature and desire. *"I will guide thee with mine eye,"* God says. Just a look will move a true servant of God, likened to a mother's "look" toward an obedient child.

In contrast, the foolish can be beaten and whipped repeatedly, only to continue in their foolishness. See Israel's foolish disobedience in Isaiah 1:1ff. Someone said, "A man convinced against his will, is of the same opinion still."

Prov. 17:11

An evil man seeketh only rebellion: therefore a cruel messenger shall be sent against him.

Unlike the wise man in vs.10, this **evil man seeketh** (strives after, desires) **only rebellion** (lit. bitterness). An evil heart seeks its own; like water, it cannot rise above its own level. We seek what we are by nature. That's why a "new nature" is essential if we're to seek God and righteousness.

Because of his rebellious craze, **a cruel** (lit. terrible) **messenger** (angel?) **shall be sent against him.** Could this be the king's emissaries of justice? Is this the police? The executioner, etc.? The Septuagint renders it: "The Lord will send a pitiless Angel." (Barnes). One thing for sure, the rebellion will meet with God's justice somewhere down the road!

Prov. 17:12

"Let a bear robbed of her whelps meet a man, rather than a fool in his folly."

Quite a radical statement! Can a fool (stupid man) really do more damage to a man than a bereaved, angry bear? Evidently it is so. Because the fool is a wicked human being, as opposed to an animal, his potential for treachery and diabolical action is unlimited. Man in his folly is worse than a beast and possibly more irrational. Animals seem much more predictable than mankind.

Animals, being subservient to man, lack the wicked, demonic nature of man. Thus, the higher creation of God (viz., man), because of sin, falls below the animals' position and has the capacity to act worse than an animal. So contact with an angry beast may be devastating and frightful, but also short-lived. Dealing with **a fool in his folly** may in some ways be far worse. Plus, the fool can effectively play with one's mind and spirit in a way that a beast cannot.

Prov. 17:13

"Whoso rewardeth evil for good, evil shall not depart from his house."

It's one thing to render evil for evil, but returning **evil for good** is another. Men not only "fight fire with fire," so to speak, but even oppress those who have done them good (e.g., Saul against David; the crowd against Jesus, etc.). See Psalm 7:4; 35:12; Prov. 3:30; Prov. 31:12.

There's a reaping factor here for the one who **rewards** (returns) **evil for good**; that same **evil** will not depart from his house, but will haunt and even curse him. The evil seed sown will not only multiply, but mark and characterize the premises perpetually.

Prov. 17:14

"The beginning of strife is as when one letteth out water: therefore leave off contention, before it be meddled with."

K&D translates this verse: "As one letteth out water is the beginning of a strife. But cease thou from such strife ere it comes to showing teeth," **Strife** and quarreling **begin** like a crack in the reservoir or dike, **letting out** a small volume of water at first. Then as the crack widens, so does the flow until it becomes a life-threatening deluge! The reference here is to the large tanks or reservoirs in Eastern cities where drinking water was stored. A crack in the wall could eventually lead to disaster.

The admonition then is to **leave off** (reject, forsake) **contention** (strife), **before it be meddled with. To "meddle with"** is the verb *gala* meaning "to expose or lay bare." The Hiph. perf. form here means "to break out (in contention)." So the idea is dealing with an issue and not aggravating it, lest it "break out" into an uncontrollable flow.

Prov. 17:15

"He that justifieth the wicked, and he that condemneth the just, even they both are abomination to the LORD."

What and whom we justify and condemn reveals our character. We justify the actions of those who do what we would do; we condemn those who are virtuous or upright when we are wicked. Only those who are godly appreciate and gravitate to those who are righteous. "Birds of a feather flock together." We gravitate to those who are like ourselves.

One may condone an employee who steals tools from work because he's done the same thing (or has contemplated it). Likewise, the same man despises the one who reveals the identity of that thief to the boss. **They both are abomination to the LORD.** Principle: We project in others what we are ourselves.

Prov. 17:16

"Wherefore is there a price in the hand of a fool to get wisdom, seeing he hath no heart to it?"

This seems to be a hypothetical question as to why a fool would even attempt to procure wisdom (for a price), when he has no **heart** or interest in it. By virtue of his lifestyle he rejects wise instruction and lives to gratify his fleshly ego. Yet, by witness of conscience, if nothing else, he knows there's a better way to live. He may "pay" for a course in "self-improvement," etc., but true wisdom will elude him. There's an ongoing conflict between what he knows is right and the lack of **heart** (desire) to do it. Cf. Prov. 1:22, 23; 8:5; 9:4-6: Isaiah 55:1-3; Prov. 14:6.

Prov. 17:17

"A friend loveth at all times, and a brother is born for adversity."

A beautiful description of true friendship: **A friend loveth** (qal. part.- constant or continuing love) at all times, **and a brother** (generic sense, companion) **is born for adversity** (times of trouble, distress). Loving friendship is not fickle nor momentary nor greedy, etc., but is constant through thick and thin; the Heb. Syntax (i.e., participle) indicates a lifestyle of being loving—an on-going mental attitude toward his neighbor.

This is likened to *agape* love in the N.T.; a one-way love, regardless of circumstance. This kind of love is an outflow from the inflow of the Holy Spirit to others, with no thought of return. It never keeps records or requires a payback, as expressed in, "You owe me one!" Indeed, this is made possible by the fruit (or gift) of the Holy Spirit (See Galatians 5:22).

I love K&D's Hebrew rendering of this verse:

"At all times the right friend shows himself loving; and as a brother is he born for adversity." Certainly a friend's brotherly love is tested and manifested in times of adversity. Every brother or neighbor has some kind of trouble and, therefore, becomes a potential object of our love. The world is filled with such, granting our opportunities to show Christ's love limitless!

Prov. 17:18

"A man void of understanding striketh hands, and becometh surety in the presence of his friend."

This is a further admonition against becoming **surety** (pledge, co-signer, security) for another. See 6:1-5; 11:15 where this issue is addressed. Transactions were made by **striking hands**; I assume that it would be comparable to shaking hands, or maybe the "high-five" equivalent in our day.

The **friend** mentioned here may not be the faithful one mentioned in the previous verse (17). Friends don't let friends get "suckered" into a bad contract.

Prov. 17:19

He loveth transgression that loveth strife: and he that exalteth his gate seeketh destruction.

Sin and strife (contention) go together! Fighting is universal because sin is universal. The love of one insures the love of the other. War is in the heart (cf. James 4:1f.), the same place where sin lurches. The warring of sin indicates alienation from the God of peace. Thus, only through justifying grace can one have *"peace with God"* (Romans 5:1) and the *"peace of God"* (Philippians 4:7).

Exalting his gate seems to refer to this man's house, primarily the door. He lives an extravagant lifestyle with an "open door" policy which draws others like himself. This leads to **destruction**, for contention breeds contention and misery. (Clarke has further description; he suggests also that the "gate" may refer to the man's mouth which spews out prideful boasting and arrogance.)

Prov. 17:20

"He that hath a froward heart findeth no good: and he that hath a perverse tongue falleth into mischief."

The **froward** (perverted, distorted) **heart findeth no good** because it (heart) seeks that which lines up with its nature. As water does not rise above its source, so the depraved heart seeks depraved things; or it takes legitimate things and perverts them. (e.g., a drug dealer uses a fine car to transport his wares). We seek and find what we really want because of the nature of our "wanter." Likewise, a believer who pursues godly things will find good because of the new nature (heart) he received when converted to Christ.

By the same token, **a perverse** (lit. overturned) **tongue falls into mischief** (evil). The tongue expresses the heart and thus exacerbates the evil externally. The tongue can "bless or curse," depending on the heart to which it's attached. (See James 3). Our tongue will reveal our true nature in time.

Prov. 17:21

"He that begetteth a fool doeth it to his sorrow: and the father of a fool hath no joy."

Possibly one of the greatest trials to face a father is to beget a foolish son. Especially is that true if the father has integrity and wisdom. One might argue, "Can that actually happen?" But experience bears it out, for there's no guarantee that a wise father will have a wise son. (e.g., Solomon bore Rehoboam).

Thus a fool's father is grieved (*tugah*- depressed, sorrowful) and has **no joy**. What a commentary on society, especially in our day. There is no lack of foolish, silly or stupid children! It is therefore imperative that a father look to the Lord alone for joy and completeness (peace), for only then can one rise above the circumstance while yet being in it. Life must go on whether one's children are wise or foolish (cf. 10:1).

Furthermore, children have little understanding of how their lives affect their parents. Hopefully they (children) will think differently when they have their own family, if the father doesn't die of a broken heart in the interim.

Prov. 17:22

"A merry heart doeth good like a medicine: but a broken spirit drieth the bones."

Certainly connected to the previous verse, **a merry** (joyful) **heart** is like **medicine** (cure) to the whole person. The inference is that the body is positively affected by inward joy. The spirit or heart condition has great bearing on the soul and body. Certainly the Good News of the Gospel of Christ would apply here. Here's the grace of God in action!

Similarly, **a broken** (smitten) **spirit drieth the bones.** Whatever the spirit's condition, it affects the body. Our bone marrow produces red blood cells, essential to good health. Somehow, a negative, grieved spirit can serve to dry up this process.

Prov. 17:23

"A wicked man taketh a gift out of the bosom to pervert the ways of judgment."

Gifts cannot always be received at face value, for wicked men have an agenda. Here the **gift** is a bribe, taken from the **bosom** (lit. fold or pocket in the garment) in order **to pervert** (bend) **the ways of judgment.** Evil men break the law, and then attempt to "buy" their way out of the consequences. "Money talks," as they say, and certainly there's nothing "new under the sun." The sinful tactics of men have never changed from the Fall to the present time.

Prov. 17:24

"Wisdom is before him that hath understanding; but the eyes of a fool are in the ends of the earth."

Wisdom is before (lit. 'near his face') **him that hath understanding; but the eyes of a fool are in the ends of the earth."** The understanding of a wise man relates with what is **before him**; i.e., the present reality of his situation. He may have vision for the future, but that does not deter him from dealing effectively with the present. While he walks with God, he is cognizant of his responsibility to work and provide for his family, to pay his taxes, rent, etc. He diligently assumes present responsibility which in turn becomes the foundation and vehicle for future dreams.

The foolish man, however, is focused on future exploits to the expense of present reality. He's looking to the "ends of the earth," i.e., what it will be someday. Without facing wisely what is right in front of his nose, his "vision" can only be relegated as "wild imagination." Solomon said further:

"Whatsoever thy hand findeth to do, do it with all thy might; for there is no work, nor device, nor knowledge, nor wisdom, in the grave whither thou goest." (Ecclesiastes 9:10)

There should be no conflict between present labor and future vision. It is possible to be so "earthly" minded, that we have no heavenly pursuit. On the other hand, we can be so "spiritually" engrossed, that earthly responsibilities are ignored or done haphazardly. Needless to say, this is not an "either/or" issue, but rather "both/and." Indeed, *"I can do all things through Christ which strengtheneth me"* (Philippians 4:13).

Prov. 17:25

"A foolish son is a grief to his father, and bitterness to her that bare him."

Just as "no man sins to himself," a foolish son greatly affects his parents. This is especially true if the parents are wise, and not foolish themselves. What **grief** (anger) **to his father and bitterness** (sorrow with anger) to his mother are caused by a wayward and ungodly son (child)! What disappointment and anguish riddle the hearts of parents who "give their lives" to instill wisdom and moral principles in their children, only to see it "trashed" along the way.

But, thank God, for hope which mollifies parental "wounds," looking for saving grace to someday seize that son or daughter. God is able! Our labors need not be in vain—the story is not over yet! There are other "instruments" of grace, beside parents, that God can and will use to confront foolish children.

Prov. 17:26

"Also to punish the just is not good, nor to strike princes for equity."

Also (and) **to punish the just** (lawful, righteous) **is not good.** To bring the wicked to justice is good, but to penalize those who do right is unjust. There are absolute laws, moral and civil, ordained of God (revealed in the Bible) which have been ignored or discarded by society. Many times the innocent suffer for or with the guilty. This is not good.

On a higher level, **princes** (rulers) who oversee justice are likewise punished ("stricken"— lit. slaughtered) for promoting **equity** or righteousness. In a depraved world, people frown on those who are upright, even those in authority. Induced by the "Cain spirit," men rebel against right, desiring to "do their own thing." Therefore, they hate those who do right, and even welcome corrupt political systems. This scenario ties in with Paul's description of the last days in 2 Timothy 3:2f:

"For men shall be lovers of their own selves...disobedient to parents...despisers of those that are good..."

Even in Jesus' day, the crowd embraced Barabbas the murderer instead of Christ, the righteous One. Things have not changed to this day!

Prov. 17:27

"He that hath knowledge spareth his words: and a man of understanding is of an excellent spirit."

Tongue control is the sign of a "perfect" (mature) man, according to James (3:1f). Likewise, Solomon relegates **knowledge** (lit. discernment) to the man who **spareth his words**; i.e., shows restraint and reserve. Only a fool "runs at the mouth." Choice and volume of words spoken does reveal one's character and discretion.

In conjunction, **a man of understanding** (translated 'skillfulness' in Psalm 78:72) **is of an excellent** (valuable, honorable) **spirit.** Evidently, this describes one who is tempered and cool in spirit; one whose words are skilled, relevant, and edifying.

Prov. 17:28

"Even a fool, when he holdeth his peace, is counted wise: and he that shutteth his lips is esteemed a man of understanding."

Someone said: "Silence is golden." That is true even for a fool, who decides to **hold his peace** or be quiet. Words reveal one's heart; thus, a foolish man may be **counted** (considered) **wise** if he keeps his mouth shut. However, the moment he begins to "chatter," he will give himself away. Some fools are astute in hiding their true thoughts in order to fool others. It could be said that they are subtly wise in their foolishness, **esteemed** as men of **understanding**; i.e., a "con-man," one who can easily gain the confidence others to get what he wants.

But I think that Solomon's main thrust here is to encourage and extol the man of "excellent spirit" (vs. 27), who reveals his wise understanding (discretion) by the quality and brevity of his words. Such a man rules his soul and rightly manages others—a "perfect man" (James 3:2). See Prov. 15:2; Job 13:5; Ecclesiastes 5:3; 10:3.

Chapter 18
A Man Who Isolates Himself Seeks His Own Desire

Prov. 18:1

"Through desire a man, having separated himself, seeketh and intermeddleth with all wisdom."

Again this is difficult wording. I think the following translation seems to capture the right thought. (ASV) "He that separateth himself seeketh his own desire, and rageth against all sound wisdom." This would also correlate with the context of verse two, regarding a "fool,"

There's an uncanny **desire** (satisfaction) for a man to separate or wall himself off from others, particularly as it pertains to taking advice. In light of vs.2, it indicates that this man is foolish when it comes to sound wisdom, desiring to do his own thing. Thus, he **intermeddleth** (breaks out in contention) against the whole (**with all**) of sound wisdom. He's an entity all to himself with no need of others or their wisdom. This pictures man's sinful pride and arrogance, and, at the same time, his utter foolishness. 19:20 says: *"Hear counsel, and receive instruction, that thou mayest be wise in thy latter end."* See 11:14.

Prov. 18:2

"A fool hath no delight in understanding, but that his heart may discover itself."

A fool doesn't have any **delight** (bent, pleasure) **in understanding** (skillful wisdom), but rather, he delights in revealing his heart to others. The phrase, **may discover itself**, means to make known, show, uncover. You would think that one would want to "take in" before speaking out—but not the fool! He rattles his empty cage (mouth), delighting not in knowledge, but in revealing his ignorance.

Pride triggers such desire to be heard, even when there's no substance. The fool believes he has the last word on a subject. This is the height of arrogance. He can't take time to study and be quiet, but must "run at the mouth." If he were quiet, some might think him to be smart, but when he opens his mouth, he gives himself away! See Prov. 12:23.

Some folks just need to keep their mouths shut; others need to speak, who have something to say. There's a big difference between having to say something, and having something to say. O, to speak out at the right time, and likewise to know when not to speak—what a virtue!

Prov. 18:3

"When the wicked cometh, then cometh also contempt, and with ignominy reproach."

A man sins because he's a sinner. "We do what we do, because we are what we are." (Bob Jones Sr.) **When the wicked** (ungodly) **cometh**, he brings his "baggage" with him. He projects who he is; he really can't be any other, even though he may act like someone else. When he comes, his **contempt** (disrespect, shame) comes with him. In conjunction, **with ignominy** (is) **reproach**. Something ignominious is disgraceful (e.g. Christ on the Cross). And this "disgrace" or dishonor leads to reproach or scorn.

But what do you do in a society where wrong is considered right (and vice-versa); when the standards of decency are all but excluded? The wicked are glorified in our day, and the righteous are despised. Yet the Word of God stands forever, regardless what the world thinks! *"Let God be true, but every man a liar."* Look at the Cross to see the depth of man's sin and rebellion. There it was that our Saviour died an "ignominious" death in behalf of wicked, contemptible, ignominious rebels! Amen.

Prov. 18:4

"The words of a man's mouth are as deep waters, and the wellspring of wisdom as a flowing brook."

There is some discussion here as to whether these two statements are parallel or contrasting. The **deep waters** may to some appear to be a cistern or holding tank for water, thus becoming stagnant, whereas the **wellspring**, or source of wisdom, is as **a flowing brook**—not subject to stagnation. But I would agree with the translators who link these two statements with an "and," making them not only parallel, but compensating or progressive.

Wise words are spoken from a "**deep**" source, which is indicated by the word, "**waters**" here. This word, *mayim* is used figuratively as "juice" and euphemistically as "urine" or "semen," according to Strong's. (see Prov. 20:5) This then becomes the "**wellspring**" or source of wisdom that is like "**a flowing** (not babbling) **brook**." There's a flow to wisdom, but it must come from some source. We know God is that Source (1 Corinthians 1:30) and by His Spirit it flows as a river. That's the filling and unction of the Holy Spirit in the believer's life.

Prov. 18:5

"It is not good to accept the person of the wicked, to overthrow the righteous in judgment."

This verse speaks to the practice of injustice—**to accept the...wicked** over the just. To **overthrow the righteous in judgment** is to "turn or thrust aside, bend or pervert" the proper verdict. The inference here is that **the person of the wicked** (his reputation, riches, influence, etc.) is unjustly accepted over the person of a lawful man (who doesn't have the reputation, money, etc.).

It's a known fact that in the justice system those with influence and money can "beat the rap" (e.g., Mafia, politicians, etc.). The poor man, though guilty, has a great disadvantage. But that's not exactly the case in this proverb. Here the wicked man is preferred over the innocent—an example of perverted justice and the depravity of a fallen society. What a picture of our world today! This was illustrated at the Cross when the murderer, Barabbas, was received by the crowd, while Christ, the Righteous One, was "overthrown," rejected and crucified!

Prov. 18:6

"A fool's lips enter into contention, and his mouth calleth for strokes."

The potential for "war" is in everyone. (James 4:1f). It takes wisdom to refrain from fighting or to handle conflict aright. **A fool's lips enter into contention**; i.e., he welcomes a fight and is very willing to argue, even to the extent of **strokes** or blows. An unbridled tongue can only lead to contention (contest) for it is a *"world of iniquity"* (James 3). One word leads to another, until fists fly! So is the way of the world and the fruit of foolishness. A warring heart will be manifested through the looseness of the lips. Foolish lips spell conflict and trouble.

Prov. 18:7

"A fool's mouth is his destruction, and his lips are the snare of his soul."

Talk about "putting your foot in your mouth"! Everyone has a "tongue" problem (James 3:1), but fools accentuate the problem—running at the mouth. Words are so powerful and revealing! How encouraging are the right words, and how devastating the wrong!

His lips are the snare (trap, lit. noose) **of his soul.** Amazing it is that those who have so little to say, speak so frequently. *"For out of the abundance of the heart, the mouth speaketh."* Some have learned to think, rather than speak; others just let it "rip." James 3 discusses the plight of the tongue. O, the power of the tongue! It can bless or destroy.

Prov. 18:8

"The words of a talebearer are as wounds, and they go down into the innermost parts of the belly."

It's been said that more wounds have been inflicted by the tongue than by the edge of the sword! How deep and lasting are the **words of a talebearer** (slanderer, whisperer). The power of life and death is in the tongue—*"a world of iniquity"* (James 3). A knife wound can easily heal, but not so with "tongue-wounds."

The word for "wound" is used only twice—here and in 26:22. Strong's says it means "a burning in"; BDB gives the meaning as "to gulp or swallow greedily." Both definitions serve to illustrate the severity and profundity of the power of words; **they go down into the innermost parts of the belly**. A sword really cannot penetrate that deeply! We're talking here about the soul or seat of emotion. A tangible instrument cannot descend that far—it takes something intangible, like words, to penetrate the depth of the soul. (see Hebrews 4:12)

Here the primary teaching is in regard to "talebearers"; i.e., bearers of evil or slanderous tales. But we must at least mention the positive power of speaking truth and encouragement, which build up rather than devastate. Let us edify one another, as opposed to tearing down. Criticism, the last I checked, is not one of the "gifts" of the Spirit!

Prov. 18:9

"He also that is slothful in his work is brother to him that is a great waster."

Laziness and wasting time, etc. (unproductivity) are "brothers" for sure. The lazy, slothful, slacker is a destroyer in the long run. Little by little he "lets up" on the job (work), milking the time clock, seeing how little he can do and still get a full day's wage. How different is a man full of integrity and purpose! Who works, not for selfish reasons, but to the "glory of God" (1 Corinthians 1:31).

Such a person is considered a **brother** (kin) **to...a great waster**. Here's a picture of kinship or relationship between the lazy man and one who is a **great** (lit. master) **waster** (lit. destroyer). If we're not building, we're tearing down. Laziness may be perceived as just "marking time," with no consequence, but not so. We may not all have the same amount of money, but we all have the same amount of time (24/7).

Time is money in the business world, and the same principle applies in the Church. How diligent some can be when there's a "buck" in it; how slothful we can be when "laboring" in the Kingdom of God! A lazy man has little or no purpose in life—no hope, no goals, other than self-gratification. That is considered a "brother" (kin) to a "master destroyer" (waster). Some people destroy purposefully (demonic), while others are wasters by virtue of not working diligently. This principle is true in the world, as well as the Church.

Prov. 18:10

"The name of the LORD is a strong tower: the righteous runneth into it, and is safe."

"That at the name of Jesus, every knee should bow... And that every tongue should confess that Jesus Christ is LORD, to the glory of God the Father." (Philippians 2:10, 11)

"All hail the power of Jesus Name, let angels prostrate fall; bring forth the royal diadem and crown Him LORD of All"! There's something about His NAME!

Solomon says: **"The name of the LORD is a strong tower..."** Jehovah's name is a memorial of His uniqueness; His honor, authority and character (accord. to Strong's). When asked by Moses regarding His name, He responded, *"Thus shalt thou say unto the children of Israel, I AM hath sent me unto you."* (Exodus 3:14). Jesus used the same name in John 8:58 when asked by the Pharisees if he had seen "Abraham's day," He said, *"Before Abraham was, I AM"!* (*ego eimi*).

This Name, which is above every name, **is a strong tower; the righteous** (saints) **runneth unto it, and is safe** (lit. high, lofty). The Hebrew reads: "A strong tower is the name of Jehovah." This portrays the emphasis of the power and strength of His name, which is as a mighty "tower," into which we can run. Sometimes we can only retreat to our position in God, finding security in Him—awaiting the next battle of life.

K&D makes the following observation:

"This name, which is afterwards interwoven in the name Jesus, is (Psa_61:4), a strong high tower bidding defiance to every hostile assault. Into this the righteous runneth, to hide himself behind its walls, and is thus lifted (perf. consec.) high above all danger (cf. Ò, Pro_29:25). "

Note also Psalm 27:5; 31:21; 61:4.

Prov. 18:11

"The rich man's wealth is his strong city, and as an high wall in his own conceit."

The conceit of riches is attended by deceit. This verse pictures the man who builds his own kingdom, but is not "rich toward God" (cf. Luke 12:15-21). How bold and arrogant is sinful man, to think he can secure himself from the inevitable: Frailty, death and judgment!

Here is a vivid picture of a man of worldly riches (sufficiency) who trusts solely in wealth as **his strong** (powerful, majestic) **city and...high** (lofty, secure) **wall.** How eager are men to build monuments to themselves (mansions, estates, etc.), trusting in manufactured security! Not far from here is a humongous, multi-million dollar mansion housing three people! It's just interesting how money reveals the heart and one's sense of value.

It must be noted here that the "rich man" in this verse has not necessarily built a fortressed city, etc. but his wealth has figuratively become that to him. In other words, his absolute faith and security is in the "almighty dollar"! (See Jeremiah 17:5-9)

Prov. 18:12

"Before destruction the heart of man is haughty, and before honour is humility.

Regarding the Christian life, someone has said, "The way up is the way down, and the way down is the way up." Indeed;

"Pride goeth before destruction, and an haughty spirit before a fall." (Prov. 16:18).

This proverb (vs. 12) is a further commentary on this truth.

Haughty stems from a word meaning "to be high or exalted." It is that self-exaltation and arrogance found in the King of Tyre, who represents Satan; his heart was "lifted up" because of his wealth. See Ezekiel 28:5, 17.

Note that this arrogance is a "heart" thing that affects every aspect of life. Such haughtiness precedes destruction and ruin. Satanic pride fills the sinful heart which makes man a target for judgment. Interestingly, the world many times clamors around haughty people, who have exalted themselves (e.g., Hollywood and T.V. stars, politicians, etc.). But how many of these "stars" have ended up in disaster?

Humility, on the other hand, leads to **honor**. The submissive, condescending individual will find proper recognition. **"Honor"** is translated from *kadov*, the word for "glory" (lit. "weight"). Weighty people are those who wait on God and His timing. Promotion comes from the Lord. See Peter's admonition in 1 Pet.5:5, 6.

Prov. 18:13

"He that answereth a matter before he heareth it, it is folly and shame unto him."

James exhorts us to be, *"swift to hear, slow to speak, slow to wrath."* Too often we are "slow to hear and quick to speak." Solomon reveals the folly and shame that may come to him that answers a matter prematurely; i.e., "before he hears or understands it." All too often listening is a lost art, or pride would lead us to "expound" on something that we know little or nothing about. It's OK to say "I don't know."

But here Solomon seems to address giving a premature conclusion before thinking through all the factors. This is both fruitless and foolish.

Prov. 18:14

"The spirit of a man will sustain his infirmity; but a wounded spirit who can bear?"

The spirit of a man... This word for "spirit" is *ruach*, usually trans. "wind or breath." But here it is used as the "seat of emotion or mind," as it pertains to mental acts or energy of life. See Genesis 6:3, where *ruach* refers to God's spirit, not as a force or wind, but the seat of God's justice and disposition. It is translated "mind" in Genesis 26:35; Prov. 29:11 and Daniel 5:20. In Joshua 2:11 it pertains to "courage."

So the infirmity (sickness) of a man is sustained, not by the flesh itself, but by his inner spirit or mind. A healthy spirit will prevail over an infirm body—even to the point of death. **But a wounded spirit who can bear** (carry, take)**?**

So there's a "spirit" and a "wounded spirit." The former is healthy and right, but the latter has been broken, stricken or offended. A wounded spirit cannot bear up or take the infirmity in the proper way. Bitterness will kill him from the inside out and he becomes unreachable (see vs. 19). At best, he will be depressed and "burned out." How essential it is to maintain a right spirit!

Prov. 18:15

"The heart of the prudent getteth knowledge; and the ear of the wise seeketh knowledge."

The prudent (discerning) heart gets (attains) knowledge; it's always on the "seek" for truth. Likewise is **the ear** (inner, spiritual) **of the wise.** Here the "heart" and the "ear" are synonymous. Jesus said: *"He that hath an ear, let him hear what the Spirit saith...."* Wise men want to know more and more of the right thing.

Prov. 18:16

"A man's gift maketh room for him, and bringeth him before great men."

This proverb may follow in the train of 17:8, 23 regarding a bribe. Such gifts do open doors otherwise closed. Could there be a legitimate usage of a gift that pleases or appeases **great men**? Is the **gift** itself the issue, or does the man receive audience with the "king," and bring his gifts of honor and appreciation? Gills note on this latter phrase (i.e., the gift that **bringeth him before great**

men) is well taken:

> "It opens a way for him into the presence and company of great men, being a fee to their servants; or with it he procures a place to wait on them. It is not necessary to understand it of a gift by way of bribe; but to introduce a person to another, and render him acceptable, and appease anger; as in the cases of Jacob and Abigail, Gen_32:20."

Prov. 18:17

"He that is first in his own cause seemeth just; but his neighbour cometh and searcheth him."

This seems to be a court scene where the plaintiff brings his case ("cause, suit") "first"; it therefore seems "just" or right, seeing that there is no challenge or opposition at that point. But then comes his "neighbor" (another person) who "searches" (investigates, examines) the matter. Thus, we have a court case with a charge (cause) and its defense or challenge. See Prov. 18:13.

Just because someone has a "cause" or controversy doesn't mean he's right. It must be open for scrutiny.

Prov. 18:18

"The lot causeth contentions to cease, and parteth between the mighty."

When **the mighty**, i.e., powerful leaders meet to make momentous choices, the "lot" (pebble, rough stone) may prevent **contentions** or fights. The lot was used to make decisions of choice (e.g., Jonah, Matthias, etc.) when otherwise those in authority would try to pull rank on each other. Especially is this helpful when electing leaders who are all qualified for the office. To give an example, this was the policy of church in Pennsylvania to choose elders who were all considered qualified to serve. (Straws with individual names were drawn by a committee). A kind of "lottery," of sorts without the gaming factor. This procedure seemed to satisfy the congregation and was perceived as "God's choice," as opposed to turning the election into a personality contest.

Prov. 18:19

"A brother offended is harder to be won than a strong city: and their contentions are like the bars of a castle."

Here is an expression of how deep **contentions** or bitterness can run among brothers (i.e., family members). How devastating are some offenses and wounded spirits. Gill suggests the examples of Cain and Abel; Jacob and Esau; Amnon and Absalsom, etc. The same principle is valid among "brethren" in the Church. How difficult to regain ground and restore a relationship with a deeply-offended brother! **Their contentions are like the bars** (e.g., gates, windows, etc.) **of a castle.** We just cannot fathom the depths of the human spirit! But thank God for His understanding and gracious power to change hearts.

Prov. 18:20

"A man's belly shall be satisfied with the fruit of his mouth; and with the increase of his lips shall he be filled."

Here the "fruit of the mouth," viz., "words," is likened to food for the stomach ("belly"). We are fed by words (good or bad); but what is produced ("increase") by our lips "fills" or satisfies our inner being. Words edify, comfort, instruct, etc.

Possibly there's a reference here to meditation (Psalm 1:2; Joshua 1:8) on the Word, which becomes "our word," audibly rehearsed. So as we edify ourselves, we edify others as well. See 12:14; 13:2; Cf. 1:31

Prov. 18:21

"Death and life are in the power of the tongue: and they that love it shall eat the fruit thereof."

In the context, the great influence toward **death or life** is in the **power** (lit. *yad*- hand) **of the tongue.** Vs. 19 bears this out regarding offending a brother. James (ch.3) effectively addresses this issue. What we say affects others for good or bad, for Satan or God, for life and death. However, it's a mistake and poor exegesis to teach, as do some, that we create with the tongue; i.e., we can speak things into existence, as did God Himself. Or some say we must never say anything negative—a "negative confession," lest it come to pass. This is spiritism and metaphysics.

They that love it (the tongue and what it speaks, etc.) **shall eat the fruit thereof.** Again, words are powerful and we must be accountable for how we use our tongues. James 3:1 challenges us not to be quick to be a teacher because we shall give an account for what we say. See Prov. 10:19; Ecclesiastes 10:12-14; Isaiah 57:19.

Prov. 18:22

"Whoso findeth a wife findeth a good thing, and obtaineth favour of the LORD."

This verse presupposes that marriage is ordained of God and is a "good" thing. (See Genesis 2:18ff.) Today this institution is being challenged by homosexual ("gay") and feminist activists who advocate "same sex" relationships. Gay "marriage" between persons of the same gender is also on the agenda. God-given marriage is a wonderful institution, despite the struggles and labor involved.

Solomon exhorts that **whoso findeth** (acquires) **a wife findeth a good** (pleasant, precious) **thing**. Some MSS (manuscripts) inject "good" before "wife" (See Barnes) which makes the statement even more appealing. However, marriage is the norm and is generally superior over celibacy (singleness). But certainly a God-given wife is without question a means of obtaining **favour** (delight) **of the LORD.** See the classic example of a beautiful, godly and efficient wife in Prov. 31:10ff.

"And they two shall be one flesh"; indeed, this "oneness" is better than "twoness"!

Prov. 18:23

"The poor useth intreaties; but the rich answereth roughly."

What a contrast between the attitude of a **poor** man, one in need, and the **rich** who need nothing! The down-and-out person "intreats," asks for help, knowing that he can make no demands. He comes with a servant spirit, willing to help where he can. I see this every day at the Rescue Mission. People come from all walks of life, but all get in the "soup line" together because they're hungry. None pulls "rank," for they're all the "same size"—same needs.

Not so with the **rich** who have no need; they can afford to **answer roughly** (harshly, rudely), for they can "demand" rather than "intreat." How significant is the connection between riches and arrogance! Wealthy people generally dominate, rather than serve.

Money speaks, even in the Church, which needs to take heed that it doesn't cater to the rich at the expense of the poor. See James 2:3 ("respect of persons").

Prov. 18:24

"A man that hath friends must shew himself friendly: and there is a friend that sticketh closer than a brother."

We reproduce in others what we are ourselves; true love finds response in others who are seeking love. People with true friends are those who themselves have demonstrated genuine friendship and concern. The phrase **shew himself friendly** has the idea of brokenness or humility. John said, *"We know that we have passed from death unto life because we love the brethren."* (1 John 3:14).

Solomon then adds, *"...and there is a friend that sticketh closer than a brother."* There are friends and then there are "friends"! Blood relationship is generally deeper and more binding than mere companionship. Yet, David and Jonathan exemplify the ultimate of true friendship (See 2 Samuel 1:26). However, we certainly envision here the Friend of Sinners Himself and Lover of our souls! See John 15:14, 15; check also Solomon's Song of Songs 2:1-4, where he extols the unique love of the Bridegroom of the Church—The Lord Jesus Christ.

Chapter 19
Better is the Poor Who Walks in His Integrity

Prov. 19:1

"Better is the poor that walketh in his integrity, than he that is perverse in his lips, and is a fool."

Here's a contrast between a man of integrity and a fool. **Better is the poor** (needy, lacking) **that walketh** (attitude, lifestyle) **in his integrity** (idea of completeness, simplicity, not as in foolishness, but single-mindedness). There are things much more important that being financially rich; it's having honest character (wholeness). Not so much what we have, as what we are!

The contrast is the one who is **perverse** (crooked, distorted) **in his lips and** (thus) **is a fool** (stupid).

The inference is that this fool may be rich materially, etc., but his bankruptcy of character is revealed by his mouth. Our tongue indeed reveals the nature of our heart. Success today is measured by a six-figure salary and the corresponding "toys" of this world. But WHO are we and WHAT are we? God is not counting as much as He's weighing!

Prov. 19:2

"Also, that the soul be without knowledge, it is not good; and he that hasteth with his feet sinneth."

Solomon goes on to say that a soul (person- *nephesh*) who is ignorant (void of common sense and knowledge) is not a good thing; and **he that hasteth** (hurries, presses) **with his feet sinneth** (*chattah* - to miss the mark). Here is the ongoing description of a fool, beginning in vs. 1 with "perverted lips"; then he has "head" trouble (i.e., ignorance), along with "feet" problems (i.e., making

305

haste) which lead to sinful actions. See Romans 3:15. Foolishness is a "total man" thing, inside and out. As a man *"thinketh in his heart, so is he."* Note the further progression in vs. 3.

Prov. 19:3

"The foolishness of man perverteth his way: and his heart fretteth against the LORD."

The foolishness (lit. silliness) **of man perverteth** (twists, distorts) **his way** (course of life); **and his heart fretteth** (i.e., to be vexed, enraged, sad) a**gainst the LORD.** Sounds like Psalm 2:2 where the heathen have set themselves against the LORD and His Anointed! *"The fool hath said in his heart, there is no God,"* (Psalm 14:1) and yet spends a lifetime fighting off His restraint and Word. Fools are not passive but active in their perverted minds and lifestyle. If you're wrong about God, you'll always be wrong about you!

Evidently, the fool destroys his life by refusing God's way, and then blames God for his failure, thus, the "fretting" and anger. He will not take responsibility for his choices, and thus acquires a "victim" mentality; i.e., nothing is my fault; I'm a victim of my environment, DNA, parentage, etc. But most of all, God let it happen, so it's his fault. See, for example, Adam in the Garden. (Genesis 3).

Prov. 19:4

"Wealth maketh many friends; but the poor is separated from his neighbour."

If you're wealthy, you may not know who your real friends are; not so with the poor. A rich man will attract "friends" or companions, but the "poor" do not have the "drawing factor," i.e., money, to cause people to gravitate to them. "Money talks," so one has said, but it sure doesn't satisfy nor buy real friends.

Success and prestige are monitored by one's wealth, rather than who he really is. The Hollywood personalities of our day are lauded and envied, but apart from their riches, they're not impressive.

When they lose their fortunes, then they find out who their "friends" are.

The poor is separated from (lit. from among) **his neighbour** (same word for "friend"). That is, he's on the "outside" of the social group—the upper crust. What a shame that people cannot be evaluated by their true worth or character, etc., but only from a financial viewpoint! There are many rich people who are poor (empty, miserable, etc.); on the other hand, there are many so-called poor folks who are rich in character qualities and true values.

It must also be stated here that some enjoy material wealth who do not love it, but use it for God's glory. These may draw the right people. Being "poor" in itself is no virtue, but there's certainly more to life than what one has in his wallet. This verse can be applied in various ways.

Prov. 19:5

"A false witness shall not be unpunished, and he that speaketh lies shall not escape."

This parallelism speaks to the fate of liars. **False witness** and **lies** go together. The former is a "testimony that's untrue, without cause"; the latter depicts one who is "breathing out lies" (deceit, falsehood). Note that in both instances, they "shall not" (emphatic-not just "will" not, but "shall" not!) prevail. The first shall not be "unpunished" or acquitted; the second shall not "escape" (slip away, or be delivered).

This "punishment" seems to deal with the judicial system of law. It smacks of a court scene. It will work as long as there's justice in the land. But today, we are "throwing out" the Commandments, while judges make their own laws which are "politically correct." The Holy has become profane; right and wrong are in the eye of the beholder (e.g., situation ethics, etc.). Thus, this verse may have to find its ultimate fulfillment in the Final Judgment.

A man lies because he's a liar! Some just "bellow" out lies, having no concept of Truth. Only the Truth Himself (Christ) can implant a heart of truth into a sinner; it's called the "new birth." But whatever the case, be sure your sin will find you out. We reap what we sow and the harvest of lying will one day be manifest. Even what was spoken in secret will one day be "shouted from the rooftop"!

Prov. 19:6

"Many will intreat the favour of the prince: and every man is a friend to him that giveth gifts."

A very familiar attitude is revealed in this verse: Men "suck up" to those in authority, especially when there's something to get for themselves. **Many will entreat the favor of the prince**, i.e., not only to "ask", but lit. "to stroke the face" of nobility. There are all kinds of worldly terms for such action, some which cannot be rightly expressed. We love to feel important by getting "next to" those of importance. How we treat politicians and celebrities measures our sense of value. Most of the time, those who make the headlines are not the most noble of people. The headlines in Heaven read much differently than on earth!

Note that "many" entreat the prince, but **"every man" is a friend to him that giveth gifts.** Very few will befriend a poor man; if fact, what we do for others who can never reciprocate indicates our true character. But here we find the well-known mentality of befriending those who freely give what we want. That is well demonstrated in every aspect of society, e.g., welfare system, graft in government, prosperity gospel, desire to find a "rich uncle" or future spouse, etc., etc. This is built in to human nature. Yet, how hesitant we are to line up with the King of Glory" who is the Giver of every good and perfect gift! Amen!

Prov. 19:7

"All the brethren of the poor do hate him: how much more do his friends go far from him? he pursueth them with words, yet they are wanting to him."

What a commentary here concerning the attitude of kinfolk and friends toward the destitute or poor! This seems explain further the truth of vs. 4—*"Wealth maketh many friends...."* There's some disdain toward the poor, whether it's that they (the poor) cannot contribute and give gifts, etc., or whether it's a "hatred" or disgust for possible laziness or lack of industry on their part. Whatever the case, being destitute is not a popular condition, with the possible exception of those who play the welfare system. Working at a rescue mission leads me to believe that some folks "enjoy" being poor, thus living off of others' wealth and generosity. Personal dignity is not a consideration to many; they will do anything but "work."

At the same time, there are those who have come to bad times and a helping hand is in order. Yet still their families may despise them, unwilling to help. So this verse states that not only is the poor man "hated" by his kin, but even his **friends go far** (withdraw themselves, leave) **from him.** It says that **he pursueth** (runs after) **them with words** (pleading for help?), **yet they are wanting** (lit. not)" So even his cry of desperation is in vain—they write him off and turn a deaf ear! What a tragedy, but so it is in this world.

Jesus said, *"For ye have the poor always with you"*; but thank God that the "poor" in spirit can get an audience with the King, even when nobody else cares! It would be great if poverty resulted in a humble, poor spirit, but such is not the case. I see folks everyday who are destitute financially and materially, but manifest a bitter and proud attitude!

Prov. 19:8

"He that getteth wisdom loveth his own soul: he that keepeth understanding shall find good."

A love of sin and foolishness is destructive to one's soul or self. There is a true love and respect for ourselves as creatures of God. Thus, what we love and hate indicates what we really are. Here Solomon exhorts us that, *He that getteth* (attains, procures) *wisdom loveth his own soul*; i.e., the best gift to ourselves (well-being) is to receive wisdom. There's nothing in this world to match it or to make us effective instruments for the glory of God.

He goes on to say, *he that keepeth* (guards, preserves) **understanding shall find good** (and not bad). Two steps here: 1) attaining wisdom; and 2) keeping or maintaining it. Some men start well and finished poorly. Wisdom not only saves us, but sanctifies and keeps us. Christ is made unto us Wisdom (1 Corinthians 1:30). How few are even interested in such a gift! Yet, this is much more valuable and important than any worldly inheritance.

Prov. 19:9

*"A false witness shall not be unpunished, and he that speaketh
lies shall perish."*

This verse is almost a repetition of vs. 5, with some variation. He doesn't just say "liars will be punished"; but rather used two negative verb forms for emphasis: **A false witness _shall not_ be _unpunished_.** That is, judgment is sure! God, being Truth, has no place for untruth! This is another reason for being "born again" by the Spirit of Truth Who places us in Christ—the Truth.

And he that speaketh lies (//--parallel to "false witness") **shall perish** (be destroyed). In a society that rubs out the line between truth and lies, only future judgment will sort it out. (See 2 Thessalonians 2:8-10; 1 Timothy 4:1, 2; 2 Peter 2:1-3; Revelation 19:20; 21:8; 22:15.)

Prov. 19:10

*"Delight is not seemly for a fool; much less for a servant to have
rule over princes."*

True luxury and pleasantness is as foreign to a fool as the possibility of a bond slave to rule over the king! So is the analogy here in vs. 10. Some who propound egalitarianism (equal outcome for all) and cry "discrimination" at every turn, should study this example of reality. Life and culture render distinctions, depending on the players. All are not equal! That's a difficult lesson to learn.

The principle here is that **delight** (lit. daintiness, luxury) **is not seemly** (becoming, fitting, suitable) **for a fool;** i.e., being a fool is not conducive to pleasantness and true prosperity. By virtue of being a fool, he makes the wrong decisions in life which nullify the blessings of God. He exists, rather than lives. But that's his problem. You can't blame his misfortune on society or God. He reaps what he sows. He's responsible for his actions and the results that accompany those actions.

The fool's chance of genuine success in life is as doubtful as **a servant to have rule** (power) **over princes** (masters, rulers). It won't happen! Fool's may be persistent in their foolishness, but that determination doesn't change their destiny. The wrong road leads to the wrong place! How different it would be if he were "wise." In fact, even the obedient servant would "rule" in his own right, while he submits to the will of the king (especially to a benevolent ruler).

Prov. 19:11

"The discretion of a man deferreth his anger; and it is his glory to pass over a transgression."

Here is a beautiful statement illustrating a true believer's ability to forgive others by the fruit and power of the Holy Spirit! **The discretion of a man deferreth his anger;** i.e., how a man thinks— the wisdom within, determines his ability to defer or prolong his anger or wrath.

Note the word "discretion" which is translated "understanding" in 13:15, "wisdom" in 1 Chronicles 22:12, and "sense" in Nehemiah 8:8. God-given "sense" and the longsuffering of the Spirit can enable a man to defer ("prolong") his anger. See 14:29 and 16:32 which extol the strength of a godly man to rule his spirit and not give in to wrath. Here is a display of the "longsuffering" of the Holy Spirit (Galatians 5:22, 23). K&D actually uses this term in their translation.

Moreover, such longsuffering to **pass over a transgression** (i.e., personal affront) **is his "glory**—lit. "beauty, honor". This word, *tifawreth,* means "ornament"; thus, to be "comely" (Isaiah 4:2) or becoming. This quality of longsuffering is an evidence of virtuous quality and godly character. Indeed, we are "forgiven, to forgive." (See Matthew 5:22-24; 6:12-15.)

Prov. 19:12

"The king's wrath is as the roaring of a lion; but his favour is as dew upon the grass."

Here we see the diverse nature of a king or ruler regarding

obedience to the (his) law. Many oriental kings were a law unto themselves, while David and Solomon followed God's Law. But in either case, the king was to be feared by the subjects; to disobey was to meet with "the king's wrath (indignation), as the roaring of a lion." This represents the justice side of his nature.

But his favour (goodwill) **is as dew upon the grass.** Here is his gracious side, which is evidenced upon those who submit to him. This principle is expressed in Romans 13:3, regarding governmental law. Prov.16:14,15; 20:2 also give similar thoughts.

Ultimately, this represents the very character of our Lord Jesus, the gentle Saviour, who graciously receives those who repent and believe the Gospel. But He is also the "Lion King" who will one day "roar" in His judgment and put down those who refuse to submit to His Law. It's sure good to be on the right side of the King of Kings!

Prov. 19:13

"A foolish son is the calamity of his father: and the contentions of a wife are a continual dropping."

To have a foolish son is bad enough, but a nagging wife is even worse! Talk about a "dysfunctional family"! And yet, in how many families is this not the norm? Everyone is dysfunctional to some degree, thus no family has it all together.

The word, **"calamity,"** has the sense of negative events or engulfing ruin (cf. Psalm 57:1; Job 6:2); it is also used for a "falling or negative desire"; i.e., utter disappointment—in this case the father. But likened to that is the contentious (lit. brawling, striving) spouse whose constant opposition is as a **continual dropping** of water. The picture is water dripping perpetually over one spot which eventually will wear a hole in any substance, cement and metal notwithstanding.

Prov. 19:14

"House and riches are the inheritance of fathers: and a prudent wife is from the LORD."

One can obtain **house and riches** (wealth) from a father's estate, but only the LORD can supply **a prudent** (wise, circumspect) **wife**. The latter "gift" is indeed the greatest value of the two. Not that wealth is not a gift from God, which it can be, but a wise and careful wife cannot be purchased. Her worth is beyond rubies and diamonds (See 31:10ff.).

Also, what a contrast to the "contentious wife" of vs. 13.

Prov. 19:15

"Slothfulness casteth into a deep sleep; and an idle soul shall suffer hunger."

Slothfulness (utter laziness) **casteth** (cause to fall, Hiph. imperf) **into a deep sleep**. Certainly this is the opposite of activity and diligence. Could this "deep sleep" be likened to Adam's? Not just "sleep," but *deep* sleep. So much is said about laziness in Proverbs. (See Prov. 19:24; 6:9, 10; 20:13).

The obvious result of such "idleness" will be "hunger" and unmet needs. This can apply spiritually as well.

Prov. 19:16

"He that keepeth the commandment keepeth his own soul; but he that despiseth his ways shall die."

How can I keep or guard my soul? Solomon's answer is to constantly "keep" or take heed to the commandment (Word of God). There is not only blessing in obeying the Word, but safety. Walking with God (the Word) is the ultimate in "eternal security"! One cannot get "off track" if he walks on the King's highway of Truth. This is the essence of abundant life (John 10:10).

On the other hand, **he that despiseth his ways shall die.** To "despise" is to treat lightly or hold in contempt. Here is a man who will not heed "his ways," i.e., the dictates of his conscience—what he knows to be right. Such can only lead to "death" (spiritual blindness and absence of life in God). Death in Scripture is not only the cessation of physical life, but the separation from and absence of spiritual life in Christ. *"The words that I speak unto you... are life,"* said Jesus; to reject them is to reject life and embrace death.

Prov. 19:17

"He that hath pity upon the poor lendeth unto the LORD; and that which he hath given will he pay him again.

Here's the recurring reference to our attitude toward the poor. To show mercy to the poor somehow "lends" to the LORD; i.e., to give to the poor is to give to God! What we do for his needy creatures is what we do for Him. Thus, He, the Lord, is "indebted" to "pay" us back!

Jesus said in Matthew 25:40:

"Inasmuch as ye have done it unto one of the least of these my brethren, ye have done it unto me."

This is an example of "laying up treasure in Heaven"; i.e., loving our neighbor as ourselves. The love of God is manifested in our attitude and actions toward others. "Love is the fulfilling of the law."

Prov. 19:18

"Chasten thy son while there is hope, and let not thy soul spare for his crying."

There's certainly a time frame for disciplining children, viz., **while there is hope.** There comes a time when "hope" or expectancy is over, and they are "out of the nest." Plus, the word chasten (*yasar*) means lit. "to chastise with blows" or fig. "with words." It is combined with reproof and correction, which must begin at an early age; (see 13:24).

Note the intense, yet compassionate, commitment to this task. Solomon says don't let your soul (*nephesh*— emotions, etc.) **spare for his crying** (lit. dying). This a great issue in our day when we have all but denied the depravity of children. People aren't evil anymore, just "sick." Thus, we have not properly disciplined our children in the home, which has led to a nation of rebels; now we throw up our hands in despair, as we build more prisons! O, to get back to God's standard of operation: Training children in truth, love and justice. (a whole book could be written here!).

Prov. 19:19

"A man of great wrath shall suffer punishment: for if thou deliver him, yet thou must do it again."

A man of great (in magnitude) **wrath** (anger, lit. heat, rage) **shall suffer** (lit. lift, take, bear) **punishment; for if thou deliver** (defend) **him, yet** (still) **thou must do it again** (*yasaph*— lit. to add, to continue to do a thing). Here's a man who has never been broken (cf. vs. 18) and one that has not received instruction (cf. vs. 20).

This is a portrayal of the "Cain spirit" which is murderous and totally consumed with self. Such temper cannot ultimately be quelled apart from the crucifying work of the Holy Spirit. (cf. Romans 6:6) God doesn't redirect or reform sinners, He *kills* them! Then raises them up as a new creation in Christ.

Prov. 19:20

"Hear counsel, and receive instruction, that thou mayest be wise in thy latter end."

It's not so much how a man begins life's journey that counts, but rather how he finishes. Hearing and receiving instruction (i.e., a teachable, humble spirit) is wise at any stage of life. Some seem to begin right, but end up wrong. A wise man will persevere to the end, disciplining his life on a daily basis. Kings Solomon and Hezekiah exemplify those who were blessed with godly wisdom, but became "sloppy" toward the end of their lives.

We only come this way one time and all that we do will carry over into eternity. Do it well!

Live skillfully! Live to the "hilt"! This is the "kindergarten of eternity," and the "right road will lead to the right place." We must not be overcome, but Spirit-filled overcomers! JFB comments: "In youth prepare for age."

Prov. 19:21

"There are many devices in a man's heart; nevertheless the counsel of the LORD, that shall stand."

Here is a decisive contrast between the scheming, self-willed "devices" (plans, intentions) of the wicked heart of man verses the eternal, righteous and steadfast "counsel" (advice) of the LORD! Man's heart is *deceitful above all things, and desperately wicked...* (Jeremiah 17:9); it is self-serving, contrary to God's desires (Word) and Sovereignty, thus can never succeed nor stand under the scrutiny of God's judgment. See Psalm 33:10, 11.

It should be noted that these "devices" may never be overtly manifested as wicked, but remain lodged in the heart. Likewise, these fleshly and egotistical thoughts may be of a religious or spiritual nature; e.g., pride of Satan, false teachers, etc.

Prov. 19:22

"The desire of a man is his kindness: and a poor man is better than a liar."

The desire (charm, attraction) **of a man is his kindness.** This is difficult to decipher on the surface. In light of man's basic selfishness, it doesn't seem plausible to say that "man's desire is to be kind." It could better be taken from an objective standpoint that what makes any man desirable or attractive is his kindness.

And a poor man (without means) **is better** (off) **than a liar.** The inference is that the "liar" has means and intentions to give but reneges. The poor man with good intentions is better, his attitude being considered some semblance of kindness. See 19:1; 11:23.

Prov. 19:23

"The fear of the LORD tendeth to life: and he that hath it shall abide satisfied; he shall not be visited with evil."

The fear of the LORD can only point one in the direction of "life" (abundant); in addition, to possess this Godly fear is to **abide satisfied**; i.e., rest in God's completeness and peace. In that state, nothing shall offend or nothing ultimately bad can come. Certainly trials and trouble invade the believer's domain, but need not overcome the one overcome by the power and blessing of God! See Isaiah 58:10, 11 Matthew 5:6; Philippines 4:11, 12. Also Prov. 12:21; Romans 8:28.

Prov. 19:24

A slothful man hideth his hand in his bosom, and will not so much as bring it to his mouth again.

Strange how wicked man will expect God to do what He has given man the ability to do; on the other hand, wicked man won't trust God to do what man can' t do, viz., deliver him from sin! Here we have an example of a lazy ("slothful") man who **hideth his hand in his bosom and will not so much as bring it to his mouth again.** It takes too much effort to eat!

It just that he can't afford to expend that much energy or is he expecting God to feed him while he "sits on his hands"? Or is this just a poetic expression of one who refuses to work for a living? (May be both).

K&D translates bosom as "bowl," depicting one who's so sleepy and lazy that he can't (won't) pick up the food to place in his mouth. Apart from the grace of God, how pathetic is pathetic man!

Prov. 19:25

Smite a scorner, and the simple will beware: and reprove one that hath understanding, and he will understand knowledge.

Whether by the "striking" of the rod or word of mouth, positive results can come. The **simple** or silly **will**, at least, **beware** (lit. "take crafty counsel") when witnessing the physical reprimand of a mocker. Likewise, the "reproof" (correction) of an "understanding" man will further his understanding of knowledge; i.e., increase wisdom. See 15:5; 21:11.

Prov. 19:26

"He that wasteth his father, and chaseth away his mother, is a son that causeth shame, and bringeth reproach."

This is Solomon's reprimand and warning given to a disrespectful son (child). He is described here as one **that wasteth his father....** Interesting term—"waste"; it is also translated "spoil," as in Jeremiah 47:4; 49:28, etc., referring to the robbery and treachery of warfare. (See this same word in Prov. 24:15, 11:3— "destroyed").

Here's a son who "declares war" on his father, robbing, violating and victimizing him as he would any other object of greed! Probably, the word "devastate" is the best rendering (Pi. part.). What despicable treatment is this!

Likewise, he **chaseth away his mother,** driving her away from the tranquility and safety of the home. He alienates himself from his mother's love and affection because of his waywardness. Such conduct can only cause shame, reproach and embarrassment to fall upon this household. The shame and disappointment affects everyone, causing a possible life-long reproach upon that family. This may explain the law of Numbers 21 whereby a rebellious son was to be put to death.

I think that Matthew Henry's take on this verse is incisive indeed and worth pondering:

> "Here is, 1. The sin of a prodigal son. Besides the wrong he does to himself, he is injurious to his good parents, and basely ungrateful to those that were instruments of his being and have taken so much care and pains about him, which is a great aggravation of his sin and renders it exceedingly sinful in the eyes of God and man: He wastes is father, wastes his estate which he should have to support him in his old age, wastes his spirits, and breaks his heart, and brings his gray head with sorrow to the grave. He chases away his mother, alienates her affections from him, which cannot be done without a great deal of regret and uneasiness to her; he makes her weary of the house, with his rudeness and insolence, and glad to retire for a little quietness; and, when he has spent all, he turns her out of doors. 2. The shame of a prodigal son. It is a shame to himself that he should be so brutish and unnatural. He makes himself odious to all mankind. It is a shame to his parents and family, who are reflected upon, though, perhaps, without just cause, for teaching him no better, or being in some way wanting to him."

Prov. 19:27

"Cease, my son, to hear the instruction that causeth to err from the words of knowledge."

In light of the previous verse (26), Solomon cries out, **"Cease, my son, to hear the instruction that causeth to err from the words of knowledge"**; i.e., stop listening to that (and/or those) which leads you astray! Words have great power and influence, whether good or bad. But the wicked heart gravitates to the wishes and schemes of other wicked men. Significantly, Solomon's own son, Rehoboam, defied his father's instruction when he listened to the evil advice of his peers, rather than the seasoned instruction of the elders. (cf. 1 Kings 12:8)

Learning more is always advantageous. Our response to what we hear is all-important. More light means more accountability. A man is never better off knowing truth if he refuses to obey it. Following the wrong crowd can only lead to disaster. James 1:22-24 clarifies this concept.

Prov. 19:28

"An ungodly witness scorneth judgment: and the mouth of the wicked devoureth iniquity."

Here is a commentary of the outworkings of a deceitful and wicked heart. **An ungodly** (*belial*—foolish, worthless) **witness scorneth** (mocks) **judgment.** No wonder people deny and spurn any sense of guilt! Justice is mocked in the land, even unto the present. None seem to face up to any wrong-doing these days; especially since we have confused sin and mental illness. Wicked people are no longer "wicked," they're just "sick." Thus, instead of needing the forgiveness of the Cross, they simply take a psycho-tropic pill, like Prozac. Then we wonder why we cannot stem the tide of rebellion and crime!

In addition, the wicked "eat up" (swallow, devour) iniquity or sin. That's their steady diet! They feast on what emanates from their hearts. Sin begets more sin. (See Isaiah 1:4-6) They love what God hates and hate what God loves! There's only one thing for a sinner to do—SIN! He does what he does, because he is what he is! O, the wonder of saving grace in Christ that can bring fruit out of a garbage pail, giving a sinner a new heart! (cf. 2 Corinthians 5:17)

Prov. 19:29

"Judgments are prepared for scorners, and stripes for the back of fools."

Justice exists for those who break God's law. **Judgments are prepared** (lit. firmly established) **for scorners** (mockers). Thus, *"...it is appointed unto man once to die, but after this the judgment"* (Hebrews 9:27). Because "God is Just," those who practice and mock (scorn) sin will be dealt with accordingly, *"for the wages of sin is death"* (Romans 6:23). The "lake of fire" is the ultimate prison house of justice for those who refuse to repent of sin.

The Lord has also made provision for justice in this world through government. In Romans 13:1-7, Paul expounds the *"higher powers* (authority)...*ordained* (appointed) *of God."* Those in high places are "ministers of God" to protect those under their jurisdiction. Therefore, we have police, prosecutors, judges, courts, etc. for the purpose of punishing people who break the law. Thus, **stripes for the back of fools**; i.e., those who refuse to comply with that which is right. This system should not only hold lawbreakers accountable, but deter others from ever getting involved in criminal behavior.

Chapter 20

Wine is a Mocker

Prov. 20:1

"Wine is a mocker, strong drink is raging: and whosoever is deceived thereby is not wise."

Wine— fermented here, not just grape juice; **is a mocker** (lit. "make mouths at" or scorn, talk arrogantly). While acceptably used for social and medicinal purpose (see Genesis 27:25; 1 Timothy 5:23), it was abused and thus "abused" its victim (e.g., Isaiah 5:11). It's therefore a subtle intoxicant that enables one to make a complete fool out of himself!

Strong drink (intensely alcoholic liquor) **is raging** (lit. make a loud sound; thus creating turmoil and great commotion). The one **deceived** (led astray) **thereby is not wise** (i.e., is a fool; not living skillfully or seeing life from a proper perspective).

Prov. 20:2

"The fear of a king is as the roaring of a lion: whoso provoketh him to anger sinneth against his own soul."

You don't want to get a king mad! He's the one in authority and ordained to deal with crime, etc. (see Romans 13) His terror or fear comes forth as the roar of a lion—it's to be avoided at all cost. To provoke a righteous king to anger is unwise and ultimately to **sin** (*chattah*— miss the mark) **against** (your) **own soul** (*nephesh*). We don't break the law, the law breaks us!

In light of verse 1 and the curse of drunkenness, so rebellion against the "king" (legal authority) ends up in judgment. The law should be a rebuke to our wrong doing, thus preventing further transgressions. We live in a day when authority in homes and communities is mocked and disregarded. Now violence and corruption and perversion are running rampant. If it's wrong, don't do it! Don't even think about provoking the "king" or breaking the law. Only fools think that they can disobey the law without reaping the consequences.

Prov. 20:3

"It is an honour for a man to cease from strife: but every fool will be meddling."

This verse may be a continuance of vs. 2 regarding the one who "sins against" himself by breaking the Law. Here Solomon extols the man who will **cease from strife** (i.e., controversy, dispute, quarrel). It indicates a peace maker rather than a peace breaker. He's a man of "honor" who can control his spirit and tongue. "Honour" here is *kadhobe* (lit. heaviness, weight), which refers mostly to God's glory. It's a man of "weightiness" who stops or refrains from quarreling, etc. This is a sign of true character and control of one's spirit.

The fool, on the other hand, reveals his lack of character by his **meddling** or contentious spirit. He has "foot and mouth" disease—always speaking before thinking. Fools love to quarrel, letting their inner thoughts "hang out" indiscriminately.

Prov. 20:4

"The sluggard will not plow by reason of the cold; therefore shall he beg in harvest, and have nothing."

A lazy or sluggish man is deterred easily by weather conditions. He'll always find an excuse for not working. For a farmer, that's critical, because without plowing, there's no preparation for seeding and thus no harvest. The "weather" never seems just right—some like it hot, and others cold, and still others moderate. But the farmer must be *"instant in season" and "out of season."* There's a time to plow and a time to harvest—both are essential, for there's not one without the other.

Because he wouldn't work at the right time, he'll be "begging" at harvest time. And if he's a fool, he'll stand there and wonder why, saying. "It ain't fair"! Then he'll head for the "welfare office," where others will be responsible to do for him what he should have done for himself! In this economy, we live by the sweat of our brow. No work, no eat! *"For whatsoever a man soweth, that shall he also reap"* (Galatians 6:7); if you sow nothing, you get nothing.

Prov. 20:5

"Counsel in the heart of man is like deep water; but a man of understanding will draw it out."

Counsel (advice, purpose) **in the heart** (spirit) **of man is like deep water**. Deep water runs still as opposed to the shallow, babbling brook (see 18:4). Everyone, good or wicked, has deep purpose and innermost thoughts. Some communicate them better than others. Others hide their intent deep within, never really expressing themselves.

But a man of understanding will draw it out. This seems to relate to a counseling situation whereby a wise person has the ability to "draw out" those deep thoughts from the heart. It takes wisdom to effectively communicate with someone who has become introverted; in like manner, one with skillful discernment can also enable the deep thinker to express himself more fully. This "man of understanding" is gifted in probing and opening (drawing out) the understanding of those who do not readily communicate.

Prov. 20:6

"Most men will proclaim every one his own goodness: but a faithful man who can find?"

How familiar is this text! It was the theme "song" of our college youth ministry in Whitmire, S.C. during the '50s. These words were reiterated at every Friday evening team meeting, prior to the weekend services. **Most men will proclaim every one his own goodness: but a faithful man who can find?** I've not been able to drift far from this message which extols the character of "faithfulness."

Men are quick to boast of their **own goodness**. One of my mentors used to say, "If you want to find out how good a person is, just ask him!" It's amazing how great people are in their own eyes! Pride and boasting are built into the fabric of our fleshly egos; how quick we are to **proclaim** (call out, preach) our own **goodness** (lit. kindness, piety).

Yet the text describes the fiber and reality of true piety which is "faithfulness" or trustworthiness. Does our life "speak" or just our mouth? God is Faithful! Do we thus manifest this pristine quality and godly character? JFB quips, "Boasters are unreliable."

My grandson Justin wrote in his journal (just before his death at 20 yrs. old): "It is easier to be a fanatic, than a faithful soul." We live in a day of "big talk" and "excitement" in the church, but where are the "faithful souls?" Where are the people that are true to their word? That "put their money where their mouth is"? That manifest the character of Christ consistently, when no one's looking? Who display the fruit of the Spirit in a day when folks are going crazy about "gifts?"

O, Lord, raise up "a few good men," who have your heart!

Prov. 20:7

"The just man walketh in his integrity: his children are blessed after him."

The character and pace of a godly man leaves a proper legacy for his children. All too often the "inheritance" of a father is material or financial. Though not to be belittled, things are not as important to leave behind as a testimony of "integrity"; thus says this proverb.

The just (righteous) **man walketh** (lifestyle) **in his integrity: his children are blessed after him.** This legacy is ongoing, not just something in the future (e.g., inheritance). The word "integrity" means "completeness" and thus spiritual prosperity; it's the result of one being right with God and thus walking in rightness. That's the key to fullness of life here on earth—the opposite of the world's thinking. Walking in fellowship with the Saviour is the essence of true life (John 10:10).

It seems that this father's character is somehow "caught" by his children who are **blessed after him**. I'm sure that the father's testimony does not bring automatic, experiential blessing to each child. Each is certainly responsible to respond to the claims of Christ personally. But to have such an example and director in the home is a true gift from the Lord.

The word "blessed" is *esher*, the Heb.pl used in Psalm 1:1; *"Blessed is the man...."* It means to be "extremely happy." It is derived from the Arabic verb meaning "to go straight." We are born "crooked" and Jesus came to make the "crooked straight." Amen. Thus we can be "complete" in Him and experience His fullness and happiness.

Now having a righteous father who walks in his integrity is a "blessing" in itself. How gracious is such a "gift" to a family. The legacy of his example is a "blessing," by which the children can know what's right and how to live—thus to follow this pattern in their personal lives. How we need such examples of integrity today in our homes and in the public square!

Prov. 20:8

"A king that sitteth in the throne of judgment scattereth away all evil with his eyes."

This proverb pictures a righteous king sitting on his throne of justice and what results: He **scattereth away all evil with his eyes**. A good and discerning ruler can disperse (lit. for "scatter away") evil (bad, unpleasant) with his eyes; i.e., glance of authority. His rightness and authority is communicated by his eyes, which can "see through" those who appear before him. He can sense the "vibes" that control his subjects and apply the law accordingly.

This king does not tolerate evil and it is rooted out quickly. People recognize authority and thus are more apt to do right when considering that they cannot escape the "eye" of the king. Likewise, those who serve under this king are more apt to toe the line as well.

One the other hand, a "wishy-washy" king will invite all kinds of evil to his kingdom. Leadership is key, for the subjects will follow their leader. That's true in government, business and the church.

See JFB's other references: Prov. 20:8 - As in Prov. 14:35; Prov. 16:10, 16:15. This is the character of a good king, not of all kings.

Prov. 20:9

"Who can say, I have made my heart clean, I am pure from my sin?"

This is the question form of Romans 3:23: *"For all have sinned and come short of the glory of God."* The universality of sin is a fact, for the *"wages of sin is death"*—and all die. Solomon asks the question as to **who can say, I have made my heart clean** (pure, innocent), **I am pure** (uncontaminated) **from my sin** (*chattah*)?

To think that anyone would ever think to ask such a question to begin with, is amazing. But sin's deception runs so deeply that man is blind and/or deceived. But the main issue here is not so much admitting sin, but taking credit for cleansing one's heart from sin. What a boast! This is arrogance on the highest level!

Of course, the direct inference here is that no one can rightly make such a boast. Cleansing self from sin is impossible with man, but certainly possible with God alone. Jeremiah says, *"The heart is deceitful above all things, and desperately wicked: who can know it?"* (17:9) Man can wash his body, but never his heart. In fact, God doesn't even "wash" our old nature (heart), but rather gives us a new one (new man). Another way of saying that he kills the old adamic nature (Romans 6:6) and raises us up in newness of life in Christ.

This whole issue of regeneration is a divine act indeed—totally out of reach for man.

"For by grace are ye saved through faith; and that not of yourselves: it is the gift of God: Not of works, lest any man should boast." (Ephesians 2:8, 9)

Thus, Christ performs in the human spirit what no other person or religion can produce. Amen!

Prov. 20:10

"Divers weights, and divers measures, both of them are alike abomination to the LORD."

There are fair business standards upon which man operates—weights and measures being fundamental. His wickedness is many times manifested by changing the standard and thus cheating or defrauding the customer. Moreover, it is an **abomination to the LORD**—the ultimate Source of every standard. How we treat mankind is directly related to how we treat God!

Divers (diverse) **weights** are lit. stones (*eben*), large or small, for measuring the weight of a substance or material (e.g., balance scale). **Divers measures** is the word, *ephah*, used for dry measure of quantity (equal to about 40 liters). Obviously, these forms of measure could be manipulated to serve the perverted desires of the merchant. All in a day's "work" is this for the crooked business man! But God sees the heart, and while the crook may "take" many, making excessive amounts of illegal money, he will one day stand before the LORD and give account.

Prov. 11:1 and 16:11 also speak to this issue. See the notes on 11:1 for the spiritual application of this principle.

Prov. 20:11

"Even a child is known by his doings, whether his work be pure, and whether it be right."

Solomon speaks of a man's inability to cleanse himself from sin (vs.9), and then his propensity to cheat (vs.10). Now he focuses on a "child" (*na'ar*) or "young lad" (cf. Genesis 22:3) who likewise can be judged (evaluated) by his actions. Thus, he says, **"Even a child** (young person) **is known by his doings** (deeds or acts)."

Evidently, young people (between infancy and adolescence) can do right or wrong. They are not innocent (Romans 3:23). Their deeds are "known" (scrutinized, acknowledged), **whether his work be pure and...right** (upright). Jesus said, *"Ye shall know them by their fruits."* (Mt.7:16f). This pertains to youngsters as well, who many times are excused from their actions under the guise of "growing up." There is only one Bible, not two. The same standard exists for children and adults.

But likewise it needs to be emphasized that there is the positive side of children who live right. They need to be recognized as well for their attitude and deeds. Thank God that not all children are rebels; there are young people who desire to be "pure in heart" and "upright" in their conduct. They need to be acknowledged as well, and encouraged to walk with God and thus glorify Him!

Prov. 20:12

"The hearing ear, and the seeing eye, the LORD hath made even both of them."

What a testimony to our All-seeing and All-hearing God! He could have made man deaf, dumb and blind, but rather chose to make him with precious and effective means of communication. Even those who may have difficulty with one or more of their senses, still magnify the glory of God's creation. For instance, a blind person may have sharper hearing than those who can see.

In a day when evolution is all but "worshipped" by the world, it's still preposterous to accept that man's complexity of intelligence and spiritual capacity evolved from a "piece of goo." God help us! A wicked, unbelieving world will not let God be God! How wonderful to just take God at His Word! Indeed, we are "fearfully and wonderfully made."

Clarke's statement on this verse is well taken:

"The hearing ear and the seeing eye - Every good we possess comes from God; and we should neither use our eyes, nor our ears, nor any thing we possess, but in strict subservience to his will."

Prov. 20:13

"Love not sleep, lest thou come to poverty; open thine eyes, and thou shalt be satisfied with bread."

It's not a compliment when someone remarks, "He loves to sleep" or "He loves to eat," etc. These necessities must never become an end in themselves. While a diligent man will enjoy his rest and food, he does not live to eat or sleep.

The warning here is to a lazy man who loves to sleep rather than work. Poverty and indebtedness will be his portion for sure. The remedy? **Open thine eyes**; i.e., get up and focus on the job so that there will be bread on the table and satisfaction (fullness) in the stomach. There's a remedy for poverty—get up out of bed and get a job! Paul said that if a man will not work, *"neither should he eat."*

Prov. 20:14

It is naught, it is naught, saith the buyer: but when he is gone his way, then he boasteth.

This pictures a bargain-hunter who lands a good deal (or a "steal," as we say) and gives the seller the impression that he (the buyer) has been "robbed." "Naught" means "bad or displeasing." The buyer is expressing his dismay with the price—"it's bad; it's a bad deal," yet down deep he knows he getting a bargain, and brags or raves about his quest all the way home!

It certainly is legitimate to barter for the lowest price for a commodity, but there's a point of dishonesty when the buyer knows he's defrauding or taking undo advantage of the unwary seller. I'm afraid that such activity is all too common.

Prov. 20:15

"There is gold, and a multitude of rubies: but the lips of knowledge are a precious jewel."

Without a doubt, there is the abundance of "gold and rubies" which are deemed most valuable by the world; however, even more valuable is the "precious jewel (lit. article, vessel)" of lips that speak true knowledge and wisdom. See 3:14-16. Jesus said, *"For where your treasure is, there will your heart be also."* What is your value system? What's really important? Clarke puts it this way:

"Gold is valuable, silver is valuable, and so are jewels; but the teachings of sound knowledge are more valuable than all."

Well said.

Prov. 20:16

"Take his garment that is surety for a stranger: and take a pledge of him for a strange woman."

This verse seems to describe the necessity of collateral, viz., **his garment,"** in a co-signing (surety) situation. Prov. 6:1f forbids "surety" or co-signing; but if one engages in such, there needs to be some **pledge** of payment from the **stranger**.

The latter phrase seems to refer to a "pledge" (lit. binding, as a rope) given to a harlot to insure her welfare. Some relate this to the story of Tamar and Judah in Genesis 38:17, 18. This may be valid in light of the next verse (20:17). See Prov. 27:13.

Prov. 20:17

"Bread of deceit is sweet to a man; but afterwards his mouth shall be filled with gravel."

Somehow stolen bread is sweeter than that gained legitimately. There's something about the power of temptation, enticing us to acquire that which is forbidden. The **bread of deceit** pertains to that which is **sweet** up front, but the "after taste" is sickening and devastating (See 9:17, 18). Things just aren't what they appear. That's why there's no substitute for obeying the Word of God.

The expression, **his mouth shall be filled with gravel**, is an Arabic statement, describing a man getting into trouble (Barnes). See Lamentations 3:16. We reap what we sow in the long run.

Prov. 20:18

"Every purpose is established by counsel: and with good advice make war."

This proverb extols the necessity of:

1. Establishing (preparing, confirming) every purpose (plan) by counsel or advice. There is "safety in the multitude of counselors" (cf.15:22). Nothing done "helter-skelter," but well thought out, etc.

2. This need for counsel is not an exhortation here, but a fact!

Only fools make major decisions without proper preparation and advice!

3. Wars are a fact of life in a wicked, selfish world. But they must be entered with the utmost preparation of "good advice" or guidance. The cost must "be counted," as Jesus said. That's true with every plan, but even necessary when considering becoming a disciple of Jesus Christ. See Luke 14:31.

4. Seeking advice from other competent and wise people is not only wise, but safe. We are not "loners" in this battle, but just one niche in the Body. We need each other and the input of those who are strong where we are weak. If nothing else, we need the confirmation and encouragement of others before launching out in a new endeavor.

5. All want peace, but sometimes there must be war to accomplish it; e.g., God declared war on sin at the Cross, so we might have His peace. We must declare war each day on the flesh, so as to experience the fruit of peace which comes through obedience. ETC., ETC.

Prov. 20:19

"He that goeth about as a talebearer revealeth secrets: therefore meddle not with him that flattereth with his lips."

There are certain people that we should not do business with, as mentioned here; viz., a "talebearer" and a "flatterer." The former is one who "goes about" (lit walks, idea of lifestyle or mental attitude) bearing tales (slandering, informing); he delights in revealing or uncovering "secrets" (*sode*—a company of persons in close deliberation, confidential counsel). The idea is sharing intimate, personal material in a shameless, unscrupulous way. There are people who thrive on this kind of wicked activity.

This seems to be connected with "flattering lips." The word here is *pathah*, meaning lit. "to be open, roomy, in moral sense." One who "enlarges" or exaggerates to entice or deceive another. Thus, a talebearer may not only slander, but flatter people to get what he wants. Don't "meddle" (engage, do business) with such a person.

You can't trust such people, for they are masters at what they do; e.g., con or confidence men.

Prov. 20:20

"Whoso curseth his father or his mother, his lamp shall be put out in obscure darkness."

Parental authority is ordained of God and must not be trifled with. Parents represent God in the child's life and thus children are "to honor" and "obey" their mother and father. How they treat their parents is directly related to how they treat God Himself. Rebellion to human authority reveals rebellion to God's authority!

Note that "curseth" here is not necessarily "cussing out" parents, but "slighting or to be trifling," not taking them seriously (*qalal*). This could be a quiet rebellion, which God hates and will punish. Result: **his lamp** (light) **shall be put out in obscure** (extreme) **darkness.** Yes, God will "put his lights out," to use a colloquial expression! Cf. Exodus 21:17; Leviticus 20:9.

Prov. 20:21

"An inheritance may be gotten hastily at the beginning; but the end thereof shall not be blessed."

An inheritance may be gotten hastily at the beginning... seems to infer the recipient's greed or unscrupulous activity. It could tie in with the previous verse (20) dealing with the dishonor toward parents. At best, it is an inheritance given prematurely, for whatever reason; the result is a blight instead of "blessing" upon the recipient. "Easy come, easy go."

So is the problem with heirs to wealth, along with those who win the lottery. *"For the love of money is* (still) *the root of all* (kinds of) *evil."* See 28:20, 22; 13:11.

Prov. 20:22

"Say not thou, I will recompense evil; but wait on the LORD, and he shall save thee."

There is a strong admonition here against avenging evil. It's common, when offended by someone, to fight back and harbor bitterness. So many believers are eaten up internally by resentment and anger! What a relief to learn to **wait** (lit. expect) **on the LORD**, knowing that He will "save" (rescue, preserve, free) us. This is an example of responding to God's provision rather than reacting to the incident of the moment. See Romans 12:17-19.

Prov. 20:23

"Divers weights are an abomination unto the LORD; and a false balance is not good."

See notes on 20:10; 11:1

Prov. 20:24

"Man's goings are of the LORD; how can a man then understand his own way?"

Man's goings (lit. steps) **are of the LORD.** There is certainly a shroud of mystery over this verse; viz., the awesome and unique purposes of God. Who really "understands his own way," much less the ways of God? (Romans 11:33). The primary issue is, as Jesus said, "...without me ye can do nothing." (John 15:5).

David said, *"The steps of a good man are ordered by the Lord"* (Psalm 37:23), but what about a "bad" man? See Prov. 16:9 and Jeremiah 10:23 which relegate the thoughts and actions of men under the jurisdiction of a Sovereign God. All I know is that "the Lord God Omnipotent Reigneth," and we are responsible for our choices and actions! Thus, DO RIGHT, because all is in God's hands! When you don't know what to do—DO the RIGHT thing!

Prov. 20:25

It is a snare to the man who devoureth that which is holy, and after vows to make inquiry.

The gist of this verse is the danger of making a rash promise (statement) or commitment without thinking it through. The word "devoureth" here (from *yala*) means "to speak rashly, wildly." It pictures one who quickly blurts out some commitment to a "holy" thing (cause, person, etc.), promising to "inquire" or check it out further at a later time.

This is a "snare" which can lead to disaster. The price of "holy commitment" needs to be considered ahead of time. See Ecclesiastes 5:4-6; Matthew 5:33. Wisdom counts the cost up front.

Prov. 20:26

"A wise king scattereth the wicked, and bringeth the wheel over them."

This verse describes how a wise king deals with lawbreakers and those who threaten civil tranquility. First, there's the preventative measure of "scattering the wicked;" i.e., dispensing and separating the troublemakers from the rest. It's like the police separating gang members from the crowd, preventing them from gathering in unity and force. Wise law enforcement does not permit the troublemakers to gain momentum, but divides them from the crowd and from each other. An example of this would be the Tower of Babel (Genesis 11), where God confused their language and created "confusion" of tongues to prevent further unified wickedness.

Second, the king performs swift justice to the guilty. That sends a further message to other potential rebels. The "wheel" here refers to the "threshing wheel" (cf. Isaiah 28:27, 28) which was used to separate the grain from the chaff. That could readily become an instrument for capital punishment.

Interestingly, the key verse in the Book of Judges is:

"In those days there was no king in Israel: every man did that which was right in his own eyes." (Judges 21:25)

Remove the "king" (Law) and crime flourishes! Fair and swift application of the Law greatly impedes lawlessness; it also fosters a sense of security and peace among the populace. How this principle needs to be implemented in our land!

Prov. 20:27

"The spirit of man is the candle of the LORD, searching all the inward parts of the belly."

We go from the "king's" (i.e., governmental) law (vs. 26) to the inner law of conscience. **The spirit of man is the candle of the LORD, searching all the inward parts of the belly.** The word "spirit" is *Neshamah*, that unique possession of man which facilitates his God-consciousness. This is the same word used in Genesis 2:7, where in the direct creation of man, God gave him *"the breath of life."* Animals do not have this quality and capacity; they do not have God-consciousness, self-consciousness, or sin-consciousness. They may have a "thinking" process, but never think about what they're thinking! This is one of the enigmas of the so-called evolution theory.

Not only did this *Neshamah* give "life" to man, but it produced a "searching" effect; viz., conscience.(i.e., "knowledge with" or God's witness within). Here is the counterpart of Romans 2:15, *"the law written in their hearts...."* Man has an inner voice that lines up with the written law (i.e., Commandments, etc.). That's why sin and judgment are unique to humans and not animals. *"...It is appointed unto men* (not cows, dogs, etc.) *once to die, but after this the judgment."* (Hebrews 9:27). Therefore, God sent the "God-Man" to die for sinful man. If we're just "animals," then there's no salvation from sin, for Christ died only for humanity.

Note that conscience searches **all the inward parts of the belly**; i.e., every inch of the subconscious part of man! Wow! That's why salvation begins on the inside, producing a "new heart"—a heart that seeks to please God.

Prov. 20:28

"Mercy and truth preserve the king: and his throne is upholden by mercy."

Mercy and truth preserve (protect, guard) **the king: and his throne is upholden** (supported) **by mercy** (love). Kings can only properly rule by the standard of truth (reality of Law), accompanied by an attitude of "mercy." That same mercy establishes (supports) his rule before the people, who need not only law but love. This sets the example for the king's subjects and makes for a healthy and respectful relationship. Cf. Prov. 3:3; 16:6; 16:12.

Jesus Himself was *"full of grace and truth,"* leaving us a legacy to follow. In a practical word, we need to be gracious in order to proclaim the truth. We need to love souls first, thus gaining the privilege to share the Gospel of God. Christ, the King, gave us the ultimate Example.

Prov. 20:29

"The glory of young men is their strength: and the beauty of old men is the gray head."

In any stage of life, whether young or old, there's a characteristic of excellence. **The glory** (lit. ornament, i.e., jewels) **of young men is their strength** (physical prowess): **and the beauty** (lit. magnificence) **of old men is the gray head.** The sunset years of life do not necessarily nullify significance. While young people are generally robust and physically strong, older people are to manifest an inner strength (quality) of wisdom and maturity.

There's something for everyone in God's economy. However, the gray head does not always signify maturity, no more than youth always possesses bodily strength. This is a general principle, and is beautiful to behold. We need to "act our age"; i.e.,, to manifest the majesty of God's gifts and provisions at any stage of life. Thank God for youth, but also the grace to grow old without losing perspective and purpose. The "gray head" needs to be revered once again in a day when respect for elders has drastically declined. Hopefully, senior (seasoned) citizens offer a reservoir of knowledge, experience and wisdom to be tapped by the young.

Prov. 20:30

"The blueness of a wound cleanseth away evil: so do stripes the inward parts of the belly."

An interesting conclusion to this chapter, regarding the effects of genuine corporal discipline. **The blueness of a wound cleanseth away evil.** The word, "blueness," refers to a "black and blue mark" from a blow. The Hebrew word is translated "bruises" in Isaiah 1:6 and "stripes" in Isaiah 53:5. Significantly, the former reference is dealing with Jehovah's discipline of wayward Israel; the latter passage is the prophecy of our Lord's atonement on the Cross, where He was *"bruised for our iniquities"* and *"with his stripes we are healed."* Amen!

Thus we have a principle of parental discipline with our children. We are to command and exhort them, but there comes a time for physical reinforcement. Such discipline can "cleanse away (used fig. to scour with detergent, purify) evil (bad behavior)."

Furthermore, **so do stripes** (blows) cleanse **the inward parts of the belly.** This is definitely a reference to the child's conscience; cf. verse 27. No, corporal punishment cannot "save" a child's soul, per se, but in loving firmness can bring deep correction, along with other means. Our present generation with its pop psychology could learn vital lessons from this passage. God's way is always the right way.

Chapter 21
The King's Heart is in the Hand of the Lord

Prov. 21:1

"The king's heart is in the hand of the LORD, as the rivers of water: he turneth it whithersoever he will."

Here we have a beautiful and practical statement of God's sovereignty. Earthly rulers or kings are subject to the Ruler of the universe who placed them in position. Those that are most absolute are under God's government; he puts things into their hearts. Revelation 17:17; Ezra 7:27 (according to M. Henry).

There's no question as to the LORD's complete control and will over the **rivers of water**, for He created them for His purpose (Genesis 1). There seems to be question, however, when it comes to God's dealings with mankind and just how much authority He has in the affairs of men. Nebuchadnezzar, king of Babylon, exemplifies one who defied the Lord's authority (e.g., golden image—Daniel 3) and was eventually judged and subdued by that same LORD (Daniel 4)!

The psalmist magnifies the Sovereign LORD in Psalm 2, *"who sitteth in the heavens"* laughing in His justice regarding the rebel kings of the earth (2:1-4) He further declares, *"Yet have I set my king upon my holy hill of Zion"* (i.e., Messiah)- vs. 6. Therefore:

"Be wise...O ye kings: be instructed, ye judges of the earth. Serve the LORD with fear....Kiss the Son, lest he be angry, and ye perish from the way, when his wrath is kindled but a little." (vs. 6, 10-12)

Prov. 21:2

"Every way of a man is right in his own eyes: but the LORD pondereth the hearts."

Everyone would like to think that their "way" (i.e., lifestyle, course of action) is right. This is how we see through our own eyes. And it may be so, especially as it lines up with the Word of God. But ultimately the LORD (Great "I Am") ponders (weighs, measures, proves) our hearts or motivation (intent). Deeds are important, but heart attitude is all-important. God is weighing hearts more than just counting deeds. Upright hearts produce upright acts (cf. 16:2).

Prov. 21:3

"To do justice and judgment is more acceptable to the LORD than sacrifice."

Here we have a contrast between religious activity and right and honest character (which results in right actions). "Justice" is basically translated, "righteousness"—doing the right and upright thing; "judgment" deals rather with the outcome or verdict attending one's actions. The former emphasizes the deeds, while the latter refers to the right decision, or proper discernment, regarding the deeds (i.e., a judge's verdict in a case).

Man's depraved nature lends itself to covering up unrighteousness with religious ritual. But God said to Saul of old, through Samuel: *"to obey is better than sacrifice"* (1 Samuel 15:22)! David said in his prayer of repentance:

"The sacrifices of God are a broken spirit: a broken and a contrite heart, O God, thou wilt not despise....Then shalt thou be pleased with the sacrifices of righteousness, with burnt offering...." (Psalm 51:17, 19)

In other words, God is pleased with our "sacrifices" when emanating out of a broken and obedient heart. Externals are important, but only acceptable when the internal (heart) is right with God. The treasurer at the church may accept your offering, but God may not! It depends on your heart attitude.

Prov. 21:4

"An high look, and a proud heart, and the plowing of the wicked, is sin."

Three conditions here are described as "sin" (*chattah*—"missing the mark"): 1) a **high** (elevated, lofty) **look**; 2) **a proud** (lit. wide, large) **heart**; and 3) **the plowing of the wicked**. The first two are easier to understand than the third. The arrogant, self-centered look coming from a lofty and proud heart is obviously sin; that was Lucifer's problem in Heaven just before he was ejected (see Isaiah 14; Ezekiel 28). Man's basic sin follows suit, the pride of doing things "my way"—the Cain spirit. *"All we like sheep have gone astray: we have turned every one to his own way."*

The **plowing of the wicked** has to do with fallow or untilled ground. Evidently it has to do with the prosperity of a farmer's labor. "Plowing" seems like such a legitimate task, necessary for one to make a living. How could it be sin? The context would indicate that the proud farmer is simply working for his own benefit and glory, rather than for the glory of God. *"For whatsoever is not of faith is sin."* (Romans 14:23) *"And whatsoever ye do in word or deed, do all in the name of the Lord Jesus."* (Colossians 3:17) So a legitimate task done by a wicked heart is still sin! That's why no flesh can please God, nor stand in His presence.

Thus the harvest of the wicked is somehow the extension of his proud heart. On the other hand, *"the fruit of the righteous is a tree of life"*—an extension of a sanctified heart.

Prov. 21:5

"The thoughts of the diligent tend only to plenteousness; but of every one that is hasty only to want."

Here's a verse that strongly encourages thoughtful planning before making important moves. It's the difference between "plenty" and "poverty." First, a diligent person thinks before he acts—not so with a fool. (That's the inference here). Second, the actions of the diligent are an outgrowth of his thought life; i.e., plan or purpose. People of purpose think, and thus do differently than those who are "hasty" (lit. under pressure, in a hurry).

I would think that the context fit the work of a farmer, carpenter, etc. It surely would apply to anyone wanting to "get rich quick," which leads to "want." (e.g., gambler, scheme artist). In a day when we want everything "yesterday" (e.g., fast food mentality), we need to focus on godly motives of the heart, building a life of purpose, to God's glory. This will lead us to "plenty" (true success), rather than the deficiency of haste and foolishness.

Prov. 21:6

"The getting of treasures by a lying tongue is a vanity tossed to and fro of them that seek death."

Here's a principle regarding dishonorable business practice and fraudulent means of gaining wealth. Some have no scruples about honesty, but will gain money **by a lying tongue**; i.e., deceptively or by sham. This is all too common in the world, even in large corporations. Presently in our beloved USA there's a moral crisis whereby some accountants no longer "count" honestly. The landmarks have been removed and disaster lurks on every side.

This verse states that such practice is **a vanity** (emptiness, vapor) **tossed to and fro** (lit. shoved around) **of** (by) **them that seek death.** This describes the tactics and character (or lack of it) of those who are headed for death and hell. Those who love life and are headed God's way are those who live honestly before men and God.

Prov. 21:7

"The robbery of the wicked shall destroy them; because they refuse to do judgment."

Here is almost a common-place axiom regarding the wicked, who's **robbery** (or violence) **shall destroy** (lit. drag away) **them**. Reason? **Because they refuse to do judgment** (right). See Psalm 7:16; Jeremiah 7:9-11.

The wicked may appear to prosper for a time, or even a life-time, but the bitter end must come sometime! It's appointed unto man once to die, but after this the judgment. Wealth is not the issue, but how it's acquired. A robber would be better off getting a legitimate job and enjoying God's provision. But instead, the wicked with their destructive spirit will do them in. They will reap what they have sown.

My mentor used to say that there's only one thing to do in any given situation, and that's the right thing. He would add, "DO RIGHT 'til the stars fall!" What looks like success to man may be an abomination to God, and vice-versa. God's laws will not be changed or thwarted by wicked men. We don't break the law, the law breaks us. It's just a matter of time.

Prov. 21:8

"The way of man is froward and strange: but as for the pure, his work is right."

The way of man is froward and strange; this describes man in his natural, sinful state—apart from the regenerating grace of God. His "way" or lifestyle is "froward"—crooked or perverted (according to God's standard). This is the great problem with society—we make our own rules as we go, forsaking the Biblical standard. A "crook" may be normal to other crooks! Thus, what appears "normal" to the world may be an abomination to God.

Man is not only perverted (froward), but "strange." This is an interesting word meaning "burdened with guilt," which causes him to be a "stranger" to God and to others as well. "He acts strange" is a statement that takes on new meaning according to this verse. What a horrible "illness" is sin which drives man to perverted attitudes and makes him a "stranger" to grace! No wonder Jesus said to a perverted religious man, *"Ye must be born again."*

On the other hand, Solomon says: **but as for the pure, his work is right** (lit. straight). Note the parallels of "froward" and "right"; natural "man" and a "pure" (clean) man; "way" and "work." You're either right or wrong dependent on your relationship to God through His Son. This is God's standard, although it's rejected by the world.

Prov. 21:9

"It is better to dwell in a corner of the housetop, than with a brawling woman in a wide house."

There surely is a difference between a house and a home! The structure and elegance of the house is one thing; the people who live in the house is another consideration. Man can build a house, but only God can create a home.

Peace and harmony cannot be built or bought. Thus, **it is better to dwell in a corner of the housetop,** (alone?) **than with a brawling** (contentious) **woman in a wide house.** I assume that this proverb addresses in part the issue of marriage vs. singleness. Not to disparage the institution itself, but rather to consider the importance of choosing the right spouse. Better to live alone, than to be married to the wrong person.

It was not uncommon for ancient homes to have towers in the corners—an upper structure accommodating one person. This would not be considered "elegant" quarters, but would be "paradise" in contrast to living in a "wide," luxurious house with a contentious spouse. Home, sweet home, must be characterized by peace and harmony. Better to live in a "cardboard box" with it than in a mansion without it!

Prov. 21:10

"The soul of the wicked desireth evil: his neighbour findeth no favour in his eyes."

Here's a comprehensive illustration of the Tenth Commandment: "Thou shalt not covet thy neighbor's house, wife, cattle, etc." King Ahab coveted Nabal's vineyard, which led him to murder his neighbor and eventually caused his own demise. It all stems from the "wicked soul" of man who "desireth" (waits longingly, covets—greed) evil, or what is not his.

This greedy desire will be satisfied at any cost. Thus, **his neighbor findeth no favour** (mercy, pity, graciousness) **in his eyes.** Greed will rob a neighbor (associate, friend, even family member) blind! O, the depth of selfishness! A wicked attitude before God will find its outlet before men. Our disregard for our neighbor is a reflection and result of our separation from God. The Cross is both vertical (man to God) and horizontal (man to man). The latter is dependent on the former; i.e., we must first be right with God if we're to rightly influence our fellow man.

In conversion and revival, one's right relationship with God will result in restitution and renewed relationship with our neighbor. Zacchaeus (Luke 19), after his conversion, paid four-fold of what he had stolen. Our heart attitude deeply affects our conduct—both ways; i.e., for sin or righteousness.

Prov. 21:11

"When the scorner is punished, the simple is made wise: and when the wise is instructed, he receiveth knowledge."

There is virtue and purpose for punishment, contrary to the thinking of modern society. It is not only a restraint and act of moral correction upon the perpetrator, but it has profound effect on some who witness it. In this proverb, the general principle is set forth that **when the scorner** (mocker, scoffer) **is punished, the simple** (foolish) **is made wise** (or becomes wiser). Indeed, mockers will be punished, in the long run, and serve to affect others who are slow to learn. A drastic display or example of the price of sin may make an impact on those who otherwise would not change.

Taking it further, **when the wise** (man) **is instructed, he receiveth knowledge.** The simple and wise both learn some things, but the process and degree may be different. Fools, if they learn at all, do so the hard way (e.g., punishment of others, or personal "hard knocks," etc.). A wise man pays attention with insight, whereby he receives (takes in) skillful knowledge. That seems to be the meaning of that last phrase. The word "instructed" has the idea of being "circumspect, prudent or having wise comprehension."

Paul talks about rebuking a disobedient elder before the congregation, that "all may fear." (1 Timothy 5:20). This can have profound effectiveness upon those who are slow to obey God. But a wise man has a teachable spirit and doesn't always have to learn the hard way. Instruct him and he gravitates to further knowledge because of the propensity of his heart. Wise men take every opportunity to become wiser. Check the following: Prov. 1:5; 9:9; 15:14; 18:1; 18:15.

Prov. 21:12

*"The righteous man wisely considereth the house of the wicked:
but God overthroweth the wicked for their wickedness."*

This is a difficult verse in that the subject or person acting is not clear. **The righteous** (man?) **wisely considereth the house of the wicked** (but God) **overthroweth the wicked for their wickedness.** K&D translation is, "The righteous (One)," i.e., God Himself, because He alone ultimately "overthrows the wicked." It does make sense if you begin with that premise.

However, the verb "wisely considereth" can refer to the actions or knowledge of a righteous man, rather than God alone. The word is *sakal* which has to do with "wise understanding or insight." Check vs. 16 where the same word is translated "understanding," or Psalm 119:99, translated the same way: *"I have more understanding than all my teachers: for thy testimonies [are] my meditation."* Again look at Jeremiah 3:15 for God's promise of understanding pastors: *"And I will give you pastors according to mine heart, which shall feed you with knowledge and understanding."*

Thus we could translate our verse: "The righteous man wisely understands or discerns the house of the wicked"; i.e., he's been in that sinful state and thus discerns their lifestyle and plight. But he also knows that only "God overthrows (lit. overturns, ruins) the wicked for their wickedness"; i.e., God judges the wicked in the finale—something that's out of reach or responsibility of a righteous human being. *"Vengeance is mine; I will repay, saith the Lord!"*

The wicked may grieve and oppose the righteous, but judgment belongs only to God. Our instrument for "conquering souls" is the Word of God, the Sword of the Spirit. This is in contrast to some Muslims, for instance, who are taught in the Koran, to "kill the infidels (non-Muslims) with the literal, physical sword." Thus, the present beheadings of hostages in the present Iraqi war.

Prov. 21:13

"Whoso stoppeth his ears at the cry of the poor, he also shall cry himself, but shall not be heard."

Compassion on the needy is a stream that runs throughout the Scripture. It reveals the heart of God's love toward humanity. It is evidenced by the coming of His Son, Jesus Christ, who met the ultimate need of man—forgiveness of sin. The story of the Good Samaritan (Luke 10) illustrates God's heart and counters the man here in vs. 13.

There's a sowing and reaping element to this verse: the one who *"stoppeth his ears at the cry of the poor* (lowly, weak)*, he also shall cry himself, but shall not be heard* (heeded).*"* The needy cry out (lit. shriek) and blessed is the man who responds properly. To turn a deaf ear is not only wrong but reaps personal consequence; when he "cries" (calls, proclaims), none will pay attention. The general rule is that the merciful alone receive mercy in return.

Prov. 21:14

"A gift in secret pacifieth anger: and a reward in the bosom strong wrath."

We have two parallel thoughts here concerning bribery and/or appeasement of anger. A "gift" is a present (*mattan*-used 5 times, e.g., Genesis 34:12; Numbers 18:12), while "reward" is also translated "bribe" (e.g., 1 Samuel 8:3; Psalm 26:10). Both can be used of gifts, but the motive behind them is the issue here.

Anger and wrath can be "pacified" (tamed or subdued) by means of a "secret gift." Evidently, this is a private affair or transaction so as not to expose the problem publicly. God only knows how many violent crimes have been thwarted through bribes. In Genesis 32:20 is the account of Jacob's appeasement of Esau; also 1 Samuel 25:35 reveals Abigail's thwarting David's wrath by gifts.

By application, we can see here the doctrine of Propitiation, whereby Christ appeased the Father's offended holiness because of man's sin.

Prov. 21:15

"It is joy to the just to do judgment: but destruction shall be to the workers of iniquity.

Joy and righteousness go together. Doing right can result in feeling right, because it lines up with truth. The Devil's lie is that "doing whatever feels good" will bring happiness. Sinners practice sin or iniquity which may yield fleeting pleasure, but ends up in "destruction" (ruin, terror).

Note that the righteous can experience joy now and eternal bliss later. While inner joy eludes the wicked both in the present and future.

Prov. 21:16

"The man that wandereth out of the way of understanding shall remain in the congregation of the dead."

A somber thought: To miss the Truth is to reside in eternal death! **The man that wandereth**, portrayed here, is not just one who occasionally strays from **the way** (course, lifestyle) **of understanding,"** but one who is perpetually out of sync with truth ("wander" is Qal act. participle, indicating a state of being). Thus, he will **remain in the congregation of the dead** (place of departed spirits). JFB notes: "remain—that is, rest as at a journey's end; death will be his unchanging home."

Note this wanderer has never been on the right road; therefore, he simply "remains (dwells, stays) in the assembly of the dead" (opposite of life). To be void of understanding is death, although one may have physical breath or existence.

Prov. 21:17

"He that loveth pleasure shall be a poor man: he that loveth wine and oil shall not be rich."

This proverb defies and counters the philosophy of the world! Pleasure, along with money, has become our god in America. Yet Solomon says (by personal experience): **He that loveth pleasure shall be a poor man.** To seek pleasure per se is to wind up a spiritual pauper! In fact, James says, *"...the friendship of the world is enmity with God."* We are in the world and must use the world without being overcome by the world.

The second part, viz., loving "wine and oil" (perfume, anointing of garments, see Amos 6:6) follows the line of worldly pleasure. Feasting and drinking, etc., are worldly pastimes which lead to wantonness and financial (and spiritual) bankruptcy. The issue is not "pleasure" itself, but the love and seeking of it apart from the Lord. Certainly, the Spirit-filled believer knows something of the glorious "pleasures at His right hand" (Psalm 16)! Here's another slant on Matthew 6:33.

Prov. 21:18

The wicked shall be a ransom for the righteous, and the transgressor for the upright.

The wicked shall be a ransom for the righteous...the transgressor for the upright. "Ransom" is lit. a "covering," used figuratively as a "price of redemption." Often in history, wicked men "cover" for the righteous, in that their wicked scheme "backfires" and comes upon them; e.g., Haman and Mordecai ((Esther 7:9). Other times, the benevolence of a heathen King will serve to "ransom" God's people. See Isaiah 43:3, 4; 44:28 (Cyrus). Check Prov. 11:8.

Also Joshua 7:26, which cites how Achan "ransomed" Israel; i.e., spared them judgment by taking the judgment for his own sin. He "covered" them. So the application of Christ who was made *"to be sin...that we might be made the righteousness of God in him."* (2 Corinthians 5:21).

Prov. 21:19

"It is better to dwell in the wilderness, than with a contentious and an angry woman."

Solomon takes the analogy of vs. 9 (housetop or attic) to another level here; viz., a "wilderness" or desert. Better to be completely separated from the same dwelling place (house) than living with a contentious and angry woman (wife).

Solomon is not encouraging marital separation here, but rather describing the pain and trouble being married to an angry, bitter spouse. Singleness may at times be preferred to marriage, especially when linked with the wrong person.

Prov. 21:20

There is treasure to be desired and oil in the dwelling of the wise;
but a foolish man spendeth it up.

Solomon, who knew by experience the futility and emptiness of riches per se, extols the proper use of material increase. Remember, it's not money that is the "root of all (kinds of) evil," but the LOVE of it! The "wise" man here recognizes that there is a legitimate **treasure to be desired** (lit. to delight in, precious)—whether gold, silver or storehouse goods. These are the gifts of God for one's sustenance and use.

Added to that is **oil in the dwelling** (home), which refers not only to literal olive oil, but general "fatness"—the abundant fruit of the harvest. The wise man is thus a steward of God's goodness, resulting from his labor. Thus, he is responsible to "lay up" (save) and/or invest it wisely. It's his personal property to use carefully— no "communism" here. (Another application of Matthew 6:33)

In contrast, "fools" (lit. silly, irresponsible) "spend up" (lit. destroy) or squander their substance. While there will always be those who are legitimately poor, you wonder how many "poor" are just irresponsible. This proverb intimates that the wise and fool had "equal opportunity," but made different choices with their substance. God is not for poverty for poverty's sake. There is a valid and "desired" use of material increase.

Prov. 21:21

"He that followeth after righteousness and mercy findeth life,
righteousness, and honour."

What we pursue (chase after) reveals our hearts! A greedy heart will be manifested by a secret obsession with money, etc. Here Solomon describes a man who **followeth after righteousness and mercy**. These words are powerful!

First, this man is literally "running after, chasing" (qal. part.-

continual action and attitude) that which is right or virtuous. Second, he is also seeking "mercy" (kindness, goodness). This word, *chesed*, is used to describe God's "loving-kindness" (cf. Psalm 40:10, 11; 51:1; 63:3, etc.) Here is a man that possesses the balance of Grace ("mercy") and Truth (righteousness), hence an example of Christ Himself (John 1:14).

The result? **He findeth** (imperf.—ongoing) **life** (abundant, reviving), **righteousness, and honour** (*kabod*—weightiness, respect). This man is wealthy indeed!

Prov. 21:22

"A wise man scaleth the city of the mighty, and casteth down the strength of the confidence thereof."

The gist here is that wisdom is more effective than brute strength. The might of a king can be overridden by the wise plan of an unknown or lowly person. Ecclesiastes 9:13-16 grants an example of this principle.

Barnes has an interesting take on this verse, applying it to the believer's spiritual warfare:

"Even in war, counsel does more than brute strength. So of the warfare which is carried on in the inner battlefield of the soul. There also wisdom is mighty to the "pulling down of strongholds" (2Co_10:4, where Paul uses the very words of the Septuagint Version of this passage), and the wise man scales and keeps the city which the strong man armed has seized and made his own."

Prov. 21:23

"Whoso keepeth his mouth and his tongue keepeth his soul from troubles."

Here's a good summary principle on the tongue's power. James 3 is devoted to this subject. What troubles and anguish result from such a small member of the body! Though the tongue be a physical part of the anatomy, its influence transcends into the soul. How many wounds of the heart are caused by the edge of a ranting, uncontrolled tongue. See Prov. 13:2, 3.

James says:

"If any man offend not in word, the same is a perfect (mature) man, able also to bridle the whole body." (3:2)

Prov. 21:24

"Proud and haughty scorner is his name, who dealeth in proud wrath."

Mockers are identified, or recognized, by their pride and arrogance. How brazen and godless are those who have no respect for authority, much less the fear of Almighty God! These **dealeth in proud wrath**; i.e., they act and judge according to their own arrogance and standard. They are gods in their own right (e.g., Lucifer – Ezekiel 28). This is the height of rebellion against God and His creation, yet they think themselves justified. How deep is sin!!

K&D translate this verse:

"A proud and arrogant man is called mocker (free-spirit); one who acteth in superfluity of haughtiness,"

Interesting take on the so-called "free thinking" of our day. Nothing is new under the sun.

Prov. 21:25

"The desire of the slothful killeth him; for his hands refuse to labour."

Talk about being one's worst enemy! Laziness can kill a man, but notice that it's his "desire," not just idleness per se. There is evidently a spirit of indolence—a deep satisfaction that loves doing nothing and furthermore "refuses to labor." Some people "work" at not working! It destroys self-respect and the purpose for which God placed man on earth. Adam worked and farmed the garden even before the Fall (Genesis 2). To refuse to labor is a sure way to die slowly and prematurely, especially when coveting what others have (cf. vs. 26).

Prov. 21:26

"He coveteth greedily all the day long: but the righteous giveth and spareth not."

What a commentary on the root and fruit of laziness! Covetousness is the universal or "bottom rung" sin of humanity. This is the "mine" or "gimme" mentality built in to the depraved nature. Paul refers to this sin that was revealed to him by the Holy Spirit who brought conviction to his heart ((Romans 7).

The slothful will not work, yet spends all day "coveting greedily." His lack of energy and ambition does not deter his eager desire to have "things" which can be "consumed by his flesh." His utter self-centeredness will not allow him to think about, much less, give to others.

In contrast, is the "righteous" man who "gives and spares not." Here's one who gives hilariously and constantly (qal imperf.) out of a new heart that is in under Divine control. Love gives, while lust gets! Giving genuine glory to God and others is only possible through the "new birth" and liberating release of the indwelling Holy Spirit.

Prov. 21:27

"The sacrifice of the wicked is abomination: how much more, when he bringeth it with a wicked mind?"

Hardly any verse deals more with man's heart than this. Religious sacrifice (i.e., slaughtered animal here) of the ungodly is an abomination (lit. morally disgusting) to the Lord. *"A broken and a contrite heart"* He will not despise, but that can only be presented by a believer (cf. Psalm 51:16f.). Outward sacrifice and worship without the faithful obedience of the heart is rejected by God.

But note how Solomon takes this to another level of depravity: **how much more, when he bringeth it with a wicked mind.** Evidently, God judges even the man's motive underlying the sacrificial offering. Many are the wicked who go through the religious ritual in ignorance and as a matter of routine. Others, as here, have an agenda, or device in mind. That's the idea of the Heb. *zimmah*, translated "mind." This is illustrated by Cain's plot to "sacrifice" his brother's blood when the Lord refused his own offering (Genesis 4:8). Certainly, Judas would fit this category and a host of others down through the centuries. See Isaiah 1:10-15; 64:6

Prov. 21:28

"A false witness shall perish: but the man that heareth speaketh constantly."

Deceptive and false testimony will eventually perish, though doing great damage. Truth will prevail in the long run, so will **the man that heareth** (*shamah*- obedient hearing), who therefore **speaketh constantly** (lit. confidently, truthfully). Unlike the first, this man has a consistent testimony of truth because he hears or heeds truth. We speak what we are. Thus, a liar lies because he is a liar.

Prov. 21:29

"A wicked man hardeneth his face: but as for the upright, he directeth his way."

Wicked determination and rebellion show up on one's face. The "Cain" spirit was obvious, being manifested by his "countenance" (Genesis 4). So it is with those who are self-sufficient and "cock sure" about the direction of their lives. The basic element of sin is to live independently from the God of all creation; i.e., to do it "my way." This was resident in Lucifer's attitude when he decided to "take God's place." (cf. Ezekiel 28:15). This is also manifested early on in children who "fight" parental authority and advice. See 28:14; 29:1.

In contrast, **the upright** (one who is right with God and desires to do right), **he directeth** (*biyn*- to discern, consider) **his way**; i.e., course of life. The true believer doesn't set his own course, but cries: "LORD, what will you have me do?" He also values the advice of other mature believers. Cf. Prov. 11:5; Psalm 119:59.

Prov. 21:30

"There is no wisdom nor understanding nor counsel against the LORD."

There is None like our God! Whether it be **wisdom, understanding,** or **counsel** (advice), He is above all!

The phrase, **against the LORD** is literally "in front of, or before the LORD;" i.e., there's absolutely no wisdom, etc. in the universe that is beyond His. He is the Author and Sustainer of all Wisdom, and Nothing can "beat" that! Isaiah cries:

> *"To whom then will ye liken me, or shall I be equal? saith the Holy One....Hast thou not known? hast thou not heard, that the everlasting God, the LORD, the Creator of the ends of the earth, fainteth not, neither is weary? there is no searching of his understanding." (Isaiah 40:25, 28)* See also 1 Corinthians 1:18-25.

Paul draws us to worship when we don't understand what God understands:

> *"O the depth of the riches both of the wisdom and knowledge of God! How unsearchable are his judgments, and his ways past finding out!"* (Romans 11:33)

Remember, the problem is with us, not Him or His Word! When we don't understand, let us Worship Him, rather than question or doubt. As we follow hard after Him, He may choose to "open our understanding" somewhere along the way.

Prov. 21:31

"The horse is prepared against the day of battle: but safety is of the LORD."

Salvation is of the LORD! Man may prepare his "horse" and himself for the day of battle, but "safety" comes only from the LORD. This is the word, *teshuah,* meaning "salvation, deliverance or rescue." We may "fight the good fight of faith," but God alone grants deliverance. We can't trust the "horses" (things) of this world, but rather the God of all things, Who may use the "things" to protect us.

On a personal level, it can be said: *"I can do all things through Christ which strengtheneth me"* (Philippians 4:13). I perform my responsibility, but the power, safety and ultimate victory comes through Christ!

Chapter 22
A Good Name is to be Chosen

Prov. 22:1

"A good name is rather to be chosen than great riches, and loving favour rather than silver and gold."

The true legacy of a man is not **silver and gold**; it's his **good name** or reputation built on godly character. His name may be hated by some because of his testimony for God, but they will not be able to deny who he is. They slander Christ's Name, but cannot deny Who He is, and will one day bow before that Name!

The world continues to collect its "toys," thinking that at the end of this journey the one with the most "stuff" wins! Not so! Wealth has its place, but wealth alone cannot make one rich. Who we are is much more important or weighty than the things we possess. Thus, **a good name is rather to be chosen than great riches.**

Better yet is to, *"seek ye first the kingdom of God, and his righteousness; and all these things shall be added unto you"* (Matthew 6:33). Seek the Lord FIRST and He'll supply all that you need. Seek things first and you may not only miss what you're looking for (things, $$, etc.), but you'll miss God too! Even if you get the things without God, they will not satisfy; only God can fill and fulfill the God-shaped vacuum in our hearts. *"For what shall it profit a man, if he shall gain the whole world, and lose his own soul?"*

Prov. 22:2

"The rich and poor meet together: the LORD is the maker of them all."

How God levels the playing field of life! **The rich and poor meet together**; they encounter each other in the course of this life. Those who prosper do so because of the needs of the lowly; the needy survive because of the ability of others to supply those needs. This is a fact of society—rich and poor always exist, and man's attempt to make all men poor OR rich is an exercise in futility (e.g., Communism has tried to redistribute wealth by force, the haves giving to the have-nots—never works for any time).

But one thing for sure: **the LORD is the maker of them all.** He has established society which includes rich and poor; but finances and wealth have never been the basis of salvation. Rich and poor are on the same footing when it comes to approaching God. Both need a Great Saviour! In fact, a poor man may be more likely to trust Jesus Christ than one who is trusting his riches. (e.g., rich young ruler).

This may be part of that "good name" mentioned in vs.1, which surpasses any wealth of this world. The world has a tendency to bow at the feet of the wealthy and despise the poor. Before God, there's no difference. Christ alone is our Footing and Foundation to approach the Lord. In a word, all men are the same size at the foot of the Cross!

Prov. 22:3

"A prudent man foreseeth the evil, and hideth himself: but the simple pass on, and are punished."

Here is an example of how differently the wise and foolish respond to the same situation or temptation. **A prudent** (sensible, shrewd—in good sense) **man foreseeth** (perceives, inspects) **the evil** (trouble, wrong) **and hideth himself** (lit. runs for cover): **but the simple** (foolish) **pass on** (lit. cross over the line), **and are punished** (suffer the consequence).

How typical is this scenario. The wise person counts the cost ahead of time when faced with evil, while the fool "jumps into the mud hole" and then thinks about it (if even then)! Prevention is much better (and easier) than the cure. Better not to "cross the line" into sin, than to suffer for sin—even if you're eventually delivered. There's something better than forgiveness, and that's innocence.

We must have foresight regarding the traps of sin and Satan. A wise man when faced with evil will ask, "Will this action glorify God? Am I ready to suffer the consequence of this action? Can this wrongdoing do more for me (and others) than obeying God?" It ties in with the age-old saying: "An ounce of prevention is worth a pound of cure," Not only that, but he'll run the other way! "Flee youthful lusts"—don't hang around! Yes, *the fear of the LORD* (i.e., taking God seriously) *is the beginning of knowledge"* (and wisdom) - Prov. 1:7.

Prov. 22:4

"By humility and the fear of the LORD are riches, and honour, and life."

What a commentary of true success is this verse! This is totally contrary to the world's definition and illustrates the "tension of two worlds" (i.e., time vs. eternity). We judge people often by earthly possessions and prestige, but God's standard of success is at another level—a different standard of measurement. How many in the world strive for "riches, honor and the 'good' life," but it totally eludes them.

True riches (wealth), honor (lit. weightiness, respect), and life (abundant, not mere existence; John 10:10) come via **humility and the fear of the LORD**. Humility, as used here, is closer to "meekness"—inner strength under control, than to just outward submission. One can appear to be humble without inward submission. Jesus was "meek and lowly." This is submission to the will of God when it hurts! This is giving oneself to others who cannot give back in return. This is one part of the "fruit of the Spirit" (Galatians 5:23).

In conjunction, **is the fear of the LORD**, an attitude of obedience, taking God seriously (see 1:7); i.e., true faith in the Lord (Hebrews 11). How rich, honorable and alive is the man that walks, not with the world, but with the LORD of Lords and King of kings! We've got to make up our minds whether we believe this or not, and act accordingly. This is the crying challenge facing the Church today!

Prov. 22:5

"Thorns and snares are in the way of the froward: he that doth keep his soul shall be far from them."

Thorns and snares (lit. a spring net for trapping birds) speak of troublesome obstacles and difficulties **in the way** (path) **of the froward** (perverted, crooked). *"The way of transgressors is hard"* and Satan uses all sorts of subtle devices to "ensnare" his prey. These are the fruit of sin. Believers have problems too, but not necessarily from the same source. Galatians 6 talks about "reaping what we sow," whether to the flesh or spirit. There will be a "harvest" one day of whatever kind of "seed" we've sown.

Here is the exhortation of not only what happens to those who pursue a wicked lifestyle, but the reward of one who **doth keep** (guard, protect) **his soul.** A believer must not be passive, but actively engaged in feeding and protecting his inner man. (Romans 12:1, 2) He's certain to have difficulties along the way, but he shall also know the delivering and sustaining power of God, ending in eternal bliss, instead of damnation and disgrace.

Prov. 22:6

"Train up a child in the way he should go: and when he is old, he will not depart from it."

Train up a child.... The word, *chanak*, means to initiate or train up. It is used 5 times in the O.T., 4 of which it is translated "dedicate" (i.e., the temple). As parents, we are to dedicate, inaugurate (BDB) and instruct our child (lad, youth) **in the way he should go.** This difficult phrase doesn't simply mean indoctrination or catechism of the Word of God. It seems to indicate the need to wisely consider the temperament and course of life (gifts, etc.) uniquely pursued by that child. He has a "bent" of interest according to his abilities and talents; thus direct or dedicate him to that end, training him in the basic tenets of life. (including salvation, morality and ethics, etc.).

Barnes has a significant comment:

"The way he should go - Or, according to the tenor of his way, i. e., the path especially belonging to, especially fitted for, the individual's character. The proverb enjoins the closest possible study of each child's temperament and the adaptation of "his way of life" to that."

Parenting is a full time job, for sure. If one ever needed to be filled with the Spirit it's a parent! In fact, Ephesians 5:18 which exhorts us to *"be filled with the Spirit,"* is in the context of the home. What wisdom is needed here. How to rightly train and influence children, without trying to be the Holy Spirit and forcing the issue is a challenge indeed. How to be firm and compassionate at the same time—a dad as well as a father. How to let them blossom in their own right, without pressuring them into your preconceived mold. How to cultivate, without manufacturing! What an impossible task without divine wisdom and grace!

The axiom continues to say: **and** (lit. even) **when he is old, he will not depart from it.** Principles and teaching instilled in youth are hard to shake and forget, even in later life. Some things learned in youth have a way of forging our thinking and actions, even to the grave. However, it must be said, that exposure to the Scriptures and God's redemption in Christ, does not guarantee a child's salvation. He still grows up to make his own choices. This verse is still a principle, not a promise; but certainly we would hope and pray that the faithful teaching of the Word by example and precept would culminate in eternal salvation of our children by the Holy Spirit's work. Amen. Matthew Henry's insight on this verse is helpful:

> "Train up children in that age of vanity, to keep them from the sins and snares of it, in that learning age, to prepare them for what they are designed for. Catechize them; initiate them; keep them under discipline. Train them as soldiers, who are taught to handle their arms, keep rank, and observe the word of command. Train them up, not in the way they would go (the bias of their corrupt hearts would draw them aside), but in the way they should go, the way in which, if you love them, you would have them go. Train up a child according as he is capable (as some take it), with a gentle hand, as nurses feed children, little and often, Deu_6:7. 2. A good reason for it, taken from the great advantage of this care and pains with children: When they grow up, when they grow old, it is to be hoped, they will not depart

from it. Good impressions made upon them then will abide upon them all their days. Ordinarily the vessel retains the savour with which it was first seasoned. Many indeed have departed from the good way in which they were trained up; Solomon himself did so. But early training may be a means of their recovering themselves, as it is supposed Solomon did. At least the parents will have the comfort of having done their duty and used the means."

Prov. 22:7

"The rich ruleth over the poor, and the borrower is servant to the lender."

Money is power, for sure. **The rich ruleth over the poor, and the borrower is servant** (lit. bondman) **to the lender.** First, there's an acknowledgement of different classes of people—some rich and some poor. That's always been the case, in spite of the determination of Communism to "equalize" society. The Word teaches a "free-enterprise" system, each man able to own his "fig tree"; i.e., house, cattle, etc. Some people work hard and others are lazy, both reaping their due reward. Still others are born into wealth and their continued state of riches is contingent on how they use or abuse their treasure.

Second, the wealthy have a definite advantage over the poor for obvious reasons. This can be positive and advantageous in a business situation where the employer hires workers (management and labor). In a tyrannical dictatorship, it would be another matter. But wealth's power to rule is just a fact of society. Money itself is not the problem, but rather the character of the one who holds it. It's the "love of money" that's the root of all kinds of evil (1 Timothy 6).

But one principle is so true in our society: **the borrower is servant to the lender.** Here's where the problem becomes acute. We live in a debt-ridden country, where people spend more than they earn. Thus, many have become "slaves" to money lenders (e.g., banks, credit cards, etc.) And what bondage this becomes! Why borrow money you don't have now, thinking you will have it a year from now (plus the interest)? Many a believer (and Christian institution) has lost spiritual ground and testimony by not living below his means. We ought not to "owe anything, but to love one another."

Note: By debt we mean money borrowed which could not be paid in full if called for. Using a credit card (OPM- other people's money) while saving your money in the bank and paying it off each month is not debt. A monthly mortgage, within means, is not debt on a house that is appreciating (i.e., going up in value). If necessary, you could sell the house to cover or pay the "debt."

Prov. 22:8

"He that soweth iniquity shall reap vanity: and the rod of his anger shall fail."

He that soweth iniquity (perverseness, evil) **shall reap vanity** (lit. trouble, sorrow—not the same Hebrew word found in Ecclesiastes; cf. Job 15:35). This reveals again the sowing and reaping principle expounded in Galatians 6:7; *"Whatsoever a man soweth, that shall he also reap."* No way to plant corn and get squash in the harvest!

Whatever is sown will "come up" for sure; only there will be much more of it in the harvest than was planted! Sow to the wind and reap a whirlwind! Thank God, this principle also works in the positive: "Sow to the spirit and reap everlasting life"! The fellow in 22:9 seems to exemplify that blessing.

The rod of his anger shall fail. Here the wicked man is eventually consumed by his iniquity (in God's judgment, if nothing else). "Rod" (stick, staff) speaks of authority (imagined, or otherwise)—his ability to "smash" other in anger. It shall fail or fade out (come to an end). It's all part of divine justice regarding the wicked. It's what Hell is about! *The wicked shall be turned into hell."* (Psalm 9:17). Consider Barnes' note here:

> "The rod of his anger - That with which he smites others (compare Isa_14:6). The King James Version describes the final impotence of the wrath of the wicked."

Prov. 22:9

"He that hath a bountiful eye shall be blessed; for he giveth of his bread to the poor."

Again, whether good or evil, the heart of a man is revealed by his deeds. Here the "bountiful (good, gracious) eye" is "blessed" and thus "gives...to the poor." This word "bountiful" indicates true prosperity (of heart and life); it is translated "prosperity" in 1 Kings 10:7; "Precious"-Psalm 133:2; "beautiful"-Esther 2:7 (of Queen Esther); "gracious"-Hosea 14:2; "joyful"-Ecclesiastes 7:14, etc.

Note that it's the "bountiful eye" that is blessed, not just the condition itself. This describes one who has understanding and vision of his true condition. He has an "eye" toward others less fortunate than himself. He understands something of the grace of God bestowed upon him; thus, he's "blessed" personally and sees the need to share that "blessing" with others. He gives of his substance (e.g., food) to help those in need.

This illustrates God's "welfare" program and how needs are met. I minister at a Rescue Mission where this principle is fleshed out every day. Those who have been blessed economically then share with others less fortunate. Thank God for those who have a "bountiful eye"—who have been blessed abundantly and see the need to help others.

It needs to be said here that the wealthy person is not blessed because he gives, but gives because he's been blessed. This is not a "seed offering" idea that some preach today. We don't give to get; we give to give and honor God—period! Agape love is one way, with no thought of return—no records kept.

Prov. 22:10

"Cast out the scorner, and contention shall go out; yea, strife and reproach shall cease."

Sometimes amputation is essential to keep the whole body from dying. So is the principle applied here in this verse. Where there's "contention" and "strife" something has to give and/or someone has to go! **Cast out the scorner...** (Qal. part. "make mouths at, talk arrogantly") Here is one who is an ongoing mocker (participle), one who perpetually runs at the mouth (same word in Psalm1:1—"scornful"). Drastic action must be taken in order for the "contention" (quarreling, brawling, and discord) to stop. War must be declared if there's to be peace!

Further, **strife** (lit. judgment, as in legal dispute or sentence) **and reproach** (disgrace, dishonor) **shall cease.** Herein is the remedy needed in many organizations, from the home and business to the Church. There must be a standard of order and conduct. Thus, the need for Church discipline which sends a sober warning to those who disrupt along with those who are thinking about it. The one "rotten apple" in the barrel can eventually spoil all the others. The 99 other apples never "convert" the one rotten one! That's a fact of life (and death) and must be faced and dealt with.

Prov. 22:11

"He that loveth pureness of heart, for the grace of his lips the king shall be his friend."

My first thought here is what Jesus said: *"Blessed are the pure in heart: for they shall see God."* (Matthew 5:8). Nothing pleases the King of Kings more than a servant (child of God) who seeks Him with pure motive and praising lips! Spiritually we know that *"there is none righteous, no, not one"*; thus purity of heart is impossible for man apart from a saving relationship with Christ. Certainly, a sinner can never "love pureness"—but only sin. But saving grace in Christ grants a "new heart" and that "grace" (lit. graciousness) which manifests itself through the "lips."

I realize that I've given the application first here. **The king shall be his friend** evidently has to do with an earthly king who uniquely acknowledges and appreciates the goodness and submission of his subjects. A king needs "friends" too, but will not be a companion with renegades. How much more our Heavenly King.

Prov. 22:12

"The eyes of the LORD preserve knowledge, and he overthroweth the words of the transgressor."

The eyes of the LORD refers to God's omniscience (All-knowing) and omnipotence (All-power) which **preserve** (guard, protect) **knowledge.** He is the Author of all knowledge and truth, particularly the Scriptures; thus, He alone preserves what He has established. The Word is "once for all settled in Heaven." Jesus said, *"Heaven and earth shall pass away, but my words shall not pass away"* (Matthew 24:35).

In contrast, we see the "transgressor" (lit treacherous, deceitful) who blatantly speaks his own words (knowledge) in opposition to God's Word; these words will be "overturned" or subdued by God, who has the "last word." Man's words will fade out, but God's, Never! So to whom shall we listen—God or man?

Just to note that "preserve" (*natsar*) is used in Isaiah 26:3: *"Thou wilt keep* (preserve) *him in perfect peace* (*shalom - shalom*, double peace) *whose mind is stayed on thee..."* Amen, what security is this!

Prov. 22:13

"The slothful man saith, There is a lion without, I shall be slain in the streets."

The lazy man has a vivid and rampant imagination to justify his indolent spirit! How fantastic can he be? A "lion" is outside? Usually, he will blame the weather (e.g., heat, cold, snow, etc.) or physical infirmity (e.g., "I don't feel good," etc.), but "a lion" that will kill me in the street? Come on! Laziness has no limit of excuses for its love of ease and disdain for work. See 26:13-16.

Prov. 22:14

"The mouth of strange women is a deep pit: he that is abhorred of the LORD shall fall therein."

The deceptive, sweet-talk of a harlot is a chasm that leads to Hell. This poetic description is unmistakable. This deep hole of destruction awaits the man **abhorred of the LORD**, i.e., one who's the object of God's indignation or anger—viz., the sinner. Falling into this pit can be viewed as the judgment or result of his rebellion against the Lord. See 23:27.

Prov. 22:15

"Foolishness is bound in the heart of a child; but the rod of correction shall drive it far from him."

In light of Jeremiah 17:9, describing the wicked and deceitful heart of man, we have here a principle regarding child-rearing. **Foolishness** (folly, silliness) **is bound** (lit. tied together) **in the heart** (spirit) **of a child; but the rod of correction** (discipline) **shall drive it far from him.**

This is a fundamental fact that is ignored or denied by modern psychology. Evolution has done its damage in making children appear "neutral" and not depraved. "I'm OK, you're OK" is the modern theme; thus, there's no sin because there was no "fall" of man. So-called "sinful behavior," therefore, is explained away as "anti-social behavior" or some form of mental disorder. Sin becomes sickness, needing only "therapy" or medication (e.g., Ritalin for ADD—Attention Deficiency Disorder, etc.). The child, being "sick," has no personal responsibility for his actions. This has led to moral disaster in our nation.

Certainly discipline (spanking with the rod) is not the ultimate remedy, but a means to instill consciousness of sin and the need to change behavior. Discipline (incl. spanking, exhortation, rebuke, etc.) can be used to "drive away" the foolishness in a child. Only the saving grace of God in salvation can ultimately remedy the situation. (viz., a "new heart" in Christ).

Prov. 22:16

"He that oppresseth the poor to increase his riches, and he that giveth to the rich, shall surely come to want."

There are those "oppress" the poor for their own gain and give to appease others who are already rich. To oppress is to defraud or take advantage of those who may have no recourse. K&D indicate that these verbs (oppress and give) are participles, which depict constant action or attitude. Here are those who take from the needy to give to those who have abundance. In God's economy, that will ultimately lead to "want" (deficiency, poverty). God is Just!

There is nothing wrong with abundance lawfully gained, but ill-gotten gain will become a curse in the long haul. On the other hand, when seeking first the kingdom of God, He will add that which we need monetarily. And while we cannot take it with us, we can send it ahead by investing it for the glory of God!

Prov. 22:17

"Bow down thine ear, and hear the words of the wise, and apply thine heart unto my knowledge."

This is a new division in the book pertaining to seeking the **words of the wise**. Note the ways of accessing this spiritual knowledge: 1) **Bow down** (lit. stretch out, incline) **thine ear**; 2) **hear** (listen to, obey) **the words...**; 3) **apply** (lit. set mind to, lay hand upon) **thine heart unto my knowledge.**

Whatever these verbs mean, the import is serious; obedience and application of the Word is paramount for spiritual success.

Prov. 22:18

"For it is a pleasant thing if thou keep them within thee; they shall withal be fitted in thy lips."

Flowing from vs. 17, words of wisdom are seen here as **a pleasant thing** (delightful, sweet) if kept or guarded **within** (lit. the womb, belly). Thus, these words will then **be fitted** (fixed, established) **in thy lips.** What is "fixed" in the heart will be "fixed" in the mouth! Cf. Joshua 1:8.

No hypocrisy or contradiction here! Our "yea will be yea, and our nay, nay." We shall speak truth because we live truth (in the heart). This exemplifies how the "truth will set us free." Our mouth consistently expresses the wisdom and truth within.

Prov. 22:19

"That thy trust may be in the LORD, I have made known to thee this day, even to thee."

Interesting phrasing here: **That thy trust** (lit. confidence) **may be in the LORD** (Jehovah), **I have made known** (taught, perceived, discerned) **to thee this day, even to thee.** Sounds like a specific revelation (*rhema*) to a specific soul or person. God opens spiritual eyes of individuals that they may trust and hope in Him. There's certainly a mystical aspect to all of this. Man left to himself is blind regarding truth. See Isaiah 53:1. Thus David prayed, *"Open thou mine eyes, that I may behold wondrous things out of thy law."*

Prov. 22:20

"Have not I written to thee excellent things in counsels and knowledge,"

Excellent things is used of a three stringed instrument (lute) or triangle shape. It also means a "three-fold measure" or a means of literary emphasis; Barnes suggests the writings of "counsel and knowledge" coming "three times"; i.e., Proverbs, Song of Solomon, and Ecclesiastes; or as some suggest, the Law, the Writings (Poetry), and the Prophets (3-fold breakdown of O.T.).

Vs. 21 further verifies God's purpose in "knowing the certainty of ...truth." Thus, the need for repetition and emphasis. e.g., "line upon line, precept upon precept...."

Prov. 22:21

"That I might make thee know the certainty of the words of truth; that thou mightest answer the words of truth to them that send unto thee?"

Hinged on vs. 20, Solomon instructs his son (inferred) as to the reason for his writings (Scripture): **That I might make thee know the certainty of the words of truth....** Interesting it is that Solomon doesn't just write the "words of truth" (lit. firmness, stability, sureness), but further desires to teach them forcibly (disciple, train) or "make them known." To "make known" here is the Hiph. form of *yada*, "to know"; it means to cause one to know; thus, it is rightly translated to "make known." Cf. 22:6.

Just a word about **the certainty of the words....** To be "certain" is the word, *koshet*, meaning "balanced, evenly weighed, real." So it is with God's Word—it is balanced and true, thus having the same effect on those who let the Words "dwell in them richly" and walk in obedience to it! See Colossians 3:16; Joshua 1:8. How precious and refreshing it is to witness a saint who walks in the balance of "Spirit and Truth." Cf. 11:1.

The purpose of all this: **that thou mightest answer** (lit. turn back, return) **the words of truth to them that send** (Qal. part., lit. "send away for, reach forth") **unto thee.** An interesting and significant expression of those who are seeking truth will "send" or reach out for others who are practicing Truth! This seems to tie with Paul's challenge to Timothy regarding discipling others in 2 Timothy 2:2. We are indeed to "counsel" others (Romans 15:14) and armed with the "Words of Truth," we become competent to do so. We cannot give what we ourselves do not have.

Prov. 22:22

"Rob not the poor, because he is poor: neither oppress the afflicted in the gate:"

These two verses (22, 23) pick up on God's protective attitude regarding the poor or helpless. The command is given: **Rob not the poor because** (seeing) **he is poor** (weak, needy): **neither oppress** (lit. crush, beat down) **the afflicted in the gate.**

The injunction here is regarding the powerful and influential taking advantage of the disadvantaged or less influential. "In the gate" describes a political scene where those in power seem free to "fleece" the underclass. Our relationship to God is revealed by how we treat those who are less fortunate, especially when it would be easy to take advantage of them. God hates this and will come to their aid; see vs. 23.

Prov. 22:23

"For the LORD will plead their cause, and spoil the soul of those that spoiled them."

God has a particular burden for the poor and will "plead" or defend their cause. This ties in with the previous verse, letting oppressors know that to what extent they "spoil" or rob them, they will be "spoiled." What we "dish out" to others will come back to haunt us, especially in regard to the disenfranchised or unfortunate ones.

Prov. 22:24

"Make no friendship with an angry man; and with a furious man thou shalt not go:"

Being acquainted with an angry man is one thing, but having him for a close friend is another. The inference here (see vs. 25) is that the traits of others can "rub off" on one who becomes too involved with them. The word "friendship" here is *ra'ah*, used of shepherding or tending sheep. The idea is feeding or grazing together—our present-day description of "hanging out" with someone.

The admonition is to refrain from an intimate friendship with an angry or furious man. As Paul says: *"Evil communications* (friendships) *corrupt good manners* (character)." All through Proverbs we note the principle of "birds of a feather who flock together"; but here there's an additional warning of not getting deeply involved with those who may influence you to be or do that which is wrong and detrimental.

Clarke has an insightful comment:

"Spirit has a wonderful and unaccountable influence upon spirit. From those with whom we associate we acquire habits, and learn their ways, imbibe their spirit, show their tempers and walk in their steps. We cannot be too choosy of our company, for we may soon learn ways that will be a snare to our soul."

Prov. 22:25

"Lest thou learn his ways, and get a snare to thy soul."

Lest thou learn (adopt) **his ways, and get** (accept, carry away) **a snare** (lit. noose, trap) **to thy soul** (*nephesh*—self). This is the result of the previous verse and is quite descriptive and logical in its conclusion. Sinful behavior can be "catching" because of the weakness of the flesh. The "body of sin" is susceptible! See Romans Ch. 6 & 7.

Prov. 22:26

"Be not thou one of them that strike hands, or of them that are sureties for debts."

Another warning against "striking hands" or being surety (co-signing) for other's debts. See 6:1; 17:18.

Yet a thought just occurred to me that Jesus became our Surety for sins; He paid the full debt of our wickedness, etc. He was abused and bruised for our redemption. Amazing grace indeed!

Prov. 22:27

"If thou hast nothing to pay, why should he take away thy bed from under thee?"

This illustrates the futility of being a "surety" (security) or co-signer for someone's loan. If you become responsible to pay back the loan and have no money, why should they take away your "bed from under you;" i.e., your possessions, leaving you with nothing? This can only be a "lose-lose" situation. Wisdom demands non-involvement in this activity. Much more is said about the subject; see notes on 6:1f.

Prov. 22:28

"Remove not the ancient landmark, which thy fathers have set."

Land or property boundaries were set by the "fathers" (ancestors) and were not to be tampered with. I assume that property lines were moved or pushed back into the neighbor's land because of greed; i.e., a man's property could be expanded unlawfully by changing the "setting" or marker. Man's wickedness seeks to encroach on other's possessions without paying the price to increase his land lawfully.

This certainly can apply to the removal of the "eternal Gospel" of grace from the church and substitute a social gospel which is not the Gospel. See Galatians 1:6. We have "moved" the time-proven markers of the Word of God in these days!

Prov. 22:29

"Seest thou a man diligent in his business? he shall stand before kings; he shall not stand before mean men."

Seest (look, behold) **thou a man diligent in his business** (occupation, employment)**? he shall stand** (lit. placed to stay) **before kings** (royalty)**; he shall not stand before mean** (dark, obscure) **men.** Diligence is rewarded with true success; i.e., produced by God rather than man. Prepared by the Lord, such a man will be positioned in strategic places, rather than languishing in obscurity before obscure people.

"Diligence" (*mahir*) has the meaning of "quick, hence skillful"; it also means to be "ready" at all times. K&D translate it "expert." It is used of Ezra (7:6) who is called a "ready scribe." He was a diligent expert in the Law. Note how he eventually stood before the king.

Also, in Psalm 45:1, David describes his tongue as *"the pen of a ready writer."* Great words! He was an expert, skillful Psalmist, among other things. So God has a "prepared place for prepared men," who diligently and skillfully do what "their hand finds to do!" What a challenge to faithfulness, "in season and out of season." See Prov. 10:4; 21:5.

Chapter 23

When You Sit Down to Eat with a Ruler

Prov. 23:1

"When thou sittest to eat with a ruler, consider diligently what is before thee:"

The obvious lesson here (vs. 1-3) is regarding gluttony or over-indulgence. However, eating with a "ruler" seems to infer a particular situation where attitude, character, and response is important for more than one reason. One could "pig out" (eat excessively) when no one's around; however, the "dainties" of the king would indicated expensive and an elegant display of food.

I gather that personal control of food consumption is a test of our character. Where etiquette and temperance are of essence, one needs to "consider diligently" (with discernment) what is on the table. Should he try some of everything or distinguish between likes and dislikes? Does he ask questions regarding various foods, or just keep quiet and eat?

I'm not sure what "deceitful meat" is in vs. 3. Is that "unwholesome" food—too much starch or sugar, etc.? Do we reveal ourselves at a table spread with sumptuous food? Whatever the case, we much not be "given to appetite"; i.e., we much eat to live rather than living to eat! A good reminder to eat the right foods in reasonable quantity.

I would think too that sitting at the ruler's table was for a better and deeper purpose than just eating. Earth shattering decisions are sometimes made over a meal.

Prov. 23:2

"And put a knife to thy throat, if thou be a man given to appetite."

A drastic admonition here regarding gluttony. **And put a knife to thy throat**—obviously a figurative statement depicting "death" to self. **A man given to appetite** is literally "a man of soul" (*nephesh*). Here's one controlled not by his spirit, but his emotions and self will. *Nephesh* (soul) mediates between the body and the spirit, which makes one "soulish," if in control. Our renewed spirit must dictate our intent to the soul and then the body (flesh).

Some are not destroyed just by the flesh, but by the soulish, which is more subtle. E.g., much of so-called contemporary music does not emanate out of the spirit (that pertaining to the glory of God), but from the soulish (emotions, self-gratifying); not to mention that which is just of the flesh (bodily orientated—heavy metal, etc.).

Prov. 23:3

"Be not desirous of his dainties: for they are deceitful meat."

The rebuke of overindulgence in vs. 2 is a general principle; but it also has to do with the social setting at the "ruler's" table. If you have a good appetite, that's not the place nor time to "indulge." First, you don't go to a dignitary's home primarily to eat. Second, vs. 3 indicates that the delicacies may be "deceitful"— a set up or a trap. The ruler may have a hidden agenda, using "dainties" (delicacies, gourmet) to "deceive."

Or it could be here that a leader may test his clients or future employees by how controlled they are at the table! Our self-discipline can be tested by how we deal with food. See also 4:17; 9:5.

Prov. 23:4

"Labour not to be rich: cease from thine own wisdom."

Caught up with riches! That seems to be the theme song of every age in history. People are evaluated by their possession of wealth. Is that a valid criterion? Money has become the "god" of the masses, yet none would deny its necessity in a free society. Furthermore, the Church is following suit today with its "Prosperity gospel." One's spirituality is being judged by his acquisition of "health and wealth."

But this proverb addresses one's motive regarding riches.

Labor not to be rich...; i.e., don't tire or exhaust yourself to accumulate riches. I don't think this has anything to do with legitimate labor for a salary or livelihood. I think this is a warning against greediness and covetousness (the gluttony of the soul). He's talking about motive and purpose here, as though wealth is equal to success.

The second part of the verse further explains the first, namely, **Cease from thine own wisdom** (understanding); i.e., desist or forsake your natural inclination for greed. In other words, riches can come in the process of serving God, but are not an end in themselves. The whole theme of Scripture is "living for the glory of God"—that's the ultimate purpose of life. *"In all thy ways acknowledge him, and he shall direct thy paths"* (Prov. 3:6). *"But seek ye first the kingdom of God...and all these things shall be added unto you"* (Matthew 6:33). O, to desire Him alone, leaving the results in His hand. Stop scheming and jockeying for money and position!

Prov. 23:5

"Wilt thou set thine eyes upon that which is not? for riches certainly make themselves wings; they fly away as an eagle toward heaven."

In the context of inordinate riches, Solomon asks: **Wilt thou set thine eyes upon that which is not?"** The word "set" and "fly away" in this verse are the same. Will you fix your sight or longingly gaze upon that which is fleeting or nothing substantial? Here's a covetous expression for illicit riches ("deceitful meat"- vs. 3). It's poor judgment, at best.

Such longing is unwise just from a practical standpoint: **for riches certainly make themselves wings; they fly away as an eagle toward heaven.** Money is illusive, it "flies away" toward the "heavens" where your eyes are fixed! It's here today and gone tomorrow. Plus it can leave behind a path of devastation and grief. This idea is supported by the present context of deceptive and shady "deals" offered by those with "an evil eye" (vs. 6).

Money is necessary to live in this world, but woe to those who make it their god. The love of it is the "root of all kinds of evil." *"For what shall it profit a man if he shall gain the whole world, and lose his own soul?"* Let us set our eyes upon our high and holy calling in Christ (Colossians 3:1ff.).

Prov. 23:6

"Eat thou not the bread of him that hath an evil eye, neither desire thou his dainty meats:"

Eating, in Scripture, is more than just taking nourishment. Unlike animals who don't want to be bothered while eating, humans are made to eat and fellowship (talk, etc.) simultaneously. It's a joyous activity to sit down at a meal among those with whom you agree and love. (see Revelation 3:20, fellowship with Jesus). But eating can also be a "set up" for evil people to get what they want. A "free meal" is not always free. That's the context here.

Solomon issues a warning here: **Eat thou not the bread** (food) **of him that hath an evil eye, neither desire thou his dainty meats** (savory food, delicacy). He's saying that we'd better discern why this individual invited us to dinner; what does he have in mind? Is it an invitation just out of kindness, or does he have an agenda—an evil scheme to ensnare you? Shrewd and illicit "business" deals are often transacted over lunch.

But this admonition can also be seen from the vantage point of lust or greed. Note that the exhortation is not only regarding the "eating" per se, but even the "desire" for his delicacies. Man's covetous spirit can get him into deep trouble, and the schemer can use his "wicked eye" and sweet talk to lure his prey. (see Psalm 141:4).

In light of the next verse (7), we must be discerning as to where people are coming from and why they do what they do. What you see is not always what you get. The deceitful heart will appear to be gracious and kind externally, while inwardly seeking to take your very life! A man is really what "he thinks in his heart," and everyone has a dark side. Only the grace of God, by which we receive a new heart in Christ, can produce genuine, unselfish love for others.

Prov. 23:7

"For as he thinketh in his heart, so is he: Eat and drink, saith he to thee; but his heart is not with thee."

What you see is not always what you get! Motives and actions don't always go together (see vs. 6). **For** (because) **as he thinketh in his heart, so is he: Eat and drink, saith he to thee; but his heart is not with thee.** This man has an agenda that is not in your interest, while offering you the "freebies," as we say.

This verse is very frequently used to explain how the thought life is what determines our actions. I have used this expression many times: "You can't live any higher or better than you think!" "What you think is what you are, etc." We need to comment on this unique word "thinketh" (*sha'ar*).

It is only used here, i.e., it occurs only one time in all the O.T. It literally means "to split open, reason out, calculate or estimate." Do you know anyone who is "calculating" in their spirit? Watch out—you're about to be overtaken! So it is with this man in the verse, who has everything "reasoned out." He knows exactly what he's doing and thus attempts to deceive his victim. How satanic!

Note this calculation is not in the brain, but in the "heart" (lit. *nephesh* or soul—mind). These are not passing thoughts or brain stimuli, but meditative, calculations of the inner man. (See Psalm 2:1 - "imagine" is the word for meditate in Psalm 1:2.) Wicked people "meditate" too, not on the Word of God, but on the demonic schemes that control their corrupt minds. Everyone seems to have some kind of hidden agenda depending on how their mind works (thinks). This is heavy (deep)!

So this man says, "Eat and drink—enjoy the free goodies," but his heart (*labe*- feelings) is not with thee. The trap is set! Beware! The impression is given that he's for you when, indeed, he's really your enemy! Remember that this is all in the context of "social friendship or pleasantry," which makes it even more deadly.

I like JFB's comment: "Beware of deceitful men, whose courtesies even you will repent of having accepted."

Prov. 23:8

*"The morsel which thou hast eaten shalt thou vomit up, and lose
thy sweet words."*

This verse continues the thought of discerning where people are coming from; i.e., evil man has an agenda when he sets forth a "free" and lavish meal. If you fall into his trap and feast unduly, you will be mesmerized for the kill! But when you "wake up," which seems to be the case here, it turns your stomach.

Because of the situation (wicked motive, etc.), the victim cannot eat much because it's not genuine fellowship where two fellows enjoy a meal together. Hence, just a "morsel" or bite causes him to "vomit" when he realizes the deception, etc. Whatever "sweet (pleasant) words" you had previously spoken are now "lost", i.e., wasted or of no value. I have to believe that this scenario is played out frequently in life, knowing the deceitfulness of man's heart (Jeremiah 17:9).

Prov. 23:9

*"Speak not in the ears of a fool: for he will despise the wisdom
of thy words."*

The characteristic of "fools" is that they don't hear (heed) words of wisdom—they despise them. The fool has no respect for wisdom because he loves silliness. So we should not be shocked and offended at such a response (or lack of). Save your breath when you come upon a mocker, lest you "cast your pearls before swine," as Jesus mentioned.

Someone said, "A man convinced against his will, is of the same opinion still." Some folks don't even have a legitimate opinion or reason for their foolishness. But, God's Spirit can "open the ears" of sinners so we can hear and understand the Word. Thank God for the miracle of the "New Birth" that can make the worst fool a wise man!

Prov. 23:10

*"Remove not the old landmark; and enter not into the fields of
the fatherless:"*

See 22:28. Boundaries and borders of land were sacred and deemed unmovable. Land owners were not to extend their land borders (rock walls, etc.) into the neighbor's property. That was dishonest and unethical at best.

But the emphasis here seems to be upon the treatment of the "fatherless" or orphans who were given "fields" for survival. God has a special love for the poor and needy (cf. Job 31:21-23; Jeremiah 22:3; Zechariah 7:10; James 1:27). The warning is not to take advantage of those less fortunate—don't enter their "fields" when you have plenty yourself. If you do, you'll have God Himself to deal with! (vs. 11).

Prov. 23:11

"For their redeemer is mighty; he shall plead their cause with thee."

Again we see the "special interest group" before God, i.e., the fatherless or orphan (vs. 10). He is their powerful "redeemer" (lit. kinsman, avenger), who **shall plead** or contends for, **their cause with** (against) **thee.**

This redemption is not primarily spiritual, but civil and protective. To treat the fatherless unjustly is to take on the Just One Himself!

Prov. 23:12

"Apply thine heart unto instruction, and thine ears to the words of knowledge."

Here Solomon again emphasizes the necessity of heart application of proper instruction. "Apply" means lit. "cause to come in, enter" (Hiph. imper.) which indicates fervent desire to receive "instruction" (discipline, doctrine). Note that "heart" knowledge is the key to right and effective action.

The parallel statement regarding "ears" also refers to spiritual ears of the heart of which Jesus spoke often. "The words (utterance) of knowledge (perception)" must penetrate beyond the outer ear. We must seek God for spiritual understanding which directly affects our attitude and conduct.

Prov. 23:13

"Withhold not correction from the child: for if thou beatest him with the rod, he shall not die."

A father's love for his child must be accompanied by wisdom and faith in order to see the whole picture. Because of the child's sin nature (which must not be overlooked or denied), the temporal pain of discipline is essential to impress his conscience. Punishment for wrong-doing is only one phase of true discipline which seeks to further instruct and develop the child. To withhold (refrain from) such correction is to bring greater pain and calamity in the long run. *"For whom the Lord loveth, he chasteneth...,"* not leaving us alone to drift into apathy and sin. Love is demonstrated by action more than mere words.

Note the assuring words that even "beating (striking) him with the rod (branch)" will not kill him! In fact, such a measure may serve to impress upon him the weightiness of sin, thus becoming instrumental in delivering his soul from eternal death or "hell." (cf. vs. 14) Loving, firm and fair discipline is really the antidote to "child brutality." To spank up front brings rest and closure, keeping parents from "losing it" and thus preventing extreme anger in them and brutality (injury) to the child. Note the two following pithy statements:

"You will not kill your son by scourging him, you may kill him by with holding the scourge." - Barnes

"While there is little danger that the use of the "divine ordinance of the rod" will produce bodily harm, there is great hope of spiritual good." – JFB

Prov. 23:14

"Thou shalt beat him with the rod, and shalt deliver his soul from hell."

A follow up encouragement and result of corporal punishment is not only that "he will not die," but may be rescued ("delivered") from Hell! Making him accountable and training his conscience now will also pay great dividend later. Yes, "beat him with the rod" (in the right place and way) and save his soul from future judgment.

This is simple instruction in letting a child know that he must submit to his Dad's authority (representing God) or one day he will be the object of God's eternal judgment. This is a vital lesson in "bringing up children in the nurture and admonition of the Lord." A child must know early who is boss! He will never have authority himself if he never learns to submit to higher authority. He must know the consequences of sin and the necessity of a broken will, along with a sharpened conscience (spirit).

A note here about the "rod," as opposed to the hand. A father's hand should be reserved for reaching out to pat, shake, hug, or comfort—rather than spank. Instead, the rod should be the symbol for spanking and used for that purpose alone. The sooner the rod is used wisely and firmly, the sooner it will not have to be used.

Prov. 23:15

"My son, if thine heart be wise, my heart shall rejoice, even mine."

From "beating" to "rejoicing"! There is indeed some connection between proper, godly discipline which yields wisdom in a child, and the joy that results in a father's heart. There is no greater joy to a godly father than having a wise son! Worldly possessions and position, etc. cannot hold a candle to the thrill of knowing a son (or daughter) is fulfilling God's purpose for his life. This is the ultimate.

Indeed, a wise, rejoicing son will produce a joyous heart in his father.

Prov. 23:16

"Yea, my reins shall rejoice, when thy lips speak right things."

This statement continues the thought of vs. 15 regarding the joyous effect of a son's wisdom upon his father. **Yea, my reins shall rejoice** (lit. leap for joy) **when thy lips speak right things.** The word "reins" pertains to the physical organ kidneys; it is used figuratively as the "seat of emotion and affection." Note how emotions are felt or sensed in the abdominal area of the body. We speak of "gut-level" reactions, etc. In this case, what a blessing to have "gut-level" joy!

Prov. 23:17

"Let not thine heart envy sinners: but be thou in the fear of the LORD all the day long."

Being yet human and in the world, there is still the temptation to "envy sinners." The word for "envy" has the idea of being "zealous for" or pursuing (in a bad sense). What sinners possess sometimes looks inviting, especially when the believer is suffering loss and struggling through times of trial. It's easy to get caught up in the moment, failing to see the big picture and the "blessed hope" that is ours.

The ultimate remedy is walking **in the fear of the LORD all the day long.** This is a walk of faith which takes God seriously, planted on solid ground. Such "fear" is the remedy of all fears. It enables the believer to "see through" the froth and tinsel of this world, because of the reality of hope in the world to come. The fear of the Lord puts all things in perspective, thus granting spiritual discernment and victory "all the day long"! This is the antidote to covetousness.

Prov. 23:18

"For surely there is an end; and thine expectation shall not be cut off."

In light of vs. 17, why envy sinners who have no hope? Walking in the fear of God intensifies our hope for the future. **For surely there is an end** (future)**; and thine expectation** (hope, thing longed for) **shall not be cut off** (destroyed). How this hope enables us to walk by faith in the present! The LORD God Omnipotent reigns; thus, all things will work out rightly! This is a sure antidote to sadness and bitterness; Our God will do justly and we need not fear.

K&D render this verse: "Truly there is a future, and thy hope shall not come to naught," I like that. Only future hope can keep us diligent and steadfast in the present.

Prov. 23:19

"Hear thou, my son, and be wise, and guide thine heart in the way."

Here Solomon again is speaking as a concerned father to his son. **Hear thou, my son, and be** (or become) **wise....** The command "hear" is *shamah* (cf. Deuteronomy 6:4ff.), meaning to "obey or hear attentively." How often do we hear the word spoken but fail to take heed! True faith obeys (e.g., Hebrews 11). Such obedience is not only safe and blessed, but lends itself to increased wisdom (skill in life's experience).

In conjunction, **guide thine heart in the way** (i.e., God's path). The word translated "guide" is *ashar*, a verb meaning "to go straight, level or right." Interestingly, it further means to "make happy" or to "advance in prosperity." This is the same word (as a plural noun) in Psalm 1:1 translated *"Blessed is the man...,"* meaning "extremely happy." O, to find the reality of this true happiness which eludes the world, but is found only through the walk of obedient faith.

Prov. 23:20

"Be not among winebibbers; among riotous eaters of flesh:"

Solomon exhorts his son not to be found in the company of drunken and gluttonous people. Intoxication can be "catching" by virtue of peer pressure. We become like those we "hang out" with. Here is the condemnation of extreme behavior; viz., excessive wine and flesh. We all have to eat and drink, but sinful lust always goes to extremes.

Prov. 23:21

"For the drunkard and the glutton shall come to poverty: and drowsiness shall clothe a man with rags."

It is significant that "the drunkard and the glutton" are named together. This ties in with the "riotous" indulgence mentioned in vs. 20. Thank God for daily provision of food and drink, but the power of sinful flesh goes to extreme; this dulls the senses and destroys incentive to work, etc. Yes, poverty will result.

The parallel expression further describes the plight of a stupefied brain: **Drowsiness shall clothe a man with rags.** Don't expect the finer things of life if you're a gluttonous drunk! Indeed, we eventually reap what we have sown.

Prov. 23:22

"Hearken unto thy father that begat thee, and despise not thy mother when she is old."

Hearken (*shamah*- obey, hear intelligently, pay attention; (cf. Deuteronomy 6:4f.) **unto thy father that begat thee.** In light of the previous verse (21), how vital are godly parents who rightly instruct their children. What heartache could be avoided if children would really listen to their parents! They are God's representatives in the home and how we treat them reflects our attitude toward God.

Note that this attitude of respect does not end because the mother is "old." Assuming she is not senile, her wisdom is not to be ignored or minimized. In fact, what a wealth is available even to an adult son or daughter who respect the hoary head! Thank God for parents who listen to God and thus become a vital and primary source of blessing to their children at any age.

Prov. 23:23

"Buy the truth, and sell it not; also wisdom, and instruction, and understanding."

We "buy" that which we deem valuable and useful. The word here means "procure, acquire, get." Although we purchase things with money, this exhortation is not about currency per se. The idea is that if we want to "buy" something of greatest value, "buy the truth"; i.e., that which is "sure, certain and stable." There's nothing in this world more important, for Christ Himself is "the Truth"! Such a "procurement" is beyond anything else in this world or the universe. When you "get" it , don't ever "sell" it! Never let it go!

Solomon places "wisdom (skillfulness) and instruction (i.e., discipline) and understanding in the same category. However, I would think that these latter qualities emanate from and are sanctified (i.e., set apart for God's use) by the truth. Significantly, the apostle John wrote:

"I rejoiced greatly that I found of thy children walking in truth....I have no greater joy than to hear that my children walk in truth."
(2 John 4; 3 John 4)

Paul spoke of the essential fruit of "faith, hope and love, but the greatest of these is love (charity)" (1 Corinthians 13:13). However, it can be said that the "greatest" of all these is Truth, without which the others would fail. Check the following: Prov. 2:2-4; 4:5-7; 10:1; 16:16. All of these deal with the possession of "wisdom." However, without the Truth, wisdom is not *true* or godly wisdom; it can only be worldly, at best.

Prov. 23:24

"The father of the righteous shall greatly rejoice: and he that begetteth a wise child shall have joy of him."

Here's a beautiful proverb describing a father's exultation over a wise and righteous son (child). In context, it's a son who is obedient and open to his parent's authority and exhortation (vs. 22). He has "bought the truth," denying falsehood (lies), taking on a Biblical world view which results in godly understanding and lifestyle (vs. 23).

The word for "rejoice" is repeated for emphasis; viz., "rejoicing, rejoice." Its root meaning is to "spin around," depicting ecstatic joy. This father is "carried away" with rejoicing over the obvious blessing upon his son. The next phrase simply enhances and compliments the former; **and he that begetteth** (bears, births) **a wise child shall have joy of him.** To father a child is easy, but being a father is tough! What a joy when that child turns out to love, respect and follow God! Such reward is all but unparalleled.

Prov. 23:25

"Thy father and thy mother shall be glad, and she that bare thee shall rejoice."

Solomon continues his enthusiastic "tirade" of parental joy resulting from the blessing of wise children (vs. 24). Mom and Dad "dance" for joy together in this verse. What greater happiness can grace the hearts of godly parents than to witness the hand of God upon their children? Worldly success and wealth are overshadowed by such. Compare Prov. 10:1; 17:21, 25.

Prov. 23:26

"My son, give me thine heart, and let thine eyes observe my ways."

The remainder of this chapter deals with Solomon's exhortation to his "son" regarding sexual impurity (vs. 26-28) and drunkenness (vs. 29-35). Significantly, these two areas of behavior still plague our young people to this day!

Here's the picture of a father pleading for his son to "listen up" with all his heart, i.e., take to heart what I'm about to say. In conjunction, **let thine eyes observe** (keep, obey) **my ways** (lit. course of life). The eyes always follow the heart; thus, in the ultimate sense, God alone can give us a new heart that follows His ways. Significantly, Solomon's son, Rehoboam, failed to heed his father's instruction. That's the enigma so often in family life as well as life in the Kingdom. How many disobedient children does God have? (See Isaiah 1) But whatever the response, the following instruction is totally valid and obligatory. *"Let God be true, but every man a liar!"*

Prov. 23:27

"For a whore is a deep ditch; and a strange woman is a narrow pit."

A young man doesn't want to face the fact that **a whore is a deep ditch; and a strange woman is a narrow pit.** The analogy here is the harlot's ability to lead one into a deep hole, making it extremely difficult to get out. The "narrow pit" speaks of a trap set up by hunters of the field.

A young man with raging hormones can easily be ensnared by sexual temptation and sin. Solomon knew something of this and so did his father, David, who said:

"Wherewithal shall a young man cleanse his way? by taking

heed thereto according to thy word; Thy word have I hid (treasured up) in mine heart, that I might not sin against thee." (Psalm 119:9, 11)

Certainly, Solomon's "son" needed to obey his father's wise injunction (word) from the heart! There's something better than being delivered from the "deep pit"; not jumping into it to begin with!

Prov. 23:28

"She also lieth in wait as for a prey, and increaseth the transgressors among men."

She also lieth in wait as for a prey.... The word "also" can be translated "moreover or yea," further describing the whore's scheming ways. Like a hungry animal ready to pounce upon its prey, so she waits in the shadows. See notes on 2:16-19.

Thus, she **increaseth** (adds, augments) **the transgressors among men** (*adam*- mankind). This is a powerful and descriptive statement! We all know the effects and influence of sex and liquor upon people—especially men. The word "transgressors" is from the verb *bagad,* meaning "to act treacherously or deceitfully." It describes a man operating constantly under cover, secretly and unfaithfully. In 25:19, this word is translated as an "unfaithful man" who cannot be trusted in a time of trouble.

I mention the technical aspect here because the English doesn't capture the thought and action. The street woman has the power to incite in men the inner force of evil and lust which dominates their lives. That's why "adultery" is not only mentioned in the Ten Commandments, but frequently in Proverbs and throughout Scripture. It is also applied almost incessantly to "spiritual" unfaithfulness and apostasy before the LORD. (See the book of Hosea). James even calls worldly believers "adulterers and adulteresses" because of their sinful compromise (4:4).

Prov. 23:29

"Who hath woe? who hath sorrow? who hath contentions? who hath babbling? who hath wounds without cause? who hath redness of eyes?"

Now Solomon moves from illicit sex to drunkenness. He builds a strong case against the devastating consequences of strong drink or alcohol. Indeed, impure behavior and liquor ("booze") surely are related. Wisely, he asks a series of questions regarding the effects of drunkenness. Who has woe (crying out)? Sorrow? Contentions (strife)? Babbling? Wounds without cause (reason)? Redness (bleariness) of eyes? Yes, he says, who does have these problems? A drunk!

Prov. 23:30

"They that tarry long at the wine; they that go to seek mixed wine."

He now answers the question posed in the previous verse. **They that tarry long** (lit. loiter, continue) **at** (by reason of) **the wine** (fermented). This pictures one having a drinking "bout" or staying up late drinking.

Not satisfied with ordinary "wine," he seeks out **mixed wine;** i.e., that with added flavor and intoxicating strength ("proof"). The drunkard is never satisfied, but, like other addicts, is always seeking a "higher buzz." So often the substance abuser is hiding from reality, attempting to "medicate" or ease the pain of guilt and hopelessness. I doubt whether anyone has purposefully planned to be a "drunk" or drug addict. But the "sliding board" of substance abuse is so subtle, taking its victim down the path of destruction one "inch" at a time!

Thank God for the power of the Gospel of God's Grace that changes folks from the inside out! Christ's death, burial, and resurrection have made it possible to be delivered from sin's penalty and power. The Scripture says, *"Believe on the Lord Jesus Christ, and thou shalt be saved, and thy house."* (Acts 16:31)

Prov. 23:31

"Look not thou upon the wine when it is red, when it giveth his colour in the cup, when it moveth itself aright."

This verse "exudes" with the power of descriptive words. It's almost like a video rendition of a potential drunk, mesmerized by the magical influence of a beautiful "reddish" liquid in the cup! Thus, the admonition, not to "look" or stare upon the substance, especially under certain conditions:

1. **When it is red**; the verb form of *adam*, meaning "growing red or reddening" (i.e., sparkling).

2. **When it giveth his color in the cup**; "color" is the word *ayin*, meaning "eye" (i.e., gleaming, clear brightness).

3. **When it moveth itself aright**; this is an interesting phrase regarding the "evenness or smoothness" of the liquid. Barnes note says it all: "The Hebrew word describes the pellucid stream flowing pleasantly from the wineskin or jug into the goblet or the throat (compare Son_7:9), rather than a sparkling wine."

How tempting it all appears! It's no wonder so many precious souls are overcome by the power of alcohol. The only real antidote is found in Ephesians 5:18: *"And be not drunk with wine, wherein is excess* (sin)*; but be filled* (lit. constantly being full) *with the Spirit,"* Only the intoxicating control of the Holy Spirit can overcome the onslaughts of the world, the flesh, and the Devil.

Prov. 23:32

"At the last it biteth like a serpent, and stingeth like an adder."

Yes, the drink looks good, tastes good and goes down the throat so smoothly; but just wait! **At the last** (end) **it biteth** (strikes) **like a serpent** (snake)**, and stingeth like an adder** (viper, poisonous snake)**.** No, this doesn't happen "up front," but later on as the victim continues to indulge and "play around" with the substance. It's just a matter of time before the "snake" lunges forward and strikes! Then other problems arise (vs. 33f.).

Prov. 23:33

"Thine eyes shall behold strange women, and thine heart shall utter perverse things."

Now the drink affects the "eyes" and the "heart," along with the mouth. The "bloodshot" eyes begin to gazed lustfully upon "strange women" or harlots; i.e., the wine releases the "brake" of restraint, permitting sexual fantasy and immorality. Along with that come "perverted" words from the heart through the mouth.

Let's make clear that the liquor doesn't produce these sinful acts, but serves as a catalyst to release the wickedness already resident in the heart of man. Jesus said that it is not what comes out of a man that defiles him, but what comes from within. *"For out of the heart of men proceed evil thoughts, adulteries, fornications, murders,"* etc. (See Mark 7:18-23). The strong drink simply facilitates the terrible sins already resident in the heart.

This fact if vitally important in dealing with "substance abuse victims." Those in Alcoholics Anonymous, for instance, may find relief over a drinking problem, but never conquer temper, lust, stealing, gossip, etc. But a new heart in Christ can and will bring deliverance over *all* of the above! Amen!

Prov. 23:34

"Yea, thou shalt be as he that lieth down in the midst of the sea, or as he that lieth upon the top of a mast. "

Not only do drunks babble perverted words, but they do crazy things. Yes, things that are likened to one "lying down in the midst (lit. heart) of the sea"; i.e., sprawled out on the deck of a ship caught in a stormy sea! That might be comparable to a man lying down in the middle of a busy freeway. He seems to have no concern or interest for the imminent danger lurking around him.

Likewise, he's acting as a sailor "lying upon the top of a mast." Certainly, this is no place to "lie down" for any reason, especially in the midst of a storm. But drunkenness blurs the sense of fear and danger, which evidently is one of the basic attractions to alcohol. In light of the turmoil of man's soul, drinking is an attempt to "quiet" the restlessness of a troubled heart. Therefore, whatever risks are taken seem worthwhile when one is inebriated by liquor.

Prov. 23:35

"They have stricken me, shalt thou say, and I was not sick; they have beaten me, and I felt it not: when shall I awake? I will seek it yet again."

In addition to his being oblivious to impending danger, the drunk has no feeling of pain. The alcohol has served as an artificial "anesthesia." **They have stricken** (whipped, wounded) **me, shalt thou say, and I was not sick** (lit. grieved or pained)**; they have beaten me, and I felt** (*yada-* to be aware, perceive) **it not.** In other words, he has probably been beaten up in a fight or scuffle, and has no recollection or bodily pain. He may be bleeding and bruised, but it seemingly has no adverse effect upon him. For sober people, pain is a warning signal that something is wrong, but that mechanism is inoperative to a drunk.

In fact, with no pain, sensitivity or guilt, he's determined to "wake up" the next day and "seek it yet again"; i.e., start the destructive routine all over again! How deceitfully sad and wicked is the depraved heart of man! Only Amazing Grace can make the difference. Amen.

Chapter 24
Do Not Be Envious of Evil Men

Prov. 24:1

"Be not thou envious against evil men, neither desire to be with them."

It's interesting how folks envy wicked people. Asaph, in Psalm 73, had this problem, which brought him to despair and depression. He had an issue with the "goodness of God" and how it was that ungodly people seem to fare better in this life than believers. It's not fair that evil folks make more money, have finer houses and cars, etc., than those who serve the Lord. But then Asaph saw their destructive end and recognized that this world was as close to Heaven as they would ever be.

Here Solomon exhorts us not to be jealous of "evil men" (those who are bad, malignant, inflicting pain and misery). In fact, he says don't even "desire" or covet to be with them. Don't even think about it!

Prov. 24:2

"For their heart studieth destruction, and their lips talk of mischief."

Reason: **For their heart studieth destruction** (i.e., violence, oppression). The word "studieth" (*Hagah*) is the word translated "meditate" in Psalm 1:2; Joshua 1:8. Also translated, "imagine" in Psalm 2:1, pertaining to the pondering, scheming heart of the wicked, rebellious heart of man!

He's not speaking here of association with sinners per se, but getting involved with malicious, conniving, evil-minded people who spend their lives "studying" how to feed their own flesh and purposes.

Note that **their lips talk of mischief** (perverseness, trouble). What's in their hearts comes out. They reveal eventually what they have been pondering. Watch out, they're trouble! Steer clear!

Prov. 24:3

"Through wisdom is an house builded; and by understanding it is established:"

Here's the contrast to "evil men" (vs. 1) who are destructive; i.e., a wise man who "builds" his house or family skillfully. The "house" here depicts not just the material structure, but the family living within. First, "established" (firmly stabilized) by "understanding" (insight), and then built up by godly skillfulness

Evil has no lasting foundation and lends itself to foolishness, which builds its house on the sand. Wisdom builds on the Solid Rock, and when the storm howls, it will stand! Many try to build a house from the second floor, which cannot be done. There must first be destruction before construction—a messy hole dug, footing laid, walls raised, etc. There must also be a straight and level foundation, without which the building will be crooked and faulty. Thank God, for the Foundation Stone Himself upon whom our spiritual house can be built!

Prov. 24:4

"And by knowledge shall the chambers be filled with all precious and pleasant riches."

Connected to vs. 3 regarding a house built "through wisdom," here is the further fruit of wisdom: **the chambers** (apartment) (shall) **be filled with all** (or wholly) **precious** (valuable) **and pleasant** (delightful) **riches** (wealth). The issue here is the fact that a wise man has learned how to live life skillfully and thus can make a living. A man who learns how to live will not have difficulty earning a living. He will thus make proper investments, one of which is a house that really becomes a home. Many folks may have a house, but only God can make a home.

These "riches" certainly may be literal wealth; however, the inference would be high quality living—which is wealth indeed. It's a house of wisdom and true understanding, well-ordered and prosperous.

Prov. 24:5

"A wise man is strong; yea, a man of knowledge increaseth strength."

A wise man (*geber*- man of strength, valor) **is strong** (i.e., bold, secure, confident). Again the fruit of wisdom is genuine and lasting power. The source of strength is not physical, whether genetics or nationality; it has little to do with wealth or sheer intellect (formal education, IQ, etc.). This is strength of spiritual character—the wholeness that comes only from God. Too little is made of this in our day! We judge people by their looks, money and "prestige," but not by character.

The compensating statement is also made: **yea, a man** (*eesh-* weak man) **of knowledge increaseth** (ongoing progression) **strength** (lit. firmness, productivity). This describes a wise man in progress, as opposed to the former declaration of a wise man's strength. It seems to infer that one can "grow" into strength who loves true knowledge (e.g., wisdom). Thank God, we can "grow in the grace (heart) and knowledge (head) of our Lord Jesus Christ!"

Prov. 24:6

"For by wise counsel thou shalt make thy war: and in multitude of counsellors there is safety."

Note that there's no argument here as to whether war has a place in human affairs. This proverb just gives advice as to how war is to be engaged; i.e., with proper counsel and guidance. Since war is "in our members" (James 4:1f.), men will fight each other (ind. or nations). Sin has produced rebellion and greed whereby one people will rise against another—that's history. Israel was always in conflict with enemies, depending on God's guidance sometimes, but not all the time. So we must *"fight the good fight of faith"* against sin, the world, self and the Devil—but the war can only be successfully engaged in the Spirit of the Word.

But this proverb simply states that only by "wise counsel" (emphasis) should war (battle) be made. The second part enhances the thought: **and in the multitude** (abundance) **of counsellors there is safety** (deliverance, victory). Counsel comes from counselors. The Word is primary (Psalm 1:1, 2), but to be surrounded by men who know the Word and its wisdom is a gift indeed.

The warning here is not to go into a battle half-cocked or unprepared. A great verse for heads of State or the Secretary of Defense. But it also applies to ordinary life and the process of decision-making. We don't have to learn everything first hand (by experience); we can listen to and learn from wise people who have gone before. It's a good idea to seek counsel from wise people before making major decisions.

Prov. 24:7

"Wisdom is too high for a fool: he openeth not his mouth in the gate."

Wisdom is out of reach for the fool! It is beyond his interest and thus his capability. He's grounded to a "low" life, not given much responsibility—he can't handle it. "The gate" indicates the opening of the city; i.e., place of responsibility and government. (cf. 22:22; Amos 5:15) This suggests political authority and decision making, which would not be expected from a fool. Thus, **he openeth not his mouth** or has nothing to say in governing the community. Being devoid of wisdom limits one's ability and opportunity to lead others.

Prov. 24:8

"He that deviseth to do evil shall be called a mischievous person."

Here's a definition of **a mischievous person**—one who **deviseth to do evil**. Mischief is a plot or device for evil purpose. Such a plot is hatched from a perverse attitude of one who "devises" to do evil. This is not referring to an innocent prank, but a deceitful plan of wickedness. This is an inventor of bad things. So he's called what he really is.

Devise literally means to "weave or fabricate" (in a malicious sense); thus one who mentally computes or conceives an evil scheme. The world is filled with such (and the church is not far behind).

Prov. 24:9

"The thought of foolishness is sin: and the scorner is an abomination to men."

Foolishness and sin begin in the mind. As a man *"thinketh in his heart, so is he."* Actions reflect thoughts. Many a crime has been "cased" and pondered in the mind, and thus was sin, even before the crime was committed. While not all sin is crime, all crime is sin; i.e., sinful acts that affect others and break the civil law.

The thought of foolishness is sin (*chattah*- "to miss the mark"). The deceitful heart (mind) is preoccupied with sin (Jeremiah 17:9). What a commentary on the basic condition of man in his depravity! Sin doesn't begin externally, but is hatched in the mind.

Jesus taught this principle to the disciples in Matthew 5:27, 28:

"Ye have heard that it was said by them of old time, Thou shalt not commit adultery (outward)*: But I say unto you, That whosoever looketh on a woman to lust after her hath committed adultery with her already in his heart."*

The Law dealt primarily with outward acts, but grace also deals with the heart—the thought life.

And the scorner (scoffer, mocker) **is an abomination to men.** I take this to refer to the same "foolish" man who now mocks wisdom and righteousness and thus is despised by those who are wise. Scoffing can be an outgrowth of foolish, unwise thinking. See the further characteristics of the scorner in Prov. 9:7-8; 13:1; 14:6; 15:12, etc. Right thinking people have no use for a mocker, even though the world is filled with such abominable people. Our own country of America continues to produce an increasing number of those who despise the Biblical foundation of our forefathers. (See Psalm 1 where those "who sit in the seat of the scornful" can never be blessed).

Prov. 24:10

If thou faint in the day of adversity, thy strength is small.

It's been said, "The test of a man's character is what it takes to stop him." Great strength holds up in trouble, while weak people faint. Interesting how some people faint just when you need them the most (e.g., sight of blood at an accident, etc.)

If thou faint in the day of adversity (trouble, lit. "tightness or tight spot, as we say), **thy strength is small.** Being faint, as used here, is not the idea of falling unconscious, but rather "to sink down, be disheartened." In the midst of trouble it takes triumphant faith to counter discouragement and assume responsibility. "Strength" here is the idea of firmness and vigor of soul. The word "small" comes from the same root as "adversity" (narrow, tightness); thus, "small" strength is narrow, as going through a tight place.

Actually this word for "small" is translated "enemy" (1 Samuel 2:32); "adversary" (Lamentations 1:10); and "trouble" (Psalm 13:4). Thus, the idea that a "tight" or troublous situation can restrict or even oppose our strength. Therefore, we must overcome by faith and resolution.

Prov. 24:11

"If thou forbear to deliver them that are drawn unto death, and those that are ready to be slain;"

This thought, along with vs. 12, seems to illustrate the "fainting" in vs. 10; i.e., one is of weak character if he **forbear**(s) (refrains, refuses) **to deliver** (rescue) **them that are drawn** (taken, carried away) **unto death, and those that are ready** (lit. shaken, tottering) **to be slain.** The context indicates a call to courage in an unjust situation; a need for righteous indignation on the part an upright man who witnesses those about to be slain unjustly.

In a day when men refuse to "get involved," this proverb calls for courageous action when others are abused. This could be an unfair trial (court), street scene (brawl), one being robbed, one being defrauded in a business scam, etc. The exhortation is to "not refrain" or hold back from getting involved in rescuing others being led to the slaughter. Certainly, this is fundamental to policemen and soldiers engaged in war.

Prov. 24:12

"If thou sayest, Behold, we knew it not; doth not he that pondereth the heart consider it? and he that keepeth thy soul, doth not he know it? and shall not he render to every man according to his works?"

Continuing the thought of vs.11, one cannot plead innocence when failing to rescue others in desperate need. Failure to do good is just as much a sin as doing the wrong thing. (James 4:17). Wisdom acts like God who "ponders" (lit. weighs, tests) the heart; He "keeps" (guards) the soul and does He not "render (lit. return back) to every man according to his works (deeds)."

Here we see the contrast between man's excuse for failing to take responsibility, and the all-knowing evaluation of man's soul and heart by God Himself. Indeed, *"all things are naked and opened unto the eyes of him with whom we have to do."* (Hebrews 4:13). True wisdom is concerned about how God sees things and how He works, with no attempt to "get off the hook" of duty.

Prov. 24:13

"My son, eat thou honey, because it is good; and the honeycomb, which is sweet to thy taste:"

Solomon, instructing his son, makes an analogy (in vss. 13-14) between the sweetness of honey and wisdom. They are good! God has given us "sweet" things, even though some refuse to take in the calories. We need the right sweetness, because the Lord has given us a taste for sweets. O, to crave the "sugar" of wisdom! How spiritually "fat" we would be!

Prov. 24:14

"So shall the knowledge of wisdom be unto thy soul: when thou hast found it, then there shall be a reward, and thy expectation shall not be cut off."

So shall the knowledge (comprehension, perception) **of wisdom be unto thy soul.** From vs. 13 we see the analogy between honey and wisdom. Honey is to the taste (good and sweet), what wisdom is to the soul.

In addition, the attainment of wisdom results in "a reward" (lit. future). **And thy expectation** (hope, i.e., the reward) **shall not be cut off** (destroyed, end). What a glorious reward from the Lord to those who walk in wisdom or the fear of God! Our hope is in the Lord! Present obedience (faith) yields future hope (Hebrews 11:1)!

K&D render this verse:

> "So apprehend wisdom for thy soul;
> When thou hast found it, there is a future,
> And thy hope is not destroyed."

Prov. 24:15

"Lay not wait, O wicked man, against the dwelling of the righteous; spoil not his resting place:"

Solomon warns against lurking in wait to ambush or harm the righteous, particularly in their home—their haven of rest. **Spoil not his resting place**; i.e., an attempt to violently assault or destroy. This relates to the 8th and 10th Commandments in Exodus 20:15, 17. But other than the breach of God's law, there's another reason why it's futile for the wicked man to assault believers. See vs. 16.

Prov. 24:16

"For a just man falleth seven times, and riseth up again: but the wicked shall fall into mischief."

Continuing the warning to the wicked in vs. 15, Solomon reminds them of God's gracious oversight and providential protection over the just. **For** (because) **a just** (righteous) **man falleth seven times** (i.e., many), **and riseth up again: but the wicked** (on the other hand) **shall fall** (for sure) **into mischief** (evil, misery).

Note that the just do fall and have trouble like others. They are not exempt from tribulation, but do have a faithful Saviour who watches over them. This is ongoing deliverance—the present aspect of saving grace. The wicked too shall fall, but into ultimate destruction. (See Psalm 1, *"the ungodly are not so...."*).

Prov. 24:17

"Rejoice not when thine enemy falleth, and let not thine heart be glad when he stumbleth:"

True love doesn't even rejoice when an "enemy falls." (1 Corinthians 13) Such rejoicing would be a form of person vengeance ("getting back"), when the Lord says, *"Vengeance is mine; I will repay."* This reflects Jesus' admonition to *"bless them that curse you, and pray for them which despitefully use you."* To love your enemy, wishing him no harm, and not even becoming "glad when he stumbles," has to be the ultimate test of inner grace.

K&D indicate the Hebrew emphasis: "At the fall of thine enemy rejoice not," etc. The idea being that even when your enemy falls, don't even think of rejoicing. Is there a consequence if we fail here? Yes! See vs. 18.

Prov. 24:18

"Lest the LORD see it, and it displease him, and he turn away his wrath from him."

Our attitude toward our enemy can backfire! Jesus was serious when he told the disciples to *"love your enemies...."* If we're not careful, we will wish them harm and rejoice in their demise (vs. 17). This displeases the Lord, and He may **turn away his wrath from him**. This may well mean that the judgment due that enemy may fall on you—the one who rejoices in the enemy's fall. Serious word! See Barnes note.

Prov. 24:19

"Fret not thyself because of evil men, neither be thou envious at the wicked;"

On the surface, "fret" seems to have the idea of "worry" or undue concern. But the word, *charah*, means "to become angry, to be hot, furious"—a forceful word indeed! The negative particle "not" is emphatic, meaning "never"; i.e., don't even think or waste time being angry because of wicked men or "envious" of them. They are in God's hands and vengeance belongs to Him! Ours is to do the will of God and let Him handle the wicked!

This is easier said than done. We have a tendency to retaliate against the wicked and then become bitter when they don't respond properly. This is a satanic trap! See Psalm 37:1, 38.

Prov. 24:20

"For there shall be no reward to the evil man; the candle of the wicked shall be put out."

Envy the wicked? No way! Why? Because **there shall be no reward** (lit. future) **to the evil man.** There's no positive future for the wicked; all they have is in the present, and that will be destroyed. In addition, they shall *"not stand* (up) *in the judgment"* (of God) (Psalm 1:6). They have no covering for their sin. Their "candle (lamp, light) shall be put out (or is extinguished)."

Thus, there's no hope for the godless, and we should never "fret over" or be envious of them (cf. Psalm 37:1, 37; 73:3; Prov. 13:9; 20:20). Let us see the "big picture" and be faithful to God and His Word. We shall reap, if we faint not.

Prov. 24:21

"My son, fear thou the LORD and the king: and meddle not with them that are given to change:"

Be careful whom you get involved with! Solomon exhorts his son to **fear... the LORD** (Jehovah) **and the king** (His representative of law and authority)**: and meddle** (lit. exchange, pledge, share) **not with them that are given to change.**

True freedom and wholeness results from obeying the Lord and those whom He has put in authority (cf. Romans 13:1f). In contrast, committing yourself unwisely to unstable people will end in tragedy (cf. vs. 22). The word "meddle" is translated "surety" in 6:1; the idea is co-signing, pledging, granting a mortgage to those with no foundation or stability of life.

Politicians often campaign with the promise of "change," but not all change is good, especially if it moves the populace away from the principles of Biblical law and sound economics. Wicked (lawless) leaders will opt for any "change" that enhances their selfish cause. Voter beware! Righteous "change," which deals properly with wrongdoing, is commendable (whether personal or governmental). But let us be wary of change simply for the sake of change.

Prov. 24:22

"For their calamity shall rise suddenly; and who knoweth the ruin of them both?"

Here is the resultant state of those "given to change" (vs. 21)—those who lack moral conviction and are thus disobedient to authority. They may appear well for a time, but **their calamity (destruction) shall rise suddenly**; life is unpredictable, and so is its end!

Thus, Solomon says, **"...who knoweth the ruin of them both,"** referring to the one not fearing God and the one not fearing the king. Whether God or king, both are to be obeyed as authorities. See Numbers 16:31f. for Korah's example. Also Prov. 16:14; 20:2; 29:1; Psalm 90:11.

Prov. 24:23

"These things also belong to the wise. It is not good to have respect of persons in judgment."

These things also belong to the wise. Solomon lists some additional statements ("these things") which are fitting to those who are wise. (They probably include vs. 23-34.) The first general saying is that it is not good to practice partiality in the justice system. In other words, perverted justice is wrong. The law must apply to all who are guilty, regardless of their station in life. Those who can afford shrewd lawyers, for instance, should not be given special consideration regarding their crime. There must be "criminal justice" for all without respect to one's wealth, race, prestige, religion, or political power. Justice must prevail for both the perpetrator and the victim.

Prov. 24:24

"He that saith unto the wicked, Thou art righteous; him shall the people curse, nations shall abhor him:"

Interestingly, even the wicked have a sense of justice. Some react when the "wicked" are held up as being "righteous." Murderers have been legally acquitted, but society will not let them forget their guilt. None can pronounce a sinner righteous without the curse and indignation ("abhor") of others. Recently a pedophile priest in jail was murdered by another inmate who despised the priest's hypocrisy.

How wonderful that God, through the sacrifice of His Son, can declare a sinner righteous by faith! But Someone had to pay the debt of sin. (See Romans 3:19ff.).

Prov. 24:25

But to them that rebuke him shall be delight, and a good blessing shall come upon them.

Here's the other side of the previous proverb; viz., that the one who upholds the law, rebuking the guilty, will be blessed. God loves justice and hates injustice. To have the same attitude is to line up with God's attitude. That's why even in an imperfect world, we have judges (and others) who stand for right (justice) and act accordingly. These people cannot be "bought" or bribed to justify the wicked. Consequently, they will reap "good blessing" or inward satisfaction for doing right. Hence, another example of the work of conscience, distinguishing between right and wrong.

Prov. 24:26

"Every man shall kiss his lips that giveth a right answer."

In light of the previous verse (25), where "delight" follows a proper verbal response, something similar occurs here. "Kiss his lips" could indicate a "smacking" of lips, expressing the satisfaction of giving a "right" or correct answer. Evidently, it signals a positive response to a matter according to the custom of that time. It must have been an expression of the "good blessing" promised in vs. 25.

Prov. 24:27

"Prepare thy work without, and make it fit for thyself in the field; and afterwards build thine house."

This proverb is an exhortation regarding the necessity of making adequate and detailed preparation for building a house (family dwelling). I assume Solomon is speaking not only of the architectural plans, but "preparing" the materials for construction and surveying the property so as to "make it (house) fit." In other words, make sure you've done all your "homework" in preparation for the building project.

This verse can be applied in several ways. First, it obviously refers to literal building plans, which takes wisdom and effort. Back in vs. 3, it says, *"Through wisdom is an house builded; and by understanding it is established,"* Check Solomon's own procedure in building the temple - 1Kings 5:17, 18; 1Kings 6:7.

Secondly, I relate this to the impeccable accuracy of the Tabernacle dimensions (Exodus 25ff.) which, among other things, illustrates the Lord utter interest in details. Applied to the believer, whose body is the temple (Tabernacle) of the Holy Spirit, every aspect (detail) has God's attention and concern. See 1 Corinthians 6:19, 20.

Thirdly, Jesus uses the analogy of one "counting the cost" before ever beginning a construction job. See Luke 14:28-30, where Jesus applies this principle of "preparation" to those considering becoming disciples.

Luke 16:10, 11 may further apply in regard to one being faithful with what God has given him before being entrusted with additional resources.

Prov. 24:28

"Be not a witness against thy neighbour without cause; and deceive not with thy lips."

Another admonition against breaking the 9th Commandment - *"Thou shalt not bear false witness against thy neighbor."* This could be in the domestic or court arena. This infers pressure coming to bear, whether by hatred or bribe, etc., upon the perpetrator. The sinful nature would destroy the reputation of others without a cause, to save face. Such is the root of character assassination, which borders on murder.

Out of guilt or greed, people will falsely accuse others to save their own "necks." And the weapon of choice is "deception" by means of "lips." They will say anything in any way to cover their sin, even after "swearing on the Bible." Again, how wicked is the wicked heart of man (Jeremiah 17:9)!

Prov. 24:29

"Say not, I will do so to him as he hath done to me: I will render to the man according to his work."

Here's another example of the flesh's desire to retaliate when offended by others. **I will do so to him as he hath done to me**; another way of saying "I will fight fire with fire." Suffering from wrongdoing is a monumental issue in society. Conflicts with others, whether at home, work, etc., are a frequent problem. How do we differentiate between personal affronts and flat out criminal behavior by others? What should our response be? Solomon has already given sound advice in this matter:

"Say not thou, I will recompense evil; but wait on the LORD, and he shall save thee." (20:22)

Thus, rather than reacting with a vengeful spirit, it would be better to "wait on the LORD" for further instruction and grace. James 1:5 adds:

"If any of you lack wisdom, let him ask of God, who giveth to all men liberally and upbraideth not, and it shall be given him."

This passage is addressed to believers, who desire to settle the conflict in a godly manner. See Matthew 5:43-45, along with Romans 12:17.

It must be said, however, that there comes a time to call the police if such conflict is criminal in nature. Certainly, in such cases, an individual, believer or not, must appeal to a higher local authority in order to preserve his life. E.g., if someone is breaking and entering my home in the middle of the night, I need immediate assistance from law enforcement. I can think later about "turning the cheek," but first justice needs to served regarding the crime committed.

Prov. 24:30

"I went by the field of the slothful, and by the vineyard of the man void of understanding;"

At the close of this chapter (vs. 30-34) we have a further description of the results of laziness. The effects of indolence occur repeatedly in Proverbs (e.g., 6:6-19). This segment is in story or parabolic form, bringing home vital lessons regarding human responsibility. Solomon says, **"I went by the field of the slothful (man) and by the vineyard of the man void of understanding."** Evidently, whoever is traveling by knows the condition of the farmer by the condition of the farm! Note that he equates "slothful" with one "void (empty) of understanding." A lazy man is a dunce! But more than that, he has no "heart"; that's the literal meaning of "understanding" here (Heb. *labe).*

Prov. 24:31

"And, lo, it was all grown over with thorns, and nettles had covered the face thereof, and the stone wall thereof was broken down."

The narrative continues: **And, lo, it was all grown over with thorns, and nettles (thorny weeds, bramble) had covered (lit. hidden) the face (of the field) thereof.** If that weren't bad enough, even **the stone wall thereof** (around the field) **was broken down."** Here's a description of the pitiful dilapidation of a property totally neglected!

Prov. 24:32

"Then I saw, and considered it well: I looked upon it, and received instruction."

Then I saw (gazed)**, and considered it well** (lit. applied it or took it to heart). Further, **I looked upon it and received**

instruction (*musar*- warning, reproof)**.** This was not just a passing glance accompanied by a critical or derogatory statement. Rather, Solomon ponders this situation and comes away with a vital lesson to share with others. What would that be? (Next verse).

Prov. 24:33

"Yet a little sleep, a little slumber, a little folding of the hands to sleep:"

Here's the platitude or proverb: **Yet a little sleep, a little slumber** (drowsiness)**, a little folding** (clasping) **of the hands to sleep** (lit. lie down)**.** It doesn't take much slothfulness, just a "little"!

So shall thy poverty come as one that travelleth (wanders, wayfarer)**, and thy want** (impoverishment) **as an armed man.** (vs. 34). The inference here is that the property is neglected because of the owner's slothfulness. It is likened to the uncertainty and insecurity of one who "wanders (travels) around" and doesn't have work responsibility. The analogy to the "armed man" or robber indicates the same uncertainty—no steady labor, but living a lawless lifestyle. See notes on 6:11 for more detail.

Prov. 24:34

"So shall thy poverty come as one that travelleth; and thy want as an armed man."

See notes on vs. 33.

Chapter 25
Further Wise Sayings of Solomon

Prov. 25:1

"These are also proverbs of Solomon, which the men of Hezekiah king of Judah copied out."

Here we have assuring evidence and example of the divine preservation and perpetuation of Solomon's proverbs through the human instrumentality of King Hezekiah's "men" or copiers. Evidently they were not passed on orally, but were "copied" or transferred from other written records. It's not enough that the Scriptures are "God-breathed" ("given by inspiration of God"-2 Timothy 3:16), but have been also preserved by the same God who gave them.

2 Peter 1:20, 21 reveals how the Scriptures came to be written: *"...holy men of God spake as they were moved by the Holy Ghost."* This same element of Divine intervention and guidance must likewise be operative in the preservation and dissemination of the Holy Scriptures.

Prov. 25:2

"It is the glory of God to conceal a thing: but the honour of kings is to search out a matter."

See here an example and beauty of the distinction between the God of the universe and human kings. **It is the glory** (weightiness) **of God to conceal a thing...**; there's a divine mystery to God by virtue of His glory—things that are concealed and never figured out by man. The LORD says, *"For my thoughts are not your thoughts, neither are your ways my ways."* We honor Him for that. **It is the glory** (*kadov*-splendor, majesty) **of God to conceal** (hide) **a thing.**

He alone knows everything and dispenses a bit of that knowledge as He wills (e.g., the Bible, mysteries, etc.).

On the other hand, kings are honored for "searching out a matter (lit. a word)." As a ruler, he examines the situation or document and conveys the meaning. The King over all (God) is revered for being mysterious, but an earthly ruler is respected for searching out (examining) a matter, even though his search may yet be a puzzle; e.g., a prophecy, which cannot be fully understood until its fulfillment.

Prov. 25:3

"The heaven for height, and the earth for depth, and the heart of kings is unsearchable."

There's a vast chasm and distance between heaven and earth! The Lord speaks through Isaiah the Prophet:

"For my thoughts are not your thoughts, neither are your ways my ways, saith the LORD. For as the heavens are higher than the earth, so are my ways higher than your ways, and my thoughts than your thoughts." (Isaiah 55:8, 9)

Paul adds:

"How unsearchable are his (God's) judgments, and his ways past finding out!"

Even **the heart of kings** (earthly) **is unsearchable** (past finding out). We can't figure out ordinary people, much less those who rule. How then do we expect to understand God, unless He reveals Himself somehow? Thus, He gave His Word and Spirit to at least begin to know Him. And to know Him is to love Him!

Prov. 25:4

"Take away the dross from the silver, and there shall come forth a vessel for the finer."

Vs. 4 and 5 go together in thought. Just as dross or impurities must be removed from raw silver to make it worthy to be forged, so the wicked must be removed from the king's (president's) cabinet to establish righteousness. Before the refiner (lit. goldsmith, founder) can make a valuable and effective "vessel" (also translated weapon, armour, furniture), the dross must be removed.

This can be likened to a believer who needs to "sanctify" himself, dealing with the impurities of sin, so as to be "forged" and used by God (the Refiner) as a "vessel" of honor in the Kingdom. (2 Corinthians 7:1). Even at the Bema Seat (Judgment Seat of Christ— 1 Corinthians 3), our works will be judged by the Refiner's fire (gaze) of "what sort they are." All believers are on the Foundation of Christ, but care must be taken how we build our ministry on that Foundation. There's two categories: 1) wood, hay and stubble; 2) gold, silver, and precious stones. The first represents fleshly works which will burn to a crisp. The latter are those labors in the Spirit which will not only remain intact, but will further be purified by the fire!

Prov. 25:5

"Take away the wicked from before the king, and his throne shall be established in righteousness."

It's a well-known principle that a nation's stability is directly linked to its leadership. An honest and upright king, as in Solomon's case, projected that personal quality on the whole Kingdom of Israel. But that integrity was not without challenge by wicked men who would undermine the establishment of the King's righteous throne.

This is illustrated specifically in Solomon's domain when he had wicked Shimei, David's enemy, executed. This just act was carried out at his father David's request, helping to establish Solomon's rule of peace. The corresponding prophetic promise is given in 1 Kings 2:45: *"And king Solomon shall be blessed, and the throne of David shall be established before the LORD forever."* (This points to the future Millennial Kingdom established in Messiah's righteousness).

Presently this principle applies to any nation at any time. Remove (**take away**) corruption and sow righteousness! Let's apply it also to Church leadership, for it's been said that "as the church goes, so goes the world." A pure church is a powerful church. Right and wrong cannot reign at the same time.

So must **righteousness** reign in our personal lives. Paul's exhortation in Titus 2:11-14 is so apropos for us today:

> *"For the grace of God that bringeth salvation hath appeared to all men, teaching us that, denying ungodliness and worldly lusts, we should live soberly, righteously, and godly, in this present world; looking for that blessed hope, and the glorious appearing of the great God and our Saviour Jesus Christ; Who gave himself for us, that he might redeem us from all iniquity, and purify unto himself a peculiar people, zealous of good works."*

Prov. 25:6

"Put not forth thyself in the presence of the king, and stand not in the place of great men:"

This proverb extols the virtue of humility, submission and respect for authority. **Put not forth thyself in the presence** (lit. face) **of the king**; the idea of the word, *hadar*, is to "swell up" or "glorify" yourself before the king. Don't presume your importance or "push" for the king's honor. Don't take "first place," because it's not yours to take. Promotion can only come from the king, not you.

And stand not in the place (lit. spot) **of great men.** Verse 7 clarifies this thought. Trying to stand with or mix with influential and powerful people does not, of itself, make you great. Honor and respect doesn't come from you, but from those in authority. Some people will do anything it takes to be noticed—pushing themselves to the forefront. But that doesn't warrant or produce greatness. The worst thing that can happen to some people is to be overlooked by the "king" and/or the crowd. Honor cannot be demanded, it must be commanded by our character.

This has a spiritual connection to the child of God who feels rejected by the world. Promotion comes from the Lord Himself, not worldly men. He that sees in secret shall reward you openly one day. Ours is to be faithful servants of Christ regardless of the clamor of the world. Those who honor God will be honored by Him. Today, for example, preachers are building their own kingdom rather than God's. They have gained celebrity status and love the world's attention. They "swell" with pride as they compete for notoriety and acclaim of the world, as well as the church. This will be sorted out one day in the Judgment.

Prov. 25:7

"For better it is that it be said unto thee, Come up hither; than that thou shouldest be put lower in the presence of the prince whom thine eyes have seen."

Truly great men do not willfully stand in the place of great men! (cf. vs. 6). Vs. 7 continues the thought of true humility and the fact that promotion is from the Lord, not men. Take a "back seat," because it's **better...that it be said unto thee, Come up hither; than that thou shouldest be put lower in the presence of the prince** (noble) **whom thine eyes have seen.**

This scenario is used by Jesus in Luke 14:8-10, to illustrate the judgment upon an arrogant attitude that would clamor to be "number one." This situation is so widespread because of man's inherent pride. It's another form of the "Cain spirit." There's something built into man that naturally wants to be first in line. How great is this greed for power! It's found not only in worldly business but also in the Church (not to mention the home).

We must not jockey for position—God knows our need (Matthew 6:33). In the proverb, the forward man may have to settle for less, when he could have sat with the king! The first shall be last and the last first! The way up is the way down. God blesses the humble in spirit—He promotes them. In fact, He dwells with those who are of "a contrite heart."

Prov. 25:8

"Go not forth hastily to strive, lest thou know not what to do in the end thereof, when thy neighbour hath put thee to shame."

Here is some practical advice regarding suing someone in court. It should not be done "hastily" (quickly, in a hurry); in fact, according to vs. 9, there's a better way to solve a conflict than to appear in a public court. This admonition is very apropos in our day when so many will sue a neighbor rather than rationally talking through the problem. See 3:30.

Solomon tells us here not to go quickly **to strive** (legal suit, contend), **lest thou know not what to do in the end thereof....** So often conflicts are flare-ups of emotion and not carefully thought through. We can easily be **put to shame** (lit. wounded, embarrassed) in the end because of a lack of evidence and/or character. We may be right, but yet use a wrong way to solve the conflict. See vs. 9

Prov. 25:9

*"Debate thy cause with thy neighbour himself; and discover not
a secret to another:"*

This is a continuance from the previous verse regarding neighborly issues. We're not to be quick to sue a friend or neighbor (fellow man), nor to even talk to others about the situation without confronting the individual alone. What a tremendous piece of wisdom!

Debate thy cause with thy neighbor himself. The first clause has to do with "contending or lit. grappling" with a "case or suit." If there's a quarrel or complaint with someone, plead your case with that individual himself alone. This is the same attitude and principle of Matthew 18:15 in dealing with offenses by those in the church. Speak to that person alone before taking it any further. Thus, the issue can be settled "secretly," without others even getting involved. The case then can be closed and fellowship restored—and all can move on!

And discover (lit. uncover, reveal) **not a secret** (familiar, intimate counsel) **to another** (i.e., a stranger to the case). The conflict need not be anyone's business but the parties involved. The courts can be left out and integrity and wisdom can prevail. Plus, these can remain or become friends, rather than enemies. See 1 Corinthians 6 for the prohibition of believers suing each other. There's a Scriptural and right way to deal with conflict. To broadcast the matter to others before dealing personally with the issue and individual at hand can lead to disastrous results. This one-on-one confrontation is not only right, but safe. See vs. 10.

Prov. 25:10

"Lest he that heareth it put thee to shame, and thine infamy turn not away."

Revealing "secrets" (lit. closed deliberation or counsel—vs. 9) can have disastrous results! Some things ought never to be shared by outsiders, 1) Because it's none of their business; 2) It can be misunderstood and used against you—to "put thee to shame"; 3) the "infamy" (evil or defaming report) may never "turn (go) away"!

The wrong information in the wrong hands can damage one's reputation forever! How powerful is the tongue (James 3)! Whispering and sharing secrets out of school, "separate chief friends."

Prov. 25:11

"A word fitly spoken is like apples of gold in pictures of silver."

Solomon portrays the value of **a word fitly spoken**; i.e., an appropriate or timely word, fitting the occasion. This is the height of wisdom and rarely occurring. Thus, it is likened to **apples of gold in pictures of silver.** Barnes suggests that this was a kingly gift of golden colored fruit arranged in a silver container or basket. Whatever the case, it was a precious commodity and illustrates the power and invaluableness of speaking a word in season.

Prov. 25:12

"As an earring of gold, and an ornament of fine gold, so is a wise reprover upon an obedient ear."

A further analogy of wise rebuke is given here—fine and exquisite jewelry. Earrings and ornaments of fine gold are very much in demand; they are sought and bought by those who can afford them (and even those who can't). **So is a wise reprover upon an obedient ear.** There is glad appreciation in the heart (ear) of a wise man when exhorted by another wise man. This attitude is far more precious than fine gold and other so-called priceless jewels.

Maybe this is the thought behind Peter's admonition for women to have "a meek and quiet spirit," rather than the emphasis on outward adorning (1 Peter 3).

Prov. 25:13

"As the cold of snow in the time of harvest, so is a faithful messenger to them that send him: for he refresheth the soul of his masters."

Not referring to a winter snowfall, but rather the process of preserving snow for cooling drinks (e.g., wine) in the summer harvest. (See Barnes for fuller explanation) Such ability to be physically refreshed is likened here to **a faithful messenger** who gladdens **the soul** (*nephesh*) **of his masters.** See 13:17; 25:25.

Faithfulness is a rare quality. When it's found in a messenger (preacher?), it yields blessing to all involved—the recipient of the message, the messenger himself, and those who sent him. See 1 Corinthians 4:2.

Prov. 25:14

"Whoso boasteth himself of a false gift is like clouds and wind without rain."

I'm assuming here that Solomon is not speaking of spiritual gifts, but rather one who makes a boastful promise of giving a gift and then fails to deliver. This is a matter of pride and deceit; an attempt to be well thought of at the expense of truth. Thus, the analogy of "clouds and wind without rain." A "blow hard," words without substance, empty talk! Just another description of a fool. One trying to be something that he's not.

But the result is also the disappointment that comes to those promised the gift. They are left "empty" by one "full" of himself! Quite a contrast to the "faithful messenger" of vs. 13.

Prov. 25:15

"By long forbearing is a prince persuaded, and a soft tongue breaketh the bone."

The idea of "long forbearing" is the ability to refrain from anger (*af*-meaning "nostril, anger"). It's the opposite of a quick and rash outburst of revenge. Longsuffering is certainly a spiritual fruit and will enable one to use a "soft tongue" (word), which can eventually "break the bone" or spirit, of that one in authority ("prince").

In 15:1, Solomon says, *"A soft answer turneth away wrath."* We cannot fight evil with evil, but overcome evil with good. This does not work in every situation, but is certainly the right principle regardless of the outcome.

Prov. 25:16

"Hast thou found honey? eat so much as is sufficient for thee, lest thou be filled therewith, and vomit it."

Too much of a good thing can make you sick! Here's an admonition to maintain self-control in eating delicacies. Obviously, honey was the choice "sweet" of the day and the tendency was to over indulge. Just because something tastes good is not a license to "stuff" oneself. Eat "sufficient" and that's all.

There are many applications to this truth in regard to temptation. Sin many times comes "sugar-coated," and thus seems irresistible (cf. 1 John 2:15f.; Genesis 3), or more in line with the text. Good things, like making money to support the family, can be perverted; i.e., greed can set in, making money a god or an end in itself. (1 Timothy 6:10).

Prov. 25:17

"Withdraw thy foot from thy neighbour's house; lest he be weary of thee, and so hate thee."

Good common sense procedure: Don't wear out your welcome! "Withdraw" comes from *yaqar*, meaning "to be valuable or rare"; thus, the idea of making your "foot rare or sparse," regarding your neighbor's house. If not, he will become "weary" (lit." filled up," or fed up) with you and become your enemy instead of a friend.

One's home is his castle and hideout—be sensitive to that when visiting someone.

Prov. 25:18

"A man that beareth false witness against his neighbour is a maul, and a sword, and a sharp arrow."

The damage done by bearing false testimony against a litigant in court is insurmountable and deadly! The instruments mentioned here in the analogy are used for murder (among other things). The "maul" (hammer, mallet), sword, and sharp arrow, picture the power of the tongue (cf. James 3). See K&D for Hebrew emphasis.

Prov. 25:19

"Confidence in an unfaithful man in time of trouble is like a broken tooth, and a foot out of joint."

People prove their character (or lack of it) in crisis situations. The "unfaithful man" here is not just inconsistent, but treacherous and deceitful (Heb. *bagad*). Confidence (i.e., trust, refuge or security) in such a man is foolish and dangerous. Such an action is described by two analogies: 1) A broken tooth; and 2) a foot out of joint. Both picture that which is dysfunctional and thus unreliable. Be careful whom you trust!

Prov. 25:20

As he that taketh away a garment in cold weather, and as vinegar upon nitre, so is he that singeth songs to an heavy heart.

One characteristic of a wise man is discernment; i.e., a holy common sense enabling him to rightly judge a situation and act accordingly. Solomon gives 3 illustrations here that demonstrate the lack of wisdom and/or common sense. First, one doesn't remove a winter garment in cold weather; second, "vinegar" is not poured upon "nitre" (*nether-* carbonate of soda; see Clarke for details). Because of a chemical reaction, it will melt or destroy it.

These two examples are likened to the third: **So is he that singeth songs to a heavy** (*ra'ah-* afflicted, distressed) **heart.** You don't do that! We don't sing to mourning people, but "weep with those that weep"; or at least sit quietly beside them, lending a comforting hand.

Prov. 25:21

"If thine enemy be hungry, give him bread to eat; and if he be thirsty, give him water to drink:"

Here Solomon extols the attitude of grace toward others, even enemies. The flesh would "fight fire with fire," extending no mercy toward those who hate us. But the grace of God enables us to minister (food and drink) to those in need, regardless of their attitude. This is also *agape* love in action (See 1 Corinthians 13).

Jesus verifies this demonstration of love in Matthew 5:44: *"Love your enemies* (and) *bless them that curse you...."* Obviously, His whole life and death was the ultimate expression of this truth. This very proverb is specifically used by Paul in Romans 12:20, 21 to teach believers how to properly respond to enemies. We can manifest a forgiving attitude (and actions) toward others by virtue of God's wondrous forgiveness extended to us in Christ! As Jesus taught: *"And forgive us our debts* (sins), *as we forgive our debtors* (those who have sinned against us)."*

Prov. 25:22

"For thou shalt heap coals of fire upon his head, and the LORD shall reward thee."

This verse supplies the motivation for dealing kindly with our enemy.

1) It will serve to **heap coals of fire upon his head**; i.e., to produce a "burning shame" in his conscience for his antagonism, etc. Angry, bitter people do not know how to handle graciousness—it disarms them. Paul quotes this thought in Romans 12:20.

JFB likens the process of smelting metallic ore:

> "As metals are melted by heaping coals upon them, so is the heart softened by kindness."

Possibly this is the thought behind the common quip, "killing them with kindness." K&D adds that:

> "Pro_25:22 accords with Pro_25:21, which counsels not to the avenging of oneself, but to the requital of evil with good. The

burning of coals laid on the head must be a painful but wholesome consequence; it is a figure of self-accusing repentance (Augustine, Zöckler), for the producing of which the showing of good to an enemy is a noble motive,"

2) Solomon also motivates us with the thought that **the LORD shall reward thee.** There is blessing in store for those who bless those who revile them. It is possible to "love our enemies" because of the fruit of the Holy Spirit. This love (*agape*) is a one-way love, without thought of return (e.g., John 3:16). See Matthew 5:38-44.

Prov. 25:23

"The north wind driveth away rain: so doth an angry countenance a backbiting tongue."

Much discussion exists over the technicalities of this verse. The basic picture here is the dark rain clouds that form from sea moisture north of Jerusalem. The north wind "drives" the wind toward the Holy City, and on to the South. This is considered a predictable weather pattern. Solomon uses this analogy to express the effect that "an angry (lit. indignant) countenance (face)" has on "a backbiting (lit. secret, hiding) tongue."

The thought seems to indicate the power of a look toward someone who verbalizes slander regarding another. Such a look can "blow away" the "cloud" of slander coming from the culprit's mouth. Often we permit people to backbite and criticize others by not responding with disdain. Thus, we become part of the problem, rather than the solution.

Prov. 25:24

It is better to dwell in the corner of the housetop, than with a brawling woman and in a wide house.

See notes on 21:9.

Prov. 25:25

"As cold waters to a thirsty soul, so is good news from a far country."

The parallel thought here is "refreshment," whether to the body or soul. How good is a cold drink to a summer thirst! Likewise how pleasant it is to receive good news from a long distance. The soldier or missionary who gets a good word from home; what joy that can bring to the heart! See Prov. 15:30. In contrast, how devastating to the soul is a bad report.

The ultimate example of this principle is Revelation 22:17:

> "And the Spirit and the bride say, Come. And let him that heareth say, Come. And let him that is athirst come. And whosoever will, let him take the water of life freely."

Prov. 25:26

"A righteous man falling down before the wicked is as a troubled fountain, and a corrupt spring."

The context would indicate what happens to a believer who compromises with the ungodly. The wicked can be intimidating, tempting us to surrender godly convictions. Something is definitely lost if and when such compromise occurs. For the saint is to be a *"well of life"* (10:11) and a reservoir from which *"flow rivers of living water"* (John 7:38). The sin of cowardice and compromise will stop the flow of blessing from our lives. This is a form of God's discipline.

Thus, Solomon likens this scenario to a **troubled** (lit. trampled) **fountain** (well) **and a corrupt** (spoiled) **spring.** Water was very precious and sparse in those days; to have a polluted well was a serious problem. Satan is bent on spoiling our "water" supply, that the Spirit's fruit be hindered from blooming in our lives.

Lot vexed his righteous soul in compromise before the Sodomites. (2 Peter 2:7) Likewise, the Amalekites fought against Israel over a new-found well of water (Exodus 17). So the Enemy fights to rob our "peace and joy in the Holy Spirit." Therefore, let us be *"strong and very courageous"* (Joshua 1:7)!

Prov. 25:27

"It is not good to eat much honey: so for men to search their own glory is not glory."

Although there is much discussion regarding the Heb. text (See K&D), there seems to be a simple explanation of this verse. Two thoughts are prevalent: 1) a preoccupation with pleasure of appetite and 2) the praise of men. Honey is good, and probably a main staple of Solomon's diet; but too much "sweet" becomes sickening.

Commendation from others can be encouraging and right; but to "search" (lit. examine) one's "own glory" (i.e. worth, honor,) ceases to be "honorable." This is the ultimate attitude of pride. In 27:2, Solomon said:

> "Let another man praise thee, and not thine own mouth; a stranger, and not thine own lips."

Sinful man lusts after a full belly and inflated ego (i.e., to be full of himself). That was Lucifer's basic problem (Ezekiel 28:15). This explanation seems the fit the context of the previous and following verse; viz., compromise before the wicked and no control over his spirit.

Prov. 25:28

> "He that hath no rule over his own spirit is like a city that is broken down, and without walls."

This thought adds further light to the previous one (vs. 27). A man out of control in his carnal appetites has little or no control over his inner spirit. Thus, the lack of self-control can only be disastrous; it is likened to a devastated city **that is broken down and without walls.** It is unproductive and defenseless.

So is a man without temperance or divine self-control. He cannot produce what he doesn't possess within. Only self-discipline can temper his gifts and energy to accomplish something worthwhile. We know that this "rule" and self-control is ultimately the fruit of the Holy Spirit. (see Galatians 5:23).

Chapter 26
Honor is not Fitting for a Fool

Prov. 26:1

"As snow in summer, and as rain in harvest, so honour is not seemly for a fool."

A fool is "unseasonable"! He's not in the true flow of things. Snow doesn't fit with summer, nor rain in harvest time. So "honour" (*kavodh*- glory, weight) is not becoming (belongs to) to a fool. Devoid of wisdom, a man has no honor or weightiness; thus he is not respected by others. He may "talk the language," but his lifestyle exposes his folly. An empty wagon makes a lot of noise, but when full it runs quietly. So with a shallow brook which babbles, while deep water is still.

Prov. 26:2

"As the bird by wandering, as the swallow by flying, so the curse causeless shall not come."

This verse seems to follow on the heels of the first. The sparrow and the swallow follow their instincts in wandering and flying; they have a distinct cause and effect in what they do (including their song). So the curse that comes upon the fool always has a cause or reason.

Another way of saying that just as the sparrow naturally wanders (move to and fro) and the swallow flies about, so there's a reason behind a curse. Things don't just happen; *"for whatsoever a man soweth, that shall he also reap."*

Prov. 26:3

"A whip for the horse, a bridle for the ass, and a rod for the fool's back."

There are some things that are appropriate and fitting: 1)**a whip for the horse**; 2) **a bridle** (bit) **for the ass** (donkey); 3) **and a rod** (stick for punishment) **for the fool's back.** Note all these are instruments to keep the beast in line and under submission. The "fool" acts like a brute beast or animal and thus needs some kind of restraint. But in all cases, there's no real intelligent response or permanent correction.

A word of rebuke is sufficient to reprove a wise man, evidenced by his positive response to correction and instruction. His wisdom makes him teachable. That's not the case with the fool, who keeps falling into the same ditch, as would an animal. What a sad commentary on man's depravity and helplessness without God.

Prov. 26:4

"Answer not a fool according to his folly, lest thou also be like unto him."

Vss. 4 and 5 here seem, on the surface, to be a contradiction—but not so. They are a mini-treatise on how to answer or respond to a fool—who is full of himself. The idea is how to respond to a fool without being foolish yourself, and at the same time exposing his foolishness. How to refute a fool and his talk, so as to "knock some sense" into his head and heart! How to be an instrument of God to break through the foolishness of a fool and make him a candidate to become wise!

We might illustrate this scenario thusly: If I were painting the front door of my house and a fool came by and asked, "Mr. Jones, are you painting your front door?" And I simply answer, "Yes," and just keep painting, I would appear to "be just like him," i.e., the fool. I might rather reply, "No, I'm mowing the grass, can't you see?" Obviously, I'm subtly rebuking his stupid question and proving that I'm not foolish myself.

Prov. 26:5

"Answer a fool according to his folly, lest he be wise in his own conceit."

This is tied to vs. 4, where both sides of the scenario are explained.

Prov. 26:6

"He that sendeth a message by the hand of a fool cutteth off the feet, and drinketh damage."

However this verse is to be broken down, it speaks to the utter futility of depending on a fool to do anything responsible. You don't trust a fool to deliver an important message to anyone; to do so is like "cutting off your foot" or "drinking lit. imbibing, as at a banquet) damage" (violence, injustice). See 13:17; 25:13 for further light.

The radical results (i.e., cutting of feet, etc.) would seem to warrant a very serious matter or message. Possibly this has to do with time of war, or a governmental or legal issue which demands a faithful messenger. Integrity and dependability are rare qualities these days—these belong to the wise.

Prov. 26:7

"The legs of the lame are not equal: so is a parable in the mouth of fools."

Here's an analogy between the frailty of a lame man and the "lameness" of a fool's brain in regard to telling a parable or discourse. **The legs of the lame are not equal**; i.e., they "hang down, languish." The picture is a dysfunctional man, unable to walk and work. He has legs but they work against him rather than for him.

So is a parable (proverb, wise saying) **in the mouth of fools.** In connection with the previous verse 6, the fool's "mouth" is dysfunctional and unreliable. Whatever so-called "wise" thing that comes from his mouth indicates "paralysis" of his mind. As a man "thinketh in his heart (mind) so is he." Again, the fool can only express what he is, nothing more. He may attempt to "wax eloquent," but it falls short, like legs that won't support a man's weight.

Prov. 26:8

"As he that bindeth a stone in a sling, so is he that giveth honour to a fool."

Giving honor (*kadhov*- glory, weight) to a fool is both unbecoming and uncharacteristic. And the one who attempts to give such honor also has a problem. He is suspect of being foolish too. The analogy is "binding (tying, restricting) a stone in a sling" (shot). How foolish is it to tie the stone (missile) in the sling-shot when it needs to be free to fly through the air, as projected by the shooter!

So honor to the fool is just as inconsistent and unwarranted as binding up that stone. In this day of egalitarianism (equal results for all), the world wants all to be "honored" equally, with no distinctions. Thus, everyone is to play on the team, regardless of their ability (and all get a "letter" as well). Forget grades at school—they only discourage and produce "low self-image," etc. How we need to get back to a Biblical world view!

Prov. 26:9

"As a thorn goeth up into the hand of a drunkard, so is a parable in the mouth of fools."

As a thorn goeth up into the hand of a drunkard, so is a parable in the mouth of fools. The understanding of this proverb is only possible in light of the previous verses (1-8). The fool seems incapable of receiving, thinking and speaking true wisdom. If truth comes out of his mouth it's an "accident"—he doesn't really know or fathom it. I know fools who preach "parables" (earthly stories with heavenly meaning), but don't have a clue as to the reality of their words!

This is likened to a thorn which penetrates the hand of a drunk who has fallen. He's oblivious of the wound because of his inebriated state (i.e., "bombed out" mind!). No sense, no feeling—the liquor serves as an anesthesia. So fools run at the mouth with no awareness or comprehension of what comes from their mouths (true or false, right or wrong, wise or foolish—it's all the same).

Prov. 26:10

"The great God that formed all things both rewardeth the fool, and rewardeth transgressors."

This verse is a real challenge to linguists and commentators. "God" is not found in the Hebrew, but added by the KJV translators. After some research, I think the present translation is best. The simple thought seems to be that God who formed all things rewards fools and transgressors alike. Now this can be positive or negative.

We know there is common grace upon all people; i.e., "the sun shines on the just and the unjust." So the "great" (lit. abundant) God graces all mankind with His common blessings. On the other hand, He "rewards" fools and sinners according to their works; i.e., they will be judged accordingly.

Prov. 11:31 adds a further challenge: *"Behold, the righteous shall be recompensed in the earth: much more the wicked and the sinner."* This verse also can be seen from both a positive and negative standpoint. One thing for sure, God is Just, and "shall not the Judge of all the earth do right"? (Genesis 18:25)

An additional thought is that God uses unsaved people for His purposes; e.g., the Pharaoh who promoted Joseph; Cyrus the king; Nebuchadnezzar in Babylon, etc. I'm glad He is the King of Kings and Lord of Lords! Amen.

Prov. 26:11

"As a dog returneth to his vomit, so a fool returneth to his folly."

A creature gravitates to his nature, whether a dog or a fool. A dog reverts back to his vomit because he's a dog; so when unrestrained, the fool turns again to his "folly" (silliness). Peter uses this former analogy to describe false prophets (2 Peter 2:22) who manifest their apostate nature by following unrighteousness.

Both the dog and the fool do what they do because they are what they are! Fools return to folly because they're fools at heart. They may attempt to act wise for a time, but soon reveal their true nature.

Prov. 26:12

"Seest thou a man wise in his own conceit? there is more hope of a fool than of him."

There are only two basic world views: Christocentric (Christ-centered) or Anthropocentric (man-centered). All Proverbs have little good to say about a fool, but here there's "more hope (expectation)" for a fool than a self-conceited man! Of course, in the final analysis one "wise in his own conceit" (lit. eyes) is the ultimate fool! His "anthropocentric" view is a rejection of his Creator, placing himself on the throne of his own life. The world is filled with such people and only the power of God's grace can change it.

Prov. 26:13

"The slothful man saith, There is a lion in the way; a lion is in the streets."

The lazy (slothful) man lets his imagination run rampant so as to justify not getting out of bed! Here he thinks of the worst scenario—**a lion** (lit. roaring one) **in the way** (his path), and **a lion in the streets.** In his mind, it would be the end of him to get up and face the day! Amazing how the fleshly mind thinks!

Thus, the believer must counter such thoughts by putting his redeemed will into operation—choosing to do what's right. The righteous also are tempted by "lazy" thoughts, overcome only by obedience.

Prov. 26:14

"As the door turneth upon his hinges, so doth the slothful upon his bed."

What a vivid picture and illustration of the slothful man: Turning back and forth on his bed like a door on its hinges! Such is about all the energy he can muster. And like rocking in a chair, no work is done (Compare Prov. 6:10; 24:33).

Prov. 26:15

"The slothful hideth his hand in his bosom; it grieveth him to bring it again to his mouth."

How lazy can you get?! Talk about a dysfunctional person—too lazy to "lift a hand." The lazy one is described here as "hiding his hand in his bosom." Some translate "bosom" as a dish or bowl, the word meaning something "deep," That does seem to correlate with lifting his hand to his mouth to eat. Even that "grieves" him (lit. wearies himself, faint); to even feed himself is too much of a strain! That's bad! See 19:24.

The "bosom" could refer to the arm pits, but the above explanation makes more sense.

Prov. 26:16

"The sluggard is wiser in his own conceit than seven men that can render a reason."

It's amazing and puzzling how conceited is a lazy fool! How smart he really thinks he is in the presence of a group ("seven"—full group) of wise men who have true perception ("reason")! How bold are the foolish, who not only reject wisdom, but would engage others in their wickedness, if they could. JFB comments: "The thoughtless being ignorant of their ignorance are conceited...." How true.

But there's something further to be said here. The influence of "seven men" with logical and righteous "reasons" as to why the sluggard should be diligent has seemingly no affect over him. This is another example of the power of sin and deception, which cannot be broken by the rationalization of men, but only by the invading power of the Holy Spirit!

Yet notice the brilliance and skill of a lazy fool, who can "outsmart" those who try to dissuade or outnumber him.

Prov. 26:17

"He that passeth by, and meddleth with strife belonging not to him, is like one that taketh a dog by the ears."

The picture here is a man passing by a group of quarreling people and deciding to offer his opinion or "put in his two cents," as we say. He's on dangerous ground because he is "sticking his nose" in other peoples' business. This is likened to the risk of "taking a dog by the ears"; i.e., angering the animal who will probably bite you.

Mind your own business is the admonition! Be a peacemaker,

rather than further agitating the situation. In this case, that means walking by the group with your mouth shut.

Prov. 26:18

"As a mad man who casteth firebrands, arrows, and death,"

One deceptive practice of human sinfulness is to justify our assaults (verbal or otherwise) on others by saying: "I was just joking"! (*"Am not I in sport?"*) Men try to cover up their true motives behind their wicked deeds; they try to make light of things that are really serious, so as to deceive others regarding their real underlying motive. The reference here to "neighbor" means fellow man—one that may not really know the culprit.

The deeds expressed here must be serious and devastating, for this transgressor is characterized "as a mad man" who throws fiery arrows and "death" (destruction)! Yet, he has the audacity to say in essence: "I'm just playing around!" Indeed, *the "heart is deceitful above all things, and desperately wicked."*

Prov. 26:19

"So is the man that deceiveth his neighbour, and saith, Am not I in sport?"

See previous verse (18).

Prov. 26:20

"Where no wood is, there the fire goeth out: so where there is no talebearer, the strife ceaseth."

No wood, no fire! There must be some kind of fuel to have a fire. So the analogy of the absence of a "talebearer" (lit. murmurer, backbiter) cannot start or sustain "strife" or controversy. Some, out of a heart of bitterness and unbelief, are bent on sowing discord (6:19); they fail to experience peace and tranquility because of the "war" in their hearts.

"Misery loves company," as the saying goes. Such people love to spread their "woes" to others. So they "stir the pot," through slander, griping, etc. Their absence is a "blessing" indeed, for there's no one (wood) to fuel the **fire**!

Prov. 26:21

"As coals are to burning coals, and wood to fire; so is a contentious man to kindle strife."

Here is a choice analogy between burning coals and wood with the "fire kindled" by a contentious person. A heart of "strife" (lit. quarreling, disputing) will produce contention (lit. brawling) for sure.

Some people seem to thrive on contention and conflict—always stirring the pot. If one responds in like fashion, then fuel is added to the fire, producing greater turmoil. See Prov. 10:12; 15:18; 29:22.

Prov. 26:22

"The words of a talebearer are as wounds, and they go down into the innermost parts of the belly."

Words are powerful! They can become a potent instrument of life or death. (cf. James 3) Solomon expresses the devastating "wounds" of a talebearer (whisperer, backbiter). Such words **go down in the innermost parts** (lit. chambers) **of the belly** (abdomen).

Unlike a stab wound, these wounds rarely, if ever, heal. Someone said that more wounds have been afflicted by the "edge of the tongue, than by the edge of the sword."

Prov. 26:23

"Burning lips and a wicked heart are like a potsherd covered with silver dross."

Some things just do not go together. Yet a disingenuous or lying spirit will attempt to deceive. Here, "burning lips (of love, inferred) and a wicked (evil) heart" do not correlate; Jesus said: "Out of the abundance of the heart, the mouth speaks." Our hearts are revealed through our lips; to fake it or cover it up is hypocrisy.

Solomon likens this to pottery (clay pot) "covered with the dross of silver." One may cover a piece of pottery with silver dross (not pure) to give it a shiny, smooth look; but regardless of the "look," it is still clay and relatively worthless. Things are not always what they appear to be and man is a master at deception.

For example, how many cubic zirconium stones are sold these days for genuine diamonds because the untrained eye cannot distinguish the difference? You can make a similar application in the religious realm.

Prov. 26:24

"He that hateth dissembleth with his lips, and layeth up deceit within him;"

A deceiver can disguise his hatred in how he speaks. The word "dissembleth" is from the Hebrew verb *Nakar*, meaning "to know or discern." A liar knows what he's doing and can discern how best to deceive with his lips; thus he can disguise his true intent, which eventually will be discovered. (see vs. 26).

Prov. 26:25

"When he speaketh fair, believe him not: for there are seven abominations in his heart."

Here is an admonition regarding the man in vs. 24, who is clever and deceitful. **When he speaketh fair** (*chanan*- "graciously, favorable, agreeably")**, believe him not.** Don't take his words at face value. Why? Because **there are seven abominations in his heart.** In this case, his words are deceitful, covering up the real intent of his heart. "Seven abominations" indicates a heart totally given over to deception (e.g., Jeremiah 17:9). Thus the need of spiritual discernment. This portrays the essence of "lying" or a liar. Beware, the world (and the church) is filled with such!

Prov. 26:26

"Whose hatred is covered by deceit, his wickedness shall be shewed before the whole congregation."

This deceiver (vs. 25) is really an angry, hateful man; he "covers" or conceals that hate by deceit; he doesn't want to be exposed for what he really is. How intent is man to "cover up" his sin! In 28:13, Solomon says:

> "He that covereth his sins shall not prosper: but whoso confesseth and forsaketh them shall have mercy."

To "cover up" sin now is to face that sin in the future. It will be "shown" (uncovered) one day "before the whole congregation," whether on earth or in the final Judgment.

But thank God for the judgment of man's sin placed on His Son Jesus Christ at the Cross! To those that repent and believe the Gospel, "uncovering" their sin before God, will find their sins "covered" by grace. If we uncover (confess and forsake) our sins now, then they will not be uncovered in the judgment. But if a sinner hides and denies his sin here, he will face it squarely one day before Almighty God. How weighty is this thought!

Prov. 26:27

> "Whoso diggeth a pit shall fall therein: and he that rolleth a stone, it will return upon him."

One who "digs a pit" is setting (plotting) a trap to snare or kill someone. Somewhere along the line, he "shall fall" into it himself. What goes around, comes around, whether in this life or in the judgment to come. *"Be sure your sin will find you out,"* says Moses.

The parallel thought refers to "rolling a stone" (millstone, see Judges 9:53) uphill, only to have it "return" to "flatten" him out! There's probably no greater illustration of this in Scripture than the saga of Haman who plotted the death of Mordecai. Building a gallows prepared for the neck of Mordecai, he ended up with the noose around his neck! (See Esther 6, 7) Cf. Psalm 7:15, 16; 9:15.

Prov. 26:28

> "A lying tongue hateth those that are afflicted by it; and a flattering mouth worketh ruin."

"Love...thinks no evil," says Paul. Thus, love doesn't speak evil either, but desires to uplift and bless others. So lying and hatred are joined together; a false witness not only "afflicts" (bruises, wounds) the victim, but demonstrates hatred, not love.

In the same vein, **a flattering** (lit. smooth) **mouth worketh** (causes) **ruin.** Much of our speaking, preaching, etc. is mere "flattery"—an attempt to impress and win people by lying. Truth is offensive, and the "smooth" tongue will avoid confrontation at any cost. Faithfulness (truth) to others is at a low ebb, even in churches. We expect a doctor to lovingly tell us the truth regarding our physical condition; why do we expect less from a preacher, especially with the consequences of eternity in view?

Chapter 27
Do Not Boast About Tomorrow

Prov. 27:1

"Boast not thyself of to morrow; for thou knowest not what a day may bring forth."

The Fall has insured that man would be full of himself—quick to brag and boast. One characteristic of a fool is to celebrate ahead of time regarding something that is uncertain. Man is a "boaster"—self-sufficient and arrogant. If you want to find out how good a man is, just ask him—he'll be glad to tell you! The problem is that his talk is bigger than his walk. Prov. 20:6 says:

"Most men will proclaim every one his own goodness: but a faithful man who can find?"

This high-minded attitude then projects into the future (i.e., tomorrow) where he has not yet gone. James has a tremendous admonition regarding such a prideful attitude:

"Go to now, ye that say, today or tomorrow we will go into such a city, and continue there a year, and buy and sell, and get gain; Whereas ye know not what shall be on the morrow. For what is your life? It is even a vapour that appeareth for a little time, and then vanisheth away. For that ye ought to say, If the Lord will, we shall live, and do this, or that. But now ye rejoice in your boastings: all such rejoicing is evil. Therefore to him that knoweth to do good, and doeth it not, to him it is sin (James 4: 13-17).

Prov. 27:2

"Let another man praise thee, and not thine own mouth; a stranger, and not thine own lips."

If there's any commendation to be done, "let it be another man"

437

who praises you, and not your "own mouth." Self praise stinks! Men are quick to "toot" their own horns, especially when no one else does. Let a "stranger" say a good word about you, if he will, but keep your lips sealed. A stranger may have a compliment because he doesn't really know you. Indeed, *the heart is deceitful above all things...who can know it?"* (Jeremiah 17:9).

If you know who you are in Christ, there's no need or desire to flaunt yourself. Only insecurity and an inferiority complex have to unduly "show off," whether verbally or bodily. For example, a hooker or prostitute exposes her flesh to sell her "product." We need to develop the "inner man" and let that be our "trademark," rather than inordinate talk and dress.

Prov. 27:3

"A stone is heavy, and the sand weighty; but a fool's wrath is heavier than them both."

What an expression of how profoundly deep and grievous ("heavy") is a fool's anger ("wrath")! We all know something of how heavy and cumbersome it is to pick up building stones. I have worked construction in my college days, mixing sand & cement, along with transporting cinder blocks for the walls. What a job! There's hardly any task I can think of that would be more difficult and physically taxing.

It's inconceivable how "a fool's wrath"(grief) could be "heavier." The weight of man's depravity and wickedness is pronounced in this analogy. It reminds me of Genesis 6:5 and Romans 1. Unsanctified anger is indeed a murderous spirit and originates with our "father, the Devil" (John 8:44)! But included here is also the idea of frustration, vexation and grief. The fool carries a "heavy load" of sin. The way of the transgressor is hard.

Prov. 27:4

"Wrath is cruel, and anger is outrageous; but who is able to stand before envy?"

Wrath is cruel. "Wrath" as used here is a different word than in

438

vs. 3—it means "hot displeasure, rage"; "cruel" means "fierce." **And anger** (lit. nose or nostril, rapid breathing) **is outrageous** (lit. flood, deluge, overflow). **But who is able to stand (remain firm) before envy?** (jealousy)!

Here's a description of the tremendous force of jealousy in a man. The idea here is that man can somehow contain his wrath and anger, as "outrageous" as they may be, but a jealous spirit is more difficult to handle, and will take him over the edge. See Prov. 6:34. Just talk to husbands who have returned home only to find someone else in bed with his wife!

Interestingly, this word "envy" has to do with "zeal or ardor." It can pertain to sexual passion(above) as well as religious fervor (see 2 Kings 19:31). In 14:30, the same word is used and is said to produce "rottenness of the bones." (arthritis?) Whatever the case, this is one powerful and devastating emotion!

Prov. 27:5

"Open rebuke is better than secret love."

How loving are the "wounds" of a faithful friend! (see vs. 6) Under the guise of "love" we often remain silent, when a word of rebuke is in order. Here Solomon states a vital truth: **Open rebuke** (correction, chastisement) **is better than secret love.** It's easier to "love" secretly, but there comes a time to "love" openly; i.e., confrontation. Real love keeps short accounts and doesn't allow his friend (spouse, brother, etc.) to backslide without a fight!

Even with children, it's easy to let things go under the guise of love, when they need to be rightfully corrected. (See Prov. 29:15). Our flesh would avoid anything negative or confrontational, equating silence with love. There are times to be quiet and wait, but there comes a time to speak the truth in love.

This too can be perverted, whereby we may feel it's our responsibility to get others "straightened out." That too is of the flesh, or even demonic. There are saints who feel they have the "gift of criticism," but that is NOT one of the gifts of the Spirit! What balance of wisdom it takes to be a real friend to someone.

While verse 6 further explains this subject, it must be said that even the reproof of an enemy is beneficial. While a friend may be silent because he doesn't want to hurt your feelings, the enemy doesn't care. They'll tell you what they think because they desire to hurt you. But God can convert that into a blessing and help, if we respond properly. If what they say is true, then make the correction; if not, then ignore it. Even an enemy can become a "friend" is they help us grow in grace.

Prov. 27:6

"Faithful are the wounds of a friend; but the kisses of an enemy are deceitful."

Faithful (true, supportive) **are the wounds of a friend.** Here's the essence of a true and honest friendship. A real friend really cares for our welfare, even if he has to "cross" us. Love wants the best for its object, even if we have to "wound" or correct that person. "Faithful" wounds are constructive, not destructive, though they may hurt one's feelings. A faithful surgeon will "cut" the patient to correct a condition, even though there's much discomfort. So a faithful friend will spare nothing to better the one he loves.

But the kisses of an enemy are deceitful (abundant). There's an obvious falseness—the kisses are over done and not sincere. The enemy wants something for himself, not really concerned for the person's welfare. Yet, it's amazing how the flesh wants to be pampered at any cost, even at the expense of truth! Hollywood and religious hypocrisy have taught us to "love lies." The "kiss" of Judas is common place, betraying the Truth (Jesus). Our sin nature wants to be "lied to"—anything but facing reality.

That's why the Word of God is hated, because it tells us the truth about who we are, etc. It's a "Faithful Friend"! But the Law then becomes "our schoolmaster to bring us to Christ." O, to desire faithful friends rather than deceitful acquaintances who are really enemies. Needless to say, Jesus is the Model Friend that "sticks closer than a brother." And while He nestles us in his bosom, he doesn't hesitate to correct and discipline us—because He's the Faithful One.

Prov. 27:7

"The full soul loatheth an honeycomb; but to the hungry soul every bitter thing is sweet."

It doesn't take much to feed a hungry soul! When one is satisfied and full even the sweetest things are loathed (lit. tread down, rejected). **But to the hungry soul every bitter thing is sweet.** How even distasteful, ill-prepared food is attractive to one who is really hungry. Some people eat from the city dump! What an all-consuming drive is hunger! The rich who have never hungered cannot appreciate the "sweetness" of satisfying an empty stomach.

This certainly can be applied to those who *"hunger and thirst after righteousness, for they shall be filled."* How many are "filled up" on religious "junk," and who have no genuine hunger for God and His Word. O, to thirst for the fullness of God's Truth and Spirit!

Prov. 27:8

"As a bird that wandereth from her nest, so is a man that wandereth from his place."

There's protection and security in a good home. Each bird has his own nest and man his own home (family). A bird who wanders from her nest may face many difficulties and even death. So man who wanders away from his home may face similar fate. The prodigal left home for the "far country" where he squandered his "substance" (money and character, etc.). Away from home he could do what he wanted, without the restraining influence of family, etc. It's easier to sin away from home than under the same roof with parents and family.

In modern context, many young people leave home for education and employment. This is understandable, but risky nevertheless. There's a balance between being a "homebody" and a "prodigal." Part of Cain's judgment was being uprooted from his family domain. Note Barnes comment on this verse:

> "Change of place is thought of as in itself an evil. It is not easy for the man to find another home or the bird another nest. The maxim is characteristic of the earlier stages of Hebrew

history, before exile and travel had made change of country a more familiar thing. Compare the feeling which made the thought of being "a fugitive and a vagabond" Gen_4:12-13 the most terrible of all punishments."

Prov. 27:9

"Ointment and perfume rejoice the heart: so doth the sweetness of a man's friend by hearty counsel."

There's more than one way to "gladden" one's heart; here we see first an appeal to the senses, i.e., "perfume"; secondly, the inner pleasantness that comes (emanates) from the "hearty counsel" (lit. advice from the soul) of a friend. The smell and touch of ointment (e.g., olive oil) and perfume (incense) which "rejoice" (Piel imperf. lit. constantly cause gladdening) the heart is likened to the deeper and more lasting pleasure of true heart-counsel of a friend.

It may be that Solomon is extolling the superior benefit of the advice of a true friend, as opposed to some of the temporal and superficial pleasures of life. Everyone has a need to be encouraged and satisfied; the issue is how is that to be done. I think here of a massage which stimulates the blood flow and pleasure of the body; then there's the "message" of a faithful friend that stimulates the pleasure of the heart. Both are legitimate and necessary, but the latter is ultimately more beneficial. Bodily exercise is profitable for a little time, says the Apostle, but better is to "exercise thy soul unto godliness," for this is eternal.

People without friends can tantalize the flesh momentarily, but how much more satisfying is a good friend; especially the One who *"sticketh closer than a brother"*!

Prov. 27:10

"Thine own friend, and thy father's friend, forsake not; neither go into thy brother's house in the day of thy calamity: for better is a neighbour that is near than a brother far off."

They say that "blood is thicker than water," meaning that family members (siblings) will always stick together in a crisis. Generally speaking, that seems to be true, yet blood relatives can be also seriously divided and unconcerned about one another. *"There is a friend that sticketh closer than a brother"*—referring to Christ; but also applied to a genuine friend (as in this context). A true and close friend of the family (e.g., "father's friend," etc.) can be of greater help in a distressful time than a blood brother who's not available ("far off").

There are several observations here: 1) Not all family members are the best of friends; 2) A faithful friend can actually be closer (in understanding, etc.) than a blood brother; 3) A friend may be better able to help than a sibling; 4) He may be more objective and wise than a blood brother; 5) The inference in the text is that this friend may be closer geographically "than a brother far off."

I don't want to read more into this passage than is valid. A good application for the Christian would be the precious gift of a godly Christian brother—connected by the blood of Christ. *"...how good and how pleasant it is for brethren to dwell together in unity!"*(Psalm 133:1). The family of God is unique—surpassing the love of even immediate family members who don't know the Lord. In this case, the spiritual "blood" relationship is "thicker" than biological blood (genes).

Overall, we have here an exhortation of the great value of genuine friends and their ministry to us in times of distress; "don't' forsake them or let them go." JFB makes a helpful and pithy statement: "Adhere to tried friends. The ties of blood may be less reliable than those of genuine friendship."

Prov. 27:11

"My son, be wise, and make my heart glad, that I may answer him that reproacheth me."

Solomon reveals the heart cry of a true father. **My son, be wise, and make my heart glad,** i.e., a son who manifests wisdom in attitude and decision-making is sure to "gladden" or lit. "brighten up" (cheer) his father's heart. There's probably no greater reward to a wise father than to have a wise son! This is far beyond the pale of money and earthly success.

But Solomon gives a further reason: **That I may answer** (lit. "turn back") **him that reproacheth** (lit. strips, exposes) **me.** Children do reflect their parents and people judge accordingly. It doesn't always follow that a wise father has a wise son, but when that's true, it is a testimony of the father's character and parental training. Such a father will find comfort and joy when others try to attack his character.

Prov. 27:12

"A prudent man foreseeth the evil, and hideth himself; but the simple pass on, and are punished."

See notes on 22:3.

Prov. 27:13

"Take his garment that is surety for a stranger, and take a pledge of him for a strange woman."

See notes on 20:16.

Prov. 27:14

"He that blesseth his friend with a loud voice, rising early in the morning, it shall be counted a curse to him."

How to turn a "blessing" into a "curse"! Just approach your friend with a loud greeting (lit. yell) early in the morning before he has sufficiently awakened; he will consider that a "curse." Here's just a matter of common sense in dealing with others, even those who love us. Sensitivity and consideration of others goes a long way in development of and sustaining relationships. Not to do so is the epitome of selfishness and folly.

Prov. 27:15

"A continual dropping in a very rainy day and a contentious woman are alike."

Solomon's analogy here is descriptive indeed. He likens a contentious, brawling woman to the constant dripping of rain water, possibly through the crack in a roof. The typical eastern houses had flat earthen roofs, easily susceptible to leakage. How constant and increasingly aggravating is such a dripping! See 19:13.

Prov. 27:16

"Whosoever hideth her hideth the wind, and the ointment of his right hand, which bewrayeth itself."

A further word concerning the "contentious woman" of vs. 15: **Whosoever hideth** (cover over, deny) **her hideth the wind.** Certainly a poetic way of saying that one could better control the wind than to control this woman! Like the wind, she will not be denied. How stubborn and selfish is sin! (Jeremiah 17:9)

The latter phrase is difficult to translate. It has to do with a hand anointed with scented oil which "betrayeth" (lit. calls out or reveals) itself. That is, a hand dripping with smelly oil cannot be hidden or silenced—it reveals its fragrance no matter what. Thus it is likened again to the woman who cannot be subdued or ignored.

Prov. 27:17

"Iron sharpeneth iron; so a man sharpeneth the countenance of his friend."

A farmer knows how to sharpen his tools by the abrasive contact with another tool. So a metal file can sharpen a metal blade. Such an analogy describes the social and spiritual interaction between friends, one "sharpening" the other. As Solomon says in Ecclesiastes, *"Two are better than one"*; one challenges and strengthens the other.

Everyone needs someone with whom he can "open up" his heart without fear of rebuke and rejection. A true friend will be that person who sparks encouragement of heart, which in turn becomes evident in the face.

Prov. 27:18

"Whoso keepeth the fig tree shall eat the fruit thereof: so he that waiteth on his master shall be honoured."

The principle here is that those who are diligent and faithful to

445

their task (vocation) will be rewarded accordingly. The farmer who **keepeth** (lit. watches over) **the fig tree shall eat the fruit.** Cf. 2 Timothy 2:6; 2 Corinthians 9:6f. *"If any would not work, neither should he eat,"* said Paul. Work is a blessing from the Lord and the means of physical sustenance.

The same is true in relationships; the servant who faithfully serves (waits on, gives heed to) his master will eventually be "honored" (*kabode* - lit. "be heavy, glorified"). Submission to authority yields authority or honor. The ultimate example is our Lord who "humbled himself and became the servant of men." He came "not to be ministered unto, but to minister." He always did that which "was pleasing to the Father."

Honor and respect is not demanded, but is commanded by a life of submission to God and others. John the Baptist said, *"He must increase, but I must decrease."* Paul said, *"Not I, but Christ..."*! The way UP is the way DOWN! The way to gain our lives is to lose them in faithful submission unto the Lord.

Prov. 27:19

"As in water face answereth to face, so the heart of man to man."

Here's a great verse on discernment or what could be called "spiritual vibes." As one sees the reflection of his face in water, so one can sense a "heart" reflection or response in another person. **Face answereth to face,** so another man's spirit answers our spirit. *"Deep calleth unto deep."*

Thus the term, "speaking heart to heart"; i.e., not peripheral or surface talk, but reaching the depth of a person's spirit. Some people say all the right things, but your spirit is troubled by your perception of their insincerity and disingenuousness.

So speaking "man to man" is to address the inner man (heart)— the real person of another.

Prov. 27:20

"Hell and destruction are never full; so the eyes of man are never satisfied."

How much is enough? To a millionaire, it's "just a little more." **So the eyes of man** (i.e., in the flesh) **are never satisfied** (i.e. filled to satisfaction, sufficient). It is likened to "Hell" (*Sheol* - the underworld of the dead and damned; see K&D), along with "destruction" which are "never full" (same word as "satisfied").

So with the lust of the eye—it never has enough (Cf. Ecclesiastes 1:8). It seems that man is born with a "God-shaped" vacuum in his spirit that can only find ultimate satisfaction in God alone! Even fleshly religion is insufficient to fill man's emptiness (e.g., Nicodemus – John 3); thus the necessity to be "born again" (lit. from above, by the Spirit).

Prov. 27:21

"As the fining pot for silver, and the furnace for gold; so is a man to his praise."

Both silver and gold are "tried" in the heat of the furnace; i.e., the quality and worth of the substance is revealed and tested thereby. So "praise" is a vital test for man, revealing who he really is—proud or humble. Cf. 17:3.

Some may "shine" in the crucible of trial, but fail the test of "praise" or commendation. The greatest test may not be failure, but success. True maturity will enable a man, when he is commended, to transfer all praise to God; the same man will also be steady and trusting in the trial of criticism and failure. (See Matthew Henry's note.)

Prov. 27:22

"Though thou shouldest bray a fool in a mortar among wheat with a pestle, yet will not his foolishness depart from him."

Bray (lit. mix by pounding) **a fool in a mortar** (vat) **among wheat with a pestle**; i.e., crush him to the fullest and discover that no matter what, his foolishness (innate depravity and wickedness) will not depart! This analogy illustrates again the utter impossibility to change a sinner's nature. That's why it takes Divine and miraculous intervention, viz., regenerating grace, to bring transformation. The old Adam must die and a new man emerge through the resurrection power of Jesus Christ. There's no way to reform a fool! (See Barnes.)

Prov. 27:23

"Be thou diligent to know the state of thy flocks, and look well to thy herds."

Solomon exhorts the farmer to **be thou diligent to know the state (lit. face) of thy flocks.** The Hebrew doubles the verb "know" for emphasis: "know while knowing"; i.e., be diligent in knowing. This is your business to know the condition of the flocks. Then he magnifies the thought: **And look well** (lit. with heart) **to thy herds.** There's a tenderness portrayed here between the shepherd and his sheep. It reminds us of our Great Shepherd who loves and cares for His own. (See John 10:3, 14, etc.) Of course, in context, this diligent care also has to do with his livelihood and future prosperity. See vs. 24.

Prov. 27:24

"For riches are not for ever: and doth the crown endure to every generation?"

Reason to be diligent in caring for the "flocks" (occupation, ministry, etc.)? **For riches are not for ever....** Faithfulness to your God-given task is far more important than material wealth or prestige ("crown"). Riches and power (earthly) are fleeting, but spiritual life and reward are eternal.

This is a word for those in ministry who lust for money and popularity, making these the goal and evidence of "spirituality." Many are more interested in the size of the membership role than the true condition of the members. The so-called "health and wealth" teaching can only end in spiritual bankruptcy and disaster. God help those who fleece God's sheep for personal gain!

Prov. 27:25

"The hay appeareth, and the tender grass sheweth itself, and herbs of the mountains are gathered."

The herdsman (vs. 23) is the recipient of God's natural provision from the land; i.e., **hay** (grass); **tender grass** and **herbs** which are gathered for food, etc. It's a further description of God's supply to his creatures, whether man or beast (cf. Psalm 104:14).

He is the *"Saviour of all men, specially of those that believe."* (1 Tinothy 4:10) *"Oh that men would praise the LORD for his goodness... to the children of men."* (Psalm 107) *"For the earth is the Lord's, and the fulness thereof."* (1 Corinthians 10:26)

Prov. 27:26

"The lambs are for thy clothing, and the goats are the price of the field."

Again here's the ongoing description of a rural family living off the "farm." The lambs (sheep) serve to supply the wool for clothing. Some even suggest that the fleece might have been also used as rent to the landlords (where applicable).

Likewise, **the goats are the price** (payment) **of the field.** This suggests that selling the goats would produce payment for the land, whether rent or purchase of new property. This might be a means to possessing real estate for security and posterity; i.e., gift to children, etc. But note that cattle were to be used for man's needs; they were part of God's provision for mankind, not to be "humanized" or put on man's level.

Evolution has served to dehumanize man, and humanize animals; thus we live in a confused society which has "thrown out" the Bible as its foundation of Truth. *"In the beginning God created...."* is essential to believe if we are to understand the order of life on this planet!

Prov. 27:27

"And thou shalt have goats' milk enough for thy food, for the food of thy household, and for the maintenance for thy maidens."

Here is the culmination or optimum results of a diligent farmer who honors the Lord. By obedient grace he is enabled to work the field and nurture the animals, etc., thus reaping abundant provision for his family. There's no magic in caring for a household; it takes responsible labor for all involved, a principle which has been all but lost in our day of free government "handouts."

This man provides abundantly for his family, along with the servants. The "goats' milk" is enough for all to eat and drink. He is a blessed and prosperous man, exemplifying how God rewards those who follow His precepts and take personal responsibility seriously. Solomon may have had this man in mind when he said:

> *"Whatsoever thy hand findeth to do, do it with thy might; for there is no work, nor device, nor knowledge, nor wisdom, in the grave, whither thou goest."* (Ecclesiastes 9:10)

Chapter 28
The Wicked Flee When No One Pursues

Prov. 28:1

"The wicked flee when no man pursueth: but the righteous are bold as a lion."

This is a great verse describing the function of conscience in the spirit of man. **The wicked flee....** The word here for "wicked" is *rasha*, "a guilty one, criminal." He runs or hides when no one is even chasing him! What a commentary on paranoia (lit. "one beside his mind"- *nous* or spirit). Prov. 20:27 says:

"The spirit of man is the candle (lamp) of the LORD, searching all the inward parts of the belly."

The word "spirit" is *neshamah*, translated "breath" in Genesis 2:7, depicting the function of conscience in man's creation. This is more than the "breathing" (*ruach*) process or air in the lungs. *Neshamah* sets man apart from all other creatures in that he has a God-consciousness and understanding. This "candle or lamp" of God brings conviction to man's spirit when he's done wrong. It's like God's red light of the heart. Romans 2:14, 15 further demonstrates this law of conscience operating in sinners as "the law written in their hearts." Thank God, for this wonderful principle in a wicked, violent world where at least there's some restraint in the sinner's heart.

But even better is work of God's saving grace through Jesus Christ who took away our sin and guilt on the Cross! Hallelujah! Therefore, **the righteous** (Justified in Christ) **are bold** (confident) **as a lion.** Through redeeming love we can face life squarely with a clear conscience. No more running from trouble, but dealing with truth. No more hiding in fear, but confessing our sins when conscience points out our wrongdoing.

Prov. 28:2

"For the transgression of a land many are the princes thereof: but by a man of understanding and knowledge the state thereof shall be prolonged."

This verse describes the tremendous importance and influence of political leadership. Here's a contrast between a stable, wise leader and those who are not. The "transgression" or iniquity (corruption) will affect its longevity and that of its leaders. Corrupt politicians come and go when the nation is corrupt. Likewise, a corrupt society will have trouble drawing the right kind of leadership. In a word, wicked nations are unstable and short lived, and so are their governments.

In contrast, one man through discernment and right knowledge (character) can insure "the state" (integrity, uprightness) of the country will be prolonged or ongoing. Thank God, for our country of America which still has a semblance of freedom and righteousness. Many are the countries of the world who lack any stability—who go from one coup or revolt to another. Leaders come and go and multitudes suffer.

Prov. 28:3

"A poor man that oppresseth the poor is like a sweeping rain which leaveth no food."

This verse doesn't fit the parallelism of other proverbs. Scholars (like K&D) argue that this "poor man" who oppresses the "poor" is one and the same. "A man—poor and oppressing the weak, is a sweeping rain, and there is no bread." (YLT). Young's translation here would be neat, but I'm not sure it's true to the text.

The problem is the thought that the "poor" oppress other poor people; it's usually some tyrant or dictator who persecutes and violates the poor. Could this first "poor man" refer to some upstart of the king who is still not financially secure? Is he poor in the sense of low character—jockeying for position and recognition? Or is this a contrast of two degrees of "poor"; i.e., one relatively poor who oppresses one who is poorer than he? I think Clarke captures this thought by illustration of the two debtors in Matthew 18—that wonderful parable of forgiveness. He says:

> A poor man that oppresseth the poor - Our Lord illustrates this proverb most beautifully, by the parable of the two debtors, Mat_18:23. One owed ten thousand talents, was insolvent, begged for time, was forgiven. A fellow servant owed this one a hundred pence: he was insolvent; but prayed his fellow servant to give him a little time, and he would pay it all. He would not, took him by the throat, and cast him into prison till he should pay that debt. Here the poor oppressed the poor; and what was the consequence? The oppressing poor was delivered to the tormentors; and the forgiven debt charged to his amount, because he showed no mercy. The comparatively poor are often shockingly uncharitable and unfeeling towards the real poor."

Like a sweeping rain - These are frequent in the East, and sometimes carry flocks, crops, and houses, away with them.

One thing for sure is that such oppression and injustice can only devastate the economy (i.e., the crops, etc.). The greed and wickedness of man can only destroy a society. That's a warning for any civilized society.

Prov. 28:4

"They that forsake the law praise the wicked: but such as keep the law contend with them."

Here's the basic war of humanity in this world! **They that forsake** (lit. to loosen, relinquish) **the law** (Torah) **praise** (*Hallel* - boast, commend, glory in) **the wicked.** How true this is! The lawbreakers love lawbreakers! The rebels hang together, as birds of a feather. In our day, the more wicked people are, the more they're celebrated by Hollywood and others. The Bible and Commandments are thrown out of our schools, while lawlessness and lewdness have invaded our society in epidemic proportions.

Like kind produces like kind. The popular politicians and clergy represent the rank and file of the people. The worst people prevail in leadership when "truth is trampled in the streets."

On the other hand, **such as keep** (guard, protect) **the law contend** (lit strive) **with them** (i.e., the wicked). Here's the ongoing conflict between right and wrong. The fight is on! This is the battle of the ages between sin and righteousness, good and evil, Cain and Abel, Heaven and Hell. The word "contend" has the idea of anger or indignation against the wicked.

We live in a society that makes its own standards—a moral relativism. They call it "situation ethics." What's moral for one, may not be moral for another; e.g., adultery and murder may be a good thing for some. "Whatever makes you happy." So the conflict continues between those who "forsake the law" and those who regard it; our attitude toward the wicked (in Hollywood, politics, religion, etc.) reveals our own M.O. (Modus Operandi). What (or who) we love and what we hate, reveals who and what we are!

Prov. 28:5

"Evil men understand not judgment: but they that seek the LORD understand all things."

Life is a matter of perspective and standard. The word "understand" here means to distinguish or lit. "separate mentally." Evil men, prompted and fueled by a sin nature, muddle the difference between truth and error (right and wrong). Genesis 6:5 is a commentary on the evil, whose "every imagination of the heart is only evil continually." Evil doing is natural to an evil man! A man isn't a liar because he lies; he lies because he's a liar!

Such evil doesn't consider what's right or wrong, but operates by "what's right for me." The judgment or justice of the Bible is of no consideration. "Whatever makes me happy" or "floats my boat" is their theme song. Then when justice *does* fall upon them, it is considered "unjust." (The word translated "judgment" here does refer specifically to a "verdict or judicial sentence").

Thank God, **they that seek the LORD** (Jehovah) **understand** (discern, settle) **all things** (the whole). It all comes out right (in the long run) when you seek the Lord and His righteousness (the Word, etc.). An evil heart and practice yields confusion and tragedy; the godly seek the Lord, which results in clarity and confidence and blessing! We have tried to rub out the line between right and wrong (e.g., homosexuality & marriage, corrupt dealings in business, etc.); it can only reap disaster over time.

Wisdom and true understanding of life's issues comes only to those who "seek the LORD"! Not only that, but there comes also the grace and power to overcome those issues (Philippians 4:13). In addition, those who seek the Lord will "have all things (they need) added unto them" (Matthew 6:33)! Hallelujah, what a Saviour!

Prov. 28:6

"Better is the poor that walketh in his uprightness, than he that is perverse in his ways, though he be rich."

"Get it any way you can"—so is the world's attitude toward money and riches. Thus from large corporations on down, the wicked find ways to "beat the system." Greed is the order of the day, even in the Church. This verse extols the "poor" man who walks in righteousness above the "rich pervert" (crook). Success seems to be measured by acquired riches, regardless of personal character. But integrity surpasses all material wealth.

This is not to say that men of integrity cannot be wealthy; Job, Abraham, David, etc. illustrate that. Likewise, this proverb does not teach that one must be rich to be blessed of God (e.g., the prosperity gospel). Saints of God all over the world walk with God and yet they have little of this world's goods (e.g., Ethiopia, Haiti, etc.). Yet many sinners and crooks have plenty! This will all be sorted out in the Judgment.

Thus we must live with eternity in view, being good stewards of all God has given us. But who we are is more important than what we have of this world. The measuring rod of the world is different than the Word's. Indeed, what may be hailed by the world as success may be an abomination in Heaven! (and vice-versa).

Prov. 28:7

"Whoso keepeth the law is a wise son: but he that is a companion of riotous men shameth his father."

Only a father knows how a father feels about a "wise son." There's nothing more heart-breaking than having a son who's a fool; that goes for even those who may be retarded, or have a terminal illness, etc. According to the text, a wise son is one who "keeps the law" or is obedient to God's Word. Thus he obeys his father as well. A father delights in an obedient son—that's worth more than any material thing that son might provide.

In contrast, **he that is a companion of riotous** (worthless, vile) **men shameth** (lit. wounds, hurts) **his father.** O, the heartache to watch a son link himself up with the underworld! Especially when you have taught him the ways of God. No man sins to himself—yes, even a wayward son. He is the product and sum of his choices, which affect his parents too. How stupendous must be the pain in the hearts of parents whose sons have turned out to be murderers, perverts and drunks! Whatever a son may do for a legitimate living, the main issue is his relationship to God and His Word. Better to be a ditch-digger or garbage man who loves the Lord, than be a godless entrepreneur or dignitary!

Prov. 28:8

"He that by usury and unjust gain increaseth his substance, he shall gather it for him that will pity the poor."

Exorbitant interest rates are nothing new! Usury or excessive interest on a loan is an ancient practice to take advantage of people—or "use" them. There's a difference between fair interest on a loan and "loan-sharking." Credit card companies come close to the latter—sometimes charging 4 times the prime interest rate.

From the context, we see the picture of a lender making his money at the expense of the poor; thus, insuring their continued poverty. No mercy is shown because of greed. There's a judgment upon such activity, whereby his "substance" (gain) shall be given to **him that will pity** (lit. stoop in kindness, show mercy on) **the poor.** Indeed, the substance of the wicked is many times reserved for the righteous. "Filthy lucre" can be turned into "sanctified shekels" by God's intervention. See Ecclesiastes 2:26.

Prov. 28:9

"He that turneth away his ear from hearing the law, even his prayer shall be abomination."

How often does one hear someone say: "I say a prayer every night before I go to sleep." Lip service to prayer is so common, yet true prayer fellowship with the true God is rare indeed! There's nothing that reveals one's character and godly attitude any more than intimate "talking" with God. This is indeed the soul's breath of a true Christian, likened to the unceasing breathing process of the body. But this proverb has a "catch"—a shocking prerequisite to acceptable prayer; i.e., obedience to the Word of God!

One who **turneth away** (lit. turns off, turns aside) **his ear** (inner spiritual ear) **from hearing** (regarding, obeying) **the law** (Torah), **even his prayer** (intercession, supplication) **shall be abomination** (lit. something morally disgusting, idolatrous). Wow! How could it ever be wrong to "pray"? I thought God "answers all our prayers"?

What a profound exhortation is this axiom. People "pray," but to whom? I said prayers for years, but never felt like I got past the ceiling. I mouthed words, but with no witness of speaking to a living God. Then Jesus came into my life and all was changed—I got through the ceiling for the first time when I cried out for His salvation and forgiveness!

Thus prayer is not just words spoken into the air, but a definite conversation and intimacy with the True and Living God. But we must emphasize here the necessity to be in touch with the written Word in order to be in touch with the Living Word. Jesus said:

"If ye abide in Me and my words abide in you, ye shall ask what ye will and it shall be done unto you." (John 15:7)

Our prayer life is vitally connected to our understanding and submission to the Word of God. Disobedience or sin "cuts the cord" or lifeline of fellowship with God.

Note however that Solomon is not just saying that if we "turn off" the Word our prayers will not be answered; rather he takes it even further by saying: **even his prayer shall be abomination**! i.e., not only unanswered, but wholly rejected as detestable and disgusting before God! What an indictment! Prayer is not a catch-all, as some may think. It's time to proclaim this truth to a sleeping, worldly, backslidden Church, as well as a pseudo-religious world! We cannot pray any higher than we live! Amen.

Prov. 28:10

"Whoso causeth the righteous to go astray in an evil way, he shall fall himself into his own pit: but the upright shall have good things in possession."

"Be sure your sin will find you out," whether what you do personally (privately) or what you do to others. There are "evil" people who delight in destroying the righteous (saints), just like they attempted with Jesus himself. The majority of sinners just "sin," but there's a remnant of sinners who are evil; i.e., they delight in the fall of those who desire to do right. Not only so, but they will attempt to "lead them astray" so they can justify their own wickedness.

But in due season this evil person will fall into his own trap, as did Haman of old, and die on his own "gallows." This principle is stated clearly in Prov. 26:27. No one will ultimately get by with sin. *"Vengeance is mine; I will repay, saith the Lord."*

But the upright (straight, lit. sound one) **shall have good things in possession** (lit. inherit good things). Note this contrast regarding the one who weathers the storm of evil opposition; he will be blessed! (Psalm 1). One who is "sound or whole" has it "together" and doesn't think of leading others astray. There's no substitute for doing right, no matter how hard the road!

Prov. 28:11

"The rich man is wise in his own conceit; but the poor that hath understanding searcheth him out."

A great word here as to how God levels the playing field of life regarding true values. **The rich man is wise in his own conceit** (*ayin*- eye, phys. or mental)." Here's a man who is wise or skillful in his own "eyes" or appearance, motivated by his wealth. Note that even a sinner or con-man can possess human wisdom (see James 3), that is elevated by riches. But that doesn't make him "rich toward God."

Significantly, a poor man can possess true wisdom and discernment ("understanding") which can search out or penetrate a con-man's scheme or true condition. Thank God, wisdom is not dependent on material wealth. In fact, true wisdom is the ultimate wealth (the theme of Proverbs).

In our day, wealth is a sign of spiritual prosperity in some camps. If you're walking with God, they say, you must prosper financially, etc. Riches=abundant blessing="Spirit - filled" life. That's rubbish! If the "health and wealth" crowd is right, then there are very few true believers in Ethiopia or Haiti! Some of those "poor" saints are rich in discernment and can see through the chicanery of false prophets.

Prov. 28:12

"When righteous men do rejoice, there is great glory: but when the wicked rise, a man is hidden."

The atmosphere is radically different between the joy of right-doing and the fruitlessness or dearth of wickedness. Solomon describes the exuberance of "righteous men" who "rejoice" (lit. jump for joy) and manifest "great (abundant) glory" (lit. beauty, honor). Note "when," not "if" they rejoice; such rejoicing is characteristic of those who live right.

But when the wicked rise (become prominent), there is no rejoicing and honor; instead **a man is hidden**- Pual imperf. meaning "to be searched for or sought out." Wickedness is not open and exuberant, but secretive and clandestine. The ungodly cannot openly rejoice because of the nature of their deeds. Sin isn't broadcast, but rather hides. (e.g., Adam-Genesis 3:8).

Prov. 28:13

"He that covereth his sins shall not prosper: but whoso confesseth and forsaketh them shall have mercy."

Sinners are in denial about their sin! We fault drug addicts for denying their habit, but the problem is universal in one form or another. But here he's addressing those who "cover" or conceal their "sins" or transgressions (lit. rebellion). This "cover up" action is participial, which denotes an ongoing attitude—not a single, isolated act. Here's one who is slow in acknowledging his sins and thus will "not prosper" or succeed. Sin separates one from God—that's the ultimate failure!

The remedy? "Confession and forsaking" sin. I'm not sure that this is addressed to the unsaved, so much as a believer who becomes sensitive to wrong-doing and the need to deal properly with sin. (See David's example in Psalm 32; 51). "Confesseth" and "forsaketh" are participles also, denoting an on-going attitude. A true saint is quick to confess (word for "worship") and forsake (turn, relinquish) his sins. He, and he alone, will find God's mercy (lit. compassion, pity). What marvelous grace is this!

Prov. 28:14

"Happy is the man that feareth alway: but he that hardeneth his heart shall fall into mischief."

God-given happiness is the only genuine and lasting happiness. The world has its "happy times," but they seem to be connected to the present circumstance or "what's happnin'." The word *asher* here is translated "happy" 18 times in O.T. and 27 times as "blessed." In Psalm 1:1, the "blessed man" is extremely happy (plural of *asher*, which signifies intensity) resulting from his separation from wicked activity due to his "addiction" to the Word of God (vs. 2). Another way of saying *"the man that feareth (God) alway(s)."*

So here we have the contrast between the God-fearing man and the one that "hardeneth his heart." Instead of being happy, as the former, the rebellious man "shall fall into mischief" (trouble, sorrow, etc.). The condition of the heart seems to dictate the resulting fruit in one's life.

Prov. 28:15

"As a roaring lion, and a ranging bear; so is a wicked ruler over the poor people."

Solomon describes here the utter depraved and wretched condition of **a wicked ruler over the poor** (needy) **people.** He is likened to **a roaring lion, and a ranging** (ravenous) **bear**, who are on the prowl, seeking prey for their greedy appetites. Yes, such is the unbridled nature of man (Jeremiah 17:9), which is even magnified and more Hell-deserving when resident within a king because of his position.

There's a "double" wickedness here seeing that a king should not only prevent the suffering of his people, but should be benevolent toward them. Sin in high places has been covered and justified, but the Day of reckoning is coming. The judgment of sin in Hell is real and must not be compromised nor ridiculed.

Prov. 28:16

"The prince that wanteth understanding is also a great oppressor: but he that hateth covetousness shall prolong his days."

The attitude and character of a ruler makes a difference in his treatment of his subjects. Here **the prince** (ruler) who lacks **understanding is also a great** (excessively) **oppressor.** His understanding has to do with discretion, wisdom, and love for his people; one who has their best in mind, rather than his own power and selfishness. This seems to be inferred from the word "covetousness" in the second part. With privileged positions of authority comes the temptation to abuse that power for self-gain. Unique indeed is one who reigns with true humility and compassion. (e.g., Jesus!).

But he that hateth covetousness shall prolong his days. Longevity and true success is suggested here to the ruler who is not only benevolent, but "hates" selfish and dishonest gain. Not all politicians and rulers are crooks, but few and far between are those who do not let power and popularity go to their heads!

Prov. 28:17

"A man that doeth violence to the blood of any person shall flee to the pit; let no man stay him."

Here's a picture and exhortation of God's justice in process. The principle of "a life for a life" (Genesis 9:6) in motion. Taking a life ("blood") unjustly is violence to the extreme, for it effaces the very purpose of God who gave that life. The perpetrator (murderer) is destined to "flee" (run) to the "pit" or grave to face God's justice.

Let no man stay (help) **him.** There is neither mercy nor grace here because no propitiation (appeasement of God's justice) is mentioned. *"The wages of sin is death"*! The murderer is simply bearing the punishment for his crime (sin) and none can "stay" that fate. But so it is with all sinners—judgment is ahead and there's none to "stay" the flames of Hell. But wait! There's a Saviour who has come to take our place! (John 3:16) Through Him the hand of God's wrath is "stayed"! Hallelujah!

Prov. 28:18

"Whoso walketh uprightly shall be saved: but he that is perverse in his ways shall fall at once."

Again the contrast between the saint and sinner. The "upright" (lit. sound, whole) is one who "walks" (lifestyle) in truth and thus will be "saved" (delivered, preserved). He will reap what he sows; but the same is true with "perverse" or perverted (crooked, distorted), whose "ways (course of life) shall fall at once (i.e., totally & completely)." See 10:9; 17:20.

Different roads lead to different places; that's why ultimately Heaven and Hell are both real destinations, depending on one's lifestyle and relationship to Christ.

Prov. 28:19

"He that tilleth his land shall have plenty of bread: but he that followeth after vain persons shall have poverty enough."

Certainly the "work ethic" shines through clearly here. **He that tilleth** (works) **his land shall have plenty of bread** (food). Note it's "his land," indicating ownership. He takes responsibility to farm it properly and is rewarded by the Lord. The real issue, however, is that he works—makes an investment in his life, cooperating with human law (e.g., sowing and reaping).

On the other hand, **he that followeth after vain** (empty, worthless) **persons shall have poverty enough** (plenty, to the full). Not only does this fool not work, but he's engaged in illicit activity with "cronies" just like himself. Legitimate work will help to keep a man out of trouble. But the human heart tends to take the path of least resistance.

Prov. 28:20

"A faithful man shall abound with blessings: but he that maketh haste to be rich shall not be innocent."

This is a progression from the previous verse. **A faithful man shall abound with blessings**; i.e., a man of moral strength and integrity, one who is steadfast in life and work (cf. 20:6; Nehemiah 7:2). Here is a man who is steady on the course of daily responsibility and thus prospers.

In contrast, is the flighty, hasty individual whose love of money overrides integrity and hard work. Here is one interested in a "fast buck" and will do whatever it takes to get what he wants. He **shall not be innocent** (or guiltless, cleared, unpunished). He will reap what he has sown! This could apply here to gambling and other "get-rich-quick" schemes.

Prov. 28:21

"To have respect of persons is not good: for for a piece of bread that man will transgress."

A "respecter of persons" pertains to one who discriminates or shows partiality for a price. It is not a "good" or godly trait; it reveals the lack of integrity and one's weakness to be bribed. And some have so little character that they will "transgress" and sell out for "a piece of bread," i.e., next to nothing.

Judas sold Jesus for 30 pieces of silver; apostates in our day sell Him out for nothing! At least Judas had enough integrity to hang himself!

Prov. 28:22

*"He that hasteth to be rich hath an evil eye, and considereth not
that poverty shall come upon him."*

Hastiness and anxiety about riches reveals a covetous ("evil") spirit. This is the driving force behind gambling and other "get rich" schemes. It seems harmless on the surface, but becomes a "monster" leading its prey to poverty. Many seem almost obsessed with getting something for nothing and finding a way to bypass the work ethic. See 23:6; 28:20; Matthew 20:15.

Prov. 28:23

*"He that rebuketh a man afterwards shall find more favour than
he that flattereth with the tongue."*

True love will do right even if misunderstood. Rebuking a man who's going in the wrong direction may be very difficult but **afterwards shall find more favour** (*chen*- grace) **than he that flattereth with the tongue.** A rebuke in season can save a man's life from destruction. Flatterers are compromisers who delight in the "smoothed" tongue so as to please men. How tough it is to confront people with truth, especially when they don't want to listen. There's no greater example than Jesus Himself. (Compare Prov. 9:8, 9:9; 27:5). Those benefited by reproof will love their monitors.(JFB)

Prov. 28:24

*"Whoso robbeth his father or his mother, and saith, It is no
transgression; the same is the companion of a destroyer."*

Parents are the first God-given authority figures to the children. How a child (young or old) treats his parents reflects his attitude toward God Himself. Thus, stealing from parents heightens the offense because of family love, trust and protection. Years ago we described the worst of thieves by saying, "He would steal from his own mother." There's something sacred about the family that operates differently than "street crime." For example, a Mafia man may readily kill others, but will respect and protect his mother to the death.

But here we have a man (or woman) who crosses the line completely, regarding his parent's wealth as his own. Familiarity seems to breed contempt, thus he justifies taking their money as though it's no real crime. Note that he may know which parent is the "easy touch," thus, the mention of both "father" and "mother" in the text. The man is indeed **the companion of a** (the) **destroyer**! He's not only a criminal per se, but an emissary of Satan, the Destroyer himself! (John 10:10)

Prov. 28:25

"He that is of a proud heart stirreth up strife: but he that putteth his trust in the LORD shall be made fat."

The man with a "proud (lit. roomy, wide) heart stirs up strife (contention, discord)." This pictures one who is covetous or self-centered. This "stirs" the pot of contention; he must have his way, at any cost to others.

But blessing and abundance ("fat") is with him who puts his trust and confidence in the LORD! What a peace and rest comes to a faithful man! Greed and selfishness can only lead to conflict and eventual disaster. There's no substitute for serving the True and Living God, *"who daily loadeth us with benefits"*!

Prov. 28:26

"He that trusteth in his own heart is a fool: but whoso walketh wisely, he shall be delivered."

The man described here is one who is characterized by "self trust"; i.e., he has a big ego, thus his confidence is in what he can do rather than having a need for God. This is the Jeremiah 17:9 heart in action! Such a person is a "fool"! But this is the "Cain spirit" which operates in all sinners, to one degree or another; only the saving grace of God can make a difference.

But whoso walketh wisely, he shall be delivered (viz., from foolishness)." Here again is a description of "lifestyle" or course of action. This is a consistent "walk" which, in turn, yields the fruit of wisdom (spiritual skill). These characters are opposite in philosophy, lifestyle and results (fruit). Fools live according to the flesh (self), while wise men walk by faith in God. Thus, the descriptions of both sinner and saint. See Romans 8:5ff.

Prov. 28:27

"He that giveth unto the poor shall not lack: but he that hideth his eyes shall have many a curse."

An abundant life yields an abundant giving to others in need. In addition, giving to the destitute or poor meets with the blessing and provision of the Lord; thus, he "shall not lack." Jesus said, *"Give, and it shall be given unto you..."* (Luke 6:38). We reap what we sow, although the reaping may not always be monetary.

This giving spirit is contrasted by the one who "hideth his eyes" from the needy (miserable). He "looks the other way" and pretends not to see. He is likewise "rewarded" accordingly, receiving "many a curse." Curses or misfortune can take on many forms, none of which are desirous.

David cries out to the Lord in his needy condition, *"And hide not thy face from thy servant; for I am in trouble: hear me speedily"* (Psalm 69:17). Having been forsaken by man, David appeals to God for His loving intervention. Praise God for His lovingkindness, that He "sees and hears" our heart condition when others have "looked the other way."

This verse is interpreted beautifully by Prov. 11:24-26.

Prov. 28:28

"When the wicked rise, men hide themselves: but when they perish, the righteous increase."

How powerful and dominant is wickedness in a wicked world! It seems to overpower righteousness at every level. When it "rises" in and through wicked men, the people "hide" or take refuge from its tyranny. This is true in government, business, religion, education, homes, etc. Yet when ungodly rulers (leaders) are removed ("perish"), the "righteous increase"; i.e., good people are free to rise and express themselves.

Wickedness and corruption are very much at home in this cursed world! History is replete with the dominance evil. Periods of revival or spiritual awakening have graced our country, whereby righteousness was exalted. But not for long! Wickedness still reigns in this world, awaiting the Return of Him who will one day dash the Enemy and the ungodly with "a rod of iron" and the "Sword of the Word of God"! Only then will righteousness be ultimately in control (cf. Prov. 28:12; 11:10; Psalm 12:8).

Chapter 29
He Who Hardens His Neck Will Be Destroyed

Prov. 29:1

"He, that being often reproved hardeneth his neck, shall suddenly be destroyed, and that without remedy."

What a warning to the ungodly who persist in their rebellion! God will *"not always strive with man."* There comes a time when the sinner crosses the "dead-line," where there's no return! This verse depicts one who has been **often reproved** and yet has **hardeneth** (or stiffened) **his neck.** He has been confronted and rebuked many times about his rebellion, but without effect. Paul says the Word *"is profitable for doctrine, for reproof... (2 Timothy 3:16)."* In mercy, God has chosen to confront man's sin through the preaching of the Word. We can never be the same after hearing God's reproof. Our response is all important—we either obey it or further harden our hearts. The same Sun that "melts butter, hardens clay."

The tragedy comes when a rebel is **suddenly destroyed** (taken down, broken) **and that without remedy** (lit. healing). When he least expects it, the "axe" of God's judgment falls and repentance is impossible! Woe unto those who flaunt their wickedness in God's face! You can only "sear" your conscience and one day unexpectantly cross God's "dead-line"! (See Prov. 1:22-32) At Niagara Falls, NY, there's a sign posted several hundred feet before the Falls which reads: "This is the Point of No Return"! There's no swimming, boating, etc. allowed; for anyone falling into the rapids there has crossed the "dead-line" and is destined to go over the Falls. What a warning is this; sinner, repent while there's time and opportunity to be saved! Let us listen carefully to God's voice within and respond accordingly. Amen.

Prov. 29:2

"When the righteous are in authority, the people rejoice: but when the wicked beareth rule, the people mourn."

The "righteous" here indicates a governmental regime (i.e., democracy or benevolent king, etc.). Solomon's reign was an example of a just and lawful authority whereby the "people rejoiced" or were glad (lit. "brighten up"). Many kings followed in Israel who ruled in wickedness, bring great grief and mourning to the people. The character of leadership makes a vast difference in the response of the people governed.

Prov. 29:3

"Whoso loveth wisdom rejoiceth his father: but he that keepeth company with harlots spendeth his substance."

What does loving wisdom have to do not keeping company with harlots? Answer: —everything! Intimacy with God's wisdom makes for right decisions and proper evaluation of life. We must be filled with something, either good or bad. To be filled with "wisdom" is another way of saying "filled with Christ" (or the Holy Spirit), thus bearing His fruit. Not only will it give overcoming grace in regard to sexual sins, but will gladden (lit. brighten) one's father who delights in children who exemplify such wisdom.

Like the Prodigal in Luke 15, the rebellious son spent his substance (wealth) in "riotous living"—with prostitutes, among others. He was totally unwise and grieved his father who had given him the inheritance. That story ended well in that the son repented and came home to his father. But in most cases, that doesn't happen.

It's interesting how often Proverbs speaks of the deadly sins of fornication and adultery. The strongest of men (e.g., Sampson, David, etc.) have succumbed to the power of women, when they could otherwise conquer armies of men! How ironic! How necessary is wisdom to be "loved" which can prevent sin from happening and gladden those who care for us. "An ounce of prevention is worth a pound of cure."

Prov. 29:4

"The king by judgment establisheth the land: but he that receiveth gifts overthroweth it."

Here's the opposite of the theme of Judges:

"In those days there was no king in the land and every man did that which was right in his own eyes."

This proverb depicts a ruler who "establishes (stands, endures) the land" by justice; i.e., there's law and standards. There's stability to a country when it's founded on the Law and system of Justice. (e.g., early America).

On the other hand, **he that receiveth gifts** (contributions, bribes, graft, etc.) **overthroweth** (tears down, destroys) **it.** Here's the conflict between righteous and corrupt leaders. As the king goes, so goes the country. How many countries are run by gangsters and mafia kings! How many cities in America have been run by Mafia-bought politicians? The Church is also greatly influenced by corrupt, money-grabbing preachers! God help us!

Prov. 29:5

"A man that flattereth his neighbour spreadeth a net for his feet."

Smooth talkers are abundant! We discovered this wicked device in 26:28: *"...a flattering mouth worketh ruin."* So, **a man that flattereth his neighbor spreadeth a net for his** (neighbor's) **feet** (steps). This can tie in with vs. 4, where the "king" can be bought with smooth words of flattery.

At any rate, we are to "speak the truth in love." Flattery is hinged to deception—not telling the truth about a person in order to divide and conquer him; it becomes a net or snare for his feet, because people love to hear good things about themselves, even if they're not exactly true. This is part of the selfish nature of sin. Amazing how this "smooth talk" is practiced by politicians and preachers and suitors! How deceitful is the human heart that "takes people down" with the instrument of the tongue! (See James 3)

Prov. 29:6

"In the transgression of an evil man there is a snare: but the righteous doth sing and rejoice."

All people are sinful but there are some who are "evil"! This verse strikes a profound truth about man's depravity. Evil (translated "wickedness" in Genesis 13:13) is sin with a scheme or a "snare." Solomon says, **"In the transgression** (lit. revolt, sin) **of an evil man there is a snare** (lit. noose, hook, trap)**."**

Some people are just weak and fall into sin—doing what is selfish, etc. But "evil" people don't usually "fall into sin," but have a wicked agenda that involves others (e.g., Mafia—look upright, etc. but wickedly ruthless).See Isaiah 1:4; Romans 1:30ff. They are not only corrupt but corrupters of others (purposefully). They not only love sin itself, but delight in getting others "hooked" into their "program."

In contrast, see **the righteous doth sing** (lit. shout for joy) **and rejoice** (lit. make glad, bright). No agenda here, but rather joyous, unadulterated praise to the Lord!! How free it is to be a Spirit-filled believer, living in victory over sin and scheming wickedness! Some saints may temporarily slide back into a wicked mentality (e.g., King Saul), but it spells bondage, defeat and misery. There's no freedom like the freedom to do right, before God and man!

Prov. 29:7

"The righteous considereth the cause of the poor: but the wicked regardeth not to know it."

Our attitude toward those less fortunate than we, reveals our heart's condition. If we are "righteous" (*tsadeek*), then we love what (whom) God loves, and hate what God hates. Thus, he **considers** (knows) **the cause of the poor** (lowly, weak). The Lord's concern for the poor is channeled through the saint of God. The believer knows how God ministered to him when he was weak and undone (see Psalm 31:7); in fact, there's a promise of deliverance to those who concern themselves with the cause of the poor. Psalm 41:1:

"Blessed is he that considereth the poor: the LORD will deliver him in time of trouble."

In Prov. 21:12, the believer even treats his pets or animals with dignity; so much more then regarding humans in need. This is the same attitude that Paul commands in Galatians 6:1ff:

> *"Brethren, if a man be overtaken in a fault, ye which are spiritual, restore such an one in the spirit of meekness; considering thyself, lest thou also be tempted. Bear ye one another's burdens, and so fulfill the law of Christ."*

What we do for those who cannot pay us back determines the depth or rightness of our character.

But the wicked (ungodly) **regardeth** (considers) **not to know it.** A picture here of no concern—no desire to get involved with the poor. There's no "return" for such expenditure in energy and means. I only help those who can "pay back" or do something for me. ("you owe me one"). Sin is selfish! I'm concerned only about #1—that's me (I)! God has a word for such an attitude:

> *"Whoso stoppeth his ears at the cry of the poor, he also shall cry himself, but shall not be heard."* (Prov. 21:13)

Prov. 29:8

"Scornful men bring a city into a snare: but wise men turn away wrath."

Scornful men bring a city into a snare; a picture of political leadership that's divisive and arrogant (bragging) which can only stir the anger ("snare") of the people ("city"). Men, filled with selfish purposes, will produce disunity and chaos. (The word "snare"-*puach*, from the word for "puff," means here to "excite or inflame").

But the wise men turn away wrath; their attitude and strategy is right and their desire is for the good of the people. Thus, the results are constructive, rather than destructive. There's peace, instead of war.

Matthew Henry's statement is helpful, as he deals with the spiritual implications of this verse:

> "Who are the men that are the blessings of a land - the wise men who by promoting religion, which is true wisdom, turn away

the wrath of God, and who, by prudent counsels, reconcile contending parties and prevent the mischievous consequences of divisions. Proud and foolish men kindle the fires which wise and good men must extinguish."

Prov. 29:9

"If a wise man contendeth with a foolish man, whether he rage or laugh, there is no rest."

Some argue whether the wise man or the foolish man "rages or laughs" in this proverb. But it seems that the wise man is the subject throughout. The wise man here seems to be in some judicial position, dealing with a foolish offender who is perverted and hard-hearted. (see "fool's" in 12:16; 27:3).

The word "contend" (*shaphat*) means "to judge, litigate, decide a controversy." In the process, the wise litigator may approach the "fool" with indignation (anger, rage) or may be sarcastic, using lightness or laughter. This is a wise judge, thus he may deal with the situation from different angles to make the point of the man's guilt. But to no avail. There's no "rest" or effective, positive outcome because the fool "despises wisdom." Thus, it remains unsettled—no quietness, whether on the part of the wise man or the fool.

Prov. 29:10

'The bloodthirsty hate the upright: but the just seek his soul."

The bloodthirsty (lit. "men of bloods") **hate the upright.** Here's another comment on the bloodthirsty spirit of "Cain" (Genesis 4)! Solomon warned of this killer's instinct in Prov. 1:11f. Hatred and bloodshed go together; interesting how those obsessed with anger are enemies of those who live right (guiltless). Misery loves company—thus they must destroy those who are upright (verbally or otherwise).

But the just seek his soul. Whose soul? The "bloodthirsty" or the "upright"? I would choose the latter. Gill renders this verse as: "men that shed blood hate integrity; but the upright seek it." That is, the just seek "integrity" or seek to protect the upright man, rather than snuffing out his life. The just gravitate to other just ones.

Prov. 29:11

"A fool uttereth all his mind: but a wise man keepeth it in till afterwards."

The ability to control the tongue is the virtue of a mature or wise man. (See James 3). Only a fool "utters all his mind (lit. *ruach* - used here for life's spirit or passion)" or constantly reveals himself. We speak of those who "run at the mouth," stemming from an insatiable desire to be seen and heard.

The wise man **keepeth it** (thoughts or matter) **in till afterwards**; i.e., for an appropriate time to come. This has to do with discernment as well as timing.

Prov. 29:12

"If a ruler hearken to lies, all his servants are wicked."

It's amazing and significant how those wicked rulers surround themselves with wicked advisors! A president or dictator appoints to his cabinet those who are basically like him. "Birds of a feather flock together."

For the ruler to "hearken to" (give heed to) lies, they must be coming from his servants (advisors?). This could be personal counsel or war intelligence, etc. For example, Ahab's false prophets told him what he wanted to hear. The "if" clause here may indicate that the ruler knows he's being lied to but follows the advice anyway.

Prov. 29:13

"The poor and the deceitful man meet together: the LORD lighteneth both their eyes."

In this world, **the poor and the deceitful** (lit. oppressor) **man meet together**. Somehow there's room for both, even though the poor are unfairly treated by those who are "usurers"—lenders of money (see K&D). Yet, the balancing factor is that **the LORD lighteneth** (illuminates) **both their eyes**; i.e., both know what's going on and are aware of God's sustaining and eventual judgment. Both will one day stand before the LORD and give account of their lives. This is where the "unfair" becomes fair and just.

Prov. 29:14

"The king that faithfully judgeth the poor, his throne shall be established for ever."

That the Lord has a burden for the poor and weak is not a secret. Thus, He promotes special blessing upon those who also care for the needy. See Psalm 41:1; Prov. 14:31; 19:17, etc. But here we have a manifestation of that caring spirit on the part of **the king that faithfully judgeth the poor**. That is, he treats them fairly and just, without condescension or taking advantage of their lowly estate.

This is really an expression of the kings' faith and obedience to God; he doesn't treat the poor any differently than the rich (who can "pay back"). Thus, this king is "established" and secured on his throne. This seems like a clear type or example of the Lord Jesus—the servant of men who "reigns forever"! For "though he was rich, yet for our sakes, he became poor, that we through his poverty might become rich."!!

Prov. 29:15

"The rod and reproof give wisdom: but a child left to himself bringeth his mother to shame."

Certainly a key principle of rearing children is this proverb. "Wisdom" or skillful living is not some ethereal or abstract experience that just comes upon a child. The parent's privilege and responsibility is to use "the rod and reproof" to enhance the process. Note the need for corporal (rod) and verbal (reproof, instruction, etc.) together which God uses to instill wisdom and understanding. It's teaching accompanied by incentive or sometimes literal force. Such is the mentality of "Boot Camp" in the Marines! (Compare Prov. 13:24; 23:13)

But to deny the child this discipline is to "hate" him and may bring "his mother to shame." This is just basic instruction in "training up a child" (20:6), thus cooperating with the Lord who alone can change children's hearts.

Prov. 29:16

"When the wicked are multiplied, transgression increaseth: but the righteous shall see their fall."

More sinners produce more wickedness! **When the wicked are multiplied, transgression** (lit. revolt, rebellion) **increaseth** (same word as 'multiply'). Peer pressure is powerful and addictive. Amazing how differently people act at a party than when they're alone. Yes, there is individual rebellion, but a crowd of rebels will multiply or fan the flame of wickedness (transgression—sinful acts toward others). They find strength and courage in numbers.

But the righteous shall see their fall. The godly will outlast the wicked and witness their ruin. Righteousness will prevail!

Prov. 29:17

"Correct thy son, and he shall give thee rest; yea, he shall give delight unto thy soul."

Because of the curse, there's a warfare to every aspect of living. Even in raising children, the rebellion (i.e., Cain spirit) must be put down and dealt with. Thus, Solomon's injunction to **correct thy son, and he shall give thee rest.** The word "correct" here, *yasar*, involves chastening (by blows and words), instruction, and training. A son left to himself will fail; in addition, the discipline yields peace and quiet in the household and in the father's heart.

What's more, to witness the progress of a son's effective training will "give delight" (pleasure) to the father's "soul" (*nephesh*). How precious and delightful it is to witness true wisdom in a son!

Prov. 29:18

"Where there is no vision, the people perish: but he that keepeth the law, happy is he."

People, like sheep, need direction from their Creator Shepherd. He has given the "law and the prophets" which reveal His will. "Visions" (*chazon*- revelation, oracle) were given to His messengers in conjunction with the Law to instruct His people (See 1 Samuel 3:1; 1 Chronicles 17:15; Isaiah 1:1, etc.) Here was a direct word

477

from God for direct action. So, **he that keepeth the law, happy** (*asher* - cf. Psalm 1:1) **is he.**

Peter mentions a *"more sure word of prophecy"* in 1 Peter 1; viz., the written Word of God itself. The Word is that Divine Vision of God, and to obey it is both safe and satisfying. Fresh "vision" is derived by the absorption and outworking of daily, fresh Manna.

Note K&D on this verse:

> "Torah (Law) denotes divine teaching, the word of God; whether that of the Sinaitic or that of the prophetic law (2Ch_15:3, cf. e.g., Isa_1:10). While, on the one hand, a people is in a dissolute condition when the voice of the preacher, speaking from divine revelation, and enlightening their actions and sufferings by God's word, is silent amongst them (Psa_74:9, cf. Amo_8:12); on the other hand, that same people are to be praised as happy when they show due reverence and fidelity to the word of God, both as written and as preached. That the word of God is preached among a people belongs to their condition of life; and they are only truly happy when they earnestly and willingly subordinate themselves to the word of God which they possess and have the opportunity of hearing."

Barnes adds:

> "The "wise man," the son of David, has seen in the prophets and in their work the condition of true national blessedness. The darkest time in the history of Israel had been when there "was no open vision 1Sa_3:1; at such a time the people "perish," are let loose, "are left to run wild.""

Prov. 29:19

"A servant will not be corrected by words: for though he understand he will not answer."

This proverb reveals the stubborn, rebellious nature of man. Here's a "servant" without a servant spirit; instead he takes after his father Cain, who heard God but refused to heed! Even though this servant "understands" the admonition, "he will not answer," whether verbally or by action. How typical this is of children and others who ignore or defy those in authority. The attempt to be "neutral" or nonresponsive is in itself rebellion! In principle, this is our response to God Himself, thus demanding repentance and the necessity of a "new heart."! See 26:3

Prov. 29:20

"Seest thou a man that is hasty in his words? there is more hope of a fool than of him."

How and what we speak is indicative of who we are. James says, in essence, that a man who doesn't offend others with his words (tongue) is a "perfect" (mature) man. Here Solomon exhorts us to watch **a man that is hasty** (lit to be pressed, hurried) **in his words**; he may not yet be a "fool" (stupid, silly), but will lose credibility and cause others to place more confidence in a foolish man. See 21:5; 26:12.

This proverb is a poetic way of describing the plight of one who "runs at the mouth," revealing his lack of intellect, wisdom and spiritual maturity. Wesley's note is well taken; "Hasty - Who is rash and heady in the management of his affairs."

Prov. 29:21

"He that delicately bringeth up his servant from a child shall have him become his son at the length."

Biological sonship is not the only kind of sonship. There is legal adoption and spiritual adoption in Christ (Romans 8:16ff.); such become legitimate or bona fide children, although previously born into another family. This proverb, however, speaks to a unique situation whereby a master so loves and nurtures his servant from a child that he becomes his "son" in the end.

This is a precious thought which illustrates that parental relationships are not always "blood" related, but can develop through a process of true love. Interesting is the phrase, **delicately bringeth up**; the word is *panaq*--piel verb, meaning "to pamper or treat delicately." It may be implied that this man had no biological son and therefore raised his servant as a son. In the end, the legacy and inheritance of the father (master) will become the servant's, who has entered all the rights and privileges of his "father." What an illustration of *"the Spirit of adoption, whereby we cry, 'Abba, Father'"*!

Prov. 29:22

"An angry man stirreth up strife, and a furious man aboundeth in transgression."

Anger and rage not only "stir up strife (contention, discord) but further result in the "abundance" of "transgression" (lit. revolt). Where there's smoke, there's fire. Ungodly anger can only reap further discord and unrest. That's why in 15:18 Solomon gives the contrast; viz., the one who is "slow to anger" and thus appeases the wrath, so that peace may result.

There certainly a place for righteous anger, standing for the right cause, but a murderous anger can only "kill" the peace and unity of those involved.

Prov. 29:23

"A man's pride shall bring him low: but honour shall uphold the humble in spirit."

It's been said that "the way up is the way down." Jesus said in Matthew 23:12 that *"whosoever shall exalt himself shall be abased; and he that shall humble himself shall be exalted,"* That's the irony of Scripture! So in this proverb, **a man's pride** (lit. arrogance) **shall bring him low**—no doubt about it; just a matter of time; even if he is locked up in Hell for eternity!

In contrast, **honour** (lit glory, *kabod*) **shall uphold** (sustain) **the humble in spirit.** Notice that the "humility" here is not just external or physical position, but in "spirit." This man is powerful and blessed, because God honors a meek and contrite heart. He hates and resists the proud, but gives grace to the humble. See James 4:6.

Prov. 29:24

"Whoso is partner with a thief hateth his own soul: he heareth cursing, and bewrayeth it not."

There's such a thing as betraying oneself. Sin is the tragedy of humanity without God; it (sin) not only alienates a man from his Creator, but reflects a hatred for his own soul! Solomon gives the example of one who **is partner with a thief**; i.e., he's involved with someone who can only corrupt him further. Paul admonishes: *"Be not deceived; evil communications* (companions) *corrupt good manners* (character)*."* (1 Corinthians 15:33). Sin is not only God's enemy, it is ours as well. It prevents a man (or woman) from enjoying the blessings that only God can bestow. To "hang out" with a "thief" reveals our character and further exacerbates our temptation to sin.

Furthermore, such companionship weakens one's conscience and ability to take a stand in other areas of life. So, **he heareth cursing and bewrayeth it not.** What does "bewray" mean here? The verb means "to expose or denounce." In a compromised position we lose the ability and will to confront or rebuke evil. We "go along to get along," and only heap sin upon sin. That is indeed the opposite of loving truth and our true person.

Prov. 29:25

"The fear of man bringeth a snare: but whoso putteth his trust in the LORD shall be safe."

If we fear God, we need not fear! Everyone fears something or someone; thus, the necessity to "fear the LORD" (cf. 1:7). *"God hath not given us the spirit of fear; but of power and of love, and of a sound mind"* (2 Timothy 1:7). Putting our "trust in the LORD" results in "safety." In other words, the fear of God and trust (faith) go together, as Siamese twins.

The fear of man is a "snare" (lit. noose, trap). But fearing or trusting God is security and freedom of soul! To fear God is to take Him seriously; i.e., to trust and obey. This dispels the "fear of man." Fear and anxiety cannot exist together with true faith.

Two birds were discussing their lot in life compared to humans.

Said the Robin to the Sparrow:

Friend, I would really like to know,
Why these humans rush around and worry so;

Said the Sparrow to the Robin:

I guess that it must be,
That they have no Heavenly Father such as you and me.

Prov. 29:26

"Many seek the ruler's favour; but every man's judgment cometh from the LORD."

Justice and reward are ultimately in the hand of the LORD. Men **seek** (lit. strive after) **the ruler's** (i.e., authority) **favor** (lit. face), **but...judgment** (justice, verdict) **cometh from the LORD.** We may seek the approval of those in authority, but, in the long run, the ultimate and personal evaluation is only in God's hands.

Those in authority may or may not think us reputable; but God alone knows what we are, and will judge us accordingly. Men do thrive on the applause and approval of other men, but it is where we stand with the Lord that makes the difference in time and eternity. See 19:21; 21:1.

Prov. 29:27

"An unjust man is an abomination to the just: and he that is upright in the way is abomination to the wicked."

What a man loves and what he hates is a revelation of his heart. God in His Word makes clear what He loves and hates; e.g., He loves righteousness, but hates sin. So a godly man, indwelt and controlled by the Holy Spirit, lines up with God's character. He loves what God loves and hates what God hates. The unsaved man has the opposite mentality; he hates what God loves, and loves what God hates.

Therefore, on the human level, **an unjust man** (lit. perverted) **is an abomination** (disgust) **to the just** (righteous)**: and he that is upright** (lit. straight) **in the way** (course of life) **is abomination** (disgust) **to the wicked.** Check out this fundamental battle ground! This is, and always will be, a line drawn between saints and sinners; just like the division between God and Satan or Heaven and Hell.

The righteous man will associate and love the unrighteous person, but will recoil within over their wicked actions. On the other hand, sinners will tolerate, to some degree, the lifestyle of the righteous, but underneath it all they have an utter contempt and disgust for godliness. Why? Because they hate the Righteous God Himself and cannot stand those who represent the righteous standard of God. See John 15:17-19.

Chapter 30
The Wisdom of Agur

Prov. 30:1

"The words of Agur the son of Jakeh, even the prophecy: the man spake unto Ithiel, even unto Ithiel and Ucal,"

In 30:1-6 we have the profession or testimony of "Agur." No one seems to be sure who he was. The name is a passive participle meaning "gathered (that is, received among the sages)." Some believe it's a "fanciful name for Solomon" (Strong's). Whatever the case, these prophetic words have found their way into Holy Writ.

The direct recipients "Ithiel and Ucal" are unknown. The prophecy here is more a "forth-telling" than a foretelling. Although in vs. 4 there is a prophetic reference to Christ the Son of God.

Prov. 30:2

"Surely I am more brutish than any man, and have not the understanding of a man."

Surely I am more brutish than any man. Agur here testifies of his utter "brutishness" or stupidity in contrast to the knowledge and wisdom of God (vs. 3f.). He says in essence "I am the least of all the brethren" (mankind). This is not a "put down" of himself, but a true vision of his unworthiness and bankruptcy apart from the God of Heaven. This was Asaph's evaluation of himself when he was faced with his unbelief in Psalm 73:22: *"So foolish was I, and ignorant: I was as a beast before thee."*

I **have not the understanding of a man.** The context demands that apart from a true relationship with God, a man is not a true man; i.e., he lacks the ability to think as a man should. Understanding separates man from beast, but apart from God , men

485

act as "animals." (e.g., "party animal, animal farm," etc.) In fact, he's worse than an animal who responds appreciatively to his master and creator (cf. Isaiah 1:3).

Prov. 30:3

"I neither learned wisdom, nor have the knowledge of the holy."

Vs. 3 clarifies the previous thought (vs. 2). He's bemoaning the fact that he has not **learned wisdom**, nor **the knowledge of the holy** (i.e., the divine or sacred; reference to God - *Chadosh*). A beast is only concerned about this world (existence), but a man is a creature of two worlds—earth and Heaven. We live in the present circumstance, but hopefully with our future destination in view. To lack the "knowledge of the holy" is to be ill prepared for either world. Thus, the utter necessity of the Word of God to find out who He is, and thus who we are in Him (2 Timothy 3:16, 17).

See A.W. Tozer's book, "The Knowledge of the Holy," which is a practical and yet profound exposition of the attributes of God.

Prov. 30:4

"Who hath ascended up into heaven, or descended? who hath gathered the wind in his fists? who hath bound the waters in a garment? who hath established all the ends of the earth? what is his name, and what is his son's name, if thou canst tell?"

This is a tremendous prophecy regarding "the knowledge of the Holy One" - Jesus Christ. (vs. 3). God has a Son, and sent Him into the world.

"For God so loved the world, that he gave his only begotten Son, that whosoever believeth in him should not perish, but have everlasting life." (John 3:16)

I thought this might be helpful to support the descriptive character of God in this proverb by using other Scripture passages. A perusal of these texts would certainly bless and edify the reader. (From The Treasury of Scriptural Knowledge—TSK)

"Who hath ascended…" Deut. 30:12; John 3:13; Rom. 10:6; Eph. 4:9, Eph. 4:10

"who hath gathered..." Job 38:4-41; Psa. 104:2-35; Isa. 40:12-31, Isa. 53:8

"what is his name..." Ex. 3:13-15, Ex. 6:3, Ex. 34:5-7; Deut. 28:58

"and what is his son's name..." Gen. 32:29; Jdg. 13:18; Psa. 2:7; Isa. 7:14, Isa. 9:6; Jer. 23:6; Matt. 1:21-23; Matt. 11:27; Lk. 10:22

These verses supply a beautiful commentary on this powerful theme of God and His Son, Jesus Christ, the Only Mediator between God and man; the One who spans the universe and holds the "wind" and the "waters" in His hand! He is "Jacob's Ladder," the One who has both "descended into the lowest parts of the earth," and has "ascended up far above all heavens that he might fill all things" (Ephesians 4:8-10)!

Prov. 30:5

"Every word of God is pure: he is a shield unto them that put their trust in him."

Every word of God is pure. The totality of God's Word is pure in the sense of "refined and tested true." The verb means "to smelt, refine, or test" (cf. Psalm 19:8). Because it is pure, the Word can purify and cleanse the soul. (Psalm 19:7). Cf. also – Psalm 12:6; 18:30; 19:8; 119:140; Romans 7:12; James 3:17.

In addition, **he** (God) **is a shield** (protector, defender) **unto them that put their trust in him.** The Word of God is not only our offense, but defense. (cf. the whole armour of God in Ephesians 6:10ff.). The word for "trust" here is used of one "fleeing for protection, thus to confide in; to have hope." Indeed, our "hope is in the Lord!"

Prov. 30:6

"Add thou not unto his words, lest he reprove thee, and thou be found a liar."

Tamper with the Word of God and He will deal with you! This is an age-old axiom of supreme importance. This is the issue of false religions and even modern translations which "add" to God's word. Man has taken liberties which have no sanction of God. How the fleshly mind lacks proper reverence for God and His Word! Such attitudes and actions are not without great price; i.e., the reproof and judgment of God.

Thus, the writer says: **Add thou not unto his words, lest he reprove thee, and thou be found a liar.** Let God be true, and every man a liar! God's reproof (rebuke-Psalm 38:1; correction-Prov. 3:12; chasten-2 Samuel 7:14) attends those who deal frivolously with God's word. Thy Word is Truth, once-for-all settled in Heaven. Irreverent men can only be fools, and exposed as liars. Unfortunately, that doesn't stop men from tampering with the Word of God.

This is a vast subject which cannot be adequately addressed here. In our day, multitudes of translations and paraphrases are in circulation, and have actually confused the issue rather than bringing clarification. The Word is spiritually understood (1 Corinthians 2:14); it is not just a matter of intellectual "simplicity" (e.g., newspaper vocabulary, like the so-called Good News for Modern Man version).

In this verse is also comfort and protection; i.e., God's reproof and exposure when we go astray. This may be the primary teaching of this text, that God is protecting His word and will deal with those who add to it (or subtract from it). Great care must be taken here. The Word is God's Special and Infallible Revelation of Himself to mankind (2 Timothy 3:16, 17). Take heed how you use it!

Prov. 30:7

"Two things have I required of thee; deny me them not before I die:"

The writer here makes a request (of God) for "two things." He pleads that that they be not denied, but become reality before he dies. (cf. vss. 8, 9 for the content of this request)

Prov. 30:8

"Remove far from me vanity and lies: give me neither poverty nor riches; feed me with food convenient for me:"

Here is the two-fold request from the previous verse: 1)

Remove far from me vanity and lies: 2) **Give me neither poverty nor riches; feed me with food convenient** (i.e., prescribed portion, due) **for me.** The first request deals with his character (moral life), while the second regards economic and physical sustenance.

He's asking God to keep vanity and lies completely away from him. Vanity is worthlessness and emptiness—a life that is of no account. Solomon speaks much of this in Ecclesiastes—*"Vanity of vanities, all is vanity and vexation of spirit."* In wisdom, Solomon did not want to waste his life; i.e., one without purpose and wholeness. He certainly did not want to live a "lie" or one of deception. He wanted truth, not falsehood. My grandson, Justin, used to say: "Life is too short to live a lie!" That's in agreement with this text.

Observe the writer's balance regarding riches—"neither poverty nor riches;" i.e., just what I need, nothing more or nothing less (incl. food and nourishment). It might be argued here that Solomon was the richest man in the world at that time and didn't have to worry about money, etc. But remember that early in his kingship when asked by God what he wanted most, he requested not riches, but wisdom to lead the people. That demonstrated where his heart was. God answered that prayer, but "threw in" the riches over and above. A great example of Matthew 6:33.

Prov. 30:9

*"Lest I be full, and deny thee, and say, Who is the LORD? or lest
I be poor, and steal, and take the name of my God in vain."*

The writer continues his thought from the previous verse (8), regarding his economic status. He realizes that even his daily sustenance is appointed ("convenient"—vs. 8) by God. Thus he pleads for a balance of provision so as not to be tempted to sin. Give me my appointed lot, **lest I be full** (excessively) **and deny** (deal falsely or fail) **thee, and say, Who is the LORD?**

The temptation in the above statement seems to center around the dulling effect of constantly having more than we need. If every meal is a "buffet," why would we ever have to pray for "our daily bread?" In other words, the soul can become as insensitive as the satiated body, thus blurring our spiritual vision and utter dependence on the LORD. Deception can overtake our simple faith now that we have so much; "who needs the LORD?—we're doing well without Him!" This scenario would be a tragic sin, lie and failure.

The other extreme is likewise wrong: **or lest I be poor** (impoverished)**, and steal, and take the name of my God in vain.** Not that he would have to steal if poor, but the temptation would be there. Stealing would dishonor the Lord's name—a failure to trust His character of faithfulness (Matthew 6:33). All sin is an affront to God's character, represented and revealed by His Name.

The thought of blaming God is involved here. Man is fickle— denying his need for God when he's full, but then being angry at God when he doesn't have enough. When I prosper, it's my "fault" (doing); but when things go wrong, it's God's fault. That's how the sinful mind thinks.

Barnes note is worth stating here:

> "The special dangers of the two extremes. Wealth tempts to pride, unbelief, and a scorn like that of Pharaoh (Exo. 5:2); poverty to dishonesty, and then to perjury or to the hypocritical profession of religion which is practically identical with it."

Prov. 30:10

"Accuse not a servant unto his master, lest he curse thee, and thou be found guilty."

Even a servant or slave has rights. The main thrust here seems to be an admonition against meddling with someone else's servant. Paul states, *"Who are thou that judgest another man's servant? to his own master he standeth or falleth."* (Romans 14:4)

The relationship between master and servant was often an endearing one. To "accuse" or slander a servant before his master could be very offensive and costly. **Lest he curse thee.** Who? The master may be the subject here—the one who is offended and threatened by the accusation of his servant. He will defend that servant to the hilt and you will **be found guilty**; i.e., the whole thing will backfire on you, the accuser.

Some make the servant the one who "curses" or treats lightly (cf.1 Samuel 18:23) the offender. That certainly could be the case. But what authority would he have to pursue the offender's crime? I should think the master himself would safeguard his servant and confront the accuser.

This certainly applies to our God and Master who intercedes for His servants. He says, *"No weapon that is formed against thee shall prosper...,"* We stand or fall before Him, regardless of Satan's slanderous attacks against us. *"Greater is He that is within us...."*

Prov. 30:11

"There is a generation that curseth their father, and doth not bless their mother."

Here is an exclamation depicting a particular "generation" (three others to follow) and its characteristics. It sounds like the present generation for sure! (Note that three other "generations" are described in vss. 12-14.) This first-mentioned is one that **curseth their father, and doth not bless their mother.** I immediately think of the Commandment to *"Honor thy father and thy mother."* Paul says that one of the signs of the last days is being *"disobedient to parents"* (cf. 2 Timothy 3:1ff.).

The word "curse" means "to trifle, to esteem lightly." There is no respect here, no fear of God, which would produce submission to those in authority, especially a father. Furthermore, there's no natural affection and adoration for mothers. "Bless" is *barak*, used both to "kneel" and "bless or adore someone" (e.g., the Lord and/or others of respect). Sin has paid its toll even in our homes where little respect and true love exist. Ironically, it could be said that those who love us the most we treat the worst.

Prov. 30:12

"There is a generation that are pure in their own eyes, and yet is not washed from their filthiness."

Another generation is **pure in their own eyes, and yet is not washed from their filthiness** (lit. excrement, dung). How proud and deceitful is the sinful heart! (Jeremiah 17:9). Lucifer paraded his sinful pride in the very presence of God (Ezekiel 28:15), denying his "filthiness." So his children do the same (John 8:44). We look into a mirror of our own making and never see the "dung" covering our faces.

In our generation we have trampled on the Word of God, which alone mirrors our true condition. Without the Law and the conviction of the Holy Spirit, no sinner will ever see his true condition, much less be cleansed from his "filthiness."

Prov. 30:13

"There is a generation, O how lofty are their eyes! and their eyelids are lifted up."

How expressive are these poetic metaphors to describe those filled with themselves: "lofty eyes" and "exalted eyelids"! Here is the high and mighty look—the arrogance of pride. It smacks of Lucifer himself, whose "heart was lifted up" because of his beauty and corrupted God's wisdom "by reason of his brightness" (Ezekiel 28:17). The "children of wrath" take on the characteristics of their spiritual father (Satan). Like father, like son! (cf. Ephesians 2:1-3)

Prov. 30:14

"There is a generation, whose teeth are as swords, and their jaw teeth as knives, to devour the poor from off the earth, and the needy from among men."

Lofty eyes bite! There's an undeniable connection between a haughty countenance and the mouth which speaks lofty things. Arrogance is manifested in the "teeth" that cut and devour. It's particularly evident in the treatment of the "poor and needy"—those who cannot stand up to the proud. This pictures those who oppress the downtrodden with the power and cutting force of their mouths.

Prov. 30:15

"The horseleach hath two daughters, crying, Give, give. There are three things that are never satisfied, yea, four things say not, It is enough:"

These two verses (15, 16) grant a vivid description or illustration of insatiable greed. "The horseleach" is a "blood-sucker" or leech. Poetically it has "two daughters" (offspring) who cry "give, give" (we want, we want...)! The picture centers on those who "are never satisfied"—who never have enough. It's like these "daughters" are bloated and ready to burst with avarice and super-abundance; yet, they are still not satisfied. He then illustrates the point from the natural realm in verse 16.

Prov. 30:16

"The grave; and the barren womb; the earth that is not filled with water; and the fire that saith not, It is enough."

Four things that are never satisfied: 1) **The grave**-*sheol*, "the underworld, grave or pit;" translated "hell" in 27:20. This is not just a hole in the ground but rather a place of departed spirits. (cf. Habakkuk 2:5) 2) **The barren** (closed) **womb**; 3) **The earth that is not filled** (satisfied) **with water**. Dry ground is always thirsty. 4) **The fire** that never says "it is enough." These are all insatiable.

Prov. 30:17

"The eye that mocketh at his father, and despiseth to obey his mother, the ravens of the valley shall pick it out, and the young eagles shall eat it."

Here's a bleak picture of judgment upon children who "mock" their parents and refuse to obey them. That rebellion is manifest through the "eye" more than just the mouth. God judges rebellion on both sides of the grave. This text suggests an untimely death with no burial; the corpse lies in an open field subject to the ravens and eagles which feed on the dead. The very eye that mocks authority is plucked and eaten by carnivorous fowl! Quite a gruesome end. The antidote: *"Children, obey your parents in the Lord"*; Why? *"For this is right"* (cf. Ephesians 6:1-3)!

Prov. 30:18

"There be three things which are too wonderful for me, yea, four which I know not:"

Here's the poetic introduction for the next verse (vs. 19—the four things). The writer is about to describe four pictures which make him ecstatic and somewhat awestruck; a scenario that he exclaims is "too wonderful" and beyond understanding.

Prov. 30:19

"The way of an eagle in the air; the way of a serpent upon a rock; the way of a ship in the midst of the sea; and the way of a man with a maid."

1. **The way** (course) **of an eagle in the air** (lofty sky). What a spectacular sight! How high he flies, cruising the air currents, etc. How far he can see from dazzling heights—a unique creature of God.

2. **The way of a serpent** (snake) **upon a rock.** So beautiful, but so deadly! (cf. Genesis 3:1f.) Yet, naturally, a great work of art, fulfilling God's purpose. This creature demonstrates subtle poise, along with its mysterious movement.

3. **The way of a ship in the midst of the sea.** It's an amazing sight to watch such a large vessel float and move across the horizon! To turn its course via a small rudder is also part of the wonder.

4. **The way of a man with a maid** (*alma* - lass, young woman, virgin). This expression of courting between a man and woman is probably the ultimate when it comes to understanding and wonder. People are indeed most fascinating and complex. How a young man woos a young lady is a world all of its own. It's filled with mystery and wonder, and no one has "a handle" on the process. There are no experts here. But how beautiful is this divine institution of marriage, which has been so desecrated in our day.

Prov. 30:20

"Such is the way of an adulterous woman; she eateth, and wipeth her mouth, and saith, I have done no wickedness."

Here's an analogy ("such is the way") between the spectacular ways of the 4 things mentioned in vs. 19 and the mystique of an "adulterous woman." Just as the legitimate beauty of the "eagle," etc. so there's a warped and subtle quality of a harlot; she can do her "dirty work" just like it's all on the up and up (legitimate). When she's done, she can eat a hearty meal, wipe her mouth (without shame) and declare, "I have done nothing wrong,"

So is the "wonder" of wickedness, which can deceive and harden the conscience—going on like sin doesn't even exist. Only the Holy Spirit can bring conviction of sin to the human, depraved heart.

Prov. 30:21

"For three things the earth is disquieted, and for four which it cannot bear:"

An interesting poetic scheme is used here regarding that which "shakes" the earth and becomes intolerable ("cannot bear" or take). Using four illustrations (citing two men and two women), he describes unbearable circumstances.

Prov. 30:22

"For a servant when he reigneth; and a fool when he is filled with meat;"

First, a bondservant who comes to a place of authority (reign); the inference is that he will become tyrannical and arrogant, expressing his bitterness for being suppressed. While resenting his servitude, when given the opportunity to rule, he manifests the same attitude which he once despised.

Likewise, "a fool...filled up with meat (food and drink);" if he acts like a fool when he's hungry, we can only imagine how asinine are his actions when he has all he needs (wants)!

Prov. 30:23

"For an odious woman when she is married; and an handmaid that is heir to her mistress."

Another troubling situation is an **odious woman when she is married.** The word for "odious" depicts one who is hated, from *sane,* "to hate." (cf. Genesis 24:60; Psalm 18:40) The inference is a difficult, selfish woman who is despised by others, and upon marriage, her distasteful attitude is magnified, especially toward her husband.

Barnes comments that this

> "odious woman (is) one in whom there is nothing loveable. Marriage, which to most women is the state in which they find scope for their highest qualities, becomes to her only a sphere in which to make herself and others miserable."

A similar attitude is evident in a handmaid (female slave) who has been "liberated," and then disinherits her mistress. The privilege and new authority "go to her head," making life unbearable for those around her. Cf. Gill's notes.

Principle: Those given authority will soon reveal who they really are.

Prov. 30:24

"There be four things which are little upon the earth, but they are exceeding wise:"

Smallness in size and/or insignificance do not negate the ability to be wise. In verses 24-28, the writer describes the uncanny prudence of four little creatures on earth who demonstrate how God equips His creatures for their ordained purpose. There's no way to explain their "exceeding wisdom" (*chakam, chakam*- lit. wise, being wise, or double wisdom) through the hoax of evolution. Rather, God has chosen to implant this prudence into His "little ones" by creative decree, redounding to His Glory!

Prov. 30:25

"The ants are a people not strong, yet they prepare their meat in the summer;"

Ants are fascinating creatures; considered a "people" (unit, congregation) because of their instinctive wisdom and diligence (cf. Prov. 6:6-8). Not to be confused with humans, of course, yet considered a phenomenon of nature. They are **not strong, yet they**

prepare their meat (food) **in the summer**. Thus, they are ready for the winter months. Here is a wise example for humans to follow.

Prov. 30:26

"The conies are but a feeble folk, yet make they their houses in the rocks;"

"Conies" are like "rock rabbits;" they are "feeble" (lit. "not strong"), yet they "make" (or set) their houses in the cliff or "rocks." In wisdom, they have chosen a place of refuge and safety.

We might make a spiritual application here. As in Numbers 2:11, 12, the rock is a symbol of Christ our Refuge. *"The name of the LORD is a strong tower: the righteous runneth into it and is safe,"* Cf. 1 Corinthians 10:4, where Christ is identified as the "spiritual Rock that followed them (Israel)" in the wilderness.

Prov. 30:27

"The locusts have no king, yet go they forth all of them by bands;"

The writer continues to describe God's natural creatures and their unique qualities. These examples serve not only to understand and marvel in God's awesomeness, but to inform and challenge man's life on earth. Much ado is made about man's need of a "king" or leader; yet the "locusts" (grasshopper?) have no king, yet go...forth...by bands" (lit. divided). Instinctively, they perform their tasks together, while divided in units. Amazing creatures, indeed. Cf. Joel 2:7, 8.

Prov. 30:28

"The spider taketh hold with her hands, and is in kings' palaces."

The spider (lit. lizard, gecko) **takes hold with her hands, and is in kings palaces.** Just another example of God's great and perfect creation which makes room for a small spider in a majestic setting (i.e., palace). Very few humans would have such privilege, but a "lizard" can go and survive in that environment. We must not despise the "day of small things, for there's a place and purpose for all that God has made.

Prov. 30:29

There be three things which go well, yea, four are comely in going:

Here's a list of four more creatures that God has made to be "comely" or stately: The lion, greyhound, he-goat and king. These further illustrate the uniqueness, majesty and purpose of God's creation. There's no way to relegate these creatures to the Godless, chance theory of evolution.

Solomon is constantly reinforcing the God-centered creationism of his father David (cf. Psalm 19:1-6).

Prov. 30:30

A lion which is strongest among beasts, and turneth not away for any;

How unique is **a lion which is strongest among beasts.** The word "strongest" is *gibbor* meaning "a brave or mighty man, champion (cf.1 Samuel 17:51)." So the lion is King of the beasts **and turneth not away for any.** He knows who he is and thus stands his ground, not backing up, backing down, or running away from any other animal. This speaks graphically and typically of the Lion of Judah and the righteous who are "bold as a lion."

It's interesting that K&D translates this verse as, "The lion, the hero among beasts, and that turneth back before nothing."

Prov. 30:31

"A greyhound; an he goat also; and a king, against whom there is no rising up."

The word rendered "greyhound" (*zarzeer)* is found only here. It literally means to be "girded or slender in the waist," probably referring to a swift moving animal. In fact the MKJV (Modern King James Version) translates it as "one girded in the loins." Whatever its identity, it is listed among God's stately creatures, along with the "he-goat" (buck).

The fourth member listed is **a king, against whom there is no**

rising up;" i.e., he is the authority whom no one resists. He is stately, in charge, majestic, etc., and none will successfully oppose him. Cf. 16:14; 20:2.

Prov. 30:32

"If thou hast done foolishly in lifting up thyself, or if thou hast thought evil, lay thine hand upon thy mouth."

The writer ends this chapter with a practical means of controlling the tongue—by placing the hand over the mouth. **If** (or although) **thou hast done foolishly in lifting up thyself**; i.e., you've exalted yourself in pride, knowing it's wrong, then use your hand, if necessary, to prevent any further damage from coming out of your mouth. In other words, "hold your tongue."

Or if thou hast thought evil; the idea here is a plot or scheme in the mind to do evil. Thus, before you speak about it, cover your mouth! Obviously, the problem is in the heart or mind; but hopefully while that is in process of being remedied, one need not aggravate the situation further by releasing words which reveal the problem.

Prov. 30:33

"Surely the churning of milk bringeth forth butter, and the wringing of the nose bringeth forth blood: so the forcing of wrath bringeth forth strife."

Here's an interesting "triplet" used in the finale of this chapter. The three words "churning, wringing and forcing" are the same Hebrew noun *meets*, meaning "pressure or squeezing" (Found only in this verse). The picture includes three scenarios, each yielding a result: 1) churning (pressure) on milk produces butter; 2) wringing (pressing) the nose will yield blood; and 3) insensible "forcing" (pressure) of anger leads to strife (contention).

This seems to be a lesson in the pros and cons of "pressure." Certainly, the production of butter through churning is positive. The "wringing of the nose" suggests some confrontation between two adversaries, although there's not enough information to make a judgment. The third seems to infer the wrong or excessive use of pressure which creates further undo pressure! It might just be a lack of discerning the situation and those involved. Whatever the case, it takes wisdom to do the right thing at the right time in the right way.

Chapter 31
The Words of King Lemuel's Mother

Prov. 31:1

"The words of king Lemuel, the prophecy that his mother taught him."

Again here, as in Ch. 30, we have an annex to Solomon's proverbs. Here is another "prophecy;" this time from "king Lemuel" of whom we have no information. (Possibly this is a symbolic name for Solomon.) Yet God has preserved these proverbs in Holy Writ with the same weightiness as the rest of the book.

Significantly, the following words were taught to him by his mother. How this emphasizes the utter importance of a mother's life and ministry in the home. What power and influence a mother has on her children! This has been all but forgotten in our 21st Century. Families are confused and shattered. The institution of marriage itself is under demonic attack, undermining God's role and purpose of strong parental leadership.

Lemuel's sound instructions are the product of a faithful Mom. He further culminates this prophecy with his own classic description of a godly woman (wife, mother, etc.) in vss. 10-31. Evidently, his mother reflected these qualities—what a heritage! O, for men and women to return to their God-intended roles.

Prov. 31:2

"What, my son? and what, the son of my womb? and what, the son of my vows?"

The king here testifies regarding the words and instruction of his mother. (vs. 1) This is a call to remembrance—a direct challenge and confrontation regarding, among other things, strange "women" (vs. 3). Thus, the mother's emphasis is 3-fold: 1) **What my son?** 2) **what, the son of my womb?** and 3) **what, the son of my vows?**

Significantly, we're struck with a meaningful description and emphasis. Lemuel was not only his mother's biological son or genetic production; he is **the son of my womb**, which exudes feeling and compassion on his mother's part. The son was at one time inside and attached to the mother, and then "given" to the world in birth.

Not only that, but she says that he was **the son of my vows**. That must have something to do with his dedication to the Lord by his mother. (Cf. Hannah and Samuel—1 Samuel 1) This makes sense in light of Lemuel's name which means "for God." Thus, this son is special, not only physically, but spiritually—given to the Lord.

BDB suggests that Lemuel may be another (symbolical) name for Solomon.

Prov. 31:3

"Give not thy strength unto women, nor thy ways to that which destroyeth kings."

We have here a warning against womanizing! It's amazing and significant how much of Proverbs is given to this subject. It not only reveals the fundamental weakness of men, but the overwhelming power of women. Godly woman have great authority and are truly "liberated." When they attempt to take the male role, they lose that authority and liberty. The same is true of men, who compromise their masculinity. God made "Adam and Eve" both for His divine purpose.

Thus the admonition, **Give not thy strength unto women, nor thy ways to that which destroyeth kings.** The driving force and need for sex will cause a man to give away his wealth (lit. force, might). Fornication and adultery are rampant to this day! But that doesn't make it right. Some things just don't change—they may just be more sophisticated, according to one's money level.

But it's this sin that "destroys kings." So the admonition continues: Don't give **thy ways** (lifestyle) **to that which**

destroyeth kings. The lust of the flesh knows no boundaries—it will take anyone down, even those in authority. You would think kings (rulers, political and religious leaders) would have more sense and restraint—but they don't. The "oldest" profession is still the "newest." How true is the Bible in its revelation of sex and sin!

Prov. 31:4

"It is not for kings, O Lemuel, it is not for kings to drink wine; nor for princes strong drink:"

Leaders must be sober-minded. Leaders must set the example for those who follow. There's a higher level of standard for those in leadership positions. "With much opportunity, comes much responsibility." The lofty position requires strict discipline of character and actions. This principle has been all but lost in our society today.

It is not for kings, O Lemuel (cf. vs. 1), **it is not for kings** (repeated twice for emphasis) **to drink wine** (fermented)**; nor for princes strong drink** (hard liquor). Wine was a common beverage with meals because of its accessibility in light of a tainted water system; drunkenness was prevalent, leading many into a debauched lifestyle. (cf. Prov. 23:29-35) But even a greater tragedy was the imbibing of those in leadership who jeopardized their capacity to lead (cf. vs. 5).

People of responsibility and strong drink do not mix! But let's not forget that we are all to be responsible and we all lead someone; thus, abstinence and prohibition are in order, particularly for the child of God.

Prov. 31:5

"Lest they drink, and forget the law, and pervert the judgment of any of the afflicted."

This continues the thought of vs. 4 regarding the prohibition of governmental leaders. They must not only be an example to their subjects, but also to prevent the horrendous results that accompany drunkenness. Two are mentioned: 1) lawlessness and 2) perverted judgment.

The scene is one of decisions made toward those in need (e.g., poor, afflicted). Drink will cause a judge to "forget" (lit. disregard, not care about) the law and to "pervert" (alter, change) proper justice. The inference is that the rich will be taken care of regardless, but the poor folks will be neglected or discriminated against.

Kings need to be sober-minded, for more than one reason. So must "kings and priests in a holy nation;" namely, believers in Christ. (cf. 1 Peter 2:9)

Prov. 31:6

"Give strong drink unto him that is ready to perish, and wine unto those that be of heavy hearts."

There is a legitimate place for "strong drink," and that's to kill pain. In our day we call it anesthesia, which is administered prior to surgery. The text seems to gives credence to the use of liquor and wine to those on the death bed or those with "heavy" (lit. bitter) hearts. Such is the case today for those who are "drugged" with medication in order to cope with the difficulties of life. But it's artificial at best.

Being poetic language, one would question whether the writer is actually advocating the usage of strong drink in light of 20:1. Drunkenness is certainly condemned, but here it seems to refer to a "last resort" medication, where nothing else works. The inference is someone facing the "jaws of death."

It is, however, in direct contrast to the king (leader) who must not indulge because of his responsibility and integrity. It's like the writer is saying: "If someone needs to drink liquor, let it be those who are down and out—who are in desperate circumstance." Vs. 7 continues this thought.

Prov. 31:7

"Let him drink, and forget his poverty, and remember his misery no more."

Since drinking (lit. imbibing) numbs the brain, etc. it seems to dull the pain of poverty and misery. People drink to forget their troubles, only to have them reappear when they sober up. I understand why people drink, for apart from the grace of God, life sometimes is unbearable. Without a great Saviour, how is one to cope with painful existence?

Again, is the writer recommending such activity or is he simply describing what people do in extreme conditions and circumstances? Certainly, in light of Scripture, drinking is not the only option in dealing with mental and physical pain. The Lord said to Paul, *"My grace is sufficient for thee: for my strength is made perfect in weakness."*

Prov. 31:8

"Open thy mouth for the dumb in the cause of all such as are appointed to destruction."

Everyone needs a mediator at times. Here is a plea to **open thy mouth** (intercede) **for the dumb** (silent ones). Stand in and up for the "cause" (justice) of all who are "appointed to destruction"; i.e., "sons or children of bereavement" (see Barnes), those who are helpless and about to be orphaned.

Someone must cry out in behalf of those who cannot help themselves; i.e., the fatherless, the unborn, disabled, etc. — this even applies to the abortion controversy. JFB states, "Plead for those who cannot plead for themselves, as the orphan, stranger, etc. (compare Psalm 72:12; Isaiah 1:17)."

Prov. 31:9

"Open thy mouth, judge righteously, and plead the cause of the poor and needy."

Many hide behind the verse, *"Judge not, that ye be not judged"* (Matthew 7:1), giving the impression that no form of judgment regarding others is valid. Yet both Solomon and Jesus speak of "judging righteously"—making a judgment call based on the facts or evidence. Matthew 7:1 deals with condemning other to Hell, which is never our prerogative. But, indeed, we are to judge unfairness, for instance, or **plead the cause of the poor and needy.**

Here's the idea of mediation or contending for others less fortunate; i.e., defending those who have been mistreated or defrauded. There is a time to "open our mouths" in behalf of others, rather than passively sitting in silence while other suffer. We *are* "our brother's keeper."

Prov. 31:10

"Who can find a virtuous woman? for her price is far above rubies."

The following and final segment of Proverbs contains the classic exposition of the "virtuous woman," the qualities of a God-fearing wife.

The question is asked, "**Who can find** (acquire) **a virtuous woman? for her price** (value) **is far above rubies.**" First, such a woman is rare, as are rubies or precious jewels. Second, such a "find" is far more valuable than gems or earthly riches.

Some would search for a pretty or attractive woman, or at least one who has riches or potential inheritance. It depends on one's sense of value. Here the writer upholds the "virtuous" woman as the greatest treasure to be gained. (cf. 3:15; 18:22) Some would be blessed just finding a wife, but how much richer is a man with a wife of virtue?

The word translated "virtuous" is *chayil*, meaning "strength, ability and efficiency." It has the idea of moral courage and excellence. It is rendered "valour" 37 times; e.g., Joshua 1:14; Judges 6:12. Also "valiant" in 1 Samuel 14:52 and 2 Samuel 17:10. This same word is translated "army" 51 times. These are powerful terms used to describe a virtuous woman. Wow!

Prov. 31:11

"The heart of her husband doth safely trust in her, so that he shall have no need of spoil."

Her character instills trust in her husband; she is trustworthy, not shirking or remiss in her wifely responsibilities. Thus, he rests in confidence that she will be faithful in properly using and dispensing the family income and provision. That confidence is such **so that he shall have no need of spoil**; i.e., no lack of gain or goods. He has no worry or temptation of doing something illegal (spoil or plundering, etc.) to provide for his family.

Prov. 31:12

"She will do him good and not evil all the days of her life."

Before Solomon describes her abilities and tasks, he established her fidelity and love toward her husband. There's an obvious sense of commitment resounding in the words, **"She will do him good and not evil all the days of her life."** It goes with the "trust" and confidence described in the previous verse (11). She is determined to treat him right and not wrong, all her days. That takes true faith in God and the outworking of God's love. What a blessed husband is this man!

Prov. 31:13

"She seeketh wool, and flax, and worketh willingly with her hands."

Notice her industry and willingness to make garments for her household. She doesn't need to buy new clothes, but "seeks" the raw materials of wool and "flax" (linen). Not only does she have "willing" hands, but skillful. In all probability she was well taught by her mother, etc. What a challenge for our present generation when few such skills are learned at home.

Prov. 31:14

"She is like the merchants' ships; she bringeth her food from afar."

The woman is likened to a traveling merchant, who "traffics" in merchandise. I like Clarke's comment:

> "If she buy any thing for her household, she sells sufficient of her own manufactures to pay for it; if she imports, she exports: and she sends articles of her own manufacturing or produce to distant countries…"

She also **bringeth her food** (grain, etc.) **from afar.** Her diligence motivates her to go beyond the local sources when necessary. She is a woman of vision and business, even to the extent of importing and exporting. Talk about "working out of the home"!

Prov. 31:15

"She riseth also while it is yet night, and giveth meat to her household, and a portion to her maidens."

Observe that her diligence and vision keep her from sleeping more than necessary. **She riseth also while it is yet night**; I would take this to be pre-dawn, getting a head start on everyone else in the household. She probably went to bed early evening so as to get up early and still be rested. Daylight was a precious commodity and she made the most of it.

She faithfully makes provision ("meat" or food) for her family and servants ("maidens"). Probably the kind of household everyone was glad to be a part of, including the servants.

Prov. 31:16

"She considereth a field, and buyeth it: with the fruit of her hands she planteth a vineyard."

This diligent and brilliant wife even "considers" (plans) a piece of land to purchase **with the fruit** (lit. reward, money) **of her hands** (business ventures)." Her purpose? To "plant a garden (vineyard)" by which she could further care for her household.

This woman is remarkable by any standard. What a tremendous pattern for true motherhood. In God's economy, she is the "queen" of the household. In contrast, she counters the present-day philosophy of so-called "liberated women," who major on a career outside of the home, being independent of their husbands (if they have one). Even the women of eastern cultures are challenged by Solomon's description of womanhood. How many women of third world countries are not the "queen" of the home, but the "work horse" and child bearer? They are still considered mere chattel or 2nd class citizens.

Barns comments:

> "This verse points to a large sphere of famine activity, strikingly in contrast with the degradation to which women of the East have now fallen," Let it be said, that God's saving grace truly "liberates" or frees women to joyfully fulfill God's ordained purpose in life. O, for a return to Biblical understanding and God's tremendous and liberating role for women!

Prov. 31:17

"She girdeth her loins with strength, and strengtheneth her arms."

This proverb is so significant in light of the ongoing craze for physical fitness and weight control. Here the diligent woman "strengthens" her arms and legs (i.e., physical body) through hard physical labor. Her tremendous home enterprise has the benefits of health and fitness built in—no trips to the gym necessary!

She girdeth (lit. puts on a belt, girdle) **her loins** (hips, waist) **with strength, and strengtheneth her arms.** This would appear to be habitual practice, yielding top-notch conditioning for all she has to do or accomplish. No "weaker sex" here.

Prov. 31:18

"She perceiveth that her merchandise is good: her candle goeth not out by night."

What a description of a savvy, confident, industrious woman! She knows that she is in the place of God's blessing. **She perceiveth** (lit. tastes) **that her merchandise** (fruit, vegetables, etc.) **is good**. There's no question of the quality of her production.

It's no surprise that **her candle** (light) **goeth not out by night.** This could refer to her diligence, which labors long and late. It could also mean that she keeps "the night light on" for emergencies, and/or tending to the family when necessary. Another possibility is her up-beat mentality when things are not always profitable. This thought is based on "night" being used figuratively as "night season," or time of adversity. (See Strong's note).

Whatever the case, this is one tremendous, classy lady— to be emulated by other woman.

Prov. 31:19

"She layeth her hands to the spindle, and her hands hold the distaff."

Not only does she seek the raw materials ("wool and flax") for clothing, etc. (cf. vs. 13), but she is skilled in spinning that material to make thread. She takes hold of the "spindle and the distaff" with strong and skillful hands to manufacture the clothing necessities of her household. An industrious woman indeed.

For further explanation of the spinning process, see Clarke's notes on this verse.

Prov. 31:20

"She stretcheth out her hand to the poor; yea, she reacheth forth her hands to the needy."

Her prosperity and diligence does not make this woman greedy. **She stretcheth out her hand to the poor** (unfortunate)**; yea, she reacheth forth her hands to the needy.** Note that she takes the initiative to "reach out" to others, not waiting for them to approach her. Also, she it is not "half-hearted" giving, but the verb implies some intensity in meeting the needs of others less fortunate. This attitude reflects her gratitude to God who has enabled her to prosper.

JFB quips, "Industry enables her to be charitable."

Prov. 31:21

"She is not afraid of the snow for her household: for all her household are clothed with scarlet."

She's not fearful or apprehensive regarding the winter months. She has made ample provision for her household, not the least of which is warm and quality clothing. "Scarlet" seems to refer not only to the color (crimson) but a quality, double-ply garment (see Barnes). This lady has gone the extra mile making full provision for the inevitable.

Prov. 31:22

"She maketh herself coverings of tapestry; her clothing is silk and purple."

No "discount" or second rate furnishings here! This woman makes the very best with the very best of materials. The "coverings of tapestry" are bed coverings (spreads? cf. 7:16). K&D renders this phrase as "pillows." Obvious this describes lavish home furnishings, along with her personal clothing which is "silk" (*shaysh*- white linen) and "purple," indicating the finest of apparel. This is another testimony of this woman's vision, ingenuity and industry.

Prov. 31:23

"Her husband is known in the gates, when he sitteth among the elders of the land."

We are told here that her husband has an outstanding reputation among his colleagues; viz., the "elders of the land" who sit in council with him. Evidently he is a politician or councilman "in the gates," used of a public meeting place (town hall?).

In context, however, I don't think Solomon is simply mentioning the husband's occupation. Rather, this indicates the confidence and effectiveness of this man's profession enhanced by having a diligent and faithful wife at home. His success has great bearing on his help meet, thus illustrating the blessedness of a God-ordained and God-honoring family. As has been said, "Behind a great man is a great woman."

Prov. 31:24

"She maketh fine linen, and selleth it; and delivereth girdles unto the merchant."

She not only "manufactures" garments, like "fine linen" (linen shirts) and "girdles" (lit. belts), but sells them to area merchants (lit. word for Canaanites). She made, sold and delivered the goods. Talk about an entrepreneur! This lady was busy, industrious, and prosperous. It seems there was hardly any household business endeavor that she did not tackle.

Prov. 31:25

"Strength and honour are her clothing; and she shall rejoice in time to come."

Now we come to the source of her industry and entrepreneurial success; namely, her inner character. She is not just adored with fine array, but her "clothing" is "strength (personal might) and honor (excellence, moral integrity)." The order of words here suggests emphasis of these qualities which are foundational to her life and ministry in the home.

The fruit of such character quality is "rejoicing" (lit. laughing), not only in the present, but in "time (days) to come." Praise God, for the fruit of the Spirit, by which we can enjoy our earthly mission, and enter into the Presence of God. Such "rejoicing" is by no means temporary, but a foretaste of future Glory. Cf. Philippians 4:4f.; 1Thessalonians 5:16.

Prov. 31:26

"She openeth her mouth with wisdom; and in her tongue is the law of kindness."

There's a progression here from the outward adorning (vs.24) to the inward adorning of her character (vs.25); now we witness the fruit of her lips revealing those inner qualities. **She openeth her mouth with wisdom; and in her tongue is the law of kindness.** The verb "open" here means to open widely or freely; it carries the idea of liberty and confidence stemming from the force of her sanctified heart. She exudes truth and counsel to others around her. She is more than just a "housewife," she is constantly engaged in spiritual ministry as well.

Notice that her expression of "wisdom" is accompanied by the "law of kindness" or mercy. She speaks the truth with a proper spirit and attitude. She says the right thing in the right way. Her tongue is an instrument of God rather than Satan. She certainly exemplifies the Lord Jesus Christ Himself who was "full of grace and truth." Let us likewise be gracious in proclaiming God's truth.

Prov. 31:27

"She looketh well to the ways of her household, and eateth not the bread of idleness."

The qualities mentioned previously enable, motivate, and equip her for household ministry. Thus, **she looketh well to the ways** (lit. going, walk) **of her household, and eateth not the bread of idleness.** The verb "looketh well" is used to depict a watchman on the wall; he is on the "look out" for anything that would harm or invade the city. His desire and responsibility is to protect the inhabitants from danger. This is an apropos description of a diligent mother and wife. A godly mother is the "watchdog" of the family!

The last phrase follows suit, for such character and responsible motivation will not allow her to "eat the bread of idleness." She has no time to be a slacker! Her diligence is both a prevention and cure for laziness.

Prov. 31:28

"Her children arise up, and call her blessed; her husband also, and he praiseth her."

Thus, **her children arise up and call her blessed** (lit. "happy" – *asher*; cf. Psalm 1:1)**.** The children, knowing her lifestyle, etc., celebrate her virtue with utmost respect, calling her "the happy one" (blessed of God)! What greater testimony and reward can a mother receive?

Furthermore, **her husband also** (rises up)**, and he praiseth her.** Interestingly, the word for "praise" is *hallel* from which we get Hallelujah ("Praise ye the LORD"). It means "to boast or brag," primarily directed to God Himself. On a human level, it indicates this husband's profound and intense commendation of his wife.

What a beautiful illustration of loving reverence and appreciation in the marital institution. How powerful a testimony to the community is such a family! How marvelously does this fulfill Christ's exhortation, *"Let your light so shine before men, that they may see your good works, and glorify your Father which is in heaven"* (Matthew 5:16).

A mother has no greater legacy than this. How tragic that in our day Satan has successfully side-tracked women (and men) from God's ordained purpose. Among the results has been the breakdown of families, along with the rise of so-called "women's liberation," which has led to disillusionment, frustration and bondage. I cannot broad-brush society's dilemma and demise, but certainly these verses address the major problem.

Prov. 31:29

"Many daughters have done virtuously, but thou excellest them all."

The following seems to be the husband's expression of commendation for his wife. He's extolling her with a flare of poetic verse: **Many daughters have done virtuously, but thou excellest them all**; i.e., others in the community also have "virtue" (strength, excellence), but you're the "best"! He's convinced, and rightly so, that she is "Tops."

How great is such a testimony, especially in our day when so much resentment and division exists among married couples. O, to get back to Bible basics, and follow hard after the fear of the Lord and His Wisdom!

Prov. 31:30

"Favour is deceitful, and beauty is vain: but a woman that feareth the LORD, she shall be praised."

Here is defined the ultimate quality that makes a woman truly beautiful and successful—the fear of the LORD. The world places great emphasis on outward physical features, but the inward spiritual condition of the heart is paramount. This is not to say that this godly woman did not have "favor" (grace, charm) or "beauty," but her seriousness in following the Lord overshadowed those outward characteristics.

Solomon makes clear that apart from inner godliness, such outward "graces" are merely "deceit" (sham) and "vain" (empty). "Beauty is skin deep," is the familiar quip, but the inward "beauty of holiness" enhances all the outward features. In fact, the most beautiful women in the world are those whose countenance "shines" with the Glory of God. Not much "makeup" needed in these cases. O, for an epidemic of such beauty in this day!

Prov. 31:31

"Give her of the fruit of her hands; and let her own works praise her in the gates."

What a finale! Solomon says, **"Give her of the fruit of her hands, and let her own works praise her in the gates."** Her husband "praises" her in vs. 28. She is "praised" for her godly character (vs. 30). Now her "fruit" and "works" praise her in the gates (i.e., the community). Just let her go, and her life and actions will speak for themselves! What a testimony of the abundant grace of God manifested from one godly, obedient woman! What a beautiful example for young ladies to emulate in a day when the sanctity of marriage and family are under satanic attack.

O, for a resurgence of such godly women in our day! O, for a true "women's liberation movement" where they take their God-given place in society, fulfilling their unique role to God's glory and to their good!

Conclusion:

Solomon's words in his last chapter of Ecclesiastes are apropos:

"And moreover, because the preacher was wise, he still taught the people knowledge; yea, he gave good heed, and sought out, and set in order many proverbs. The preacher sought to find out acceptable words: and that which was written was upright, even words of truth.

The words of the wise are as goads, and as nails fastened by the masters of assemblies, which are given from one shepherd."
(Ecclesiastes 12:9-11)

The Book of Proverbs, although written to Israel, is applicable to the New Testament Church and present-day society. The repetition of these precepts is obvious and purposeful. It's "line upon line, here a little and there a little." The preacher today must also "find out acceptable words...of truth," and fasten these "nails" of God's wisdom to the heart's door of each listener. In a time of widespread corruption and apostasy, skillful living is in greater demand than ever.

Sources Consulted

Adam Clarke, **Adam Clarke's Commentary on the Holy Bible – Abridged Kindle Edition** (Amazon, 1983).

Albert Barnes, **Barnes' Notes on the Old and New Testaments** (Kregel Publishers, 1980).

Brown, Driver, and Briggs, **Index to Brown, Driver, and Briggs Hebrew Lexicon** (Moody Publishers, 1977).

C.F. Keil, F. Delitzch, **Keil and Delitzch Commentary of the Old Testament** (Hendrickson Publishers, 1996).

Holy Bible, King James Version, 1611(400th Anniversary Edition).

John Gill, **A Body of Practical Divinity or a System of Evangelical Practical Truths Deduced from the Sacred Scriptures** (Baptist Standard Bearers, 2001).

John MacArthur, **MacArthur's Study Bible** (Zondervan, 2006).

Matthew Henry, **Matthew Henry's Commentary on the Whole Bible: 6 Volumes** (Hendrickson Publishers, 2014).

R.A. Torrey, **The Treasury of Scripture Knowledge** (Hendrickson, 1990).

Robert Jamieson, A.R. Fausset, and David Brown, **Commentary: Critical and Explanatory of the Whole Bible** (1871).

Strong's Exhaustive Concordance: Updated Edition, KJV (Hendrickson Publishers, 2009).

Index of Words and Phrases

About the Author

 Pastor, teacher, and presently Biblical instructor at the Discipleship Academy in Youngstown, Ohio, Bill Finnigan has been engaged in active ministry for over Fifty years.

A native of Newark, New Jersey, Bill received a call to ministry while in college. The ensuing years were spent in intensive study to learn and sharpen ministry skills. Attending several universities, he holds a number of degrees, including the Doctor of Ministry. For over twenty seven years, Bill held pulpits in Pennsylvania and New Jersey, reaching people with God's life-changing Word.

His outreach experience has included radio, prison, and Bible conference ministries. He has served as a college professor, and director of a Biblical counseling center. He has authored other publications, including *Healing for the Mind*, offering comfort and remedy for mental turmoil; also *Forgiven to Forgive*, which serves as an antidote to resentment and bitterness.

Along with his wife, Chris, Bill continues to be busily engaged in the Lord's work, considering himself "refired," rather than retired.

CPSIA information can be obtained
at www.ICGtesting.com
Printed in the USA
FFOW01n1737021116
28898FF

9 780996 259163